P9-EFG-087

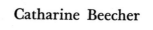

Catharine Beecher

REUTER-STEWART

Catharine Beecher

A STUDY IN AMERICAN DOMESTICITY

Kathryn Kish Sklar

NEW HAVEN AND LONDON, YALE UNIVERSITY PRESS, 1973

Designed by Sally Sullivan
and set in Baskerville type.
Printed in the United States of America by
The Colonial Press Inc., Clinton, Massachusetts.

Published in Great Britain, Europe, and Africa by
Yale University Press, Ltd., London.
Distributed in Latin America by Kaiman & Polon,
Inc., New York City; in Australasia and Southeast
Asia by John Wiley & Sons Australasia Pty. Ltd.,
Sydney; in India by UBS Publishers' Distributors Pvt.,
Ltd., Delhi; in Japan by John Weatherhill, Inc., Tokyo.

To Susan, Leonard, and Bob
Beautiful Anti-types

Contents

Illustrations

Acknowledgments

My intellectual debts for this book begin with the late Perry Miller and Alan Heimert of Harvard University, who taught me that scholarship means commitment. John Higham of the University of Michigan initially directed my research and gave generously of his acute historical insight. Gordon Wood and Sam Bass Warner, now respectively of Brown and Boston universities, provided important reassurance in the early stages of my writing.

Many librarians and archivists rendered essential assistance. Joseph Van Why and others at the Stowe–Day Foundation, the marvelously supportive staff at the Arthur and Elizabeth Schlesinger Library on the History of Women in America at Radcliffe College, Doris Cook at the Connecticut Historical Society, Anne Edmonds at Mount Holyoke College Library, and John Dann at the Clements Library at the University of Michigan were especially important. Archivists at the Library of Congress, the Cincinnati Historical Society, the State Historical Society of Wisconsin, Yale University Library, and Yale's Beinecke Rare Book and Manuscript Library were patient and helpful.

The assistance and friendship of Lynn Weiner, now of Boston University, considerably brightened and lightened the last stages of manuscript preparation. Marilyn Blatt Young, Ann Douglas Wood, Joseph Kett, Gail Thain Parker, and Carroll Smith Rosenberg gave thorough and merciful criticisms of the manuscript. Merle Spiegle and Judy Metro of Yale University Press offered constant support and expert assistance in transforming this manuscript into a book. My parents, Elizabeth Sue and William Edward Kish, along with Lilyn and Leon Sklar, encouraged the emergence of a zealous historian from the chrysalis of their dutiful daughter. The dedication of this book includes Robert Sklar, but words fall far short of evoking my gratitude. He and the two other beautiful people to whom this book is dedicated allowed me to love them and my work at the same time. For a woman preoccupied with nineteenth-century concerns, there could have been no greater act of human benevolence.

Introduction

On a sunny summer day the kitchen of the Stowe house in Hartford is filled with light. It streams in from southern and western exposures onto a perfectly engineered set of counters, sinks, and cupboards. Although inhabited by one of the most famous women in America during the later decades of the nineteenth century, the Harriet Beecher Stowe house was similar to thousands of others built in that era. Based on a design that was widely disseminated as early as the 1840s by works such as Catharine Beecher's *Treatise on Domestic Economy* and Andrew Jackson Downing's *Cottage Residences,* the house embodied the spirit of what had become an American domestic orthodoxy.[1] A well-ordered self-sufficiency was the central tenet of that orthodoxy, and the Stowe house celebrated this notion in both design and furnishings. The kitchen, like the rest of the house, is self-contained, efficient without being crowded, and provides ample access to the outside without seeming vulnerable to values other than its own. The parlor furnishings, replete with artifacts, hanging plants, and family mementos, keep the eye moving actively and convey a sense of fullness. A spray of growing green trails in front of a window, and before it a table reflects the image of a statuette. Everything is arranged to make the most of the natural light. A porch seems to extend the living space into the outside landscape. It is a house in which one is content to be inside even on a glorious day.

In one sense the house exemplifies the Victorian abhorrence for unfilled voids. It demonstrates the belief that for every space there is an object, for every question an answer. It speaks of interrelated certainties and completion. In another sense the house exemplifies a new set of social boundaries constructed and inhabited by nineteenth-century Americans. It defines a new kind of space within which they forged their identities and around which they organized their social and political interaction.[2] More than a sanctuary, this domestic enclave provided a secure base from which men, women, and children could venture into the world. It fostered a particular set of loyalties that were applicable outside as well as inside the home.

The most important characteristic of this new domestic space was its ability to integrate personal and national goals. It fostered uniform communities, molded socially homogeneous human beings, and produced a set of predictable habits among contemporary Americans. To do this and at the same time to defend the virtues of self-reliance, freedom of choice, and independence of mind required considerable ingenuity. Catharine Beecher was among the first to engage in the contradictory task of both nationalizing and personalizing the American domestic environment. Like others so engaged, she found the key to her task in gender roles. The dichotomies of masculine and feminine identity could be orchestrated to agree with both a standardized cultural score and a specialized personal calling. Womanhood could be designed to engage all one's creative energies, yet simultaneously to smooth the edges of one's regional, lineage, or class identities and to articulate the similarities one shared with other women. The same could be done for American manhood. In a nation tentatively evolving new democratic forms, gender roles were an effective way to channel the explosive potential of nineteenth-century social change and bring it at least partially under the control of a national elite.

Although the Beechers were not firmly established in that elite when Catharine was born in 1800, her growth to maturity paralleled her father's rise to national prominence as a spokesman for resurgent evangelicism. Lyman Beecher's prominence was achieved and maintained only through struggle and conscious effort, however, and for the first twenty-five years of her adult life Catharine shared his sense of urgency and mission and worked to fortify their status within local and national elite groups. From 1829 to 1849 she was more widely known than either Harriet or Henry Ward, both of whom rose to fame in the vortex leading to the Civil War. The family's passion for cultural dominance was rooted in Lyman's work of the first decade of the century and lasted until Harriet's death eighty years later. The Beechers were a formidably energetic group, ceaselessly generating qualities of tension and anxiety that they aimed outward into their culture, leaving a deep imprint on the nineteenth century and keeping their mutual loyalties miraculously intact. Their insatiable enthusiasm for public life, their quick response to cultural nuance, and their ability to orchestrate the basic themes of popular democracy, made them a phenomenon unto themselves. Like the Adams family in the eighteenth century and the Kennedys in the twentieth, they welcomed the role of cultural interpreters and relished the chance to forge their own unity out of the manifold variety of American culture.

Much of the effectiveness of the Beecher family lay in its ability to seize the power of social definition during a time of widespread change. Very early in life Catharine was attracted by and became adept in using this power. As the oldest child she was the first to struggle with the meaning of her father's drive for cultural dominance. All the Beecher children were influenced by the power of Lyman's example, but Catharine did much to create the mold that her younger siblings followed. For her the questions attached to her father's mission were real and compelling. How was his power created? How diminished? How increased? How might she perpetuate it? As much as she dodged these questions, she could never avoid them or the implications they had for her own life. Torn constantly between her evangelical loyalties and her personal needs, she mixed innovation with conservatism, honesty with dissemblance, and feminism with antifeminism in her lifework. Yet what concerned her most was the power of social definitions and their ability to affect behavior.

Catharine Beecher's female identity constantly intruded into her consciousness and her career. It excluded her from the main vehicle of contemporary social influence, the church, and it persistently relegated her to a marginal social status when she sought a central one. Over the course of her lifetime she accumulated a tremendous amount of animus against male cultural dominance, but she usually expressed this anger indirectly. Her political assumptions led her to oppose the women's rights movement. Nevertheless her efforts to overcome the marginal status allotted to women constituted a central theme in her career. It caused her to innovate, to seek new channels of cultural influence, and to design an ideology that gave women a central place in national life. The home and the family, she believed, could be redefined as the social unit that harmonized various national interests and synchronized different individual psyches. She used this ideology to promote both cultural homogeneity and female hegemony.

One of the most impressive functions of the American family in this period was its role as mediator between the expanding thrust of Jacksonian Democracy and the continuing social need for coherence and stability. The new domestic code bound individual family members together with sentiment, and it established a moral norm against which a wide variety of other groups, ranging from political parties to reform movements, could be measured.[3] The family's role cannot be easily summarized as a purely conservative one, however, for it contained the seeds of its own destruction. The ideological justifications that facilitated the family's new functions frequently affected human lives in unanticipated ways. Far from instilling obedience, the ideology of domesticity could, for example, lead women to repudiate both heterosexuality and their familial responsibilities.[4] The tension inherent in a society that rapidly extended new opportunities to men, but sought severely to limit those open to women, could not be completely obscured by ideological justifications, no matter how compelling. Historians have noted the ways women subtly subverted their assigned roles, but we are still far from understanding the origin or consequences of their resistance. This book is an effort to examine those origins and consequences in the life of one woman.

Much of the ideology of domesticity is still with us. Perhaps the most powerful tenet supporting it today is the principle of female self-sacrifice. Women have always been praised for their readiness to put the needs of others before their own, but not until Catharine Beecher's lifetime were they led to accept self-sacrifice as a positive good and as the female equivalent to self-fulfillment. As American culture developed new forms of self-realization in the nineteenth century (exemplified in the image of the frontiersman and the writings of Emerson), it attached a male label to these experiences and called women selfish and unnatural if they wanted the same set of personal goals. For them another set applied: devotion and service to others, selflessness, sacrifice. Catharine Beecher was especially attracted to this formula since it described her own experience and since it focused the spotlight of cultural virtue on women. Self-sacrifice, more than any other concept, informed both the triumphs and tensions of nineteenth-century womanhood, and Catharine Beecher was its major theoretician.

In the recent reassessment of the historical experience of women the middle decades of the nineteenth century have emerged as a critical period. Here the first movement for women's rights was born.

Here too the genteel cult of the lady and the encumbering customs of domesticity took hold. This book is a study of that era through the life of one woman. It is also an effort to use the biographical density and motivational impulses of one person to uncover and isolate significant questions about the relationship between women and American society.

Part I

A CALVINIST GIRLHOOD,
1800–1823

❧ 1 ❧

His Powerful Influence, 1800–1809

Catharine Beecher's earliest memories were of riding in her father's open carriage as he toured the farm settlements of his Long Island parish. Lyman Beecher had fashioned a small chair for Catharine so she could safely accompany him on these ventures over the still-rugged landscape near East Hampton. These exciting trips were Catharine's first encounter with social power. "I was his constant companion," she later wrote in an autobiographical fragment, and "as the only daughter and eldest child was much petted by the good people where we stopped."[1] Lyman Beecher was by far the most powerful personage in the region, and Catharine learned to feel the confidence that power brings.

Lyman Beecher supervised the quality of morals, the attitudes toward politics, and the arrangements of domestic life as well as the religious state of his parishioners' souls. The community owed him their current state of tranquillity since he had nearly single-handedly, and in little more than three years, suppressed a dangerous outcropping of deist and Jeffersonian opinions among the region's youth. By the time Catharine was old enough to share his pastoral jaunts, Lyman Beecher had restored orthodoxy of mind and habit to East Hampton and its environs.[2] Beecher's spectacular success in the battle to save the young testified to his effectiveness as a revival preacher and a community organizer. Catharine was nine when the Beecher family left East Hampton, and by then she had absorbed a powerful lesson in the dynamics of social power. She had been tutored by an expert, and she learned not only how to exercise the art of social influence, but to identify with those who were on the winning side.

In the quiet but intense struggle waged within the domestic life of the Beecher family itself, Lyman triumphed over his wife, Roxana, as decisively as he conquered irreligion in his parish. Catharine was born in 1800, when Roxana and Lyman had been married barely a year. The difference in their personalities — so important

3

in shaping Catharine's own personality — was rooted in their respective childhoods. Like most people in Connecticut at the beginning of the nineteenth century, Roxana and Lyman Beecher could trace their ancestry back to the first settlements of the colony in the 1630s.[3] Although Lyman and Roxana were born in the same town, the circumstances of their upbringings were far from similar. Roxana's family was the more prominent since it was part of the town's privileged group of educated and professional families. Roxana Foote's father was a lawyer, and when he died during her early adolescence, she and her ten siblings were raised in the home of her uncle, Andrew Ward, who had served as a general in Washington's army. The Ward home, called Nutplains because it stood in the center of two hundred wooded acres, was a comfortable if not elegant farmhouse, and the family set itself above the "commonality," attended the Episcopal rather than the Congregational church, spoke French, and read English novels. Before her marriage to Lyman Beecher, Roxana was accustomed to a leisured but not an idle life. She rose with the sun, spent much of the day at her spinning wheel overseeing the play of her younger brothers and sisters, and in the evening played the guitar, read, and sewed.[4] Roxana was raised in a traditional culture, and she fully expected to transmit it to her own children.

The circumstances of Lyman Beecher's childhood and the nature of his chosen career required far more of him than the passive transmission of his inherited culture. Lyman's mother died during his premature birth, and although his father, a prosperous blacksmith, soon remarried, he would have nothing to do with the baby and sent him to live with relatives. Lyman was raised in the otherwise childless home of his mother's brother. The affection of his aunt and uncle did not compensate for the loss of his father's love, and his childhood left him with an almost insatiable desire for intense familial relationships. He had thirteen children whom he loved voraciously, and Catharine, as his first child, was the special object of his vigorous, generous, and sometimes crushing affection. Lyman left his uncle's farm for Yale when he was sixteen. There, under Timothy Dwight, he became a fiercely dedicated servant of God and a master of withering Calvinist and revivalist rhetoric. "I was made for action. The Lord drove me, but I was ready," he said. Beecher moved through life at full speed, in many ways a driven man, reckless of consequence and fired with belief. Periodically, however, his internal fire died and he suffered moods of deep depression. Beecher "felt as if the conversion of the world to Christ was near," and his millennial and apocalyptic beliefs lent an urgency to all his actions. His hopes for his church and his children were extravagant, and their fulfillment, he felt, depended largely upon his own efforts.[5]

The evangelical movement in American religion, of which Lyman Beecher was so important a part, coincided very closely with the growth of popular democracy in the United States. The movement was an effort by organized Christianity to seize the cultural initiative at a time when American society seemed open to new definitions. It was an important aspect of American life in the first half of the nineteenth century, and for Lyman Beecher, it was everything.

Lyman Beecher courted Roxana Foote with the tenets of Calvinism rather than the poetry of romance. The six months after their engagement was a season of passionate religious communion between them, during which Roxana surrendered her mild Anglican faith and Lyman guided her through the anguished stages of a Calvinist conversion experience. Whereas she had always been comfortable in her "propensity to see every thing in the most favorable point of view, to clothe every object in the brightest colors, to make all nature wear the face of hope and joy," Lyman caused her to fear this propensity. Roxana had been raised to believe that she was "an object of God's mercy and goodness," but Lyman awoke in her the "distressful apprehension" that she was "an enemy to God" and an object of His loathing. Lyman's efforts were finally rewarded with Roxana's conversion, at which time she realized her wickedness but felt assured of God's compassion. Later that year, in the winter of 1798, they were married, and Roxana learned that her marriage demanded not only that she submit to the will of the Calvinist God, but also to the will of a quick-tempered husband. Soon after their marriage Lyman told her that he expected implicit obedience and no back talk from her. "She entered into my character entirely," Lyman said, and he considered this her greatest virtue.[6]

They were married two weeks after Lyman was ordained, and they moved immediately to his "parish across the water" from Connecticut, on the northeastern tip of Long Island. East Hampton was a Connecticut outpost separated from the mainland by a span of water wide enough to discourage visitors and to eliminate all transient traffic. Besides the laborious boat trip across the Sound, the only connection with Connecticut was through the post office, and the one nearest East Hampton was seven miles away. There was not a store in the town, and all purchases were made in New York through a small schooner that ran once a week. Although the town's commercial ties were with New York, its cultural ties lay with Connecticut, whence its original settlers had come and from which its ministers and social traditions still sprang.[7]

Lyman Beecher looked toward the future but considered himself part of a living tradition that began with the founding of New England. From her early childhood Catharine Beecher was highly conscious of her family's ties to the traditions of New England. "East Hampton where I was born and lived till nine years old," she wrote, "was settled by people from New England and [was] so secluded a spot that it fairly represented the society and customs of the early puritans."[8] In piety and manners Catharine Beecher's early years may have superficially resembled a seventeenth-century Puritan childhood, but a more important similarity between the two was their seclusion, their isolation from the mainstream of contemporary culture. In her early years on the tip of Long Island, Catharine Beecher experienced an unusually intense family life. For neither the church, nor the wider society, nor her peers acted as a counterbalance to her experience within her family. In the isolation of East Hampton Catharine's father loomed larger than life, while her mother seemed out of place.

Catharine's earliest memories of her mother were of a woman who would go to enormous lengths to overcome the cultural isolation of the town in which she lived. Catharine later recalled that "a carpet was in the whole town unknown, and the floors were sprinkled with sand, first in lumps and when trodden down, stroked with a broom in waving or angular lines."[9] Roxana Beecher refused to adopt this style of seventeenth-century simplicity, however, and the high price she paid in time and energy to make her own carpet was indicative of the strength of her desire to bring the culture and comforts of the mainland into their rude home. It was also a measure of her own sense of social dislocation.

When Catharine was born, Roxana not only called her mother and sister to her side and hired a nurse, she also arranged to have a five-year-old Negro girl "bound" to the family. By the time Catharine was five years old and her mother had begun a "select" school in their home, the family had three full-time black servants, two of them "bound." [10] There was little danger that Roxana would allow the family to adopt the local rustic ways.

Roxana may have been preoccupied with the babies that arrived almost annually during Catharine's early years.[11] She may have devoted whatever free time she had to domestic improvements. She may simply have lacked affection and warmth in her personality. In any case, Catharine felt the absence, if not the deprivation, of her mother's affection. In comparison to Lyman, Roxana was in Catharine's eyes a distant and abstract person: "For my father had that passionate love of children which makes it a pleasure to nurse and tend them, and which is generally deemed a distinctive element of the woman," Catharine wrote. "But my mother, though eminently benevolent, tender, and sympathizing, had very little of it." Catharine could not remember ever seeing her mother "fondle and caress her little ones as my father did." [12] Her father "was imaginative, impulsive and averse to hard study," Catharine recalled, "while my mother was calm and self-possessed." Her mother had the mind of a mathematician, Catharine believed, whereas her father had the mind of a poet.

Catharine felt an early antipathy to her mother's domestic accomplishments and was a reluctant pupil. "Oh, the mournful, despairing hours when I saw the children at their sports, and was confined till I had picked out the bad stitches, or remedied other carelessness, or had completed my appointed 'stents!' " "Some of my own natural traits were decidedly the opposite of those of my mother," she concluded.[13]

All the affection that would ordinarily have gone to her mother Catharine gave to her Aunt Mary, Roxana's younger sister who joined the family at Catharine's birth. "She was both guardian and playmate of infancy and childhood," Catharine recalled, "and her image returns to me as my highest ideal of a guardian angel." [14] Roxana's sister stayed on with the Beechers throughout most of their life in East Hampton. From Mary, Catharine received the personal attention she did not get from her mother. "Most observing and most sympathizing was she with all the little half-fledged wants and ambitions of childhood," Catharine wrote. For Mary, Catharine was happy to perform simple domestic tasks and services. "She secured my enthusiastic devotion by the high appreciation she seemed to have of my childish services." Mary introduced Catharine to the romantic imagination of Scott and Burns, and Catharine called her "the poetry of my childhood." [15] Whereas Roxana drilled Catharine in the fine arts of domesticity, Mary groomed Catharine in the style of one of Scott's heroines. "She never allowed my hair to be cut and dressed it in fanciful ways, while all the other children wore close cropped hair," Catharine recalled.[16] Mary was frequently the channel through which Catharine reached the affection of her parents. On one occasion she called Roxana to come and see how lovely Catharine looked while reading Scott with her ringlets drooping on the open pages.[17] Later she felt obliged to remind Lyman that he should pay close attention to Catharine and not only admire her intelligence but also give her his love.[18]

Lyman's affections toward Catharine during her childhood did not need to be prompted. From his initial greeting to her at her birth — "Thou little immortal!" — to the end of her childhood, Lyman lavished his daughter with affection. "I remember him more as a playmate than in any other character during my childhood," Catharine later wrote, and their "play" was sufficiently rugged to scare off any but the most dedicated of daughters. "I remember once he swung me out of the garret window by the hands, to see if it would frighten me, which it did not in the least. Another time, as I was running past a washtub he tipped my head into it to see what I would do." [19]

The isolation of East Hampton exerted a decisive, yet subtle, influence on Catharine Beecher's early attitudes toward her parents. Living removed from other male relatives in a town where all social and religious authority fell uncontested to Lyman Beecher, Catharine developed an early and intense devotion to her father. Yet paradoxically the isolation of East Hampton meant that Catharine saw less of her mother than she might have in a more refined environment. Whereas Lyman flourished in the rusticity of East Hampton life and gave free rein to his natural exuberance, Roxana struggled to re-create mainland improvements, and this was a constant drain on her time and energies. She was uninterested in Catharine's and Lyman's rides to "another place with an ugly Indian name," and she rarely accompanied them.[20]

Catharine and Lyman both relished the element of wildness in the East Hampton environment. Some of her most vivid memories of early life were of the ocean "only half a mile from the house, whose roar we could hear any hour of day or night." From her room Catharine could see "the vast ocean, the white crested billows, and the flying ships." [21] Although the townspeople were mostly farmers, they hunted whales that they could sight and pursue from the shore. Catharine and Lyman shared a love of these whaling expeditions, and although Lyman joined the men at the oars and Catharine could only watch, her description of these events surpasses in vividness any of her other childhood recollections. The drama of the event appealed to a girl who preferred Scott to embroidery:

> Men and boys flocked to the beach, the harpoons were brought and boats were launched and the wild chase for the whale was watched by anxious wives and mothers recalling the history of some friend or neighbor once thus drowned or killed by the whale.

She recalled her fascination upon coming to the beach while men were cutting up a captured whale. "It looked like an acre of red meat sunk deep in the sand and men and boys were cutting it in huge hunks and dragging it off for manure or for oil," she said.[22] There was nothing squeamish about Lyman Beecher, and his daughter took after him. In appearance as well she had his angular features, chestnut hair, and lithe physicality along with his mental curiosity and enthusiasm.

Catharine Beecher was adventurous when she was young, and in her fishing expeditions with her father, in her delight in getting drenched by the ocean "from the mere love of excitement," and in her fondness for practical jokes, she was following Lyman's example. Even while she was in her mother's school, her father stole her attention. "Sometimes, in school hours, when he had got tired of writing," Catharine recalled,

> he would come out of his study and go into the sitting room under the schoolroom and begin to play the violin as loud as he could. . . . Mother would come into the room, quietly walk up to him . . . and would take the violin out of his hands, go upstairs and lay it on her table in the schoolroom.[23]

This anecdote also reveals the contrast Catharine felt as a child between her father's lively, even disruptive, playfulness and her mother's quiet restraint.

It was Lyman's combination of love and authority that made him the dominant parent in his daughter's eyes. "It has been said the children love best those that govern them best," she recalled and admitted that this was verified in her own experience.

> Mother was gentle, tender, and sympathizing, but all the discipline of government was with father. This strong and decided government was always attended with overflowing sympathy and love. His chief daily recreations were frolics with his children.

When the time for frolicking with her father had passed, Catharine gladly gave up this intimacy for his "intellectual companionship." "Gradually I began to share with mother in his more elevated trains of thought," she wrote, and she considered this more important than what she learned in her mother's school. Through him, Catharine said, "our house became in reality a school of the highest kind, in which he was all the while exerting a powerful influence upon the mind and character of his children." [24] For Catharine, Lyman Beecher was the source of learning, authority, and love. He was far more vivid to her than her mother, and he was a powerful model as well as a powerful influence.

Catharine Beecher never fully escaped the dominating force of her father's personality, and in her career she struggled to come to terms with the intellectual, social, and religious issues he raised. Lyman Beecher's career was a remarkably consistent one, and from its beginning in East Hampton three central concerns were evident: the creation of a unified society, the merging of piety with morality, and the modification of orthodox Calvinist doctrine. These three concerns were posed to Lyman Beecher by the historical circumstances in which he, as an orthodox clergyman, found himself at the beginning of the nineteenth century. His response to these circumstances raised more questions than it answered, however, and Catharine inherited these questions. Many of the issues that she would later contest, absorb, and finally transform originated in her father's career in East Hampton. There was more to her early religious experience than the pleasant companionship of the jaunts in her father's chaise.

Lyman Beecher's children were not the only ones in East Hampton to feel his "powerful influence." His leadership in the commu-

nity was vigorous and aggressive and by no means limited to his
Sunday sermons. The year of Catharine's birth was one of a remarkable religious revival that extended throughout much of the new
nation. In East Hampton as elsewhere the Second Great Awakening
waxed and waned for many years, but by the time it ended, evangelical religion had incontestably become part of American life.
This revival rescued the Calvinist tradition from the decline it had
suffered during the postrevolutionary period when various forms of
deism and rationalism had gained wide popular support. Timothy
Dwight (1752–1817) in New Haven had set the example for the new
Calvinist offensive and was the first to use revivals as the means to
restore religious orthodoxy. Previous to Dwight, Calvinist orthodoxy had barely condoned popular revivals and had preferred the
persuasion of more formal measures. Religion in New England was
rarely divorced from wider social and political matters, and Dwight
fought Jeffersonian democracy just as bitterly as he fought religious
infidelity.

Beecher adopted the program of his mentor, and in East Hampton he used revivals to rebuild the church and to reshape the social
and political attitudes of his parishioners.[25] First he restored the
social cohesion of the community, emphasized each person's duty to
obey established authority, and came dangerously close to an unorthodox equation of morality with religion. Meanwhile he sought
conversions among his people, pursuing every hint of personal
awakening with a singular and "almost indescribable" ardor.[26]

One of the first fruits of Beecher's ministry, and an essential part
of the social matrix he hoped to build, was the restoration of family discipline and devotions. He emphasized the necessity of family
cohesion not because he thought it more important than other
human institutions, nor because he believed that the religious instruction of the home was more efficacious than that of the church,
but because the family was one of many mutually reinforcing social
institutions that unite to form a consolidated culture.

He also stressed his parishioners' duty to support civil and religious institutions. He told them to obey the laws, to uphold civil
and religious institutions, and to act for the general good.[27] "The
general good" was not an empty phrase to Beecher. It had meaning
as the larger social entity to which the individual was subordinate.
Beecher's goal was social consolidation, and all his life he struggled
against social fragmentation and disruption. One of the most dis-

tinctive aspects of his East Hampton ministry was the creation of societies that would unite the community's moral sentiments.[28] He equated virtue with social cohesion and sin with social disarray. "Sin is in its nature antisocial," he said. "It will sunder the ties of society, lead us to bite and devour; to be hateful and hate one another." The purpose of the Moral Society he founded in 1803 was not only to suppress vice, but to build a united and virtuous public opinion.[29] Lyman Beecher saw no distinction between secular and clerical concerns. To him the church and the society were bound together by countless ties of mutual interest. Catharine Beecher's later thought and career also treated the individual as a subordinate part of a larger social whole. Yet, unlike her father, Catharine could not so confidently equate clerical and social concerns. She could never command the kind of clerical authority her father did, and much of her career was devoted to a search for other sources of social authority and other grounds to justify the subordination of the individual to that authority.

In spite of Lyman Beecher's efforts to embody morality in social institutions, he was profoundly committed to the Calvinist doctrine of salvation by grace alone. There was a deep tension in his thought between the moral strictures of his social philosophy, which urged people to lead virtuous lives, and his religious doctrine, which claimed that virtue was meaningless unless accompanied by the experience of conversion. "Overt action and continuance in well-doing" was not enough, Beecher declared, to achieve salvation. "New affections are demanded."[30] This ancient Calvinist dilemma between morality and religion endured to plague the new generation of which Catharine Beecher was a part. Her father clearly saw the need to link the two, and in 1803 he warned his congregation: "There is currently a crafty distinction made between immorality and irreligion — one hurting others, one only the self. This is not true. Irreligion is at the heart of immorality."[31]

Morality was not to Beecher "a mere act of the understanding"; he believed "the *heart* decides and is never neutral."[32] Following Beecher's logic, then, a converted heart would be consistently virtuous, an unconverted one persistently sinful. Yet this was patently not the case. For Catharine Beecher this issue posed by her father was inescapable. The pure heart and the moral act were to her forever linked, yet conversion lay beyond her grasp. In her later thought, after Catharine had recast her Calvinist heritage into a form more appropriate for the Victorian era, she removed morality from the sphere of the church and treated it purely as a social entity. Yet the heart and its motivations remained at the core of her moral philosophy. Between Catharine's final conclusions and her initial experience, moreover, lay a long struggle with this and other components of her New England religious tradition.

Lyman Beecher's overriding concern in East Hampton was to make religious doctrine relevant to the lives of his listeners. This concern led him off the path of strict orthodoxy and into a turbulent career marked by controversy and heresy trials. In 1807 he asserted his single most important modification of orthodox doctrine and claimed that the human will was able to choose God, that man was able to choose salvation, and that God judged human souls according to how well they exercised this choice rather than according to a predestined plan.[33] Lyman Beecher never admitted to being unorthodox and insisted rather that he was only interpreting doctrine so as to make it more understandable. Doctrine was not, Beecher insisted, something that "God had locked up and frozen from all eternity." [34] Lyman Beecher reinterpreted Calvinist doctrine not because he had less faith in it than orthodox men, but because he believed that the Calvinist tradition was vital and strong enough to bear the changes necessary to preserve it. He was a man who was keenly aware of the criticisms leveled at the church by deists outside it and by the growing liberal movement led by W. E. Channing (1780–1842) within it. These movements had put Calvinism on the defensive, and Beecher was determined to take the offensive and meet their criticisms from a doctrinal position of strength rather than weakness. In addition to his revised doctrine of election, Beecher reinterpreted the doctrine of original sin — the weakest spot in the Calvinist armor and the one most vigorously assailed by its opponents.[35] Beecher insisted that although men had a natural propensity to sin, this did not mean that God condemned infants and other "helpless, unoffending creatures to eternal torment." [36]

Beecher had a remarkable facility for responding to the changing religious temper of his culture while maintaining the essential structure of Calvinism. "As demands were made by events, I met them to the best of my ability. My ideas were all my own," he said. Yet he was convinced that his revisions strengthened the cause of Calvinism and made it a more formidable faith. In his own words he was "harnessed to the Chariot of Christ, whose wheels of fire have rolled onward, high and dreadful to his foes, and glorious to his friends." [37]

Lyman Beecher thus presented to his daughter a faith that was malleable but not easily breakable. Later when she was faced with the alternatives of either seeking an accommodation with it or breaking completely with it, Catharine found that she could change it but not desert it. For many of her contemporaries the latter alternative was easier, and they escaped from Calvinism more painlessly than Catharine by rejecting the faith in its entirety because they were offended by some of its parts.[38] Catharine Beecher was not so easily released. Her religious tradition could not be shrugged off as part of a dead and irrelevant past. Her devotion to her father and his particular role in making that tradition relevant meant that she had to meet it on terms other than outright rejection.

※ 2 ※

Sociality, 1809–1821

By 1809 Lyman Beecher had become too prominent in Connecticut affairs to remain in a small Long Island parish. His successful revival efforts in East Hampton had established his reputation among the clerical leadership of New England and New York, and his extraordinarily popular sermon on dueling (after the death of Alexander Hamilton) made his name a rallying cry for Federalists throughout the eastern United States.[1] When the East Hampton church refused to increase his salary to an amount that would accommodate his large family in their accustomed style, he took the occasion to cast about for "a wider sphere of influence." The town that finally delivered the family from cultural isolation and financial debt was Litchfield, a Federalist stronghold in northwestern Connecticut. No place could have been better designed to consolidate Catharine Beecher's place in New England tradition. If East Hampton had preserved Puritan traditions by its seclusion, Litchfield had maintained the old religious and social order by concentrated effort.[2]

From its beginning the town had had a conservative character. Like the rest of that region of Connecticut, Litchfield had been settled only decades before the Great Awakening. Yet Litchfield stood aloof from the religious enthusiasm that swept the other new settlements around it.[3] Initially Litchfield's ministers staunchly opposed Edwardean theology. Yet after the popular vitality of the revival movement had died, the Litchfield church found that conservatism and the Edwardean tradition were quite compatible; it joined that tradition rather than the old-school liberalism of the eastern part of the state. Conversion became a respectable experience in Litchfield.[4] When the Beechers moved there the town was at its zenith. After the Revolution a number of wealthy lawyers, merchants, and prominent political families settled there and lined the two intersecting main streets with Federal-style mansions. In the first decades of the nineteenth century, Litchfield's prosperity

15

continued to attract settlers, and by 1820 it was the state's fourth
largest town.[5]

Since the turn of the century Litchfield had grown famous as the
seat of the nation's best law school, and it attracted ambitious
young men like John C. Calhoun of South Carolina and the son of
Rufus King of New York. Like the rest of the town, the law school
was ardently Federalist, and even before New England Federalists
threatened rebellion over the War of 1812, a director of the Litchfield Law School was summoned for seditious utterances in Jeffer-
son's administration.[6] The town's other cultural attraction was Miss
Pierce's school for young ladies. From a small beginning in 1792
the school was by 1810 one of the most celebrated in the United
States. In that year, when Catharine Beecher entered, Miss Pierce's
school had more than one hundred girls in attendance, some drawn
from as far away as Savannah and a good number from New York
City.[7]

Prerevolutionary manners were still alive in Litchfield. Some of
the older generation still wore powdered queues, white-topped
boots, silk stockings, and breeches with buckles. David Daggett,
once Lyman Beecher's tutor at Yale and influential in calling him
to Litchfield, was now a chief justice and one of the gentlemen who
retained this style of dress. Litchfield's leaders assumed upper-class
prerogatives and considered themselves above the multitude.[8] Yet
the younger generation studying at the law school and Miss Pierce's
were taken into their wealthy homes as boarders and shared in all
the social privileges of the community. Leisure, as the prerogative
of the wealthy and the delight of the young, united both the old
and the young and made the town an unusually convivial one. The
students strolled about the town alongside the local aristocracy.
Catharine Beecher in her adolescence was among the groups of
"young people passing and repassing through the broad and shaded
street to and from the favorite Prospect Hill." Romances abounded
and the atmosphere of the town lent itself to innocent social amusements.[9]

In Litchfield, Catharine Beecher later wrote, "there was a free
and easy way of living more congenial to liberty and sociality than
to conventional rules." [10] The town was remarkably well suited to
her needs and talents. It was sufficiently self-assured to condone a
cultivated worldliness among its residents, and it was pious enough
to lend credence to the ideals of the Beecher family. It sanctioned

both the romantic attitudes Catharine learned from her Aunt Mary and the deep devotion she felt for her father. The fragments of Catharine's childhood came together in Litchfield to form a perfect whole. Catharine grew up in a traditional environment but remained unoppressed by it. The town rewarded just those accomplishments in which Catharine excelled, and she became one of its most prominent young women. Sociality was the key to Catharine's Litchfield experience, just as seclusion had defined her East Hampton years.

As soon as the family was settled in Litchfield in the fall of 1810, Catharine entered Miss Pierce's school. She was ten years old. Miss Pierce's school was chiefly dedicated to training the social instincts of its pupils. All of the young ladies were required to keep private journals at Miss Pierce's, and although Catharine's prizewinning journals have not survived, many others remain to reveal the strong social orientation of the school experience.[11] It was only natural that Catharine should have received "instruction on those rules of delicacy and propriety so important for every young woman," and that she should have learned "lady-like manners" and "cultivated and refined conversation." [12] Given the proximity of the young men in the law school and the emphasis in the society on marriage, self-interest alone would cause the girls to master these social graces. Yet the journals reveal even a more pervasive social consciousness. For they show that all the religious and moral instruction the girls received was primarily meant to make them agreeable to their elders and their peers. "Candor, Truth, Politeness, Industry, Patience, Charity and Religion," were urged upon them as social usages and only secondarily as the path to holiness.[13] The best journals were frequently read aloud to the school, and self-analysis, in these circumstances, could not be honest or profound. Catharine Beecher, like the rest of her companions, learned to record her private thoughts for public perusal and to interpret her personal experience in socially acceptable terms. Indeed, she must have developed a special facility in this medium since her journals received the praise of her instructors.[14] Unlike some of her companions, Catharine did not shrink from having her journal made public, and she took pleasure in what others considered a public ordeal.

For Catharine Beecher, who was to transpose Puritan values into Victorian attitudes, this early social consciousness was an invaluable asset. Yet for a girl who was still in the Calvinist tradition, this worldly facility could only hinder her when her time came to stand alone before God. Catharine Beecher could never have the luxury some of her friends enjoyed of forgetting religious doctrine. One girl's journal recorded that in a recent sermon Lyman Beecher had said "that we must repent and believe and explained how we should repent and believe, but my memory is so poor that I cannot remember it." [15] For this girl a pleasant religious demeanor in society was sufficient. Within a few years Catharine suffered some anguish in deciding whether this was also sufficient for her.

Catharine easily rose to the top of her class, partly on the basis of her self-confidence and partly through her sociability. Her native intelligence could have carried her effortlessly through the school's undemanding academic course, yet even in her studies she preferred to use her social rather than her intellectual talents. She claimed later that she bluffed her way through her schoolwork and did not really earn the academic honors she received. Her classmates aided in various schemes that gave her the right answer at the right time in recitation.[16] When she won the school's first prize in 1814, one of her instructors noted that "for a small girl [she] shows great fertility of genius and strength of memory," and he was probably not deluded in his estimate of her since the prize was awarded after a four-day public competition.[17] Yet Catharine decidedly preferred the friendship of her peers to real academic achievement. "In school and between schools I was incessantly busy in concocting or accomplishing plans for amusement," Catharine recalled, and her "fun-loving associates" encouraged her.[18]

Catharine gained a reputation as "the busiest of all creatures in doing nothing." [19] Yet in fact she was busy exploring her new role of social leadership. At the end of each term Miss Pierce's school was turned into a theater, and the community gathered to watch the young women perform. These events were respectable because the dramas presented, usually written by Miss Pierce, were based on Old Testament themes. They were in the New England tradition of typology in which the trials of the Israelites stood for the trials of the people of New England. The morals drawn were heavily Federalist, as some of Catharine Beecher's lines in the starring role show:

> Here we have lived a peaceful, happy life.
> The rude inhabitants, thy father's virtues
> Have humanized, refined and taught the worth

> Of civil laws and righteous government.
> Their barbarous manners softened into virtue.

In dramatics Catharine discovered the perfect vehicle for her social skills. During her years at Miss Pierce's she wrote several short dramas, and she and her friends acted them out for their own pleasure. "Dramatic writing and acting became one of the 'nothings' about which I contrived to be busy and keep others so," she recalled.[20] Dramatics necessarily demand more form and structure than other casual social amusements require. Catharine provided that structure. Through theatricals she formalized her role as the leader of her group of friends, and she also found a comfortable means whereby she could order experience. For Catharine did not take experience casually as it came to her but tended to impose a form or order upon it. Catharine's dramas were conventional rather than daring, yet they show that she could grasp the common social forms of her community and recast them to interpret her own experience.

Although she had shown that her social skills were effective outside her home, the focus of Catharine's life nevertheless remained within the Beecher family. During Catharine's school years life in the Beecher household was relaxed and buoyant. Catharine called these years from 1810 to 1816 "a period of more unalloyed happiness" for the Beecher family than any other that preceded or followed it. "As I look back to those days," she recalled, "there is an impression of sunshine, love, busy activity, without any memory of a jar or cloud." [21] The family was a gregarious one, and Catharine was at the center of activity, constantly devising family games and amusements and writing poetry for the entertainment of the family and their friends.

By her fifteenth birthday Catharine was the older sister to seven siblings. Harriet, Henry Ward, and Charles were the youngest and barely out of infancy. George and Mary were nine and five years younger than Catharine and looked to her to enliven their play. Edward and William were nearest Catharine's age, but since they were boys they were expected to contribute their brawn rather than their wit to the family welfare, and they did not compete with Catharine for the role of family merrymaker.

Besides her seven siblings, Catharine also had the company of her father's sister and mother, who had moved into a small house

nearby. Catharine's beloved Aunt Mary died from consumption in
1813, but until then she remained Catharine's close companion,
sharing her room and accompanying her on walks and horseback
rides. Roxana's brother, Samuel Foote, a shipowner and captain
who sailed to Spain and South America, visited Litchfield after
each voyage and brought Catharine Moorish slippers, told of his
adventures in the Spanish Empire, and read aloud with Mary the
new tales of Washington Irving and the poetry of Lord Byron. The
household was large and varied, and it included several boarders
who lived with the Beechers while they attended the law school and
Miss Pierce's school. Lyman took great comfort in his close friendship with Tapping Reeve, the founder of the Litchfield Law School.
Tapping Reeve was the closest friend Lyman Beecher was ever to
have, and Litchfield was the only place where his confidants were
also the town's elite. After each church service the Reeve and
Beecher families came together, and, while the men discussed their
plans for preserving the religious and political establishment that
ruled Connecticut, the ladies read to each other from English evangelical writers like Hannah More and William Wilberforce. Catharine relished the expansive social atmosphere of the family during
these years. Litchfield society appreciated Roxana's domestic virtues, and she was content to dedicate herself to her home and children and to let Lyman and Catharine represent the family in the
Litchfield limelight and dominate the home amusements. She herself was uncomfortable in large social gatherings. Whereas Roxana
was the source of the family's domestic comforts, Catharine was the
undisputed center of the family's gaiety. "Making fun for everybody," was Catharine's forte.[22] The "unalloyed happiness" of the
family during these years was doubly rewarding because of her own
role in creating it.

In 1816 Roxana died of consumption and the family's spell of
serenity was broken. Roxana's death was in keeping with the self-
control and placidity that characterized her throughout her life.
Six weeks before her death, when no one suspected that she was
ill, Roxana surprised Lyman by saying that she did not expect to
be with him long. She declared her willingness to die, and "her
more than willingness to leave him and her children." [23] This attitude was commonly known and praised as "Christian submission,"
and in the context of Calvinist life it was altogether admirable.
Even approaching her death, Roxana did not allow herself to ex-

press her affection for her children. Her death came quickly and she never lost her composure. She left eight living children, the youngest less than a year old.

After Roxana's death Catharine drew closer than ever to her father. She withdrew from school and expanded her role at home. For her father she enthusiastically performed the domestic duties she had been reluctant to do for her mother. "He stimulated my generous ambition to supply my mother's place," Catharine related. Lyman's affection was unstinted, and Catharine was showered with it now as she had never been before. Her father had a remarkable faculty, Catharine continued, "of discovering and rejoicing over unexpected excellence in character and conduct." He not only felt pleased and grateful when kindnesses were done to him, "but he had the *gift of expression*." Lyman "made known his pleased approval," and Catharine responded. "Thus stimulated, I for the first time, undertook all the labor of cutting, fitting and making all the clothing of the children as well as my own." She also learned to cook and took charge of the younger children, "cheered and animated by the consciousness that it comforted father." [24]

It was only natural that Catharine should have resented her father's remarriage the following year. In the fall of 1817 Lyman Beecher went off to Boston on an extended visit, and Litchfield buzzed with rumors that he had gone wife-hunting. In this uncomfortable situation Catharine behaved with great propriety and wrote her father only that his family missed him and longed to see him.[25] When he returned with the news of his betrothal to Miss Harriet Porter, Catharine immediately dispatched an elaborate but stilted letter of welcome to her prospective stepmother. Lyman had approved Catharine's letter, but he had not missed its affected and strained tone. "My daughter has written to you with my approbation," he explained to Harriet Porter and apologetically added, "I hope however we shall not overwhelm you with our letters and exhaust your patience." [26]

All the sentiments in Catharine's letter were exaggerated conventional ones. In this difficult circumstance Catharine chose to play her social role as stepdaughter to its utmost extent. Even at the age of sixteen she was capable of defending herself by erecting an impregnable shell of social rectitude. Catharine stressed the loss of Roxana as her guide and model, the sacred qualities of motherhood, and her desire to win her new mother's affections. Although she said she now looked to Harriet Porter as "a guide" and "a pattern," the rigid formality of Catharine's letter conveyed her intention of defining her own character.[27]

After her father's remarriage, Catharine admitted that "at first" Harriet's presence "was a trial for me" and that she resented her new mother.[28] Yet these feelings either faded or were repressed, for Catharine soon accommodated herself to the new household regime. Harriet had all the credentials to make her acceptable to Litchfield society. She was staunchly orthodox in her religion, was related to the ardently Federalist family of Rufus King, and behaved, in Catharine's words, like "a model of propriety and good taste." Into the Beecher household Harriet "introduced a more complete and refined style of housekeeping" and "a quiet and lady-like rule." If she was not affectionate, she was orderly and gentle. In concluding her estimate of her new mother, Catharine ruefully commented in her *Reminiscences:* "That she sometimes failed in manifesting pleasure and words of approval at the well doing of subordinates, only proved that the best of women have opportunities for improvement." [29]

Catharine continued to stay at home and to care for her younger siblings. Mrs. Beecher described her as "a fine-looking girl and in her mind I find all that I expected. She is not handsome, yet there is hardly anyone who appears better." [30] Catharine's rather fierce feeling over her father's marriage was an unusual breach of her normal congeniality. It showed how strongly she felt about her own position in the Beecher family; when she reoccupied that position, in spite of her stepmother's intrusion, her brightness returned.

During her Litchfield years Catharine wrote a good deal of poetry and acted as the family's poet laureate. Her dramatics and her role as the family's eldest child were some of the means whereby Catharine ordered experience. Poetry was another: it gave her the opportunity to stylize or formalize family and social events. For the wedding of a family friend, for example, Catharine wrote a long comic poem describing the ceremony and its participants. On the death of her infant half brother, the death of her mother, taking leave of a friend, and other similar occasions, she composed suitable, usually sentimental, verses. When a party was to be held in her honor, she described the event beforehand in a poem entitled "The Bumble Bee's Ball," characterizing each person as a genial insect and herself as "Katy-Did." These were not necessarily pretentious or even serious poems, and Catharine's wit often made them amusing.[31] By the time she was twenty, Catharine had developed a penchant for seeing herself and others in a stylized rather than a direct way. She could more easily place her experience in a cultural context than she could analyze its interior parts. Perhaps she was so thoroughly socialized to respond to others that she rarely investigated her own feelings or considered them divorced from the immediacy of a social encounter.

Catharine's poetry arose from her enjoyment of the society of others, not from her withdrawal from it. As a lively, personable young woman she formed many close friendships with girls her age who were studying in Litchfield, and she also enjoyed the company of the town's young men. Sleigh rides in winter and strolls under the elms in balmy weather occupied the young people when there was no formal social gathering. Whenever she needed an escort for these occasions, Catharine felt close enough to one young man to ask him to accompany her. She became an expert rider, and her horseback excursions took her through the hilly countryside of western Connecticut. Although she was aware that she "was expected to throw off the character of a girl and assume that of a woman," at this time she was enjoying an intermediate stage.[32] Moonlight walks and romantic fantasies were as much a part of her experience as they were for any other adolescent.

In the spring of 1819 Catharine took her first extended trip away from home. For six months she visited relatives in Boston and Portland. In her letters to an intimate friend, she revealed the state of her mind in these adolescent years. She was not so grown-up as to be above practical jokes, and she and her Bostonian cousin, Lucy, one day donned the kitchen girls' hats and rigged themselves "like dowdy country girls." Since no one knew her in Boston when she first arrived, Catharine sallied around sedate Boston, acting "the simple country wench to perfection." This form of hilarity abruptly ended, however, when the two cousins began to receive the attention of a pair of young Bostonian men. At the end of the first evening that the gentlemen called, Catharine felt "quite acquainted" with them, and before they left, Lucy and she "went out and walked in the court with them some time." Even in Boston propriety did not prevent the girls from calling on the gentlemen, and Lucy and Catharine would stop by one of their homes, exchange "some witty remarks," and return home.[33]

Mr. Hobart and Mr. Willis squired the girls around Boston, and
one Saturday afternoon they took them into the "State house."
They had, as usual, a "charming time": "Lucy and I seated ourselves in the speaker's chair and Hobart and Willis made speeches
to us quite in legislative style." All these excursions were apparently
unchaperoned. Catharine found the attention of the young men
"quite convenient," since they could not move "about Boston much
without beaux." Yet Catharine had other thoughts in her mind
besides convenience. One day her uncle hired a carriage, and the
whole family toured the Massachusetts countryside. Lucy and
Catharine climbed a hillside for the view and at the top "shouted
for joy" at the lovely spot they had discovered. "I was glad there
was no gentleman with us," Catharine confided, "for I should most
assuredly have fallen in love in such a beautiful romantic spot." [34]
Later in June their beaux accompanied them on an evening stroll.
"It was a calm and bright moonlight and I never had so delightful
a walk. . . . Oh, it is enough to make one's *hair bristle* to see it." [35]
At nineteen Catharine was beginning to experience romance and
think of marriage. She had every reason to anticipate a happy
future.

From Boston, Catharine wrote her father that she was "mad with
joy." He responded with a gentle reminder of her unconverted state
and said: "Should you return a Christian from your journey I
should be 'mad with joy.' " [36] During these years Catharine had not
neglected religion, but as the daughter of Lyman Beecher she had
cultivated an insider's view of the quarrels and conflicts in which
the churchmen of her time were engaged, and she gave remarkably
little thought to her personal religious feelings. She occasionally
still accompanied Lyman when one of his many evangelical projects
carried him outside Litchfield.[37] The Beecher home was often
filled to overflowing with visiting clergymen who stayed for days
discussing their strategy against their various enemies. "This is a
confused and noisy week," one of Catharine's visiting cousins wrote
from the Beecher house sometime in 1818. "Kate and I expect to
have to sleep on the sofa every night this week in order to accommodate more ministers." Thus, when Catharine visited Boston's
pulpits, she listened more with a critical mind than a pliant heart
to what the minister said. As an insider, she was more inclined to
judge the quality of the sermon than to apply its message to her-

self. Catharine gave her critical assessment of the Bostonian
churches in a letter to her father, and he replied:

> I am glad my child that you feel the difference between the Gospel
> preached plainly and that despicable, pitiable stuff, called or meant
> to be called, fine writing, as much at war with common sense as it is
> with fidelity and simplicity of real revival preaching.[38]

Catharine had learned to discriminate among the varieties of Calvinism then being preached, and she adopted her father's condemnation of those who opposed or differed with him.

Lyman Beecher had strong opinions about other ministers because to him the church was more than a religious institution — it
was the mainstay of a social order. He had bitterly resisted the
disestablishment of the Congregational church in Connecticut, but
after it was accomplished in 1818, he accepted the new political
reality and devoted himself to maintaining the social power and
influence of the church through other than political means. The
English pattern of evangelical societies, popular tracts, and magazines was one means he adopted. Reforms such as temperance were
another. Revivals were a third.[39]

Catharine grew up highly conscious of the social thrust of her
father's religion. She had been present at too many ministerial
conventions not to know that they were engaged in a struggle for
social supremacy. Yet in Litchfield, where the "best people" were
also the mainstay of the orthodox church, she felt none of the
urgency her father felt as he watched the social gains of the
Unitarians in Massachusetts and the Episcopalians in other parts
of Connecticut. Catharine's family, her school, and her community
all reinforced her strong sense of the stability of her own social
position.

After her return from Boston in the fall of 1819, Catharine spent
the next year and a half cultivating the ornamental accomplishments appropriate to a well-bred young woman in the early nineteenth century. Although she had neglected the piano during her
school days, she now devoted herself to long hours of practice and
within a year became known as an accomplished musician.[40] In her
elegant composition book with red morocco binding, she carefully
wrote the music to the pieces she had mastered. In Litchfield's
literary coterie she was considered quite the equal of the other

native poet, John Brace, Miss Pierce's nephew and an instructor
at her school.[41] Catharine wrote romantic ballads in the style of
Scott and ghostly poems in Irving's gothic style. Lyman placed some
of her poems in an evangelical magazine he had founded.[42] While
her younger brother Edward began to study at Yale and prepare for
a professional career, Catharine devoted herself to the fine arts at
home and prepared for her future calling — marriage. To aid the
family finances she left Litchfield in the spring of 1821 to teach
the domestic arts of needlework, drawing, and painting at a school
for girls in New London.

Catharine continued to enjoy Lyman Beecher's extraordinary
paternal affection. His letters to her are filled with small tokens of
the ties that bound these two so closely. When Catharine's coach
had a slight accident on her journey to Boston, Lyman responded:

> Your account of your journey *affected me much* and though you gave
> a humorous description of your appearance and that of your com-
> pany, I hope you regard the good hand of God in your preserva-
> tion. . . . Your long cold also gave me some uneasiness, though you
> said it was passed away. You must, as you say you do, take especial
> care to clothe warm. You ought, if you do not, to wear flannels in
> that new and raw climate. Purchase or make you some and I will
> pay for them.[43]

Lyman Beecher was a man literally exhausted by his many responsibilities, but he always found time to write to Catharine when
she was away. "My dear Catharine," he wrote on one occasion:

> Though I have written since the receipt of a letter from you . . . I
> wish to let you see that I can write from affection without the im-
> mediate stimulus of a letter. I have concluded to give you half an
> hour this morning — the very cream of the day.

This letter continued to relate the small events of the Beecher
household. "Write to me freely and fully on all subjects interesting
to you," Lyman concluded. On another occasion he wrote, "Be
assured that you have not and cannot have a friend and confidant
more affectionate and trusty than your father." [44]

Yet even before she left for New London Catharine's relationship with her father had begun to change. An eligible Connecticut
bachelor had requested the pleasure of her friendship, but marriage
seen so close did not appear as exciting as it had during her lark
in Boston. She viewed with mixed feelings her father's eagerness

to promote the match, and her confusion increased when Lyman Beecher began to urge that she experience a religious conversion before she left home for good. Catharine was for the first time faced with the full force of the Calvinist insistence that religion was a private change of heart rather than a social style.

❧ 3 ❧

Handling Edge-Tools, 1821–1822

During the years immediately preceding and following her twenty-first birthday Catharine Beecher underwent the full rigors of a New England initiation into adulthood. For her the difficulty of the ritual was compounded by the fact that its major ingredients — religious conversion and marriage — required her to abandon and even denounce the experience of her childhood and youth. In marriage she was asked to transfer her loyalties from her father to her husband, and in a religious rebirth she was asked to forswear her past as encrusted with sin and offensive to God. Both experiences required submission to wills other than her own. These two years were the most traumatic in Catharine Beecher's life. They instilled in her a strain of resistance to her inherited cultural patterns and forced her to begin the search for alternative social forms.

In the spring of 1822 all of Litchfield was talking about Catharine Beecher's engagement to Alexander Fisher. Horace Mann, a law student in Litchfield at the time, met Catharine at one of the town's spring festivities and wrote home about the fashionable young woman to whom "Professor Fisher of New Haven has been *making love*." Horace Mann described her as "a lady of superior intellect," who "writes very good poetry and will probably make the Professor a very good help-mate." [1]

Alexander Metcalf Fisher, like Horace Mann, was born on a farm in Franklin, Massachusetts. Fisher's native intelligence and dedicated scholarship had carried him far beyond his modest origins. In 1819, when he was twenty-four years old, Fisher was appointed to Yale's Professorship in Natural Philosophy. When Catharine Beecher met him in 1821, his reputation as a brilliant scientific thinker had spread throughout the northern United States. Fisher was not only a man of science. Nathanael Emmons (1745–1840), New England's foremost Edwardean theologian, had prepared Fisher for Yale, and after he graduated in 1813 Fisher returned to

28

Franklin to study theology with Emmons. Although he later resumed his secular studies at Yale, Fisher's mind and character remained strongly influenced by New England orthodox thought. He
was also a serious student of music theory and the psychology of
music. All Fisher's actions were characterized by a high moral
rectitude and an earnest sobriety. In spite of the rapid rise of his
academic career, his bearing was straightforward and unaffected.[2]

Fisher's attentions were first drawn to Catharine by a poem of
hers published in Lyman Beecher's evangelical magazine, *The
Christian Spectator*.[3] As an admirer of Lyman Beecher, Fisher had
donated money to Beecher's evangelical causes and contributed
articles to *The Christian Spectator*.[4] Early in 1821, when one of his
clergyman classmates went to preach for Beecher in Litchfield,
Fisher asked to be taken along and introduced to Miss Beecher.
He met her after the morning sermon, walked home with her, and
was invited to stay for Sunday dinner. Later he escorted Catharine
to the afternoon service. In the Litchfield manse that Sunday,
Catharine and Alexander Fisher sang and played the piano together
and both recited poetry.[5] Such attentions were not casually given or
lightly received in the early nineteenth century. The Beecher family
considered Fisher's attentions the beginning of a serious courtship,
and, indeed, within a year the two young people were formally
engaged.

Almost immediately after Fisher's first visit to Litchfield, Lyman
Beecher began to press Catharine to seek the salvation of her soul.
When a young woman of an orthodox family was preparing for
marriage, she was also expected to prepare for her future existence
in heaven. In Connecticut at this time, conversion after marriage
was considered unlikely — presumably because worldly cares became
too engrossing.[6] Another factor that turned Lyman's attentions to
the state of Catharine's soul was her impending departure from
home. That spring she was leaving Litchfield to teach in New
London. Since this departure signified an entrance into the world,
Lyman believed that his daughter's conversion could no longer
safely be postponed.

As a fervent revivalist, Lyman Beecher had strong and somewhat
unusual views about conversion. In the Calvinist tradition his

stance was slightly unorthodox, because redeeming grace was to him no mysterious gift from God to His elect, but a spiritual awakening that men themselves could induce. Beecher believed that conversion was the only path to salvation. Whereas some Calvinists were comfortable in the belief that good works were a means to grace, or prepared the soul for grace, Beecher held that good works were quite irrelevant and that a change of heart was essential to salvation. In the great argument among Calvinists about the use of means to induce grace, Beecher disclaimed all means save that of the heart's total submission to God. Each person was responsible for achieving his own regenerative experience, Beecher believed, by voluntarily submitting himself to God.[7]

Lyman Beecher entreated his children, with all the intensity of his most ardent revival sermons, to experience conversion. He focused this attention on each of his children as he or she left home to study or work. Since Catharine's two younger brothers had departed before her, she was the third child to receive his exhortations. William in 1819 was the first to leave, and Lyman described his feelings about his children in a letter to him.

> While I am as successful as most ministers in bringing the sons and daughters of others to Christ, my heart sinks within me at the thought that every one of my own dear children are without God in the world, and without Christ, and without hope. I have no child prepared to die; and however cheering their prospects for time may be, how can I but weep in secret places when I realize that their whole eternal existence is every moment liable to become an existence of unchangeable sinfulness and woe.[8]

At that time William had already begun to show hopeful signs, and Lyman reminded him "that the most perfect honesty and the most correct morality are nothing, and will profit you nothing in God's account, without love, repentance and faith." Lyman intended to concentrate on his children one at a time until he saw them all sanctified. "I talked and prayed with Edward before he left home," Lyman continued in his letter to William, "and shall attend to Catharine, and Mary and George and Harriet with the hope that God will bless them with salvation." A year later, in 1820, Edward was on the brink of conversion, and Lyman wrote him:

> I shall not cease to pray, my dear son, for your conversion nor to deplore the mighty ruin which all your capacities and improvement

will constitute in another world, should they continue under the dominion of a heart unsanctified and unreconciled to God.[9]

In the spring of 1821, with his two oldest sons well on their way to conversion and with Catharine about to leave for New London and probably soon to marry, Lyman turned his attentions to her. Although Lyman Beecher believed that the sinner's main avenue to conversion was "instant submission," conversion was, in fact, a more complex and prolonged experience than this term indicates. The classic description of conversion — a description approved by Lyman Beecher and one with which Catharine was thoroughly familiar — was Philip Doddridge's *The Rise and Progress of Religion in the Soul.* This popular book had guided private devotions in England and America since the middle of the eighteenth century, and Catharine had studied its pages from the time she could read. She knew its formula well.[10] For Doddridge the path to conversion passed through many stages, beginning with the soul's awakening to its neglect of God, followed by a profound conviction of its sinful state, and finally the soul's repentance of its sins and full submission to God. In this final stage all self-dependence was banished, and the soul was wholly committed into the hands of God.[11]

In response to her father's urgings, Catharine took the first step along this path in March 1821 by resolving to turn her thoughts away from the world and toward God. Catharine's conversion did not proceed as easily as her brothers', however, and her struggle seemed to involve more complicated issues than those her brothers had faced. For Catharine, as a marriageable young woman, could hardly fail to remember what the spirit of submission had meant to her own mother. A young man might exercise briefly his submission to God and then recover his sense of independence and self. For a woman, however, submission to God might be but the prelude to a lifetime of earthly submission to a husband. Such indeed had been the case with Roxana Beecher, and Catharine, like her own mother, was expected to accept conversion and marriage together. Her initiation into the adult world was, like her mother's but unlike her brothers', one that involved a temporary commitment to the will of God and a lifetime commitment to another person. Forced to choose between her mother's example of submerging herself in the character of another and her father's example of personal autonomy, Catharine chose her father. The forces operating against this choice were powerful, but Catharine's resistance was firmly rooted. The whole episode stands as a testimony to the difficulty with which female personal autonomy was achieved in circumstances like Catharine Beecher's in the early nineteenth century.

In the spring of her twenty-first year, Catharine composed a set of religious resolutions designed to aid her concentration on the task of saving her soul. "I will allow no schemes of pleasure, no worldly plans or amusements so to engross my mind as to banish the subject of religion," she wrote. She resolved also "to endeavor to withdraw from that society and those pursuits that will have a tendency to destroy my interest in religious concerns." Catharine admitted that a spring and summer thus spent would be "irksome and disagreeable" to her and that she would be tempted to give up her efforts as a "useless and vain attempt." Yet she accepted the unanimous family opinion that the time for such an effort on her part was ripe and should not be postponed.[12]

Catharine vowed to seek the salvation of her soul, but she seemed, in fact, bent on failure. For the daughter of one of New England's most committed revivalists, Catharine's attitude toward her personal religion was remarkably cool, and her resolutions were filled with clichés instead of piety. She resolved to believe that the so-called better things in life were mere transient pleasures and that in God alone could lasting happiness be found. She acknowledged "the awful probability that this is the last time that God will awaken my attention to the voice of his word," and hoped that "the encouragement of the present time" would indeed be effective.[13] Yet Catharine seemed throughout these vows to be going through the motions of a form in which she did not believe. Although she admitted to worldliness, she did not characterize herself as a lost sinner. Although the exertions she prescribed were conscientious, they were not strenuous. Under the circumstances, her father expected more of her.

Catharine had already begun to disagree with Lyman over two issues that dominated their later theological dispute: the amount of guilt she should feel for her sins and the degree to which she felt able to commit herself to God. She could feel passionately neither her guilt nor her lack of commitment. A week after she had written her resolutions, Lyman wrote to Edward: "She feels so strongly her inability that she can not feel her guilt; and I have had much and assiduous labor with her on that point, and hope she is quiet.[14] Her anxiety is great at times," Lyman added, and he took that for a good sign. She was, he felt, "at the very threshold of heaven" and needed only to feel more strongly and exert herself a little more to enter.

Yet a year later, after she was engaged to Fisher, the condition of her soul remain unchanged. To Edward, who had recently been converted, Catharine wrote that she simply could not feel as she ought and asked him how she could force herself to feel. Edward replied that she would never feel properly when her *"whole* soul" was not committed, and he tried to impress Catharine with the scene she would face when all her family was in heaven and she was shut outside. "O how would the excuses which now paralyse your efforts disappear," he said, "should you see the gates of glory close against you excluding you from all whom you held dear on-earth." Then he said she would ask herself, "This must I endure and this have I lost because I could not make myself feel?"[15]

Believing that her time of grace was passing quickly by, Lyman in the spring of 1822 continued to press God's case with Catharine. Catharine still resisted her father's exhortations, though by now at the price of considerable internal tumult. In April Lyman wrote to Edward: "Catharine has been sick for three days. The first in acute distress. I had been addressing her conscience not twenty minutes before. She was seized with most agonizing pain. I hope it will be sanctified."[16] Yet in this case, as in all others during the past year, the most strenuous exhortation failed to improve Catharine's religious prospects.

During the same year Lyman was pressing God's case with Catharine he was also pressing Alexander Fisher's. On her way to New London in the spring of 1821, Catharine and Lyman traveled together to New Haven. Presumably due to the demands upon Lyman Beecher's time, he did not continue with Catharine to New London. Instead he arranged for Alexander Fisher to take her the rest of the way in his carriage.[17] Although Catharine could not help feeling flattered by the attentions of one of Connecticut's most prominent young men, she had serious doubts about Fisher's qualifications as her husband. Measuring Fisher's personality against her father's, Catharine initially found him wanting. She was determined that her marital home should be as affectionate as her childhood home, and Fisher seemed lacking in affection. He also appeared to be unsuited to the kind of social life Catharine enjoyed. Only after Lyman Beecher's timely intervention and reassurance on these points did Catharine agree to a betrothal.

From the first Lyman was sympathetic to Fisher's courtship, but Catharine felt otherwise, and from New London she described her feelings to her father. "It always seemed to me that devoted and exclusive attention to the abstract sciences almost infallibly will deaden the sensibilities of the heart and destroy social habits," she began. Catharine said she knew the coldheartedness of scientists was a popular myth, but nevertheless she knew no reason why she should "not apply the principle in this case." "It was true," she continued, "that intellect with me ought to be a cardinal point, but I could in the trials and vicissitudes of domestic life better . . . far better dispense with it than I could with a social disposition and an affectionate heart." Catharine reminded her father that she had already discouraged one suitor whom she had found wanting in "the sensibilities of the heart," and said she was skeptical that a scientist could succeed where another had failed. It was her resolution that an "affectionate disposition" was the one qualification she could not dispense with "for any possible consideration that could be offered." [18]

Catharine did not want to enter a marriage that would provide her with less emotional nourishment than she had with her father: "I could not live to be forgotten or neglected by the one for whom I should leave such a father and such a home," she said. "It would be a sorrowful consolation for the want of the thousand kindnesses and little attentions of affections that give comfort to domestic life . . . to know that in return for the loss I could reflect that I was the wife of the greatest mathematician and philosopher in the country." [19] She concluded by saying that she had consented to a friendly correspondence with Fisher and that their relationship could be ended at any time if she chose not to write him.

Fisher for his part seems to have courted best through the mails. Catharine found him unresponsive in person, but his postal responses were more than adequate. He replied the same day to every letter she sent him. Catharine admitted to her close friend Louisa Wait, "The fact is he does write confounded pretty letters and has shown more good judgment and delicacy than I should have thought possible in such a kind of man as I used to think he was." Catharine was beginning to wonder whether she had misjudged his capacity for affection. "What kind of a man I think he is now," she concluded, "I really don't know." [20]

Catharine was not happy in New London, and she wanted to return home. Edward, home for a vacation from Yale, wrote that he missed her. "Indeed I did not think you filled so large a place till you left it," he said. Catharine was reluctant to see her childhood home disbanded. Before she had left for New London she had written that she "could not bear to have [Edward] go away" and that she "used to be scared sometimes to see how like men and women we four oldest children looked." [21] These sentiments were perhaps natural to one who had experienced such a full and happy childhood and youth, surrounded by the activity and excitement of her large family. New babies continued to arrive in the Beecher home, and the family life in Litchfield was as vital as it had been ten years earlier. But Catharine and her older siblings had become marginal members of that life. It would necessarily take several years or even a decade of married life before Catharine and her husband could re-create such a rich and intense family life as the one she was leaving. In July, after she had been in New London for four months, Catharine wrote her father that she would soon return home. But he replied:

> You speak with confidence of returning in the fall to spend the winter at home. On this subject however . . . my opinion and advice is that you make us a good visit in your vacation and return to prolong your earnings through the winter. You will need assistance which you can perceive my circumstances will not enable me to afford. Though were my finances equal to my affections I should doubtless leave you little to ask or desire. . . .

The financial assistance Lyman was referring to was the money Catharine would need for a trousseau. Lyman believed that she would soon be married, and by his tone he tried to create a new distance between them. Yet Catharine felt restive in New London and was not in a compliant mood. She freely criticized the town's orthodox minister as "unanimated," and Lyman warned her to keep her judgments more secret lest her remarks wound the minister and injure her relations with the community.[22] She was "entirely

without society of any kind," she said, and keenly felt the loss of
Litchfield's social liveliness. "As for the young gentlemen," Catharine wrote Louisa, "they are polite enough, but pretty shy, for
from the ominous circumstances in which I came to town . . . it
is pretty generally supposed I am engaged." [23]

Catharine resented the paternal and social pressures pushing her
toward a socially and financially desirable match and in her rebellious mood hinted that she might break off her correspondence
with Fisher since her postal courtship had grown less and less
satisfying. Lyman sternly replied: "Let no caprice or inconsistency
on your part becloud a prospect so deservedly a subject of com-
placency to your friends and so full of promises of earthly good."
Her father assured her that she could return home permanently in
the spring of the next year, and that her sister Mary was preparing
herself to take Catharine's place in New London.[24]

In the fall, however, Catharine took matters in her own hands
and told Fisher she would no longer exchange letters with him.
Lyman, dismayed by his daughter's decision, wrote her a letter
highly critical of her conduct and visited Fisher in New Haven to
try and mend their relationship.[25] Lyman proposed that Catharine
join Fisher in New Haven for a few days to reassure him of her
affection, but Catharine refused to go and instead suggested to her
father that she return home immediately and receive Fisher there.
Whatever the logic of Catharine's maneuvering was, she was home
for good a month later.[26] "I brought matters to a crisis, as the
doctors say," Catharine wrote Louisa in January 1822, and "I am an
'engaged woman.'" Fisher came to Litchfield in December, and after
"a long string of misunderstanding," Catharine wrote, "we finally
both found out that we both loved each other too well to quarrel
any longer, and we soon met on such terms as all lovers should
meet." Catharine went on to say that her earlier doubts about
Fisher's "sensibilities of the heart" had vanished.

> He staid two or three days and I soon felt no doubt that I have gained
> the whole heart of one whose equal I never saw both as it respects
> intellect and all that is amiable and desirable in private character.
> I could not ask for more delicacy and tenderness.[27]

Catharine had not initially encouraged Fisher's courtship, and
she was at one time willing to end it. Her dominant desire in New
London was to return home rather than to encourage Fisher. Yet

once she was home she was more easily reconciled to her father's desire to see her married, and to her suitor's qualities of heart.

Catharine's only regret, she wrote Louisa, was that they must soon be parted, for Fisher was scheduled to sail for England on the first of April and spend a year touring European universities. For his part, Lyman was happy to have had his way. "We have lately had a visit from Professor Fisher," he wrote to the Foote family, "which has terminated in a settled connection, much to my satisfaction as well as of the parties. He goes to Europe in the spring, returns in a year, and then will expect to be married." [28]

Two months later, upon arriving in New Haven for a conference of clergymen, Lyman Beecher heard the first news of Alexander Fisher's death at sea. His ship, the *Albion,* had lost a rudder and crashed into the cliffs on the west coast of Ireland. There were only two survivors, and Fisher was not among them.[29] The news had just reached New Haven nearly five weeks after the event occurred. Catharine's father wrote her:

> My Dear Child, — On entering the city last evening, the first intelligence I met filled my heart with pain. It is all but certain that Professor Fisher is no more. . . .
>
> Thus have perished our earthly hopes, plans, and prospects. Thus the hopes of Yale College, and of our country, and, I may say, of Europe, which had begun to know his promise, are dashed. The waves of the Atlantic, commissioned by Heaven, have buried them all.

After some comforting words on how to live with sorrow and a hopeful speculation on the state of Fisher's soul at the moment of his death, Lyman dramatized the alternatives before Catharine's own soul:

> And now, my dear child, what will you do? Will you turn at length to God, and set your affections on things above, or cling to the shipwrecked hopes of earthly good? Will you send your thoughts to heaven and find peace, or to the cliffs, and winds, and waves of Ireland, to be afflicted, tossed with tempest and not comforted? [30]

Lyman clearly expected Catharine to make a new effort to experience conversion, but Fisher's death did not weaken her resist-

ance. "Will you let this warning also pass unimproved," Edward
wrote his sister. "What more can God do that he has not done to
detach you from this earth?" [31] Lyman and Edward made it impossible for Catharine to express any feelings of personal loss at
Fisher's death, for they made the theme of her loss their own and
used it against her. Whatever feelings of personal distress Catharine
felt (and the fact that she spent much of the next winter with
Fisher's family revealed a more than superficial regard for his
memory), she repressed in the presence of her own family and turned
to meet Lyman and Edward on more solid and purely doctrinal
grounds.

Though living for the next year under considerable stress, Catharine persisted in the course she had taken before Fisher's death.
She had no deep sense of her sin or guilt, and she could not bring
herself to submit to an angry God. With the salvation of her soul
hanging in the balance, Catharine struggled to reconcile her own
feelings with her father's religious doctrines, but at the end of a
year she was still unconverted and so she remained.

This confrontation between Catharine and her religious heritage
was the most formative experience of her life. It so profoundly engaged her mind and emotions that, even while she resisted certain
doctrines of her father's religion, she became irrevocably committed to the larger issues of that heritage. Engrossed in her father's
arguments, Catharine never imagined a completely different intellectual or emotional framework from the one her father provided. Her ability to find her own answers to the arguments her
father considered irrefutable only attached her more firmly to the
basic outlines of her religious heritage. Rather than devising new
terms or totally rejecting those used by her father, Catharine re-
shaped the old ones to suit her present needs.

Among these needs was some kind of confirmation of her female
identity. The "rebirth" or "new birth" experience of conversion
had classically enabled men and women to establish psychic contact with their interior self, or at least to resolve contradictions
within their sense of self. Yet during Catharine's whole *rite de
passage* Lyman and Edward Beecher seem to have heightened rather
than resolved the contradictory elements of her identity. Catharine's
passage through these rites was especially rough precisely because
she refused to pretend that the contradictions were resolved when
they were not.

On the one hand she had been encouraged to invest a great deal of herself in the family life of her childhood and youth. Indeed many of her difficulties now arose from her unwillingness to leave her childhood home. Yet she was now required to condemn this past as a sinful attachment to worldly concerns. Moreover, this condemnation was not, as in the case of her brothers, a prelude to some new life outside the home, but a prelude to the resumption of those same feminine domestic responsibilities.

When faced, therefore, with her father's view of original sin, Catharine now said that she had her own ideas about that doctrine and that her views were sanctioned by experience. Catharine's description of the grasp of past socialization on present character contrasted sharply with Lyman's belief that conversion can overcome and obliterate the past. She was guilty, she admitted, of sinful self-regard, but she felt unable to change herself voluntarily or to feel that she was totally responsible for those sinful propensities. Whatever she was, her past had made her so, and she could not now alter it. The principle of selfishness, for example, was "implanted" within her "as powerful and inveterate as the love of drink," and by now it was "altogether involuntary." She argued that if she was born with an inclination toward the sins she was guilty of, then she should not be held wholly responsible for them. "I feel all the time as if there was *something wrong* — something that is unreasonable," she wrote to Edward.[32]

Perhaps as a woman Catharine was more attuned than the men in her family to the powers of socialization and the difficulty of overcoming them in order to begin a new life. In any case, she refused to use Lyman's and Edward's line of reasoning even when the cost of maintaining her own was emotionally very high. Given the vigor of her father's persuasive powers, Catharine's strength of resistance was remarkable. Lyman exhorted Catharine while she sat sobbing in his study, her face swollen by days of crying.[33] Still she refused to submit. "I am greatly afflicted," she wrote Edward. "I feel no realizing sense of my sinfulness, no love to the Redeemer, nothing but that I am unhappy and need religion; but where or how to find it I know not."[34]

Lyman himself admitted to Edward, "I have at times been at my wit's end to know what to do." He concluded that "nothing safe can be done" but to urge the full force of all the doctrines Catharine resisted. He asserted "ability, and obligation, and guilt upon

divine authority" and tried to knock down "the indefensible positions which depravity, and fear, and selfishness, and reason set up."
In other words, he said, "I answer objections and defend the ways
of God." In Catharine, however, Lyman admitted that he may have
met his match. "She is now," he wrote to Edward, "handling edge-
tools with powerful grasp." [35]

Indeed, Catharine did handle the edge-tools of depravity, guilt,
and responsibility with a strength equal to her father's. Even among
the New England ministry, few besides Lyman Beecher relished the
task of wrestling with the logic of these divine matters. The de-
fenders of Calvinism had argued many points of theology into
a dead end by the 1820s, and what had begun in the seventeenth
century as a positive assertion of God's glory became in the early
nineteenth century a collection of negatives that was increasingly
out of touch with such basic forces as the growth of popular
democracy and the ideology of individual freedom. Perhaps one
reason Lyman Beecher emphasized conversion so passionately was
that it was at least a positive achievement wrought by anyone who
would turn his or her will to the effort. In a set of contemporary
doctrines given to ambiguity and to the avoidance of evil rather
than the celebration of good, conversion represented a saving
remnant of the seventeenth-century spirit of joyous conviction.

Lyman Beecher's theology was more democratic than most because it located spiritual and moral initiative in the individual.
Yet because he retained the minister as the ultimate spiritual authority, Beecher's system remained fundamentally hierarchical. By
designing multiple sources of moral authority, two of which were
the family and the school, Catharine's later writings leveled this
hierarchy. She came to celebrate even the homeliest of earthly
virtues as contributing positively to God's purposes, and the
Americans who bought her books must have agreed. Catharine's
system had greater democratic potential than her father's, but it
eliminated the strain of visionary insight that had periodically
revitalized New England orthodoxy. If the change in American
popular attitudes in the nineteenth century can be defined largely
as the transition from a Calvinist to a Victorian or realist ethic,
Catharine's contribution to this change began in her sense of "something wrong" with the moral sensitivity of the Calvinist system —
a system that invalidated the worldly circumstances she had so successfully mastered as a child and young woman. [36]

Lyman and Edward grew increasingly frustrated with Catharine's theological debate, however, and by August 1822 they were not above reprimanding her for arguing too closely about points better left to God and to men trained in the ways of God. "I think you are in danger of speculating too much," Edward wrote her, and after arguing himself to a standstill on a fine point of guilt and original sin, he asserted: "I do not expect to throw light on this dark spot, so as to make all things clear; nor ought you to expect to be entirely unembarrassed, where none within the range of my knowledge are free from perplexity." If mere reasoning could make the issues clear, Edward concluded, "I might protract these remarks much further." [37]

Having engaged in a purely doctrinal argument with Catharine, both Lyman and Edward treated her crisis as a religious "case." They were either unsympathetic or deaf to Catharine's signals that her distress involved personal issues besides religion. Edward cut off his correspondence when Catharine said that her preoccupation with her inner self prevented her from surrendering to God. Lyman seems never to have thought that her prolonged crisis was her way of calling for the affectionate and understanding attention of a father instead of the annihilating voice of a Calvinist God. In a remarkable note to her father, Catharine described God in terms that could well have stood for Lyman:

> I am like a helpless being placed in a frail bark, with only a slender reed to guide its way on the surface of a swift current that no mortal power could ever stem, which is ever bearing to a tremendous precipice, where is inevitable destruction and despair.
>
> If I attempt to turn the swift course of my skiff, it is only to feel how powerful is the stream that bears it along. If I dip my frail oar in the wave, it is only to see it bend to its resistless force.
>
> There is One standing upon the shore who can relieve my distress, who is all powerful to save; but He regards me not. I struggle only to learn my own weakness, and supplicate only to perceive how unavailing are my cries, and to complain that He is unmindful of my distress.[38]

In his reply Lyman spoke for God in the first person, but his assurance was not the kind of paternal affection Catharine desired. He devastatingly answered that he had deliberately destroyed her happiness and that he had already come as near to her as he intended:

I saw that frail boat with feeble oar, and that rapid current bearing onward to destruction an immortal mind and hastened from above to save. . . .

It is many days, many years, I have stood on the bank unnoticed. I have called, and she refused; I stretched out my hand and she would not regard. At length I sunk the bark in which all her earthly treasure was contained, and, having removed the attraction that made her heedless, again I called, and still I call unheard. My rod has been stretched out and my staff offered in vain. While the stream prevails and her oar bends, within her reach is My hand, mighty to save, and she refuses its aid.

Catharine's reluctance to experience conversion drew her into a state of extreme inertia that lasted till the end of August. "Thus," she wrote, "my hours are passing away as the smoke, and my days as a tale that is told. . . . I lie down in sorrow and awake in heaviness, and go mourning all the day long. There is no help beneath the sun, and whether God will ever grant His aid He only knows." [39]

☙ 4 ❧

Brow of Iron, 1823

Even when Catharine was at the height of her spiritual crisis, she never fully abandoned her worldly roles. Edward's letters frequently left their high theological plane to ask her to mend his trousers and to have his shirts pressed. "Trust in him and he will give you that peace which passeth all knowledge," he wrote to her, and added in almost the next breath, "I wish the striped pantaloons I send to be lengthened as the other pair was." Another time he added to his religious exhortations, "I wish you would be *very particular and very certain* to have my shirts, vest, cravats and stockings washed and sent down on Monday." [1] Catharine was his older sister, currently in spiritual distress, but still apparently responsible for the care of his wardrobe. Yet in spite of Edward's domesticity-as-usual attitude, Catharine must have found that her normal family role was complicated by her religious crisis.

Toward the end of August, therefore, Catharine ended her seclusion in the Litchfield manse and visited her stepmother's sister in Boston. There Catharine's spirit revived. When she was engaged once more in social activities, her depression of the last three months lifted. After reading John Newton, an English evangelical writer who stressed God's compassion and His willingness to save even the most reluctant sinners, Catharine felt a mental and emotional composure that had been impossible for her under her father's more demanding presence.

In Boston began the first in a lifelong series of female friendships that she sought to comfort her in times of mental distress. She did not take part in any of the social amusements that characterized her visit to Boston in 1819 but stayed close to another young woman who, like herself, felt forsaken. Julia Porter, Catharine's distant cousin, was also staying with Catharine's aunt. "She is homeless and forlorn," Catharine wrote to Edward and said she took pleasure in comforting Julia.[2] Catharine's affection for her cousin increased when Julia became ill, and Catharine took charge of Julia's protracted convalescence. In these circumstances Catharine was kept too busy to devote her time to religion. She explained defensively to Edward: "I have greatly enjoyed her society — much more than I wished to, for it has been a great temptation and diversion of mind from a subject which I wished should have my whole concern." The temptation of Julia's companionship was too great for Catharine. She decided that since "it seems to be my duty to be with her," and since she "struggled against the temptation," she now only "hoped that in the path of duty I should not be led astray."

Duty and convenience combined to relieve Catharine of her pressing religious concerns. Catharine's description of Julia's companionship reveals how happy Catharine was to return to her former social self. "She is a very interesting girl," Catharine said. "I don't know where I have ever come in contact with one more congenial in habits, tastes and feelings." The two were constantly together during Catharine's six weeks in Boston. "The more I become acquainted with her," Catharine wrote, "the more I esteem and love her."

In Boston Catharine revealed that her quarrel with her father had been an internal Calvinist or familial quarrel and that she remained strongly allied with him against his external enemies. Bitterly as she might argue with her father's strain of religion, she never placed herself outside the cultural tradition he represented. The alien Unitarian context, Julia's sociable and religious companionship, and the absence of the severe pressure she had endured in Litchfield, all revived her sense of position within her father's religious culture. When she was placed once more in a social rather than a purely devotional context, the beliefs she held in common with her father became more important than their disagreements.

In Boston Catharine read books that she never would have read in Litchfield. Catharine Sedgwick's *New England,* currently enjoying an enormous popularity in Boston, was one of these. *New England* ridiculed Calvinist theology for its unreasonable doctrines and attacked the Calvinist clergy for its single-minded rigidity.

Catharine's criticism of Sedgwick's book was highly revealing, for she attacked Catharine Sedgwick as a traitor to her social position and tradition. Descended on her mother's side from a prominent family in the aristocracy and orthodoxy of the Connecticut River clans of western Massachusetts, Catharine and her brother Theodore were one of the first converts to William Ellery Channing's new Unitarian beliefs. "I think every one who has heretofore known Miss S. will feel both grieved, surprised, and indignant, at the course she has pursued," Catharine wrote. "If there ever was one who with their eyes open and in the full blaze of truth turned traitor and denied the Lord, it is her." Catharine Beecher could not think of a circumstance to palliate or excuse her. "She has long been a church member of Dr. West's church and was considered as one of its brightest ornaments, and she has long associated with many of those who are the excellent of the earth," Catharine said, "and *she knows better.*" Catharine did not object to Miss Sedgwick's opinions as much as she deplored the fact that by stating them publicly she had aided the enemies of orthodoxy and aligned herself with them. "For the sake of gaining the admiration and applause of a party," Catharine said, "she has sacrificed her integrity and she ought to be made to smart for it."

Catharine thought the review of *New England* in the *Christian Spectator* had not attacked Miss Sedgwick strongly enough. The book was gaining great influence in Boston, and Catharine believed that it was certain to do great injury to the Calvinist cause. "For it may be said and it is said," Catharine wrote, " 'Here is Miss S. who has known and associated with those whom the Calvinists consider their best and truest representatives, who has been educated a Calvinist, who is a woman of superior discernment and who has had every advantage to learn the truth and see how she thinks and feels about Calvinism and its influence.' " Catharine's horror was fully aroused by Catharine Sedgwick's betrayal of her social leadership and religious heritage. She fully allied herself with her father against his Unitarian enemies. "I believe she has done more injury to the cause of truth," Catharine concluded, "than Dr. Ware or Professor Norton, and I believe she has done it wilfully and with her eyes open." [3] Edward replied that he thought Catharine exaggerated Miss Sedgwick's importance, especially by comparing her with Ware — that Unitarian usurper of Harvard's divinity professorship.[4] But to Catharine, Sedgwick's social betrayal was more significant than Ware's theological betrayal. "The cause of truth" was to Catharine more than a set of doctrinal beliefs; it was a social establishment and a set of loyalties. Her quarrel with Calvinist doctrines had for the present left her allegiance with the Calvinist way of life and its social leadership intact. Indeed her doctrinal unorthodoxy may even have intensified her social orthodoxy, for the ferocity of Catharine's attack on Sedgwick bespoke a certain anxiety on her part. The prospect of a wellborn young woman attacking the entirety of Calvinist culture was deeply disturbing to Catharine, perhaps because she feared that she herself had come dangerously close to such an act of symbolic patricide.

Just before she left Boston in October to spend the winter with the Fisher family, Catharine received a letter from Lyman blasting the tranquillity she had enjoyed after reading the gentler English evangelicals. Their tradition was not hers, he said, for they neglected the New England emphasis upon depravity and guilt, and they did not insist upon a complete submission to God in a conversion experience. "Now who are right," Lyman asked, "the Old or New England Divines?" After reclaiming Catharine's loyalty for New England, Lyman warned her against relaxing her spiritual vigilance, as she so obviously had in Boston. "Guard against those seasons when the clouds clear away, and present an inviting, smiling world," Lyman warned. "I dread such clearings off. Had rather you should walk in darkness and see no light till you trust in the Lord." [5]

In spite of the harsh wording of her father's correspondence, Catharine looked forward to receiving his letters and requested him to write to her at the Fishers' so a letter would be there when she arrived. Lyman complied. "I shall follow you, step by step, in your comfortless way," his first letter to her at Franklin began.[6] Catharine's correspondence and debate with her father was beginning to assume a life of its own apart from the theological issues they were discussing. What others might have taken as an unbearable assault on their minds and emotions, Catharine seemed to relish. She would have preferred a more kindly God (and father) who looked to her individual needs instead of imposing a doctrinal formula, yet if neither Lyman nor his God supplied the quality of attention she desired, Lyman was rendering her an enormous quantity of intense attention. Her letters invariably closed by urging Lyman to reply to her letter immediately, or by requesting him to "answer this speedily and *in all its particulars*" just as he would in conversation, and she often underlined her requests.[7] Catharine's opposition to her father did not take a sulking form. Instead, she engaged in the very activity for which Lyman himself was best known — a vigorous, even extravagant, assertion of deeply held convictions. He was the pattern of her protest.

※※

In Franklin, Massachusetts, among Fisher's literary remains, Catharine found another pattern.[8] This was one of quiet distress in religious failure, a distress relieved by only one spectacular outburst. Fisher had been a divided man who had loved science but had feared he was displeasing God. Nathanael Emmons, the Edwardean preacher of damnation, had prepared Fisher for Yale and instructed him in divinity after his graduation. Fisher had continued these studies at Andover for a year and then suffered a brief period of insanity before he had returned to Yale and secular pursuits. His mental derangement may have been known only to his family, and although Catharine must have discovered its evidence among his papers, she never mentioned it, and she may have attributed it to his genius.

In keeping with his meticulous honesty, Fisher wrote a long description of his insanity. It lasted only a few weeks in 1815 after he left Andover and before he assumed the duties of a tutor at Yale. His "delirium," as he called it, consisted of an overwhelming elation and a fanatical concentration on designs to save the universe through science. He often went for four days without sleep while he filled notebooks with schemes for a man-made millennium. His religious melancholy gave way, he said, to a conviction that he was "the master of the world."[9] Fisher's excursion into the fantastic was brief, but it revealed the enormous strain created by his decision to leave theological for secular studies. At Yale Fisher devoted himself wholeheartedly to his scientific career, and each year found him further removed from his desired goal of conversion. Fisher, like Catharine, clearly recognized what God expected of him, but he too felt incapable of meeting God's demands. He had none of her doctrinal objections, but rather "an incapacity . . . of making moral truth the subject of steady contemplation." Sabbath after Sabbath from 1815 to 1820 he plaintively recorded his failings in his diary and resolved to make greater efforts. He prescribed "meditation, devotional reading, writing and prayer" for himself but found that he could not persevere in his resolutions. "The subject of religion has been more nearly than ever banished from my thoughts," he wrote in 1818. "In respect to the performance of religious duties [this year] has been a blank," he wrote in his diary in 1819. Finally he concluded that he had developed an "inconceivable blindness of mind and hardness of heart," and he stopped keeping a diary.[10] In the meantime, however, he was a highly conscientious teacher, and his virtue and morality were exemplary.

Fisher's example renewed Catharine's conviction that worldly virtue as well as divine grace could earn salvation. "When I think of Mr. Fisher, and remember his blameless and useful life, his un-exampled and persevering efforts to do his duty both to God and man," Catharine wrote her father from Franklin, "I believe . . . that God . . . does make the needful distinction between virtue and vice; and that there was more reason to hope for one whose whole life had been an example of excellence, than for one who had spent all his days in guilt and sin." In her dead fiancé's papers Catharine found proof that she was not alone in her inability to experience grace. "Year after year with persevering and unexampled effort, he sought to yield that homage of the heart to his Maker which was required," Catharine wrote, "but he could not; like the friend who followed his steps, he had no strength, and there was none given him from above." [11]

Lyman agreed that "there is more reason to hope for one whose whole life has been an example of excellence than for one who has spent all his days in vice and sin" but said that Fisher's main claim to salvation lay in his humble attitude toward God. In spite of Fisher's feelings of inability, Lyman said, he never murmured against God for not helping him but "took the blame and shame upon himself." This was, he told Catharine, "exactly the opposite course from what you are taking." Fisher was unwilling to submit to God, but, Lyman said, "he maintained just and honorable views of God, his law and gospel, and of himself as able and accountable." Lyman had read Fisher's diary earlier in the summer but had postponed telling Catharine of its existence, fearing its effect upon her. "I have some hesitation now as to the expediency of your perusing it," he said. If Catharine's "aversion to effort" continued, and if the environment in Franklin produced more "wild dis-order" in her thoughts, Lyman concluded, "it is my opinion de-cidedly that you must withdraw from the town immediately." [12]

Fisher's example of moral rectitude coexisting with an unredeemed heart did have an enduring effect on Catharine Beecher's attitude toward morality and religion. Although Lyman and Edward both began to fear for Catharine's sanity when she prolonged her religious crisis into the new year, Catharine was in fact thinking more clearly than ever and was now firmly convinced that there was another path to salvation besides the one her father advocated. Perhaps she too could lead a virtuous life, remain unconverted, and yet be saved.

Nevertheless the effect of Fisher's example upon Catharine can be exaggerated. As much as she desired to believe they would meet again in heaven, Catharine was more concerned with her own case than with Fisher's. Her preference for morality over piety can also be overstated. Her belief in the efficacy of moral behavior never devolved into an Arminian doctrine of salvation through good works alone. The affections of the heart remained as important to her as they were to her father.

Catharine's resolutions of these issues were not really completed until the end of the decade, when she wrote a text on moral philosophy. For the present Catharine fell back on Newton's view of a compassionate God, which permitted her to remain passive rather than energetic in her love to God and allowed her heart to remain her own.[13] Lyman was incensed and refused to let her off easily at the end of their two-year debate. "What has altered your feelings toward God?" he wrote and insisted that she had avoided a change in her own heart by devising a spurious "change in the divine character." Her "presumptuous reliance upon [her] own supposed consciousness," he said, would cost her her soul.[14]

Catharine's faith was not in any compassionate Methodist or Episcopal God but in herself and her own convictions. She concluded that "arguments equally powerful with those advanced by you and Edward and ten thousand times more so" would not be strong enough to move her. "Consciousness," she said, "would be that brow of iron that would resist them all."[15] With this their debate ended. Catharine had won the right to define her own religious and emotional life and to inhabit her own moral universe. She had turned the rites of submission into a ritual of endurance.

By January Catharine began to consider herself qualified to engage in adult worldly pursuits. She said she had fervently desired to find "a better and more enduring good" and to wean her heart "from this fascinating world." But having failed, she said she

would "almost from *necessity,* return to the world to receive its
dregs of happiness." Worldly happiness would not be equal to the
greater happiness she might have found in God, she said, "but the
heart must have *something* to rest upon and if it is not God, it
will be the world." [16]

At Franklin with the Fishers Catharine had already begun to
establish modest connections with the outside world. The Fisher
family treated her as their son's "greatest mourner," and this role
gave dignity to her predicament. It also drew her into worldly concerns, for she spent most of December and January composing an
epitaph for a monument Mr. Fisher was erecting in his son's
honor. Sponsored partly by Yale and partly by the Fisher family,
the monument was to stand in Franklin. Professor Kingsley of Yale
was chosen to write a Latin epitaph for one side, and, "in com-
pliance with the wishes of the family, the other side" was to be
"inscribed by the hand of the greatest mourner." [17] Catharine had
to defend her inscription against the objections of the men at Yale
who were responsible for the college's share of the monument. A
member of the Dwight family feared that her personal sentiments
would mar the effect of the classical Latin lines, and he asked Mr.
Fisher to omit Catharine's epitaph. Mr. Fisher quickly rose to
Catharine's defense, however, and her lines were inscribed.[18]

Catharine thus played a part in the public ceremonies of mourning that followed Fisher's death. At Yale and Columbia black arm-
bands had been worn for a month. Yale commissioned Samuel
F. B. Morse to paint Fisher's posthumous portrait, and it was hung
in the room where Fisher lectured. Fisher's scientific accomplishments and moral rectitude were eulogized in magazines, from
pulpits, and at academic ceremonies.[19] In August Edward had
urged Catharine to attend Yale's commencement, when a special
memorial ceremony for Fisher would take place. For undisclosed
reasons, probably due to her hostility toward Kingsley and Yale,
Catharine declined Edward's invitation.[20]

After the Fisher family gave her the opportunity to express her
grief in a public way, Catharine more fully explored the meaning
of Fisher's death. Catharine's role in the memorial rites seem to have
made his death and her present situation clearer to her. After organizing and formalizing her emotions toward the event, she was
able to see herself as a woman with an earthly future and to speak

of what worldly pursuits would engage her before she was reunited in heaven with Alexander Fisher.

By the time Catharine left Franklin she was energized as she had never been before. The chief inspiration for her self-confidence and enthusiasm arose from her immersion in Alexander Fisher's scientific papers. Upon her arrival Catharine had agreed to replace Alexander as tutor to his siblings, and her most ambitious tutee was twenty-six-year-old Willard, whose neglected education Catharine meant to correct. For aid in the scientific lessons she was giving Willard, Catharine often wrote Edward Beecher at Yale, requesting information about the nature of electric fluids, the movement of hot and cold air masses, and experiments with the chemical composition of wood.[21]

Catharine was especially eager for Edward to have Alexander Fisher's scientific papers sent from Yale to Franklin so that she could refer directly to them for information she needed in Willard's lessons. She impatiently refused the request of Fisher's successor that the papers remain at Yale.[22] In obedience to the family wishes, all of Fisher's scientific papers were returned to Franklin, where Catharine pored over them and began to realize that her intellectual abilities ran deeper than she had imagined and that they had been only superficially tapped by her past education.

Among Fisher's papers were several texts on mathematics, the earliest one composed when he was eleven years old. As Catharine studied these and other currently popular texts for the lessons she gave the Fisher daughters, she developed an appetite for serious intellectual exertion. "Beside completing Daboll," she recalled, "I went through Day's Algebra, a few exercises in Geometry, a work of Logic, and two small works prepared for schools, on Chemistry and Natural Philosophy." Having begun with the "pleasing mournful task" of filling the place Fisher had left vacant in his family, Catharine began to have grander ideas on how she might follow in the footsteps of her fiancé.[23]

Signaling that the time of mourning for her soul and for Fisher had drawn to a close, she consulted Lyman in February about her "future employment." Catharine now anticipated that "the world will soon engross my thoughts," and she agreed to leave Franklin and meet her father in Boston, where he was conducting a revival. In answer to Lyman's hint that she might now consider some kind of gainful employment, especially since the Beecher family finances were in another period of crisis, Catharine consented to the obvious option of teaching. But with Fisher's example before her and with her own intellectual development well under way, Catharine believed she could make more of this employment than she had before. "Generally speaking there seems to be no very extensive sphere of usefulness for a single woman but that which can be found in the limits of a school-room," she admitted, but she now meant to accomplish a great deal within those limits. "There have been instances in which women of superior mind and acquirements have risen to a more enlarged and comprehensive boundary of exertion," she continued, "and by their talents and influence have accomplished what, in a more circumscribed sphere of action, would have been impossible." Thus Catharine consented to her father's wishes that she not remain at home, yet hinted at her new intellectual ambitions. "I have always supposed that the distinguishing characteristics of my own mind were an active and inventive imagination, and quick perceptions in matters of taste and literature," she said. "Yet I think there is reason to believe that in more solid pursuits there is no deficiency." Her memory, she said, was "quick and retentive," and the only reason it was not stored with knowledge was "the neglect of the past." All her knowledge, she said, "as it were, *walked into my head.*" [24] For the past year Catharine had pitted her mind against her father's, and this experience together with her winter in Franklin had revealed her intellectual competence and had shown her how satisfying intellectual pursuits could be. A school of her own would give her the chance to continue her intellectual growth.

In July Lyman had taken Catharine to Hartford to talk with the Reverend Joel Hawes (1789–1867), pastor of the First Congregational Church, feeling that Catharine might accept the theological arguments of someone outside the family sooner than she would accept them from her own father. While they were there, Hawes had "lamented the want of a good female school." Catharine chose to ignore this remark when it was made, but now she returned to it. "This and your advice have led me to wish to commence one there," she concluded in her letter to Lyman. Another reason for wanting to go to Hartford was that Edward was also operating a school there as a means to finance his theological studies. With Edward's help and with the assistance of her younger sister Mary,

Catharine thought the school would not be too great a burden and that she might "have considerable time for improvement" of her own mind.[25]

Within a month Lyman had canvassed the Hartford community, obtained definite commitments from scholars for the school, and arranged for it to open within six weeks. "I came here Tuesday evening, and began my inquiries next day about opening a school and [have] been pushing them as fast as such matters can be pushed until now," he wrote Catharine. The "principal people" who have growing families in Mr. Hawes's congregation have been consulted, Lyman said, and "approve and desire the attempt." Although some of their children are currently committed to other schools, "they will in due time be placed in your school," he believed.[26]

Whether Lyman felt that Catharine had only reluctantly agreed to return to teaching, whether he took her intellectual ambitions as a sign that she would use the school as an opportunity to pursue her own studies to the neglect of her students, or whether he feared that Catharine would put Edward and Mary to work in the school while she engaged in other things, he in any case wanted to be sure "before a definite engagement" was made that Catharine understood the nature of the obligation she was assuming. In the first place, he said, "it will not . . . answer for you to engage in it listlessly, expecting yourself to superintend and do a little, and have the weight of school come on others." Mary, he said, was not strong enough to sustain the weight of the school, for she had been ill recently, and Edward found keeping school "irksome," since it affected his health. If he could obtain a loan of two hundred dollars from her, Lyman said, he would support Edward at home, where he could help in the revival effort. Catharine must bear the weight of the school herself, he admonished: "It cannot to you in any way be a sinecure." [27]

Catharine was currently in Boston, and Lyman, after conferring with Hawes, told Catharine to "go immediately to Mr. Emerson at Saugus and get from him all the information concerning his system of instruction" that she could. Emerson's school was one of the most famous in the country for encouraging more than ornamental female accomplishments. Lyman suggested that she go there, "staying long enough and going into his school and perhaps taking notes as an assistant till you are well possessed of his plan."

Emerson, being a friend of her father's, would, Lyman concluded, "gladly indoctrinate you in his system." [28]

As one of the first marks of her new independence, Catharine declined to take advantage of Mr. Emerson's wisdom, and when she entered Hartford a few weeks later to make arrangements for boarding and for a place for the school, she came equipped with only her own ideas.

On her way to Hartford, Catharine stopped in New Haven to inquire about the two thousand dollars left to her in Fisher's will. "Of this money I will thank you to make no disposal until I see you," Lyman wrote. He needed some of it immediately for himself, and he thanked her in advance for her loan of two hundred dollars.[29] Lyman continued to treat his daughter as a dependent minor, and although she was twenty-three years old, she found it as hard to assert psychological independence as to establish financial independence.

Catharine Beecher had been raised to believe in herself as a strong and distinctive person. For twenty-one years she had derived emotional and psychological satisfaction from her relationship with her father. Yet in her crisis of 1822 Lyman made it clear that he would no longer sustain this relationship, and her anguish arose as much from his abrupt and contradictory treatment of her as from her belief that God seemed cruel and unreasonable. It was one thing for Lyman Beecher to encourage the potential and admiration of a child; quite another to condone uncustomary behavior in a young woman. Once she passed through the portals of adulthood as they were defined in early nineteenth-century New England, Catharine found that her father developed an almost deliberate inability to sympathize with her predicament. Suddenly shut off from her usual paternal model, Catharine passed through a period of bewilderment but was finally fortified by the alternative model she began to pattern herself after in Franklin. Her attraction to Fisher's role was at least strong enough to provide the pivot whereby she began to reorient her life along a separate course from that of her father.

Nevertheless this reorientation was not complete, and in later years the contradictions between the dependent feminine role encouraged by her father and her culture in 1821 and the assertive role she had been raised from childhood to imitate marked Catharine's life with deep psychological tensions. Her life became a pattern of strong assertion and sudden withdrawal. She was enormously ambitious but could not see any project through to its successful conclusion. Yet the success that lay immediately ahead in Hartford was important proof that she could work creatively within these tensions.

Part II

CAREER BEGINNINGS,
1823–1831

⚓ 5 ⚓

A Source of Earthly Good, 1823–1829

Catharine Beecher rented a room above a harness shop in the center of Hartford, and her school opened there in May 1823. It was an enormous success. Within five years the Hartford Female Seminary was housed in its own imposing new structure, maintained a staff of eight teachers, and drew its trustees from among Hartford's leading citizens. By 1831, when Catharine left the school, it had become one of the most celebrated academies in New England. Her contemporaries believed and historians have since held that Catharine Beecher's school constituted one of the most significant advances made in early nineteenth-century education for women.[1]

For eight years this seminary dominated Catharine Beecher's life. Yet the school was for her always a means rather than an end — the means whereby she could define a new relationship with the culture in which she had been raised. Her school enabled her to assert social, religious, and intellectual leadership. In so doing, she was also prompted to clarify her own social, religious, and intellectual beliefs. Even before she emigrated to Cincinnati with her father in 1831, the school had fulfilled its purpose for her and outlived its usefulness to her. By 1830 she was already planning a larger and different enterprise.

From the first Catharine had viewed her academy as an opportunity to continue the intellectual progress she had begun at Franklin, and her own studies outside school were much more important to her than her teaching inside the school. Most of Catharine's intellectual energies were initially dedicated to her Latin studies with Edward. "The only pleasant recollection" she said she had of her first term at Hartford was "that of my own careful and exact training under my most accurate and faithful brother Edward." Boarding in the same Hartford home, Catharine and Edward read Virgil, Cicero, and Ovid together in the evening. In comparison with this pleasant intellectual exercise, Catharine found the hours she spent in school "painful and distracting."[2]

After a term she was ready to leave her academy. Catharine proposed in December that she leave the school entirely in Mary's hands and return home. Catharine's ties to Hartford and to teaching were tenuous, but her ties to her Litchfield home were still strong.

Lyman now made it clear to Catharine that he considered her stay in Hartford a permanent one. He strenuously opposed her plan to leave Hartford, and although he admitted that he would approve of Mary's return home since her health was poor, he said that there was no place in Litchfield for Catharine. "It will not answer for you to leave that school," he wrote. "You must not think of it." [3]

Catharine could find temporary comfort in the fact that the four Beecher children in Hartford constituted a family annex. George Beecher was a student in Edward's school, the Hartford Grammar School, and Catharine, Mary, Edward, and George boarded in the same home. They wrote collective letters to Litchfield and received frequent and affectionate letters from home. Lyman wrote that "the idea that we are all one establishment" so strongly tied the family together that their division between Hartford and Litchfield did not really separate them.[4] Nevertheless in the fall of 1824 two events occurred that, together with her father's decision of December, solidified Catharine's relationship with Hartford. First, she decided against another betrothal and began to explore the role of an independent unmarried woman, and, second, Edward left Hartford, transferring the leadership of the Hartford family annex to Catharine.

In August 1824 Catharine wrote Louisa that "before a great while" she might be married and have a home of her own. Whether by her own or her suitor's decision, however, the engagement never took place. In September Catharine wrote, "I have pretty much concluded not to take . . . a matrimonial home." [5] Edward began theological studies at Andover that fall. Harriet and Henry Beecher, eleven and thirteen years younger than Catharine, came to study at her school. Catharine was now responsible for four younger siblings and was no longer able to defer to Edward's counsel and example. Autonomy was thrust upon her.

Catharine's career began in earnest in the fall of 1824: she could not hope to resume her place in Litchfield, she had apparently decided against marriage, and she no longer was sustained by her brother's fellowship. The new independence was exhilarating. She immediately moved her school to a larger room, began a new social life, and found greater and greater intellectual satisfaction in her role as a teacher. Catharine's goals and beliefs were still unformulated, and she still remained a part of the Beecher "establishment," but she was for the first time seriously engaged in the life of an intellectual single woman.

Catharine began to order her academic and social life. She arranged the school's schedule so that she taught in the morning and Mary taught in the afternoon.[6] Catharine heard "the recitations in Rhetoric, Logic, Natural and Moral Philosophy, Chemistry, History, and Latin," and she instructed a class in algebra. "By the bye," she wrote to Louisa, "I know a good deal more about some of these matters than I used to."

Confined in her school for only half the day and feeling more competent in the topics she taught, Catharine had time once again for a social life. She began to reassert her social leadership and initiated a series of Saturday evening gatherings in her room. "Several young ladies who are among the first in this place" met there every week "for social worship." [7] Catharine not only cultivated the friendship of Hartford's leading young women but also came to know well the men who directed the town's major institutions. Hartford was a center of benevolent activity, and as the principal of the Hartford Female Seminary, Catharine socialized as an equal with the leaders of the other schools, the pastors of the churches, and the directors of such institutions as the school for the deaf and dumb and the insane asylum.[8] She developed an especially close friendship with Mrs. Lydia Sigourney, a woman who stood near the top of Hartford's social hierarchy and who was an important spokeswoman for the town's social and moral attitudes.[9]

By the spring of 1825 Catharine's social life was completely transferred from Litchfield to Hartford. "You will find Litchfield much altered in society since you were there," she wrote Louisa that spring. "I feel almost like a stranger except in our own family. Some are dead, some married, some gone away and it seems almost lonely there to me. I have many more attachments in Hartford than in Litchfield." [10]

Catharine grew more purposeful not only in her approach to her school and her social environment, but also in her view of herself.

She now believed that her role as a teacher was vitally linked with her intellectual pursuits. No longer were her studies outside school at odds with her teaching. "I was never driven to mental effort till affliction came," she wrote Louisa in December 1824, "but except for the comforts of religion and of friendship I find no so pure and interesting a source of earthly good as the exercise of the mind in acquiring and communicating knowledge." Learning and teaching were both satisfying mental exercises for Catharine. "The exercise of the mind," she said, "imparts a pure elevation of thought and character. It turns the mind from the contemplation of trifles to the realities of truth." Catharine had reconciled her role as a teacher with her intellectual ambitions, and the resolution of these two formerly incompatible roles lent a new purpose and a new dynamic element to her life. She described intellectual growth to Louisa as a kind of conquest. "That march of the mind in the knowledge of God and of his works," she said, "shall continue to enlarge and expand our faculties through the interminable ages." Just as there was no end to the expansion of human knowledge, so there was no end to what Catharine herself might achieve through her mind. "The exercise of the mind," she continued, "makes us realize the high faculties and immortal destinies of our nature." [11] The exercise of the mind had become for Catharine an important means for ordering her experience. For it not only created a present role for her, but also seemed to assure a grander future.

Catharine's school brought her both social prestige and intellectual satisfaction. By the end of 1825 she had created a place for herself among Hartford's social and intellectual leadership, and that December she considered renting a home of her own and striking deeper roots into her community. This was an important financial and personal step for her since it meant that her savings would be spent in equipping her own home and not reserved for a future marital home. Setting up her own household was taken as a sign that at the age of twenty-five she disavowed any intention of marrying.[12] More positively seen, however, her own home would provide a focus for her life and would place her on an equal footing with the men and women of her social standing.

Catharine asked her father's opinion of such a step, and he agreed that "a hired home" of her own would be "profitable, pleasant, and expedient." He warned her, however, that if she had any thought "of getting married and bearing children," then she should instead reserve her money for her future needs. Lyman agreed that there were "providential indications" that she would serve her generation in other ways than raising a family, but he was not as certain as Catharine was on this issue. "The strong hand with which God has turned back your family course may and it may not indicate his purpose as to the way in which he intends to resolve your service," he said. Yet since Catharine so strongly wanted her own "establishment," Lyman granted his approval.[13]

In the spring of 1826 Catharine rented a house owned by the Olcott family and advertised for boarders. Mary, Harriet, and Henry Beecher moved into the house with Catharine, and Aunt Esther Beecher came to manage the housekeeping. "We expect to live very pleasantly," Mary wrote Edward. "Our prospects are *very flattering*," she continued, for in addition to their new home they also had rented a more commodious schoolroom "under the North Meeting House." [14]

The North Church was built only the year before, and its basement provided a large room, complete with stove; its grounds offered a "nice large playground" for outdoor recreation. There was no secondary school for girls in Hartford that could rival Catharine and Mary Beecher's.[15] To mark the growing stature of her school, Catharine ordered from a Philadelphia optical firm in June 1826 "an Improved Magic Lantern" and some "astronomical slides" to use with the lantern. She also requested this firm to send "any other articles of apparatus which would answer my purpose for illustrating either chemical or philosophical subjects." [16] By the spring of 1826 Catharine Beecher was in full control of her personal and professional life. A home of her own enabled her to organize her private life around her own interests, and she no longer had to accommodate herself to the routine of someone else's home. Her competence as an educator was steadily growing, and she now began to innovate with and expand her pedagogic materials.

In the spring of 1826 Catharine Beecher was in a position to build upon the social and intellectual leadership she had already established in her school and community. A variety of paths were open to her to do so. She could follow the example of Lydia

Sigourney and her own social inclinations and form a salon. She could concentrate upon her career as an educator and expand the scope and scale of her influence upon American education. She could become a leader in the many benevolent activities that abounded in Hartford. Yet Catharine chose a course more dramatic than any of these. Regardless of her unconverted state, she fostered and led a religious revival.

In initiating her own revival Catharine was playing with psychological and cultural fire. In terms of her personal needs, she seemed to be exploring the boundaries of her new-found independence and asserting an autonomy parallel to her father's. Subservience was for her no longer an alternative. She was for the first time in her life willing to compete with him on his own ground — as a preacher, prayer-leader, and cultural standard-bearer. She who had been asked to submit now assumed a male role and asked others to submit to her as their spiritual mentor. The step was an important one in Catharine Beecher's life, and it had taken three years to develop.

As soon as Catharine moved into her own home she used it for prayer meetings rather than for social pleasures. In her school that fall she did not concentrate on scholarly accomplishments but sought the conversion of her students. The religious revival that Catharine Beecher inspired and led was an extension of rather than a break with the leadership role she had already developed in Hartford. For her greater goal beyond the conversion of her students was the expansion of her social influence. The only new element that her revival revealed was Catharine's desire to imitate her father's style of social leadership.

Catharine had never entirely neglected religion in her school. At the end of her first term in 1823 she had addressed her students on their need to seek God as a shelter from the disappointments of life. Catharine's remarks had been drawn from her own recent experience. "The time may come to some of you, even now in the morning of life," she said, "when instead of the gay colours that adorn each scene, every object will be inscribed with 'mourning and lamentation and woe.'" Such changes, she said, "are known each day among your fellow men and who shall say they are not in store for you?" She urged her students to "seek something that will endure when earthly expectations fail."

You can not now realize and I pray you may never experience how bereft, how lonely, how desolate is a heart that has no portion in Heaven, when the hopes of this world pass away, when the bright visions of life are shrouded in darkness, when the midnight pillow is bathed in tears of lonely bitterness, and the dawn of day brings no light to the soul.17

Catharine's highly autobiographical remarks show that she was in 1823 more concerned with her personal trauma of the previous year than she was with religious experience per se. The heart bereft, not the soul converted, was the subject of her address. Her school at its beginning had enabled her to reverse her roles and become the dispenser rather than the recipient of advice, and this stylization of her experience may have aided her in assimilating the events of the past two years. Yet she may subsequently have realized that her stance as a woman who had known disappointment and bitterness was not an attractive or forceful one. Her address as a whole had all the weakness inherent in the sentimental poetry that Catharine's friend, Lydia Sigourney, was then beginning to write.

Catharine did not long follow this sentimental course, nor did her own experience continue to dominate her religious attitudes. By contrast, in 1826 she addressed her students on their need to maintain a mood of high religious fervor and act as powerful religious examples to their unconverted schoolmates and to all of Hartford. This change was the result of the new relationship Catharine had developed with her father between 1823 and 1826 — a relationship based on the alliance she formed with him in his evangelical battles of those years. Catharine had always sympathized with his style of social and religious leadership, and in the spring of 1826 she adopted this style as her own.

In the fall of 1823 Catharine had joined her father's church. She calmly announced her "wish to join the church" during her vacation, and Lyman as calmly approved. Earlier Catharine had concluded "that if I can not *be* a Christian I will try to be as near *like* one as I can." 18 Her desire to become a church member was in keeping with this sentiment, and her admission to church membership, anticlimactic though it was, temporarily suspended her religious disagreements with her father and began a new alliance between them. Catharine expressed a new excitement in her father's sermons.

"Yesterday I heard two of father's very best sermons. The afternoon sermon perfectly electrified me," she wrote to Edward in the summer of 1824. "The fact is," she continued, "I never hear any body preach that makes me feel as father does; perhaps it may be because he is father. But I can not hear him without its making my face burn and my heart beat." Lyman began to send her copies of his sermons, articles, and reviews, and she read them closely and admired them enormously. He looked forward to her praise and gently chided her when she was slow in delivering it. "I suppose you are proud enough of the sermon already," he wrote in the spring of 1824, but he said he still could stand to hear more praise of it.[19] Lyman Beecher had embarked on an effort to "put down" the Unitarian criticism of Calvinism and founded a weekly newspaper, *The Connecticut Observer,* to aid in that effort.[20] Catharine shared her father's enthusiasm over the success of the paper. "The paper goes on finely. Father has prepared some rare pieces for it," she wrote Edward early in 1825. "He is much animated with the success of the paper," she said. "There is nothing makes me feel so happy as to be with him, and nothing so stimulates my intellect as his conversation." Every visit home during these years strengthened Catharine's attachment to Lyman. "You can not imagine how much I enjoy this visit at home," she wrote Edward in one typical response to a Litchfield visit. "You know how happy it makes us to be with father. His society seems always to give a new impulse to the affection of the heart, and to every intellectual power." More and more Catharine made Lyman's causes her own. "He is now very much engaged in finishing off his answer to the review," she wrote in 1825, "and I think his last will make all smoke again." [21]

At the end of 1825 Lyman Beecher's career reached an important turning point, for he decided to carry his struggle against Unitarianism into Boston itself. Catharine was with him in Litchfield when he decided to move to Boston. Although there was nothing she could do to aid him there, she encouraged Edward to go "as a fellow-labourer with Papa to that peculiarly interesting and desolated field." Lyman Beecher sought in Boston more than the conversion of souls. He was engaged in a social struggle against the influence and prestige that Unitarianism had gained at the highest levels of Boston society. His revival in Boston was designed not only to bring souls to God, but also to restore the social influence of evangelical religion. In a letter to Edward he revealed the dimensions of his struggle. "It is here [Boston] that New England is to be regenerated, the enemy driven out of the temple they have usurped and polluted, the college to be rescued, the public sentiment to be revolutionized and restored to evangelic tone." [22]

Lyman Beecher was particularly eager to gain converts among the socially prestigious Unitarian congregations. Every victory of this kind was described in detail in his letters to Edward. "Two accomplished young ladies . . . [who] belong to Unitarian societies," "an intelligent young man of Mr. Ware's Society," and "a young man of intelligence from a Unitarian society" all received special attention from Lyman Beecher when they indicated to him their possible conversion to Calvinism. Beecher encouraged those who were "cultivated in intellect and refined in taste." [23] Unbiased observers of the Boston scene noted however that Lyman Beecher's congregation did not include Boston's wealthier and socially prominent citizens.[24] Although his task was a difficult one, Beecher showed no signs of discouragement. He was creating "no small stir among Unitarians," he wrote Catharine, and he had great hopes for the future.[25]

When Catharine arrived in Boston on her first visit in the spring of 1826, Lyman wrote William Beecher that "she has been and is a comfort to me." Catharine fully shared her father's view of the importance of his work. "The Lord I think is raising a standard there and calling his children to gather round it," she wrote Edward. "With the moral influence which He may enable such men as Papa and you to exert, we may hope for great things in Boston." [26]

Catharine returned from her visit to Boston and began to raise God's standard in her own school. Within a fortnight of her return she wrote Edward that "the state of feeling preparatory to a revival was begun" in her school. The first step toward such a feeling had been the conversion of one of Catharine's students who boarded in her home. "Four other of my scholars I trust have also been renewed in the temper of their minds," she continued to Edward. "This is only the beginning," she felt, and she increased her labors. A week later she wrote that "the state of things in my school still continues interesting" and that she now anticipated the conversion of "fifteen or more" of her students.[27]

Catharine immediately sought to carry the influence of the revival beyond her school. Her first means of doing so was to engage the aid of Reverend Joel Hawes. Catharine was very disappointed when Mr. Hawes initially ignored her revival. "I have been greatly tried by the absence of Mr. Hawes," she wrote Edward at the onset of her revival. "He was aware of all the circumstances of my school . . . yet he thought best to go to Northampton to spend a week or ten days . . . to assist in a great revival there." Catharine believed that Hawes had "greatly misjudged" the importance of her own revival. "I felt like crying all day after he went away," she continued to Edward. "I and my little church in school have been laboring *all alone* this fortnight past." Yet Catharine was determined to succeed. "God has been with us so that we have had no cause of fear or discouragement. Pray for us," she concluded.[28]

Hawes returned to find that Catharine's revival still flourished in her school and was beginning to make itself felt in the wider community. "There are eight or ten in town who have lately as I trust become pious," Catharine wrote in the third week of her efforts. She began to use her home as a second center for the revival, and by this means draw in the adults of Hartford. "Our house is literally a house of prayer," she wrote. "Most of its inmates are pious and faithful in this duty." Every day after school "from twenty to thirty" of her scholars met to pray and examine their spiritual progress. Once a week Catharine held "a special prayer meeting of our acquaintances and particular friends." Mr. Hawes attended these meetings. In addition Catharine arranged a monthly "union prayer meeting" for the "ladies of the three churches" of Hartford. "So you see," Catharine concluded to Edward, "we have been able to do as we desired and consecrate our house to the service of God." [29]

Catharine looked to her brother and her father for aid in promoting her revival. "It is a critical time with us," she wrote Edward, and urged him to come and preach in Hartford. She needed all the help she could get, she said, in sustaining the intensity of the spirit of the revival.[30] To her father Catharine described the religious excitement that had been aroused in her school and asked how she could now best increase her efforts.

Lyman's reply must have disappointed Catharine, for although he encouraged her praise for his own evangelical work, he did not encourage her to imitate him. It was one thing for her to admire and follow him, but quite another for her to duplicate his efforts and assume for herself the prerogatives and burdens of leadership. "Your last letters, giving an account of the state of things in your school, have been read with deep interest and much thanksgiving, though not without some solicitude," Lyman began. "The very high state of excited feeling, though extremely natural among young Christians, and powerful in its effects while it lasts, is too hazardous to health to be indulged, and necessarily too short-lived to answer in the best manner the purpose of advancing a revival." Catharine had asked for his advice, but probably had not anticipated his answer. "You must," he said, ". . . instantly put yourselves upon a different system . . . or you will all be prostrate." For herself, he said, she should adopt a "mild" state of mind. She should cease being agitated, and rather be "strong and steady." Her state of feeling should be "a genial warmth of heart, of steady benevolent temperature," and not "the more intense heat and flashings of holy and animal affections and passions, all boiling at once in the heart." [31]

Lyman's advice to Catharine was now quite different from his urgings of 1822, when he implored her to feel and feel deeply. "The excitement and agitation of too much emotion" could be "fatal" to her health, he said. She should not assume the "overpowering weight of responsibility and care" involved in a revival, he continued. "Settle it in your heart, therefore, that you are to exercise your best judgment, and perform in the best manner you can your duty and leave the whole in the hands of God," he said. "You can not be accountable for consequences." Do not anticipate a greater success, he admonished, for that "may never happen." Lyman concluded: "Be therefore quiet. Let not your heart be troubled." [32]

Catharine replied by asking him to come to Hartford and stand in her stead as the leader of the revival. Lyman's reply, when it finally came, was a reprimand. "Nothing but the urgency and goodness of your motive saved you from the reaction of vexation and rebuke that you should think of such a thing," he wrote. He was far too engrossed in his own "preeminently important post of duty" in Boston to "come on to Hartford." [33]

Nevertheless, Catharine struggled to carry her revival beyond her school. In an address "To Those who profess or have the hope of Piety in Miss Beecher's School," Catharine described how this

might be done. "The success we have received has laid us under
new obligations and responsibilities," she said, for "God has showed
us that he is ready to hear prayer and to bless our efforts." Her
students, she continued, "should know and feel this responsibility"
and turn their attention outward toward "the public mind." If
they were faithful "in devotedness, in prayer and in labours this
week," she believed, "the current of feeling will set the right way
. . . and the public mind" will be made "really to feel as if God
was among them." Devote the whole week, she said, "to labours for
the salvation of your fellow men as the *great object of interest and
thought*." Be not afraid of spending too much time for God, she
urged them, for

> this week I feel as if it would probably *be decided* whether the good
> work begun so auspiciously should be extended in the school and
> from the school to the churches in this place, or whether the excite-
> ment shall be transient and the world and the church should turn
> aside a little moment to see what [God] is doing for us, and then pass
> away. I feel that it almost entirely rests with us, my dear young ladies,
> and I wish you should know and feel this responsibility.[34]

Exactly how she and her students were to influence "the public
mind" was a delicate issue, however, for a real revival was God's
work, not the product of its human leader, and if they were to
extend the revival it would be by the power of their example, not
by exhortation. "Now I do not wish that you should talk about the
situation of our school at all except as *still* and *secret* as possible,"
she said, but in the next breath she added: "But oh my dear fellow
Christians be faithful in prayers, in labours and in interest for the
school." Catharine ended her address with a revivalist exhortation
in the style of her father.

Catharine succeeded in making her revival felt throughout the
town. By the summer of 1826 all the Congregational churches were
engaged in it, and Joel Hawes in the Center Church had assumed
the leadership of the revival.[35] What Catharine Beecher had begun
among the town's young women, Hawes continued among the young
men. His sermons of 1826 were printed the next year as *Lectures to
Young Men* and enjoyed an enormous popularity. Yet Catharine
Beecher's efforts did not exactly parallel Hawes's, and the difference
between them was revealing. Hawes's volume of practical religious
advice and simple moral precepts was addressed to the "mechanic"

class.[36] Catharine Beecher did not turn her attention to the middle class but sought to influence the daughters of Hartford's patrician families.

The social goals behind Catharine's religious revival were made apparent in her efforts to convert one of her most socially prestigious pupils, Sarah Terry. The Terry family, one of the most important in Hartford, regularly held posts in the town's government and contributed financially to the church and other benevolent enterprises.[37] Catharine made Sarah Terry the special object of her attentions. "The present is a time in which I am looking about among my scholars and selecting such as I feel a particular interest in, to make them the subjects of my particular efforts and prayers," Catharine wrote Miss Terry. "You have often occurred to my mind as one whom I love and whom I long to see a child of God." Catharine said that at first she had felt intimidated. "You have had so many advantages and know all about these things so well," she said, "that I could not say anything you may not have heard till you are *tired of it*." Nevertheless, Catharine continued, "I cannot rest in peace till I have made *one* trial at least." Both through her letters and her meetings in prayer with Sarah Terry, Catharine guided her pupil through all the states of a classic conversion experience. She watched and analyzed her feelings and prescribed the next step to be taken in Sarah's spiritual progress. Finally she wrote, "Do not wait to *feel more*" but immediately submit to God.[38] Sarah Terry's subsequent conversion put the Terry family much in Catharine's debt, and the next year they contributed their prestige and their money to help Catharine enlarge her school.

Catharine's revival was important to her in two ways. It showed that she could profoundly shape her pupils' lives and that she could widely influence the society around her. Although her revival efforts had not won her father's approbation, through them she had demonstrated her ability to imitate his style of cultural leadership. The revival had been a formative experience for Catharine, and she continued to sustain its spirit in her school. "For several years every term witnessed what would be called a 'revival of religion,'" she wrote in her *Reminiscences*, but she never again sought to expand it beyond her school. "Like the kingdom of Heaven which 'cometh without observation,'" these later revivals, she explained, were "quiet and gentle as the falling of the dew." [39]

Perhaps she accepted her father's advice and felt she was an inappropriate leader for a thoroughgoing revival. Her one experience had told her all she needed to know, however, about her ability to lead. Although in her first exercise in leadership she had turned to the model closest at hand — her father — she soon embarked on a more independent course. The revival had perhaps functioned as a substitute conversion experience for her — an occasion of psychic rebirth in which the sins and omissions of the past were canceled and the future made clear. She had participated in the conversion experience as the leader, not the supplicant. This reversal of roles was symbolic of Catharine's lifelong skill in altering the forms of her own culture even while she insisted that she was preserving them.

After the revival Catharine devoted herself to her career as an educator. She published articles and became known as an educational reformer, and she expanded her school to a full-scale seminary. In the wake of these activities, however, Catharine's desire to exert a profound influence upon the minds and characters of her students reemerged, and her desire to expand her moral and social influence beyond her pupils also revived. Two years after her revival Catharine took up "Mental and Moral Philosophy," a discipline that combined and recast all the intellectual, social, and religious currents of her life.

Even before the fervor of the revival had subsided, in the fall and winter of 1826, Catharine embarked on an ambitious plan to transform her private school into an endowed seminary. She envisioned a new building, a full staff of teachers, and a series of educational reforms. By February 1827 she had raised nearly five thousand dollars through the sale of stock subscriptions, and in the fall of that year her seminary opened in its own handsome neoclassical building.[40] Yet Catharine's seminary was built as much by social and religious influence as it was by financial subscriptions. From the beginning she appealed to the social aspirations of Hartford's citizens, and she used her own social and religious influence, recently increased by the revival, to good advantage.

In that winter of aroused religious sentiment, Catharine took her plans to the leading members of Joel Hawes's First Congregational Church. At the height of the revival Catharine, Mary, and Harriet Beecher had joined Hawes's church.[41] Lyman Beecher no longer led the Litchfield church, and there was no reason for his older daughters to transfer their church membership to Boston. The lay leaders of this, Hartford's oldest church, were among the town's wealthiest citizens and held positions of social prestige and political power. The men Catharine approached to act as trustees for her subscription fund, and subsequently as trustees of the seminary, were decidedly the most important men in Hartford. Her access to them was through the First Church. She had established her position as a leader in religious affairs, and she now sought to use this position for the benefit of her school. She had not donated large sums of money to the church as these men had, but her revival efforts had lent her an authority of a different kind. Financial, social, political, and religious leadership in Hartford rested in the hands of a few men, and Catharine had put herself in a position to employ their power for her own ends. Catharine's educational success in Hartford grew directly out of her religious success. She managed to achieve in Hartford what her father was struggling unsuccessfully to gain in Boston — the religious support of the town's leading citizens and their social ability to affect other nonreligious institutions.

One man, Daniel Wadsworth, stood preeminent in Hartford's religious, social, and financial affairs. A descendant of one of Hartford's original founding families which had become wealthy in banking even before the Revolution, Daniel Wadsworth was the chief financial supporter of the First Church. He paid over one thousand dollars for a pew at the front of the church when it was rebuilt in 1809. Wadsworth had inherited his wealth and was an art patron and amateur architect.[42] He was the first person Catharine approached with her plan. He agreed to design a facade for her proposed seminary building. He drew a front elevation appropriate for either one or two stories, with four Ionic columns and a plain pediment in the new neoclassical style.[43] The building resembled a small Greek temple. Armed with this sketch as a sign of her high purpose and presumably bearing Wadsworth's sanction, Catharine next approached "some of the leading gentlemen" of Hartford and asked their aid in having "such a building erected by subscription." All of these leading gentlemen were mainstays of the First Church.[44]

Seth Terry and Eliphalet Terry were two of Catharine's ten trustees.[45] The Terry family, whose daughter Catharine had been so careful to convert, owned and occupied the only pew in front of Wadsworth's in the First Church. The Terrys were one of Hartford's patrician families who sponsored Assembly balls where dancing continued until two in the morning. Conscious of its aristocracy, Hartford citizens elected men from the Terry family to serve as mayor, committeemen, and justices of the peace.[46] Henry Hudson, James H. Wells, and Oliver Cooke were also prominent church members who supported Catharine's subscription drive and later served as trustees.[47] In addition to two other laymen, Thomas Day and William Ellsworth, Catharine gained the support of Hartford's three Congregational ministers and included them among her trustees. Thomas Day and William Ellsworth were both eminent Hartford lawyers who had attended Litchfield Law School. Day was the son of a Congregational minister and a descendant of one of the original founders of Hartford. He was currently Chief Judge of the county court. William Ellsworth was a deacon in the First Church and an intimate friend of Joel Hawes's. Subsequently, in 1829, he was elected to Congress, and a decade later he became governor of Connecticut.[48] These men constituted an upper-class establishment. Catharine Beecher's experience with this establishment was to have an important influence upon her later career in the West, where she mistakenly expected to find the same kind of social, political, and financial leadership concentrated in her church.

Yet even in Hartford it was not easy for Catharine to gain the support of this establishment. The "leading gentlemen" were not initially enthusiastic about her plan. "Many of them were surprised and almost dismayed" by it, she said, and they called it "visionary and impracticable." Behind Wadsworth's facade Catharine planned a structure large enough to contain "a study hall to hold one hundred and fifty pupils, a lecture room, and six recitation rooms." Many of the gentlemen thought the plan overly ambitious and were not prepared to support it. "The absurdity of it was apparent to most of the city fathers," Catharine said, "and with some [it] excited ridicule." [49]

Under these circumstances Catharine knew exactly where to turn. She had, as it were, prepared a back entrance into this establishment, and she entered it through her friendship with their wives. She carried the plan to the women who had gathered in her home for prayer meetings during the revival. To her evenings of "social worship" Catharine had always invited women who were "among the first in this place." When she now turned to them for help they did not disappoint her. "The more intelligent and influential women came to my aid," Catharine wrote in her *Reminiscences,* "and soon all I sought was granted." [50]

Catharine had learned an important lesson in the uses of social power. "This was my first experience of the moral power and good judgment of American women," she recalled in 1874, "which has been my chief reliance ever since." The consolidated nature of Hartford's leadership, and its susceptibility to feminine persuasion were important contributors to Catharine's success. "My affairs go well," Catharine wrote her father in February, 1827. "The stock is all taken up, and next week I hope to have out the prospectus of the 'Hartford Female Seminary.' " [51] She expected the building to be completed in June.

Catharine's arguments in behalf of her plan were pedagogically sound and socially astute. In the spring of 1827 she published an article in the newly established *American Journal of Education* and described there her proposed reforms and the reasons behind them.[52] The article was an appeal to the public to alter its attitude toward female education. Doubtlessly she used the same arguments when she appealed to Hartford's leading gentlemen and their wives.

Her argument was based on the assumption that parents wanted their daughters to receive a "refined" education. No parent who sent his daughter to Miss Beecher's school would be likely to disagree with this traditional goal of feminine education. In Hartford this tradition had been established long before Catharine's school had begun. Oliver Cooke, one of her trustees, had paid for the publication in 1799 of a volume entitled *A Mirror for the Female Sex: Historical Beauties for Young Ladies Intended to Lead the Female Mind to the Love and Practice of Moral Goodness.* "Designed principally for the use of Ladies' Schools," this was merely a reprinting of an English text and contained no hint of the existence of America. Its "refined" bias was evident. "Politeness and good-breeding are such requisite introductions into genteel society that it is absolutely astonishing any one can gain admittance into it who are deficient either in the one or the other," the book asserted in a typical passage.[53] It was the dissolution in 1819 of Mrs.

Lydia Sigourney's fashionable school, where such books were read, that had originally created the need for Catharine's school.[54] Catharine did not completely abandon this tradition of refinement, but she did significantly alter it.

Catharine added a new dimension to this traditional goal by insisting that young women should not be educated to be genteel ornaments. Their refinement had a larger purpose. "A lady should study, not to *shine*, but to *act*," she said in her article of 1827.[55] By insisting upon action rather than ornament as the goal of "refined" women, Catharine had transformed this traditionally passive quality into an active one. This transformation was critical to Catharine's later attitude toward women and the cultural role they play. In 1827 she was one of the few professional educators who maintained that the purpose of a young woman's education was to enable her to translate her knowledge into action.[56] "To come out in *conduct*," Catharine said, a girl's education must reach deep inside her and shape "her principles and the formation of her habits." Parents were misguided, she said, in seeking only the veneer of refinement for their daughters rather than the real understanding that creates genuine refinement. "Both parents and pupils sometimes thus demand the superstructure and ornaments of an education before the indispensable foundations are laid," she concluded. They were satisfied with the appearance rather than the reality of learning. Real learning was especially important for "the young lady destined to move in higher circles," for she could exert an influence "upon the general interests of society." Catharine believed that many educational reforms were needed, such as the creation of endowed institutions, "where a regular course of study is demanded — regular periods for entering and leaving established — a proper division of labor effected, and suitable facilities and accommodations provided for instructors." [57]

In the course of the last few years, Catharine continued, "public sentiment has advanced so much on the subject of female culture that a course of study very similar to that pursued by young men in our public institutions is demanded for young ladies of the higher circles." Yet although the curriculum was similar, the educational facilities and teaching techniques of girls' schools were vastly inferior to those of male colleges. One or two teachers in a female school were expected to rush through the curriculum that several professors divided among themselves in a man's college.

Moreover they were expected to do so in one crowded room containing pupils of a variety of ages and abilities and without proper teaching aids or books. Chemistry, for example, was learned from a "compend" or summary rather than a full textbook, Catharine said, and was taught without the aid of classroom experiments. In these circumstances, Catharine said, "the whole process of school keeping consisted in trying to discover how much each pupil had committed to memory," and it was impossible to know how much was clearly understood and how much was mere "parrot learning." "To preserve order while attending to recitations all in one room, to hear such a succession of classes in so many different studies, to endure such a round of confusion, haste and imperfection," she said, was exhausting and unrewarding work.[58]

Catharine's reforms had a double aim. She meant to raise the quality of education in her school and to make her own life more pleasant as its director. "The greatest evils incident to female schools of the higher order at the present period," she wrote, "result from the fact that far too many and too varied duties are necessarily demanded from one person." [59]

In the fall when Catharine's seminary opened in its new building, her educational career was no longer confined to the classroom. As the director of eight other teachers she was freed from the routine of teaching. Almost immediately she began to explore the implications of her published remarks of 1827. Her teachers were responsible for the "foundations" of learning, and she made herself responsible for translating this learning into "conduct" and molding the principles and the beliefs, the habits and actions of her students. She began to teach a course in moral philosophy.

❦ 6 ❧

The Rule of Rectitude, 1829–1831

Catharine did not originally plan to teach "mental and moral philosophy" in her new school, and she assigned this class to one of her teachers "who claimed to be much interested in it." [1] This teacher boarded in Catharine's home and, Catharine said, "constantly appealed to me for aid" in answering the questions raised in the class. "Eventually I took the class myself," she wrote in her *Reminiscences,* and "soon I became deeply interested in this study." For the next three years Catharine devoted her intellectual energies to "mental science and moral philosophy," and in 1831 she published a remarkable work entitled *The Elements of Mental and Moral Philosophy, Founded upon Experience, Reason and the Bible.*

In this occasionally rambling, often contradictory, but always revealing volume, Catharine Beecher began to integrate the three themes around which her past experience had centered: the salvation of the soul, the reshaping of social forms, and the experience of women in each of these activities. Catharine discovered that these themes could be woven together to create a powerful new cultural design. This design anticipated the new morality and social vision that historians sometimes term "Victorian" — that matrix of consolidated social institutions and web of personal interdependencies characterizing the late nineteenth century and contrasting with the exuberance and openness of the early part of the century.[2] Although the basic contours of the early and late nineteenth century differ profoundly, important contributors to the Victorian matrix do emerge early in the century, and Catharine Beecher was one of these.[3] Three crucial elements form a skeletal structure to which she and others later added. These include the transposition of the drama of salvation from theological to social grounds, the creation of a moral code designed to check behavior even without the existence of an angry God, and the assertion of a new class of moral guardians empowered to enforce this code. All of Catharine's later thought was based on this volume of moral philosophy.

Some important personal considerations shaped Catharine's new approach to moral philosophy. All her thinking on topics related to psychology and morality up to 1827 took place within a Calvinist mold. "At the age of twenty-seven," Catharine said, she "had never read a work on Mental Science, owing to want of interest in the subject." Yet reading only briefly in the field enabled Catharine to say in her first class on moral philosophy that character, not conversion, was the answer to the question "What must we do to be saved?" [4]

There are professional and personal reasons why Catharine made this important shift of emphasis and why her class on mental philosophy was not conducted in a revival atmosphere. Catharine's seminary attracted many more students from outside Connecticut than had her one-room school, and it quickly gained a national reputation. From 1828 to 1831 the proportion of students from "abroad" increased by sixty percent. Previously her school had been patronized by families belonging to Congregational churches in Hartford, but in 1827 it drew a much more heterogeneous group of students.[5] Conversion was an experience from which many people in such a mixed group would be excluded. Catharine's decision to emphasize proper character formation rather than conversion may have arisen from her need to find a more inclusive and universal principle around which she could organize the studies of her class. In this sense the national prominence of her school encouraged her to transcend regional mores and to design a more appropriate national system of morality and ethics.

There were also signs that Catharine herself had happily suspended the kind of introspection associated with conversion. When Edward wrote her in 1828 that he now thoroughly understood his "inward man," Catharine replied: "I wish I could catch my *inward woman* and give her such an inspection and exposition, but she is such a restless being that I cannot hold her still long enough to see her true form or outline." [6] Catharine had concluded in 1822 that worldly success would have to serve as an alternative for the conversion she could not experience, and the substantial worldly success she enjoyed by 1827 may have lessened her need to achieve conversion herself or promote it in other people.

On a more personal level Catharine found great satisfaction in her role as the moral caretaker of others. "I am so much engaged in moulding, correcting, and inspecting the character of others," she

wrote Edward, "that I sometimes fear that my own will be a 'cast
away,' but I then comfort myself with the reflection that 'he that
watereth shall himself be watered' and I cannot say but the promise
has in a measure been verified to me." The New England tradition
of introspection and self-scrutiny was still alive in Catharine's
generation and was about to reach a new intensity in Emersonian
transcendentalism. Catharine's younger sister Harriet wrote in 1833
that her "pernicious habit of meditation" upon "this inner world
of mine" had burned inward till it seared her soul and left her
"withered and exhausted." [7] Catharine turned this tradition of self-
analysis outward upon others rather than inward upon herself.
Although she was reluctant to analyze her own "inner world,"
she happily analyzed the internal world of other people. In doing
for others what she could not or would not do for herself, she
made emotions and beliefs the subject of an objective rather than
subjective study. Her study of mental and moral philosophy was
the channel through which she redirected Puritan self-analysis and
codified it into a set of mental and social rules. In this way Catharine bypassed what was for her a destructive process of Calvinist
introspection and fashioned instead moral rules more compatible
to her social predisposition. In one sense she had claimed her
"inner world" as her own and accessible to no one else. In another
sense she had discovered that her inner self was profoundly interdependent with her students and that it quickened in interaction.
Her own leadership role and the supportive female context of her
work may have been additional contributing factors to this shift
away from the inner workings of piety to the outward manifesta-
tions of morality. In her book Catharine generalized from her own
experience and began to design a moral system in which women
inspired and shaped the moral standards around them.

Catharine Beecher's *Elements of Mental and Moral Philosophy*
was one among several early ventures into a new kind of American
philosophical writing. Many of Catharine's contemporaries, Francis
Wayland being perhaps the most well known, were at the same
moment engaged in writing texts of "moral philosophy" based on
the intuitive psychology of the Scottish philosophers Dugald Stewart

and Thomas Reid. This school of American philosophical writing emerged to perform a very difficult but necessary task for mid-nineteenth-century social conservatives. It endorsed the American belief in democratic individualism and the ability of each person to work out his destiny, but to counteract the political and social anarchy that this school feared American democracy might generate, it prescribed a system of morality in which the "conscience" dominated all mental and moral judgments and stood ready to guide the individual through the chaos of the times if he would but listen to its small, steady voice of internal virtue. Dominating American academic philosophy from 1840 to 1870, the Common Sense school of thought paid homage to the resources within each human conscience for making virtuous judgments, but it also emphasized that the conscience had to be cultivated and especially equipped for its task since it was not naturally good and since it had constantly to fight the inroads of vice and immorality.[8]

Common Sense philosophy was used by liberal and conservative alike as a tool for restraining Jacksonian Democracy. For amid widespread social change and dislocation, it provided a handle on such questions as social leadership, the philosophical basis of social authority, and the nature of moral responsibility. Eighteenth-century rationalist conceptions of natural rights and limited government were notions believed too narrow to embrace the turbulent ebb and flow of American society in the first half of the nineteenth century, but the comprehensive vagueness of Common Sense supported a multitude of moral assertions — speaking generally to a person's duties and obligations rather than his freedom and rights. Bypassing Enlightenment thought, Common Sense philosophy drew instead on the issues central to the Calvinist tradition: the importance of the social community, and the nature of the relationship between internal piety and external morality. Nothing could have been more useful to Catharine Beecher's purposes than this philosophical system.

For Catharine as for other writers in this genre, two pressing questions emerged: Who was to create the cultural norms necessary to guide the individual conscience through its difficult journey between morality and immorality? and How could society reinforce those norms, rewarding the virtuous and penalizing the vicious? The system did not rely, as Calvinism had, on the omnipresence of

a vengeful God. Neither did it uphold the clergy as the guardians
of the community's morals. New agencies of moral authority had
to be found that could speak to emergent democratic values. The
individual conscience was one of these agencies; all Common Sense
writers agreed on this. Several competing agencies were designed
to guide the conscience, however, and it is on this point that Catharine Beecher's volume was most innovative.

The two dominant wings of American Common Sense philosophy
— the conservative Evangelical wing represented by Francis Wayland, and the liberal Unitarian wing represented by William Ellery
Channing — answered the question of social leadership and moral
guardianship in very similar ways. Although Francis Wayland acknowledged the important role of Evangelical institutions such as
the American Tract Society (which sponsored the publication of
his text), the fundamental source of moral leadership was for
Wayland the emerging commercial class of property-minded but
respectable young men who linked "commercial honour" and
"personal virtue." [9] Both Wayland and Channing wrote at the beginning of the period when a secular commercial class was making
unparalleled claims to moral and social leadership in the United
States. This cultural strain, always present in American life, now
fully flowered under the opportunities presented by Jacksonian
politics and laissez-faire economics. Channing too, though a patrician Bostonian, paid homage to this group. He and other Unitarian
moral philosophers have been described as trying to work "with and
through the consolidating commercial plutocracy, transforming it
into a cultivated, socially responsible, stable aristocracy." The bargain that both wings of moral philosophers struck was that they
"would provide the rationale for capitalism and the protection of
property," if the merchants would in turn adopt the moral attitudes
and socially stabilizing norms designed by the moral philosophers.[10]

This consolidation of commercial and moral values may have
made "common sense" to the men involved in this bargain, but
it was not Catharine Beecher's brand of common sense. For she
was quick to recognize that this was an exclusively male definition
of cultural leadership, and she saw, moreover, the weak spot in the
system whereby women could assert their own claim to that leadership.

Common Sense philosophy was built on a contradiction. Combining "an exalted view of man's potential with a determination to preserve traditional values," [11] it fostered an energetic moral leadership, yet discouraged assertive, bold, or innovative behavior in the society as a whole. Rather than endorse one kind of behavior for the leaders and another for the rest of society, Catharine Beecher chose one quality — submission of the self to the general good — as appropriate to exemplary moral leaders and their followers alike. She turned self-sacrifice and submission — traditional values associated with women — into signs of moral superiority and leadership. The willingness to "select that which will produce the greatest amount of general happiness, irrespective of its own individual proportion," constituted, Catharine said, "one universal and unvarying system" around which the whole society could be united.[12] Whereas Francis Wayland argued that the submissive behavior of women removed them from the mainstream of American experience and denoted their dependent status, Catharine Beecher described female qualities of submission, purity, and domesticity as traits that placed women closer to the source of moral authority and hence established their social centrality.[13]

The transition from piety to morality as the basic system of belief in the United States was congruent with an increasingly democratic and individualized ethos, but it also translated what had theretofore been merely superficial behavioral modes into rigid moral determinates. For the emphasis on moral behavior created new distinctions between men and women not previously inherent in a system based on piety. Piety was not necessarily manifested differently in men and women. The steps toward conversion were the same for each, and "joyous love to God" was a psychological state, not a set of conduct rules.[14] Yet in popular attitudes as well as academic philosophy, Americans came to value overt behavior as the measure of moral worth. Sexually differentiated definitions of morality were thereby heightened, since so-called natural and unnatural behavior could now be equated with the moral and immoral. Thus what might be deemed virtuous modesty in a woman could be unhealthy self-doubt in a man, and the different interpretations on what was conceivably the same behavior was conferred by the united forces of "nature and revelation." [15] Wayland's writings typically condemned an "angered and turbulent" woman as unnatural, but nevertheless praised righteous "indignation" among men.[16] Seeing that these "natural" gender distinctions could be invidious as well as favorable for women, Catharine Beecher tried to crystallize the largest number of positive interpretations she could draw from the raw material of gender differences.

Just as Common Sense philosophy marked a shift from piety to behavior it also signaled the change from external to internal enforcement of values. Censure and approval came not from an angry God, but from the promptings of one's own conscience, and this new school of thought agreed that the family was the chief agency for shaping the conscience. The Scottish philosophers believed that "the family, rather than the individual, was the fundamental unit of society," and everywhere Scottish philosophy permeated American thinking, it brought an "intensified awareness of the function of the family in society." [17] Traditionally patriarchical, the family seemed an excellent model for establishing a sense of social order and hierarchy in a frequently too exuberant democracy. Here too the new philosophy was building on ground seemingly unfavorable to women, yet easily shifted to their advantage by Catharine Beecher, who saw this new emphasis on the family as a means of elevating the status of women rather than confirming traditional patriarchy. By the 1840s, when most of American society shared her views on the family, she had been working for a decade to define the role of the woman in the family, and, by extension, in the society as a whole.

Although Catharine Beecher's text on moral philosophy was often derivative and imitative, some of the details of her more innovative arguments not only illuminate her attitudes toward women but also locate her within the social structure of nineteenth-century American life.

Catharine Beecher's text, like others in its genre, began with the assumption that human beings are oriented primarily toward the social context in which they live rather than toward a life hereafter. On every possible occasion she emphasized that social interdependencies dominate and define human life. "If all intercourse and relations between minds should cease, and all hope of them be removed, happiness would be destroyed," Catharine wrote. The main springs to human activity were the rewards granted by society to the individual. "To gain the esteem and affection of other minds is what regulates the actions, the plans, and the hopes of all mankind," she insisted.[18] Yet as highly social creatures, humans faced special problems in a democracy. Since in a democracy each person is free to exercise his own will, and since happiness depends upon the interactions among wills, unhappiness easily results because there is no "universal and unvarying system" to guide the free will in its social context. Suffering rather than happiness was often the result of such "a constitution of things," Catharine wrote, and she claimed that there was only one rule — self-sacrifice — that could properly form the basis of a democratic morality.[19]

Catharine Beecher's definition of self-sacrifice as the "rule of rectitude" was appropriate to the interweaving of personal and social dependencies that characterized the Victorian era, and during the course of the next two decades she emphasized it more and more. Yet it is an idea that reaches into the past as well as the future and is, in fact, an outstanding example of the way Catharine Beecher gave new meaning to inherited Calvinist concepts. Selfishness — "the greatest and most terrible evil to be dreaded," as Catharine described it — had been consistently condemned in Calvinist thought as the opposite of "benevolence," or love of God.[20] In the eighteenth century and particularly in the theology of Jonathan Edwards, benevolence meant "holy love of Being in general," and since it was only experienced by the redeemed soul, it was taken as a sign of true virtue and redemption.[21] By the time Catharine was born, however, benevolence had lost this meaning and revivalists like Lyman Beecher associated it with evangelical good works. Benevolence devolved to a social activity similar to Benjamin Franklin's civic benevolence rather than to a "holy affection" and love of God. Catharine once more crystallized the meaning of benevolence by calling it "a willingness to make sacrifices of personal enjoyment." [22]

This was a negative definition expressing self-denial rather than joyous love of God. Still the opposite of selfishness, it was a new image of secular human fulfillment, designed to function entirely in a worldly milieu and to promote voluntary self-restraint in that milieu. As a conservative democratic social theory it was unparalleled, and as a means of establishing the moral leadership of women it was ingenious, for it rewarded most those whose restraint was greatest. Self-sacrifice became a kind of grand achievement, and a goal worthy in its own right as well as a means of promoting the greatest social happiness. In the 1850s Catharine concluded that no act was moral if it was not an act of self-sacrifice and that moral rectitude consisted wholly in self-sacrifice.

Catharine's moral system assumed the existence of a coherent society willing to abide by a set of moral norms. This certainly did not describe the regionally diverse, racially varied, and culturally heterogeneous society of the United States in the 1830s. Even Connecticut, "the land of steady habits," was itself rife with doctrinal disputes and traditionally unwilling to identify its welfare with that of any other part of the nation.[23] A nationwide system of institutions and leaders was needed to nourish, exemplify, and enforce any unified set of cultural norms. Catharine Beecher, along with others of her generation, gave most of the rest of her life to creating such institutions and acting as such a leader, but in this volume in 1830 she merely suggested two tests for determining whether a person was truly moral or not. Both tests were more easily passed by women than by men, and both subtly shifted moral centrality away from the male clergy and placed it on women laity.

One sure sign of deeply rooted moral character, Catharine wrote, was the individual's continued striving after purity. Every moral philosopher of the Common Sense school emphasized how impressionistic the human mind was and recommended that constant scrutiny be exercised to prevent the mind from falling into the grip of sin. Francis Wayland employed a metaphor of infection to describe this process: "We should dread the communion with anything wrong, lest it should contaminate our imagination," he wrote, "and thus injure our moral sense." [24] What Wayland described as a proscription, Catharine turned into a prescription for virtue. Vice was, of course, to be avoided, she said, but she gave far more importance to the cultivating of purity for its own sake to provide a kind of natural immunity to sin. The truly redeemed soul was, she concluded, marked by its ardent "longing for purity," and this quality of character, which was thoroughly identified with the "natural" character of women, was used to distinguish the hypocritically moral from the truly moral.[25]

Similarly the difference between consistent and occasional morality was often revealed in the way a person behaved in his own home and family. Some men, Catharine wrote, "labour diligently for the general interests of men, and forget their own vineyard, in the heart and in the family circle, where rank weeds are speedily discovered." Such a man "awakens the suspicion that all his efforts for the public good are the offspring of a desire for notoriety and the praise of men," Catharine said. Coming very close to equating domestic virtue with holy virtue, Catharine described the home as the crucial testing ground of the person's soul. Removed from the influence of the home, a man was not likely to be redeemed by God, she said. "A man that has been drawn from the social ties of home, and has spent his life in the collisions of the world," she concluded, "seldom escapes without the most confirmed habits of cold, and revolting selfishness." [26] It may not have been deliberate, but it was surely significant that all Catharine Beecher's examples of failed domestic virtue were men. Women, she assumed, were perforce versed in the arts of domestic virtue.

Catharine Beecher's discussion of mental and moral phenomena was based on her own experience. She had a strong desire to order and control her life, and her philosophical and psychological studies gave her a vocabulary for doing so. The general laws of the mind she found in Locke and the Scottish writers assured her that the mind, properly understood, was not a mystery, but a machinery that could be regulated to allow the individual to control his or her own destiny. This destiny was for Catharine a profoundly social one. In 1822 Catharine had argued against her father's insistence on instant obedience to God. Yet in 1830 she designed a hardly less demanding morality of social obedience. She enthusiastically endorsed submission to social forms and seemed herself fully able to meet the requisites of this new socially-defined redemption.

Yet the realities of Catharine's social context were not as pliant as the pages on which she poured out her socially conscious moral theory. Catharine was and remained a middle class woman, and although she harbored upper class aspirations, she never comfortably or fully acknowledged them. Her dilemma was nicely revealed toward the end of her book, where she noted that a simple division of mankind into two classes of the saved and the damned seemed inappropriate. Mankind seemed to exist in "gradual gradations of character" rather than two extremes of sinful and saintly, Catharine said, and she found it especially difficult to envision the damnation of the socially prestigious. "When the lines are drawn among the amiable, the refined, the elevated, and intelligent, many a heart will demur, and question the sufficiency of the grounds for such distinctions," she concluded.[27]

In many ways Catharine was attracted to the upper class refinement and social manners of the Unitarians and Episcopalians. Mrs. Lydia Sigourney, Catharine's close friend in Hartford, was a model of social ambition and pretention and was also a convert to the Episcopal church. Catharine Beecher was far from willing to condemn these people for their worldly virtues, and yet she could not wholeheartedly endorse or identify with their style. Catharine Beecher's stance toward these people of worldly virtue was ultimately ambiguous. Her own personality harbored too much of the evangelical enthusiast to feel fully in accord with upper class satisfaction in the status quo. Yet Catharine's evangelical style and her covert upper class aspirations created a tension in her thought that was not resolved until she left New England for the new social context of the West. This tension was an important one for Catharine Beecher's career, for it impelled her to find new ways to merge refined culture with evangelical morality.

Although for the present the upper classes seemed not to share her feeling of urgency about moral reform and about the need to build and proselytize a new moral theory, Catharine felt that any cause could be better fought allied with this class of people. She still identified with her father's cause sufficiently to share the keen pain he felt upon being rejected by upper class Bostonians. "What adds greatly to the danger" threatening the evangelical cause, Catharine wrote, was that "the character of many who are found advocating [antievangelical attitudes are] the learned, the intelligent, and the amiable; those who are exemplary in all the external duties of religion; those who are seriously and honestly believing that they are contributing to enlighten and benefit mankind." [28]

Ultimately Catharine's solution to this dilemma was to design a single standard of conduct that would incorporate both middle class evangelical earnestness and upper class Unitarian or Episcopal assurance. Although she was still feeling her way toward it in 1830, Catharine asserted that one "true standard of rectitude" could be created to promote the "happiness and usefulness" of all classes of Americans. In a nation quickly abandoning eighteenth-century status definitions and evolving a new social structure especially vigorous at the middle levels, Catharine Beecher's desire to include

as many people as possible within these boundaries laid the ground-
work for her relevance to the American society of the mid-
nineteenth century. Meanwhile in her own school she had begun
to explore some ways in which evangelical and upper class ethics
could be combined and how this new combined standard could be
carried forward by American women.

☙ 7 ☙

Modes of Moral Influence, 1829–1831

The Elements of Mental and Moral Philosophy was published anonymously at Catharine Beecher's expense in the fall of 1831. While she was writing her book, Catharine was simultaneously attempting to raise an endowment of twenty thousand dollars for her school. In the process of writing and studying mental and moral philosophy Catharine's ambitions for her school had grown and assumed a new shape. Earlier in 1827 she had based her campaign for a new school on intellectual principles. To act and think properly, she said, young women needed to be better instructed in the fundamentals of learning, and she had claimed that truly refined character went hand in hand with intellectual development. She had not mentioned moral training as a primary or distinct goal of her school. In 1829 she revised the goals of her school and devised a new alliance between evangelical morality and feminine refinement. Catharine Beecher's educational career during these years was remarkably congruent with the conclusions she had reached in her moral philosophy.

As early as August 1828 Catharine Beecher began to think of adding a new dimension to her school. "My school is not yet what I intend to make a school before I stop," she wrote to Edward. "I must take *one more step* and that as great a one as stepping from my private school of 30 to 40 to the charge of an endowed Seminary of 130 to 40." She said that she had "many plans and some very good ones" but that she would defer mentioning them until she had the "time and opportunity to talk with [Edward] face to face." [1]

In 1829 Catharine revealed these plans to the Hartford public. She wanted to expand greatly her school's emphasis on moral instruction and to add an associate principal to the school who would not only direct the course in mental and moral philosophy, but who would also be engaged in a more thoroughgoing attempt to mold the character of her students. Early in 1829 Catharine published an essay entitled *Suggestions Respecting Improvements in Education*.

In it she described the new goals of her school. "The improvements made have hitherto related chiefly to *intellectual acquisitions*," she began, "but this is not the most important object of education," she now concluded. "The formation of personal habits and manners," she said, "the correction of the disposition, the regulation of the social feelings, the formation of the conscience, and the direction of the moral character and habits, are united, objects of much greater consequence than the mere communication of knowledge and the discipline of the intellectual powers." [2]

Two things were necessary to accomplish these more important objects, Catharine said. "The formation and correction of the moral character and habits" must be made into a "distinct department" and one well-qualified person must be employed to head such a department. In addition, a boarding home must be built for the teachers and students, for it was there that the real shaping of moral character would take place. The hours spent outside the classroom, Catharine said, "are the hours of access to the heart, the hours in which character is developed, and in which opportunities for exerting beneficial influence are continually occurring." [3]

No contemporary female seminary provided room and board for its students since the alternative of boarding in nearby private homes was believed more efficient and less costly. However, George Bancroft and Joseph Cogswell had since 1823 conducted a very successful experimental boarding school for boys at Round Hill, Massachusetts. The aims at Round Hill were to create a "controlled environment" in which the students were "constantly under observation and care" and thereby educated morally as well as intellectually.[4] Catharine's proposed experiment may have drawn on the example of Round Hill; certainly it was influenced by the pioneering efforts of Emma Willard since 1818 to create such boarding facilities at her Troy, New York, seminary. With the exception of Emma Willard's seminary, boarding plans were not successful until later in the decade when the American schoolhouse was seen as an appropriate institutional location for women. Only then did parents consent to transfer boarding students out of local families and into the school's own facilities. This change in socialization patterns was simultaneous with the shift in women's career options to include teaching as well as homemaking.[5]

Catharine may have had personal reasons for wanting such a boarding house or residence hall. She found that her own rented house was an expensive and tiring enterprise. Mary Beecher had married a Hartford lawyer, Thomas Perkins, in 1827, and Aunt Esther was frequently in Boston. The burden of the housekeeping fell on Catharine, and she was eager to be rid of it. A residence hall, financed by seminary funds, would have been an expedient solution to Catharine's own housing problems. Lyman Beecher assumed this was the case, and he believed that Catharine advocated a moral department only to make her proposal of a boarding hall more attractive to potential financial contributors. Catharine's main goal, he assumed, was to build a home where she and her teachers and students could live more cheaply and more comfortably.

Lyman frequently urged his daughter to save her money and make sure she could support herself in her later years.[6] Housing and finances were always problems for Catharine, and undoubtedly her own interests did play a role in her plea for a residence hall. When Catharine failed to raise the money for it, she subsequently gave up her own home and thereafter boarded with Mary and Thomas Perkins.[7]

Yet Catharine's scheme for thoroughgoing moral instruction was more than a front for her campaign for a residence hall. Catharine knew exactly whom she wanted to employ as an associate principal, and her letters to this woman reveal what kinds of moral instruction she envisioned for her school. Catharine's choice was Zilpah Grant — currently the associate principal of Mary Lyon's Ipswich Academy, one of the best-known educators in New England, and an ardent and orthodox Congregationalist. In 1828 she had been dismissed from the principalship of an academy in Derry, New Hampshire, for overemphasizing religion and urging too zealously the conversion of her students.[8] In May 1829 Catharine Beecher asked Zilpah Grant to "unite with me as principal of this institution" and "to be its chaplain and direct and control its religious teaching."[9] Catharine assured Grant "a thousand dollars a year" in such a position — much more money than Miss Grant could expect to make anywhere else. Yet to Catharine's surprise, Zilpah Grant declined the offer, believing it to be too worldly an undertaking. Catharine pressed her father and Joel Hawes to plead her case with Grant, and Catharine explained further the reasons she wanted to introduce a person of real religious convictions into her school. Her Hartford school, she wrote to Miss Grant, drew "pupils from families of wealth," and under Zilpah Grant's influence this wealth could be put to evangelical uses. "A woman of piety and active benevolence, with wealth which enables her to take the lead in society, can do more good than another of equally exalted character without it," Catharine wrote.[10] Through her moral department Catharine meant to unite upper class influence with evangelical beliefs. This was the category of "character" Catharine wanted to promote.

Lyman Beecher's letter to Zilpah Grant enlarged on this theme. "Hitherto," Lyman said, "religion had been associated with poverty and ignorance, or, at best, with solid, strong, coarse, unpolished orthodoxy." He continued: "I do not expect that taste and refinement will convert the soul, but who can tell how many have been repelled from religion by a want of them." The association of "taste and refinement" with religion would be a powerful combination against God's enemies, he concluded. Zilpah Grant now understood fully the nature of Catharine's scheme of combining middle class evangelical enthusiasm with upper class style of leadership, and she now definitely declined the offer on the grounds that she preferred straightforward, not polished, beliefs. Pointing to the emphasis on wealth and refinement that already dominated Catharine's school, she asked, "Would that school be such a model one as is needed in New England?" and answered readily, "No." [11]

Immediately upon receiving Grant's refusal, Catharine suffered a nervous collapse and left Hartford.[12] The success of her scheme to promote the moral influence of women by merging upper and middle class virtues into a moral imperative depended upon widespread social support. Now that a prominent fellow educator had rejected it and others seemed wary of a plan so patently designed to replace the role of the male clergyman with a female moral instructor, Catharine saw that instead of establishing herself as the leader of women's education, she had isolated herself from her supporters. The next innovative step in women's education came from Mary Lyon at Mount Holyoke, where girls began in 1836 to care for their own domestic needs in the school's boarding facilities.[13] Yet it took Mary Lyon two years of full-time fund-raising to set up this facility, which was primarily devoted to learning habits of domestic economy and not, as Catharine would have it, to character development.

The social influence Catharine wanted to create for women seemed for the moment obstructed. She felt that her moral department would fail unless she found a dedicated evangelical to help direct it, and yet it was the very zeal of Miss Grant's religious principles that prohibited her from joining too worldly a school. The Hartford community did not support Catharine's endowment-fund drive; perhaps they were unwilling to remove young women from the influence of the families in which they lived either as daughters or as boarders and disapproved of a plan in which these young women would reinforce one another's character under the influence of an unmarried woman. Although part of Round Hill's success was its ability to create a "male oasis" nurturing the character of young men through peer interaction and through the moral example of bachelors Bancroft and Cogswell, an equivalent environment of female mutual support was not condoned by Hartford's potential donors.[14]

A sizable portion of the community feared that their daughters would be overeducated for the traditional roles they were expected to fill. They linked "philosophical" study with intellectual and marital independence, roundly condemning all three. "I had rather my daughters would go to school and sit down and do nothing, than to study Philosophy, etc.," an editorial commented in the *Connecticut Courant*. "These branches fill young Misses with *vanity* to the degree that they are above attending to the more useful parts of an education," it continued, adding that vanity would then pervade the entire character of the young woman. "She will be a dandizette at eighteen, an old maid at thirty." [15]

Catharine's state of mental depression lasted throughout December 1829. Her spirits may also have been affected by the failing fortunes of Edward and Lyman Beecher in Boston. Edward's Park Street Church was "determined," Lyman said, "to get him dismissed." [16] Seeing Edward fail as a "fellow labourer" to Lyman's evangelical cause did not help Catharine face her own failure in Hartford. For she also viewed her work as a complement to her father's. Lyman's letters to Catharine often mentioned her work in these terms. After her successful fund drive in 1827 Lyman had written her: "I am glad that your plan is likely to succeed and I am glad that there is a Beecher in Hartford that the Episcopacy may not bind them all hand and foot there while they sleep. Your academy will be a discomfiture of their plans." Lyman said that if the Episcopals "were evangelical I would not care how much they prospered," but as they were not, he said, "the good people of Connecticut have as much cause to resist their ambitions as we have here to resist Unitarian encroachments." [17] In December 1829, however, a general mood of gloom replaced this earlier ebullience of the Beecher family, and this may be another reason Catharine reacted so strongly to Zilpah Grant's refusal and Hartford's rebuff.

Harriet Beecher, then eighteen years old, assumed the school's leadership while Catharine was in Boston, and her daily letters to Catharine demonstrate how much of the school's attention was currently focused on the notion of "moral character." "This morning I delivered a long speech on 'modes of exerting moral influence,' showing the ways in which an evil influence is unknowingly exerted and the ways in which each and all can exert a good one," Harriet wrote. "The right spirit is daily 'increasing.' " [18] Harriet took it upon herself to resume the joint prayer meetings with her students and members of the First Church, and she happily reported to Catharine that four students wished "to make a public profession of religion." Harriet meant to lift her sister's spirits and said: "I feel willing to devote my whole life to this institution, as I never did before." She believed that the school itself had generated so much moral energy that it no longer needed Zilpah Grant. "If only the resources you already have are employed, you need not give up for want to Miss Grant," Harriet wrote. Touching as Harriet's letters were, they missed the point of Catharine's moral aims. Though temporarily lacking an effective institutional means, the end Catharine sought for her students was not conversion, but social influence.

Catharine returned to Hartford, disbanded her boarding house, and she and Harriet moved into a small room in the Perkins's home. By February Catharine had recovered her composure and reasserted her aims, but now in a significantly different form. Rather than engaging an associate principal to direct a separate moral department, Catharine assumed this responsibility herself. Moreover the aim of that moral instruction would be broader than inducing wealthy young women to adopt evangelical beliefs. In the spring of 1830 Catharine turned her attentions away from Hartford and focused on a larger national scene. She planned now to turn her seminary into a training school for young women who would learn proper social, religious, and moral principles and then establish their own schools elsewhere on the same principles. She sought out a new group of teachers "who will agree to devote three years of their

lives to effecting this object." To Mary Dutton, one of her favorite
pupils and assistant teachers, Catharine wrote: "We could train
both principals and teachers to go forth and establish similar institutions all over our country." Catharine felt sure that "almost
anything can be done with *almost any mind*," if she could "*control
the circumstances*" of the learning experience. "I feel no doubt the
thing can be done and the plan perpetuated," she concluded. The
prospect was exciting to Catharine. She now spoke of the national
rather than the local influence of refined and moral women. "I see
no other way in which our country can so surely be saved from the
inroads of vice, infidelity and error," she said. "Let the leading females of this country become refined, pious and active and the salt
is scattered through the land to purify and save." [19]

From 1828 to 1830, therefore, while Catharine was writing her
mental and moral philosophy, she was also developing a new channel for her career. She saw the possibility for vastly enlarging the
scope of her educational activities and endowing them with moral
energy. The evangelical impulse was an expansive, outward thrust,
and Catharine Beecher's thought and career manifested those qualities. Yet there was a second factor essential to the development of
her career during these three years. Catharine Beecher became
increasingly conscious of women and their special roles, and the
shifts in her aims during these years was as much a product of this
consciousness as it was of evangelical expansiveness. Catharine
Beecher not only wanted to "save" the nation, she wanted women
to save it. In her appeal to the Hartford community in 1829 she
emphasized the moral role of women. "Woman has never wakened
to her highest destinies and holiest hopes," Catharine said. "She has
yet to learn the purifying and blessed influence she may gain and
maintain over the intellect and affections of the human mind."
The time was coming, Catharine continued, "when educated females
will not be satisfied with the present objects of their low ambition."
Catharine felt that woman had no object "of sufficient interest to
call forth her cultivated energies and warm affections." The object
that will call forth these energies and affections, she said, "[is] the
immortal mind whereon she may fasten durable and holy impres-
sions that shall never be effaced or wear away." When women learn
how great their "power over the intellect and affections" of others
is, Catharine said, then they will begin to use this power. "The cul-

tivation and development of the immortal mind shall be presented to woman as her especial and delightful duty." [20]

In 1829 Catharine meant that this duty should be exercised primarily in the home. Yet within a year she came to see the role of the teacher in these terms. These statements of 1829 were partly rhetorical and designed to justify her department of moral instruction, but by 1830 Catharine had become convinced that women could indeed effect such a power and that they could best do so as teachers. "To enlighten the understanding and to gain the affections is a teacher's business," Catharine wrote Mary Dutton in 1830. Since "the mind is to be guided chiefly by means of the affections," Catharine said, "is not *woman* best fitted to accomplish these important objects?" [21]

Again Catharine's own practical problems fitted nicely into her pedagogic vision. Teaching was important to Catharine also because it provided women with a respectable alternative to marriage. The single woman need no longer become merely a spinster aunt who was dependent upon her relatives for support. Teaching, Catharine said, "is a *profession,* offering influence, respectability and independence." Woman, Catharine said, can "discern before her the road to honourable independence and extensive usefulness where she need not outstep the prescribed boundaries of feminine modesty." [22] In expanding the options open to women, Catharine hoped she could use traditional values to her own advantage, but, if not, she was fully able to redefine these traditional "boundaries" when they interfered with her plan.

Teaching was in 1830 not a woman's profession. Although Emma Willard had for a decade linked her curriculum at Troy with preparation for a teaching career, Catharine Beecher was the first to envision teaching as a profession dominated by — indeed exclusively belonging to — women. Demographic and economic developments in the United States during the next two decades supported Catharine Beecher's vision. A rapidly expanding population demanded more teachers, but a swiftly developing economy had relatively fewer males available for nonindustrial or noncommercial work.[23] Several forces converged in the 1830s and the 1840s to form a matrix of support for Catharine Beecher's ideas. These were the creation of a leisured middle class of women, the institution of tax-supported common schools, the expansion of population in the

West and its need for new schools, and the glorification of female qualities of nurture throughout the United States. The hints of these events were barely audible in 1830, but when they had gathered to a chorus a decade later, Catharine Beecher was ready to orchestrate this cultural crescendo and use it for her own and, she believed, her sex's advantage.[24] Meanwhile, during the last year of her Hartford career, Catharine's school did become a training ground for teachers.

Angelina Grimké was one young woman who considered entering Catharine Beecher's school to train for a teaching career. In the summer of 1831 she visited the Hartford Female Seminary, and she vividly recorded her experiences there in her diary.[25] Since Angelina was a Quaker and a Southerner, her account is valuable as an outsider's view of Catharine and her Hartford social environment.

What most impressed Angelina Grimké was the gentility of Catharine Beecher's society. "They are very genteel in their manner," she said of the whole Perkins household. Although twelve pupils in addition to Catharine and Harriet Beecher boarded in the home, Angelina could say that the house was "as quiet as though there were neither young children nor boarders in it." Mary Beecher Perkins was "quite the lady in her deportment" and Catharine Beecher had "very sociable manners." Nevertheless, Angelina said, Catharine Beecher taught her scholars "to feel that they had no right to spend their time in idleness, fashion and folly, but they as individuals were bound to be useful in Society after they had finished their education, and that as teachers single women could be more useful in this than in any other way." Many of her pupils, "though quite independent" financially, "had become teachers simply from the wish of being useful," Angelina said. The genteel air of the Hartford Female Seminary was not therefore the gentility of leisure, but was dedicated to social usefulness. To Angelina Grimké Catharine also stated her belief that minds "well managed would never turn out badly."

Angelina found Hartford full of benevolent activity, and Catharine accompanied her on tours of the "reformed" state prison, the school for the deaf and dumb, and the Insane Retreat. At Lydia Sigourney's home Catharine introduced Angelina to a young Greek who had left his country during its recent war and who was heralded as an ambassador of freedom and supported by Mrs. Sigourney while he studied at a small college in Hartford. In Catharine's school interest in benevolent activity ran high, and pupils had in the past sent bandages and money to Greece. The main focus of Catharine Beecher's benevolent activities was the Cherokee Indians, who in 1827 had been ordered out of Georgia. From 1828 to 1830 Catharine had formed a women's auxiliary to aid her father and other Boston ministers who opposed this Jacksonian measure. She arranged public meetings in behalf of the Cherokees, circulated petitions to be sent to Congress, and wrote a widely distributed pamphlet entitled "To the Benevolent Women of the United States" to forward the cause.[26] Yet in Hartford the leadership of benevolent activity fell not to Catharine Beecher but to Lydia Sigourney. Mrs. Sigourney combined "wealth, beauty, refinement, talent and religion in one beautiful assemblage," Angelina wrote in her diary, and meeting her was one of the high points of her Hartford stay.

Angelina accidentally uncovered Catharine Beecher's attitude toward Alexander Fisher's death. "I read that beautiful and touching piece of poetry written by EK after the decease of the young man she had been engaged to, and dear Catharine soon became convulsed with agitation and it was not difficult to perceive that some tender string had been touched," Angelina wrote. "When the piece was finished after a little silence she remarked that her case had been very similar." Catharine then related the story of her engagement and Fisher's death, and "went on to say how this affliction had been blessed to her and how completely the whole course of her life had been changed by it." Catharine said, Angelina wrote, "that she had been uncommonly wild and thoughtless, living without a thought of religion but since that time had been an altered character."

Catharine was now able to place Fisher's death in the larger context of the development of her own character and to see it as a blessing in disguise. She continued to wear her hair in the short ringlets of her girlhood and seemed in other ways to have developed an enviable capacity for cloaking her mature responsibilities in the audacity and independence that characterized her youth. Living a life very much of her own design, and not often in the company of those who might reprove her, Catharine felt it natural that she should dominate her surroundings. Men more used to wifely submissiveness were put off by her manner, but to Angelina and many other women, she was an imposing example of female self-sufficiency.

The great event of Angelina's visit was a school excursion of about ten miles to Daniel Wadsworth's country retreat. "About 50 of Catharine's scholars were to go and about 8 o'clock the barouches began to assemble at the Seminary," Angelina wrote. The procession began with "Catharine at the head of the party on her fine white horse, Rollo — she wore a green riding dress and the contrast was handsome — she is an expert rider and altogether the cavalcade made an imposing appearance." Wadsworth's country property was "a most elegant spot fitted up for the purpose, it would seem, not of selfishly enjoying it himself only, but of generously affording to strangers and visitors the opportunity of beholding Nature in one of her most engaging and lovely forms." Wadsworth had built a tower and "a dwelling house" in the Gothic style, and in addition to these his property included a boathouse, a lake, and an abundance of pathways by which the hills were to be climbed, the views enjoyed, and the woods explored. Catharine Beecher had included the "emotions of taste" in her analysis of mental phenomena, and she knowledgeably discussed the contemporary aesthetic of the sublime, the beautiful, and the picturesque.[27] Wadsworth's country retreat was based on these aesthetic principles and every perspective was designed to offer an aesthetic experience. The outing was then more than a trip to the countryside. It was an exercise in the cultivation of the aesthetic emotions.

The whole afternoon was one of refined pleasure and Angelina Grimké was charmed by it. From the top of a hill she looked down to see the young ladies scattered through the scenery in groups of six or eight, "in pink and white dresses." At the picnic lunch in the Gothic house, "our kind friend Catharine Beecher presided over the table and sent round the lemonade and dishes so that we had a plentiful meal," Angelina continued. Before the party returned to Hartford the girls "decorated their barouches with branches of trees."

Such pleasures were a regular part of Catharine Beecher's life. The general graciousness of her Hartford life included daily horseback rides, "weekly levees" when she received "her own friends and those of her pupils," piano recitals, and poetry readings.[28] Yet by 1830 these pleasures had begun to pale for Catharine Beecher.

Hartford encouraged gracious manners and social amenities; it sustained Catharine's aim of producing "refined, well-educated" women but was not willing to support Catharine's further aim of altering the moral character of women. This was considered the prerogative of the church. What Catharine was aiming at in 1829 was neither the traditional refined goals of a female academy nor the traditional conversion goal of the church. In 1827 she had begun to speak of refinement as an active rather than a passive quality, and her moral philosophy carried her further into the study of mental and moral activity. By 1829 she had created a theoretical model of female character formation that required neither the church nor the traditional seminary. Just as Lyman was uncomfortable about Catharine's revivalism, so Hartford was uneasy about the activism she seemed to be urging upon young women. Catharine's desire to enlarge her own role as well as the role of women was unfulfilled in Hartford, but her discouragement and depression of 1829 were temporary. Catharine's letter to Mary Dutton in 1830 demonstrated how eager she was to bring her theoretical model into practice. "I feel a confidence that if an institution could be formed on the plan I propose and five or six ladies could, associated with me, adopt my views and fairly bring them to the test of experience, we could *prove to the world,* to the very most skeptical and cavilling, that characters can *be made over,*" she said.[29] Women would first themselves be made over and then they would reshape the society.

The principles of Catharine Beecher's moral philosophy were never fully brought "to the test of experience" in Hartford. As early as the spring of 1830 she wrote, "[I] foresaw that my career there was coming to a close,"[30] and in July 1830, seven months after Catharine had temporarily abandoned her school, Lyman Beecher revealed a way for both of them to escape their recent reversals. They could emigrate to the West.

At the Presbyterian General Assembly in June, the trustees of Cincinnati's Lane Theological Seminary had asked Beecher if he would be interested in accepting the presidency of the seminary. Edward Beecher had already left Boston for Illinois, and Lyman Beecher's own fortunes in Boston were failing fast. Catharine was the first person to whom Lyman revealed his new plans. "While at

Philadelphia and since, my interest in the majestic West has been greatly excited and increased," he said. Lyman described the West in terms that were sure to appeal to Catharine. "The moral destiny of our nation, and all our institutions and hopes, and the world's hopes, turns on the character of the West, and the competition now is for that of preoccupancy in the education of the rising generation in which the Catholics and infidels have got the start of us," he said. "I have thought seriously of going over to Cincinnati, the London of the West, to spend the remnant of my days in that great conflict, and in consecrating all my children to God in that region who are willing to go," he added. If Lyman went, so, he hoped, would the whole Beecher establishment. He implored Catharine, "Write your thoughts to me as soon as you have time, and I will find time to write back to you, [for] if I go, it will be a part of my plan that you go." [31]

The West as Lyman described it was the perfect place for Catharine to test her theory of moral education, and she had no desire to stay longer in Hartford. The summer term of 1831, when Angelina Grimké visited, was Catharine's last term as principal of the Hartford Female Seminary. She resigned in September 1831, even before her father had formally accepted the Lane offer.

In the fall and winter of 1831 Catharine was busy sending and delivering copies of her newly published *Elements of Mental and Moral Philosophy* "to leaders of thought in both the literary and religious world." [32] Through friendly intermediaries Catharine sent the work "with a request for full criticism." All these leaders were led to assume that the author was a gentleman. In a gesture that later became characteristic, she solicited comments from people who avowedly opposed her own beliefs. Prompted mainly by a genuine desire to learn why and on what grounds these people disagreed with her, Catharine hoped to take their criticism into account and enlarge her readership to include her critics. She believed that it was possible for her writings to have a universal appeal, and partly in the hope that she had already achieved this universality she sent copies to Henry Ware, her father's chief Unitarian opponent in Boston, and to Archibald Alexander, her father's old school Presbyterian opponent at Princeton — the polar extremes of American religious thought of the 1820s.

Henry Ware thanked "the Author" through an intermediary for

"the opportunity to peruse an unpublished book in which I have found so much to admire and approve, together with some doctrines which *are far from my own views of religious truth.*" Ware said he would be happy to see it officially published, "believing that free and unreserved discussion" prompted "the discovery and the establishment of truth." [33] This was faint praise indeed, but it was more than a Beecher might have expected from Henry Ware.

Catharine not only revealed her identity to Archibald Alexander, but she also invited herself into his home. In October 1831 Catharine visited Philadelphia, where she tried to have her book adopted in some private schools. Before leaving Hartford she wrote to Alexander: "I took the liberty several months since of forwarding to you a work which I had prepared for the use of the higher class of pupils in the institution under my care." She explained that she had sent her book to other gentlemen "most of whom, however, were personal friends to myself or my father." Her hope, she said, was "that *some* of them would find time at least to read *parts* of the work and that in this way, among them all, I might gain valuable suggestions on all the subjects discussed." One of her father's close associates in Boston recommended, she said, "that I should converse with you on certain points and to this my own feelings responded. I am about to make a journey to Philadelphia," she continued, "and of course I shall pass Princeton, but as I have no claims upon the hospitalities of any family there, and being a lady, cannot leave my protection and stop at a public house, it will afford me no opportunity to seek what I desire." Yet, she said, she had been told "that Dr. Alexander is a man not studious of etiquette — that I might without being considered intrusive, address him a letter stating my wishes" and "he would offer me the privilege of visiting for a day or two under his roof." [34] This was the first of many occasions when Catharine assumed the role of a traveling intellectual and freely invited herself into the homes of teachers, writers, and clergymen. The details of Catharine's visit with this old school Presbyterian are lost, but the result of it was that Catharine cut out some pages of her book because they offended orthodox beliefs. Many Hartford citizens had also expressed concern at some of Catharine's "views supposed to be contrary to the established orthodoxy," and she said that she "deemed it prudent to cut out the heretical pages." [35]

Both Catharine's moral theory and its practical application had run into opposition in the East. Yet Catharine Beecher knew how to turn her "afflictions" into blessings. When she set out for "the majestic West" with her father, she carried along fifty copies of her book.

Part III

ACHIEVEMENT AND RETRENCHMENT, 1832–1843

⚜ 8 ⚜

So Fair a Prospect, 1832–1835

In the spring of 1832 Catharine and Lyman Beecher traveled to Cincinnati to take their measure of the city. "It will not . . . be prudent" to decide to emigrate "until I shall have surveyed the premises," Lyman said, and he and Catharine went by stage to Wheeling and then took the riverboat up the Ohio to Cincinnati.[1] Cincinnati was then one of the most attractive cities of the West. On the hills rising from the river's edge, large Georgian houses declared the city's pride and prosperity.[2] Lyman and Catharine had but a short walk from the boat to one of the most elegant of these mansions, the home of Samuel F. Foote. Foote was Roxana Beecher's brother, and the dashing uncle whom Catharine remembered from her childhood in East Hampton as the bearer of exotic gifts. Foote had made a fortune in ship trading in the last days of the Spanish Empire, and he retired with his brother John in Cincinnati to invest his money in western public works.[3]

Catharine and Lyman stayed in his home, one of the major centers of Cincinnati social life, and from the first day of their arrival Catharine could barely contain her delight about her future prospects in Cincinnati. "Uncle John and Samuel are just the intelligent, sociable, free and hospitable sort of folk that everybody likes and everybody feels at home with," Catharine wrote home to Harriet. "I know of no place in the world where there is so fair a prospect of finding everything that makes social and domestic life pleasant." [4]

Her uncles were not the only familiar faces in Cincinnati, for the city was full of New Englanders whom Catharine had known in either Litchfield or Hartford. It seems, she said, "that everybody I used to know is here or coming here." Catharine was especially pleased with the women she met, for the quality of her professional and social life depended largely upon their character. "I have become somewhat acquainted with those ladies we shall have the most to do with, and find them intelligent, New England sort of folks,"

Catharine wrote to Harriet. "I think a very pleasant society can be selected from the variety which is assembled here."

The prospects for a new school were excellent. "The folks here are very anxious to have a school on our plan set on foot here," Catharine wrote. "[Everybody is] ready to lend a helping hand," and she and Harriet could expect to have "fine rooms in the city college building which is now unoccupied." "Indeed," Catharine emphasized, "this is a New England city in all its habits," and she was eager to complete their move West. "We have finally decided on the spot where our house shall stand," she added, ". . . and you cannot . . . find a more delightful spot for a residence." [5]

Catharine Beecher's career in Cincinnati lasted more than a decade. During her first two years she established a place for herself among the city's social elite and began a new female seminary. In Cincinnati Catharine tried to duplicate the kind of leadership she had exerted in Hartford. Yet she failed to realize that Cincinnati was only superficially a New England city and that the tactics that led to success in Hartford were inappropriate for Cincinnati. Cincinnati society consisted of several disparate elements held together only by the concerted efforts of those who put the town's prosperity and stability before all else. Catharine entered an already established society where New Englanders, Middle-Atlantic state emigrants, and Southerners were dedicated to suppressing the issues that could potentially divide them. Slavery and abolitionism, and questions of regional loyalties were all potentially divisive issues in this border city, and the leadership of Cincinnati sought to prevent them from erupting to the surface of the city's life. [6]

For a variety of reasons the Beecher family became the focus of just the kind of controversy Cincinnatians sought to avoid. Catharine Beecher's fall from their social esteem was as swift as her initial ascent, and she spent the last half of the 1830s struggling to restore her damaged prestige, and, when that failed, struggling to create a new alternative career. Her immersion in Cincinnati's highly volatile culture forced Catharine to revise her mode of leadership and alter the set of issues she stood for. In Cincinnati she learned in practice what it took to implement her theory of cultural unity. Through her bitter defeat on that local scene, she forged a fuller national achievement.

In the winter of 1832–33, when the Beechers were finally established in Cincinnati, Catharine gained an easy entrance to the socially elite circles of the city. She had special access to three families who stood at the center of Cincinnati society: the Nathaniel Wrights, the Edward Kings, and the Samuel Footes. Nathaniel Wright was a New Englander who had emigrated to Cincinnati in 1817 and was by 1833 president of the Board of Trustees of Lane Seminary, an elder in Lyman Beecher's Second Presbyterian Church, and one of the city's most important legal and financial figures. Later he was responsible for much of Ohio's railway development.[7] Edward King, the son of Rufus King, New York's leading Federalist, was a graduate of the Litchfield Law School and one of Catharine's earliest beaux. Harriet Porter Beecher was related to the King family, and Catharine considered Edward her cousin. Edward had strong political aspirations and had married Sarah Worthington, the daughter of the governor of Ohio.[8] Samuel Foote, Catharine's uncle, had wide investments in public works in Cincinnati and elsewhere, and his judgments on all aspects of the city's development were sought after and respected.[9]

Catharine spent her evenings in the company of these families and their friends. One of the most remarkable aspects of Cincinnati culture was its literary clubs. The Semi-Colon Club, Cincinnati's preeminent social and intellectual group, was founded by Samuel Foote and other New Englanders.[10] The Semi-Colon "soirees" consisted of polite conversation, music, poetry, and usually an essay written for the occasion by one of the members. Catharine Beecher enjoyed these gatherings enormously, and for one of them she presented an elaborate sketch "of the ground plan of Castle Ward, the residence of my ancestors on my mother's side." [11] This kind of upper class pretentiousness characterized most of the Semi-Colon activities, and Catharine's own pretensions were apparently not questioned by Samuel Foote, who knew that Castle Ward was nothing more than a Connecticut farmhouse.

In addition to the Semi-Colon Club, Catharine joined the literary evenings sponsored by Daniel Drake, a Kentuckian who was one of Cincinnati's most cosmopolitan and respected citizens. Called "the Franklin of Cincinnati" for his interest in public institutions, Drake had founded Cincinnati College, the Medical College of Ohio, the Cincinnati Hospital, and served on the boards of several other institutions. His literary group was begun "for the benefit of his daughters, then just growing into womanhood," and Catharine was invited to discuss with their guests "questions belonging to society, literature, education and religion," with "an occasional piece of poetry or a story to diversify and enliven the conversation." [12]

By the fall of 1834 Catharine Beecher counted among her associates the most important people in Cincinnati. She rode to church in the carriage of Mrs. Burnet, the wife of the former head of the legislative council for the Northwest Territory who was at that time a judge on the Supreme Court of Ohio and one of the most prominent members of Lyman Beecher's congregation.[13] Catharine went on excursions to nearby Ohio towns in the company of Charles Hammond, the editor of the powerful Whig newspaper, the *Cincinnati Gazette.* In the summer she joined Cincinnati "society" in Yellow Springs, where the town's wealthy families vacationed to avoid the cholera that often reached epidemic proportions in the city.[14] Whether directing summer theatricals in Yellow Springs or leading the conversation at a soiree at the Kings', Catharine Beecher was at the center of what she felt was an exhilarating and elegant social setting.

For more substantial literary and intellectual pursuits, Catharine had access to the *Western Monthly Magazine,* a literary journal modeled after regional magazines such as the *New England Magazine,* Philadelphia's *Port Folio,* and the *Southern Literary Messenger.* Harriet Beecher began to publish stories and essays in this magazine almost as soon as the Beechers arrived, and the *Western Monthly Magazine* seemed a likely outlet for Catharine's writings as well. Harriet's first contribution, signed "B," was widely assumed to be from Catharine's hand.[15] Many of the early issues of the magazine were devoted to articles promoting Western education, and although none of these articles shared Catharine's New England biases, she had no reason to think the magazine would not support her educational ideas. When Catharine established a new school in Cincinnati, she included the magazine's editor, James Hall, among her trustees.[16]

The other cultural association in which Catharine took a keen interest was the Western Literary Institute and College of Professional Teachers, an organization that grew out of a conference on education held in Cincinnati in 1831. Literary men, clergymen, teachers, and other professional and intellectual men met annually thereafter to discuss all aspects of Western education and published in the Western Literary Institute *Transactions* the text of the papers presented at the annual meeting.[17] Since the group included prominent men from throughout the Ohio and Mississippi valleys, they acted as a self-appointed advisory board to those engaged in educational activities, and they frequently took stands on issues and sought to influence western educational policy. Resolutions on such topics as female education, moral instruction, and seminaries to train teachers were brought before the group, studied, discussed, and acted upon. Since the membership was restricted to men, Catharine Beecher could participate only as an observer, but in her father she had an active ally. Lyman Beecher quickly became one of the institute's most important members, and the institute frequently met in his Second Presbyterian Church.[18] This organization gave Catharine the potential opportunity to publicize her ideas, for papers by women were occasionally included in the institute's agenda and read before the group by a male member. Given the strong evangelical bias of the group, Catharine could feel confident during her early years in Cincinnati that the group would turn to her for aid in shaping the educational institutions of the West.

After two months in Cincinnati Catharine Beecher began to organize her own school, but given the other opportunities open to her, it was not surprising that she wanted to conserve her energies for them in addition to her school. She proposed to Mary Dutton and some of her other favored Hartford pupils and teachers that they come to Cincinnati and operate "a school which should be open to my direction and advice and which in some way should be connected with *my name*," but in which she would not herself teach.[19] "The ladies of this place who are pious are all exceeding anxious to have a school got up under my auspices," she said, "[but] I cannot teach myself." Harriet also preferred to remain free to pursue her writing. "I should love to come and *preach* and sometimes to *teach* and Harriet would like the same, and if we assumed no obligation or responsibility, we could do it without feeling burdened," Catharine wrote to Mary Dutton. She assured Mary that she "could not find a more interesting and intelligent and *influential* circle to commence with" than the one she had already cultivated. "Your school," Catharine explained, "would have all the influence of the Lane Seminary connection and of the parish connection which with all their various ramifications is no small concern." As an afterthought Catharine dispatched another letter that made it clear that she intended to remain in charge of the "pecuniary responsibilities" of the school and that Mary Dutton and the other teachers would be her salaried employees.[20]

A month later, in the spring of 1833, Catharine advertised the establishment of the Western Female Institute, a school dedicated not merely to the "technical acquisition of knowledge," but to "mental and moral development." [21] Catharine raised five hundred dollars for equipment for the school, and it began that spring with Catharine and Harriet as associate principals and Mary Dutton and Anne Tappan as teachers. Catharine did spend enough time at the school to make it necessary for her to board downtown with the Wright family rather than to remain in the Beecher household two miles out of town in Walnut Hills.[22] This for Catharine was no sacrifice, however, since it gave her easier access to Cincinnati's social life. Harriet, whether by choice or necessity, gave the school nearly all her time. "Harriet is well and is keeping school as assiduously as if she liked it," Mrs. William Beecher wrote to Mary Beecher Perkins in Hartford. Catharine, on the other hand, was involved in a wide variety of activities. "Cate is very well," Mrs. Beecher concluded, "and keeps the world going busily, as usual." [23]

Cincinnati and its immediate vicinity had several well-established girls' schools, and the most prominent of these, in Oxford, Ohio, invited Catharine to teach a class in moral philosophy from her own text.[24] William McGuffey was a professor at Miami University in Oxford, and since Catharine developed an immediate friendship with him, he may have had a hand in offering this invitation to her. During her first two years in Cincinnati Catharine lived the life of a cultured woman with financial independence through her school, and yet with only light responsibilities and with much of her time given to social diversions.

Yet there was a curious disparity between Catharine's potential opportunities and her real accomplishments during these years. With the exception of a temperance song she wrote for the Youth's Temperance Society of Cincinnati, the *Western Monthly Magazine* did not become an outlet for her writing. The magazine's educational articles tended to glorify the virtues of the common man and did not share Catharine's concern for moral education as the means of civilizing a crude democracy. The Western Literary Institute was similarly disappointing for Catharine, since it discussed female education in either traditional or sentimental terms. Although the institute's *Transactions* published an essay on female education by Lydia Sigourney, the group did not turn to Catharine's more ambitious and more aggressive ideas on women as the moral educators of the nation's youth.[25]

Catharine's first major address since her departure from Hartford was delivered not in Cincinnati but in New York. In the spring of 1835 she was invited to speak before a group of women there, under the auspices of the American Lyceum. Her address, *An Essay on the Education of Female Teachers,* was subsequently published by the American Lyceum in both New York and Cincinnati. In this essay Catharine put forward for the first time a detailed plan for shaping a national morality.

Essentially Catharine called for the creation of a corps of women teachers to civilize the barbarous immigrants and lower classes of the West. Her proposal played on Eastern fears, but it was not designed to win her friends in the West, and its strident tone belied the meliorative female influence she attributed to her plan. In 1835 Catharine stood at the brink of subtle cultural changes that would in a few years permit her to recast her proposal in far more acceptable terms. In the next two years Angelina and Sarah Grimké emerged on the national scene with more radical and insistent female voices, setting a background against which Catharine could seem to speak for social harmony and a comparatively modest extension of female influence.[26] As the potential options open to women in the nineteenth century became further clarified in the third decade, Catharine generally participated in the bargain then being struck between women's social role and domesticity. If women would agree to limit their participation in the society as a whole, so the pact has been described, then they could ascend to total hegemony over the domestic sphere.[27] The terms of this compromise were not fully clarified until early in the 1840s, and although Catharine Beecher made qualified use of it then, she fell back in 1835 upon her father's formula of asserting the need for evangelical leadership to meet the threat of national wickedness and corruption.

Catharine described the threat posed to American democracy by a whole generation of uneducated lower-class people. The conditions of American liberty freed this class from the moral influences of the church, but to avoid moral dissolution and civic anarchy some substitute influence must be found. "The great crisis is hastening on, when it shall be decided whether disenthralled intellect and liberty shall voluntarily submit to the laws of virtue and of Heaven, or run wild to insubordination, anarchy and crime," she said. "The education of the lower classes is deteriorating, as it respects moral and religious restraints. . . . and at the same time thousands and thousands of degraded foreigners, and their ignorant families, are pouring into this nation at every avenue." [28]

In the West children were not only growing up without moral education, they were growing up without any education at all. "In one of the best educated western states, one-third of the children are without schools," she said. Ninety thousand teachers were immediately needed, Catharine estimated, to teach those currently destitute of schools, and she further insisted that this need could only be filled by women. "It is chimerical to hope," she said, that men will become teachers "when there are multitudes of other employments that will . . . lead to wealth." A teacher will never become wealthy, she predicted, and therefore men will never become teachers in large enough numbers to meet the national need. "It is woman who is fitted by disposition and habits and circumstances, for such duties, who to a very wide extent must aid in educating the childhood and youth of this nation," she said.[29]

Catharine's plan for a national system of moral education called for the creation of teachers' seminaries where those women "who have the highest estimate of the value of moral and religious influence" shall be trained; some of these women would in turn train other teachers in their own seminaries elsewhere. This plan was initially to be financed privately, with an agent employed "to arise and enlighten the people." When the people were sufficiently awakened, "legislative and national aid" was to be sought. Mere intellectual learning in the common schools, Catharine concluded, was not sufficient to create a virtuous democracy. "Moral and religious education must be the foundation of national instruction," and "energetic and benevolent women" must be its mainstays. She spoke this way in the East, where some people were willing to believe the worst about the West, but these fear tactics alienated Cincinnatians, who grew less and less willing to sponsor her educational plans.

The success of Catharine's plan for national moral education was, in 1835, contingent upon her local success in Cincinnati. For it was there that she planned to create, from her Western Female Institute, the first model seminary for the national system. Early in 1835 Catharine had begun a fund-raising campaign in Cincinnati, and her *Essay on the Education of Female Teachers* was designed to promote that campaign. In it she called for "men of wealth" to "furnish the means" for such seminaries. "Men of patriotism and benevolence can commence by endowing two or three seminaries for female teachers in the most important stations in the nation," she said, and Cincinnati was clearly the first "station" she had in mind. In June Catharine gathered together some of Cincinnati's wealthy citizens and arranged for Nathaniel Wright to chair the meeting. Wright was to impress upon the committee the ambitious plans Catharine had for the Western Female Institute, the success of which depended upon their initial local support. "The citizens of Cincinnati," she hoped, would "furnish the funds necessary for a building and apparatus for the school," and "after this is done it is my intention to make efforts among the friends of education *abroad* to raise say thirty thousand dollars to endow the Seminary for Female Teachers." [30] Only fifteen thousand dollars was needed from Cincinnati citizens to place the seminary in its own building and give it the appearance of a more solid educational institution. Yet Wright's committee failed to take any action on Catharine's request. As a sign of her inability to gain the support of Cincinnati leaders, Catharine's major public appeal was made in the name of Thomas Gallaudet, the Hartford innovator in teaching the deaf and dumb, who visited Cincinnati in the summer of 1835. Even prestigious Gallaudet could not move Cincinnatians to contribute to Catharine's building fund. The campaign for funds failed, Catharine said, because "the committee were absorbed in their own affairs," [31] but there were other more important reasons for Catharine's failure than the preoccupation of the committeemen.

The reasons behind Catharine's failure were almost as complex as Cincinnati culture itself. In 1834 the issues of abolition and regional loyalties erupted into two violent controversies that were directly connected with Lyman Beecher and Lane Seminary. In the winter of 1834 Catharine, far from trying to ameliorate the controversy over regional loyalties, had only fed the flames of the dispute. Although she did not realize it at the time, she was the last person to whom Cincinnatians would give their financial support. In the summer of 1835 Catharine was dropped from the ranks of the Cincinnati elite.

The collapse of Catharine Beecher from social eminence began as early as the autumn of 1834 when Lane Seminary became the center of an abolitionist controversy. Theodore Weld, a Lane professor and a dedicated abolitionist, carried out his principles into social action. He and the Lane student abolitionist group went into the large free black community and put into practice their principle of "social intercourse according to character, irrespective of color." This mingling created strong feelings against them, and Lyman Beecher warned Weld against such practices. "If you want to teach colored schools," Beecher said, "I can fill your pockets with money but if you will visit in colored families, and walk with them in the streets, you will be overwhelmed." [32] Yet the students and Weld persisted in activities that the trustees viewed as divisive in the extreme and liable to incite a riot. In the fall of 1834 Nathaniel Wright and the other Lane trustees ordered the antislavery society disbanded. Rather than submit to this, Weld and his supporters left Cincinnati to found their own institution at Oberlin. Beecher was at that time out of the city and managed not to take a stand on either side of the issue, but the onus of the episode lay at his door, and he and his whole family were popularly regarded as troublemakers if not abolitionists. [33]

This incident had barely passed when Lyman Beecher became the center of yet another issue that threatened to divide the city into opposing factions. In Boston Beecher appealed for money for Lane by drawing a frightening picture of national danger arising from an increasing Catholic population, especially threatening in the West. He was reported in the eastern papers, soon unfortunately to reach Cincinnati, as speaking of the westerners' "limited means of education, and of the importance of introducing the social and religious principles of New England among them." He called upon New England sons to go among the westerners, "not in a mass to encite an envious feeling — but to mix with them as leaven in the loaf and thus produce a saving and enduring influence." [34] James Hall ridiculed Beecher and his speech in the December 1834 issue of the *Western Monthly Magazine,* and when the text of Beecher's speech was published as *A Plea for the West* in 1835, Hall pointed out the discrepancy between the published text and the text as it was reported in the eastern papers, for Lyman Beecher had edited out the offensive passages.[35]

Lines began to be drawn between those of New England loyalties and those strongly committed to an independent West. Daniel Drake, the spokesman for the latter group, came to Hall's defense. Drake considered his *Discourse on the History, Character, and Pospects of the West* (1834), wherein he predicted that the West would create her own institutions without any of the corruptions or artificialities of the East, a thorough rebuttal of Beecher's *Plea for the West.*[36] Catharine entered this battle on her father's side. Her own *Essay on the Education of Female Teachers* had nearly duplicated her father's sentiments, and if his *Plea* was not vindicated, her own reputation might similarly suffer. Most of Cincinnati's leaders were eager to drop the issue, however, and to let the matter rest with a mild reproof to Hall for ridiculing a clergyman. But Catharine kept the issue alive, and she sought not only to vindicate her father, but to use the issue to gain ascendancy in Cincinnati society.

Catharine violated the major rule of polite society and tried to erect social barriers between the New Englanders and the westerners. She proposed that the Semi-Colon Club adopt the motto "The March of Intellect," to imply that the club progressed in an established intellectual path, one presumably originating in the East.[37] Catharine began a campaign to exclude Hall and Drake from the elite homes of Cincinnati. Sarah Worthington King, the daughter of Ohio's governor and the daughter-in-law of New York's leading Federalist, was a central figure in Cincinnati culture since she bridged both the eastern and western groups, and Catharine concentrated on turning her against Hall and Drake.

Yet the Kings refused to cooperate in this plan to divide Cincinnati into western and eastern camps. "Tell Catharine Beecher," Edward King wrote his wife in December 1834, that she is "a guest and not a director" in our home. Tell all the Beechers, he said, that "if they choose to visit and partake when invited, it is well," but "not as our advisors as to when and how and with whom they are to mingle at our fireside." The whole fabric of Cincinnati culture was threatened by Catharine's actions, he believed. "I earnestly hope that the Club may go on," Edward said, "and let the disciples of 'The March of Intellect' see that they are not to rule in every household." He assured Sarah King, "You have a fair and indisputable right to entertain your friends in such way as you think may be most amusing and instructive, and that you need acknowledge no right in any person to interfere in the selection of your society." [38]

The difference between Catharine Beecher and Edward King was a class difference inherited from the eighteenth century. He, as a high-born Federalist aristocrat, considered himself superior to Catharine's middle-class ambitions and machinations. "Now our policy is to be above such matters, not even to seem to know them," King wrote his wife in December 1834.[39] Catharine, soon forced to accept the King family's invulnerability to her influence, learned the limits of her more simplistic evangelical manners, and a decade later she evolved a style that obliterated eighteenth-century class distinctions and created a new cultural category. Whereas the superiority of the old aristocracy arose from its high place on a natural "chain of being" that moved from lower to higher forms of intelligence and order, the later supremacy of the Victorian middle class sprang, for Catharine at least, from its greater capacity for interpreting and orchestrating themes of cultural and personal guilt.

For the present, however, Catharine had met her match in Edward King who scoffed at her efforts to understand their unfamiliar aristocratic living style. In an extremely revealing letter Edward King described how awkwardly Catharine's frank vitality fit into the household of an ultra Federalist family. Catharine visited the Worthington home in Chillicothe in 1835, and Edward King accompanied her on a horseback tour of the countryside. With patrician disdain Edward King described Catharine's inexhaustible curiosity as if it were a form of ill-bred enthusiasm. "She expressed great delight at the splendid views and asked more questions than any one could answer in a day," King began. "Why the fields were so square! Why there were not better houses! Why the current ran where it did! Whose property was this and that! Whether the land was good!" After a gibe at Catharine's manners at dinner when they returned home — "She devoured all before her and *licked her fingers!*" — King related more of what he believed to be her ill-mannered inquiries. "She asked innumerable questions about the house, how long it had been built, why the walls were so thick, when everybody slept, why Lizzy slept in that room, whether mother managed her farm, whether she gave orders to the men, whether labour was diffi-cult to procure, what was the price of *help*, why this fence was built and that." [40] Catherine Beecher behaved as though she were, like Harriet Martineau, a traveler from abroad, plying the natives with questions about their way of life.

This incident also reveals the degree to which Catharine was a stranger in the West. In rural Connecticut she would not have had to ask such questions, for she would have known the answers. Per-haps even more important, it reveals Catharine's capacity for assert-ing herself in a strange environment and overcoming its strangeness by absorbing it intellectually. Catharine had the will and the ability to conquer and dominate her surroundings, and she was not likely to yield the control of any social or intellectual situation to those who either knew more than she did or spoke with greater social authority. She was attracted to upper-class styles of life, was keenly aware of social distinctions, and frequently asserted upper-class prerogatives herself, but she was never so wholly at ease within this style as to let down her intellectual guard and cease to attempt to dominate it. This blindness to the limits of her own social and in-tellectual authority was paradoxically Catharine's greatest personal asset, and although it was to blame for her failure in Cincinnati, it led her to greater success elsewhere in the 1840s and 1850s. This char-acter trait was most effective in situations where Catharine asserted herself briefly and then moved on elsewhere. In Cincinnati, where Catharine had now lived for two years, this trait contributed to her undoing.

Edward King decided Catharine was an intellectual and social upstart. He was outraged when Catharine asserted her social su-periority to his niece. "She asked Lizzy how she liked her riding dress, if she had ever seen one like it, and that she made it and set the fashion in Cincinnati," King continued to his wife. "On the whole she did not add much to her reputation as a learned or well mannered lady." Catharine was then in the midst of her attempt to assert her control over Cincinnati elite society, and as King escorted her to her coach back to the city, Catharine asked his aid in displac-ing Hall and Drake from their position of social and intellectual authority. She "broached the everlasting subject of the Western society," King said, and she predicted, he said, that "Hall would

bring me into difficulty, that he quarreled with everybody and had
no friends." King took this as an opportunity to put down Catharine's social ambitions. "As she began the matter I gave her my
opinion very freely and told her that the difficulty had begun with
them, in endeavouring to assume all the society, intelligence and
literature of the city," King said, "and that I for one should promote the Western Society until the emigrants thought proper to
yield to the customs and habits of the people amid whom they might
come and not endeavour to establish their own rules for the regulation of society." [41]

Catharine hoped not only to ruin Drake's western literary group
but to oust Hall from the editorship of his journal. "The plan of
putting Hall down and passing the review into the hands of those
who would be more favorable to their views," King told Catharine,
"would not succeed." "After he had been assaulted and pecked at
by all the jackdaws of literature," King said he did not blame Hall
"for pulling out their feathers and exhibiting their baldness." King
disdained Catharine's idea that the whole nation should imitate
"the good education of the Yankees," and delighted in the fact that
Sarah King's mother, the previous evening, "broke out with force
against the abolitionists and peace destroyers in the church." "Therefore," he concluded in a letter to his wife, "I think *cousin* had on
the whole a hard time." [42]

King's verbal chastisement in August 1835 came close upon the
heels of Catharine's failure to rouse Wright's committee to any action in behalf of her school. Mrs. Worthington's remarks on abolitionists and the "peace destroyers in the church" revealed to Catharine how deeply she was implicated in the turbulence that then
swirled around her father. Lyman Beecher was currently being tried
for heresy by the Cincinnati synod, and this, in addition to the
antislavery imbroglio at Lane and the recent controversy with Hall,
had earned Beecher the reputation of a troublemaker. By identifying so strongly with her father on the Hall issue, Catharine too was
seen as a disrupter of the civic peace of Cincinnati. Catharine realized too late that the social eminence she enjoyed in Cincinnati
was contingent upon her willingness to cooperate in maintaining
Cincinnati's delicate balance of social power. In pushing the prerogatives of her social position beyond their limits, she had threatened to upset the balance between the eastern and western interests
in the city. And since Hall and Drake carried more social weight

than Catharine and the Beechers, the only result of her actions
would be to demolish her and her family's social position. After her
social stratagems to salvage her own and her father's reputation had
backfired, Catharine turned to other means.

𝕐 9 𝕏

The Storms of
Democratic Liberty, 1835–1837

The 1830s have been characterized by Americans during and after that decade as an era of unprecedented change. Although some conservatives still could rail about the rise of popular democracy and the decline of a culture based on deference and led by gentlemen, patently reactionary views were frowned upon by the entrepreneurial leadership and deemed counterproductive.[1] This leadership had more to gain by channeling, not checking, the course of events. People of many political persuasions could see a driving inevitability behind the march of progress and flocked to view Thomas Cole's series of paintings, begun in 1836, allegorically depicting how the rich fertility of the natural environment gradually succumbed under the artificial imposition of an advanced civilization, but then reemerged triumphant after the commercial and sophisticated culture ripened from consummation to chaos and self-destruction. Cole's graphic representation of "Jacksonian fears about the corrupting influence of wealth and power" had a few prose equivalents among politically radical Americans who spoke out against the exploitation of the laboring classes and the brutality of slavery.[2] But in socially and politically conservative circles, the rapid course of change was tentatively viewed as beneficial — especially if the rising entrepreneurial class could maintain its grasp on the reins of change and direct events onto a course that avoided the pitfalls of class conflict and regional rebellion.[3] A variety of social and political theories emerged to counteract these potential disruptions, and Catharine Beecher's writings of the mid-1830s were among them. Like several other conservative spokespersons, Catharine Beecher addressed problems created by the changing nature of class structure and the intensification of sectional conflict. But Catharine's proposals were uniquely her own, arising from her peculiar circumstances as a woman and as an evangelical embroiled in the tensions of Cincinnati in the 1830s.

The issues of class and status that stood behind much of the controversy responsible for the Beecher family's fall from favor in Cincinnati were revealed in an exchange of letters between Lyman Beecher and Nathaniel Wright in 1840. Beecher, in a passionate letter to Wright, denounced the social practices of polite Cincinnati society and called upon Wright, as one of the chief offenders and one of the leading church elders, to give up the lavish entertainments and family balls that characterized the social life of his congregation.[4] Beecher claimed such amusements obstructed his own efforts to convert the young people. "My heart is sick with hope deferred and dies within me in the prospect of my unsustained and obstructed ministry," Beecher concluded. Wright replied that he was shocked to learn that he, who had supported Beecher in all his difficulties in Cincinnati, was viewed as an obstacle to the success of his ministry and that Beecher considered it a matter of such importance "whether our children are made to romp with a measured or unmeasured step around our parlor." [5] Wright implied that Beecher was overstepping the boundaries of his authority and that dancing and family balls were only denounced by those people "who look *up* to it as a novelty or as above their rank."

By the late 1830s, if not before, polite Cincinnati society had come to view the Beechers as a cut beneath them in manners and social style. When Catharine came to Cincinnati she relied upon Wright and King and Foote to smooth her entrance into elite society, yet by the end of the decade the first two of these had been thoroughly alienated, and Samuel Foote placed himself above any Beecher criticism or influence. Catharine had plenty of free evenings for writing in the mid- and late-1830s since she no longer had a place in polite society.

The Beechers were middle-class Yankee evangelicals, and their moral edges were often too sharp to move smoothly in genteel Cincinnati society. This was a flaw that might easily be forgiven, but it made it impossible for the Beechers to assume social or moral leadership in the community. To retain their leadership they needed a theoretical base different from simple evangelicism. It was to this need that Catharine addressed her writings of the mid-1830s. Although it was in fact too late for her to revive her own and her father's fortunes on this local scene, Catharine's effort to do so impelled her to design a set of beliefs that prepared her for a national role. Intending to meliorate local divisions, Catharine in a sense overshot her target and hit upon ideas that could be usefully employed to foster national cultural unity.

Catharine's three writings on religious topics, one written to defend her father in 1836, one designed in 1838 as a common school text on "moral instruction," and the third a serious theological summation of all her moral writings, were intended to reconstruct the evangelical and upper-class alliance so ineptly impaired by herself and her father. Her tactic was to provide one moral theory applicable to both groups, and in addition to show how, by joining together on this base, they could more effectively meet criticism raised against them by the lower classes.

Catharine's first such writing, *Letters on the Difficulties of Religion* (1836), was on the surface both a gesture of allegiance to her father in a time of great trouble for him and an attempt to explain in layman's terms the controversies then raging in the Presbyterian church. The exodus from Lane to Oberlin had left Beecher with only a handful of students, and his seminary had failed to become the vanguard he had hoped to create for the evangelical conquest of the West. In accepting the ministry of the Second Church, Beecher had placed himself under Presbyterian discipline, convinced that he could imbue the Presbyterianism of the West with his own New Divinity Congregationalism. The Presbyterian and Congregational churches were at that time bound together under the "Plan of Union," but southern Presbyterians were beginning to suspect that New Englanders, through the union, were undermining the church with heresies and abolitionism.[6] The union was on the brink of dissolution in 1835, and the final split of the Presbyterian church into southern and northern factions in 1837 was one of the first indications of the growing rift between the two regions. This conflict was played out on a smaller scale in Cincinnati between Lyman Beecher and Joshua Wilson. Wilson, born in the South but for decades the leading clergyman in Cincinnati, opposed Beecher from the beginning and in 1835 succeeded in bringing him to trial for heresy before the Presbytery of Cincinnati. Beecher's adroit arguments in his defense saved him from expulsion from the church, but Wilson continued to press his attack and, after Beecher's acquittal in Cincinnati, brought him to trial before the synod and finally before the general assembly in Pittsburgh early in 1836. Ultimately Wilson instituted a civic lawsuit for Beecher's removal from Lane.[7] Lyman Beecher's boisterous and self-confident rebuttals led many to regard him rather than Wilson as the originator of the controversy and the chief disturber of the peace of the church. The trials were widely reported in the secular press, and this publicity did not endear Beecher to decorous Cincinnatians.

By reinterpreting the dispute in layman's terms of mental philosophy, Catharine hoped to quiet the animosities it had created in Cincinnati. She spoke as a conciliator, writing: "I have great respect for the piety, the talents and the sincerity of many on both sides; and I do verily believe that the . . . party spirit and evil feelings generated in this painful collision . . . could be quieted." She expected that her own work would be seen as trying "to soothe the combatants" and promote communal harmony. But few of her readers failed to notice her barely disguised theological partisanship, and Joshua Wilson claimed in a pamphlet that Catharine Beecher was as much a heretic as her father.[8]

Catharine's conciliatory volume sought to restore her own prestige as well as Lyman's, and much of it was devoted to an explanation of her own religious and moral beliefs. She hoped to demonstrate that Cincinnatians had nothing to fear from these beliefs, that she did not consider doctrinal questions as important as moral questions, and that she was the farthest thing possible from a religious fanatic. Written as a series of letters in answer to criticism of evangelical religion, Catharine's book argued in measured, calm, and reasonable tones for the necessity of some external law against which moral acts could be measured. Episcopals, Baptists, Congregationalists, Methodists, and Presbyterians were united in believing in the existence of moral laws and in the fact that one unified social and moral system of belief could be created to override their sectarian differences. The system of belief proposed in this and her other two moral writings of this decade was designed to promote unity among differing social and economic classes. The most telling argument, present in all three works but most pervasive in the second, *The Moral Instructor for Schools and Families: Containing Lessons on the Duties of Life, Arranged for Study and Recitation, Also Designed as a Reading Book for Schools* (1838), was an argument devoted to the morality of material success.

Catharine's formula for interpreting economic success forged a connection between the possessors of material comforts and leisure on the one hand and on the other hand the hard workers, who are not necessarily rewarded with social or economic advancement during their lifetime. The old justifications for such class differences were breaking down in the 1830s, and the realignment of class structure during the Jacksonian period created a sharp need for new theories to justify or condemn social and economic inequities. The perennial American dilemma of how to interpret success in a basically sinful world puzzled Americans even more after "success" became democratized and every individual became thereby a candidate for the morally ambiguous circumstance of living amid material sufficiency rather than spiritual austerity.[9] Why, for example, should the poor defer to the wealthy as their social betters when this wealth might be but a recent acquisition and when virtue in any case lay in work rather than in material possessions and leisure? From a different perspective, how could the national ethic of hard work be maintained as the key to a virtuous life when its chief benefit, success, brought a release from hard work? Catharine Beecher's moral system had answers for these vexing questions.

First she emphasized the contingent nature of material achievement, not from the traditional Christian perspective of contrasting transient worldly success with otherworldly glory, but simply as an economic fact of life. "No one can tell who is to be rich, or who is to be poor, or where we are to live ten years from hence," she said. Therefore, she felt that everyone, regardless of station, should develop habits of industry and self-denial in case these traits should be needed, though they need not be used by those temporarily able to do without them.[10] The unstable quality of economic life united all Americans and made the work ethic pertinent to all, if temporarily inapplicable to some. Comfortable middle-class parents should prepare their children for a future as unpredictable as that of an impoverished family. Meanwhile they could, in their provisional security, enjoy the material pleasures afforded by their class and status; similarly the poorer classes should respect their betters and at the same time practice habits of thrift and hard work to alleviate their current distress and ultimately perhaps to elevate their economic status. By emphasizing the capricious nature of economic life, Catharine managed to embrace both the wealth of the rich and the hard-working habits of the poor within one internally consistent system. This solution fitted perfectly the unsettling economic mobility responsible for the disruption of class equilibrium in the first place.

If Catharine's first answer to the dilemma of success was to reconfirm the virtues of hard work (especially for the poor), her second answer established a new criteria for justifying the superiority of the well-to-do. The social and moral superiority of the "better" classes did not, she said, arise from their material possessions, but from their greater exposure to moral temptation and therefore their greater opportunity to resist and overcome moral temptations. Anticipating the orchestration of guilt themes that accompanied the Victorian culture of the 1870s and 1880s, Catharine Beecher in the 1830s constructed a moral system based not on virtuous deeds or heavenly redemption, but on guilt, pure and simple. If a person merely behaves virtuously, she said, but has no counter-desire to behave sinfully, then he is in fact not a moral person.[11]

Catharine was trying to delineate a moral theory inspired by evangelical religion but devoid of its doctrinal controversies. The nature of sin, the source of human guilt, and the capacity of the will to refrain from sin were all strongly contested doctrinal issues that Catharine hoped to eliminate altogether from her moral system. In an ingenious fashion Catharine incorporated guilt into the very motivation of every moral act, without drawing upon theological doctrine in any form. She said that in every moral act taken with reference to biblical moral law, there is an initial temptation not to obey the moral law. Her "idea of virtue" as she now described it involved three steps: "a feeling of obligation to perform certain moral duties, temptations to violate such obligation, and a strength of principle that enables a person to overcome such temptations."[12] No moral act was complete without the temptation to avoid doing it. Catharine had never accepted her father's view of imputed guilt from Adam's fall or from a corrupt moral nature. In 1822 her own inability to feel this kind of guilt had been the chief block to her conversion. Now, however, she had found a way to incorporate the notion of universal guilt into her own moral philosophy. In one sense Catharine's notion of guilt was more benign than her father's, for "strong principles" presumably usually overcame temptation. Yet in another sense Catharine's notion was more oppressive, for Lyman Beecher's theological guilt was absolved by the act of conversion and rebirth, but Catharine's was a constant, inescapable guilt that played a role even in the performance of virtuous acts.

Catharine's theory made it possible for economically comfortable Americans to feel confirmed in the sense of guilt that accompanied their release from hard work and austerity, yet her system dignified and even exalted this guilt. Seeing the temptations around oneself and recognizing the guilt attendant on such temptations was as good as — indeed better than — eliminating those temptations. One could therefore experience a higher level of moral activity by choosing, for example, between an untrimmed muslin shirt and a more highly desired lace-trimmed muslin shirt than by giving one's unnecessary clothes away to the poor. It was the temptation overcome that mattered, not the virtue left undone. Objective realities such as the needs of the poor had no significance when placed against the richness of the drama of subjective desires.

As in her discussion of economic capriciousness, Catharine had managed to perpetuate the social dominance of the "better" classes while at the same time she paid homage to the democratic belief that one set of rules should apply equally to all people. By reorganizing moral theory along an axis of guilt instead of redemption, Catharine attempted to resolve the contradictory values of Cincinnati society. The evangelical emphasis on redemption was still respected by a large portion of Cincinnati opinion represented by Joshua Wilson, but it was a message now scarcely heeded by more genteel families like the Nathaniel Wrights. A matrix built around material success, temptation, and guilt was a bold invention that could command the attention of both constituencies. It had a familiar enough ring for the traditional evangelical, and for the genteel it addressed the compelling realities of the present rather than the abstract possibilities of the future.

Although forged to meet an immediate local need, the ideas in Catharine Beecher's *Moral Instructor* fit into a burgeoning national literature addressed to the problems of child-rearing and education. Along with most of such literature composed in the 1830s, her volume rested on the seemingly contradictory wish to release Americans from old agencies of social control — represented by magistrates and clergy — and yet to consolidate new ties of social obligation and economic interdependence that might counteract the potential anarchy of American democracy. Like Lydia Maria

Child, Almira Phelps, and several others, some of whom filled the pages of new journals devoted to the question of democratic education, Catharine Beecher resolved this contradiction by demonstrating that "character" was the key both to individual success and to social interdependence. For one's character was shaped for an unknown and self-reliant future not through introspection, but through sensitivity to the expectations of others. This theme dominated antebellum attitudes toward child-raising and education, and by 1860 "character formation" had effectively replaced religion as the primary basis for learned moral behavior in both the school and the home.[13]

Catharine completed the first of her moral writings in the early months of 1836, but fortunately for her own ego she did not wait to gauge Cincinnati's reaction to her *Letters on the Difficulties of Religion*. In this, as in her two other moral treatises, Catharine's efforts met with more local ridicule than understanding. On this occasion her volume, dubbed "Miss Beecher's difficulties," was seen as fuel for the fires of controversy rather than as the meliorative gesture the author had intended.[14] No matter what its potential importance, moral theory alone could not persuade the dubious, and Catharine, unlike the male members of her family, was excluded from the institutional forms of the church where she might have successfully nurtured and implemented her theory.

Henry Ward Beecher, for example, still a theology student, was able ten years later to exert a far more extensive influence on American moral attitudes because he was able to invest his ideas with the moral authority of his office as pastor of the Brooklyn Heights Plymouth Church and because he was able to interweave his ideas with the institutional needs of his congregation.

Sensing perhaps the importance of the institutional realities within which people live and the need of any set of abstractions to be translated into concrete human experience, Catharine set out at the first sign of spring in 1836 to test her ideas in a reality more congenial and more substantial than her second-floor room in the Beecher house in Walnut Hills. She began to explore a new institutional identity that could translate her ideas into reality. Returning to her 1830 notion of training female teachers for new

common schools in the West, Catharine Beecher toured throughout
the East in the spring and summer of 1836 to promote this idea
and suggest what institutional forms it might take. Her idea was
not a new one, and it was not implemented until several years
later. Yet this brief interval of success, compressed though it was
between two periods of unrewarded labor, was one she fruitfully
built on later.

Included in her original plan for her school, the Western Female
Institute, was "some agency that would bring teachers to Cincinnati,
where they could be trained for their difficult duties, so that those
seeking teachers would come to this establishment, and the parties
thus negotiate face to face." [15] Although in 1836 such an agency
was in fact remote from reality. Catharine traveled throughout
New England representing this nonexistent "agency" and disregarding the failing fortunes of her school. She began in Boston, moved
on to cities in Vermont, New Hampshire, and Connecticut, and
made extended stops in Albany, New York, and Philadelphia.[16]
From these places the growing problems of the Western Female
Institute seemed less urgent, and she told Mary Dutton not to
trouble her with the school's problems, for she was engaged in
more important matters.[17]

The tour was an exhilarating one for Catharine. She was received as a spokeswoman for the West, and in contrast to her
social exclusion in Cincinnati she was welcomed into the homes of
prominent clergymen and educators at each of her stops in the
East.[18] On this tour, lasting from April to October, Catharine
sought the names of young women who were willing to go to the
West and teach. At each stop she issued a statement:

> Miss Beecher informs those who have addressed her on the difficulty
> of finding situations as teachers that she is engaged in an effort to
> secure some organization and means, that will enable all who are
> willing to teach to find suitable places and suitable means and op-
> portunities of reaching such places. She hopes before six months are
> past that something of this kind will be effected, but until this is done,
> it will not be in her power to do any thing more than obtain the
> *name, character* and *residence,* of those who wish to be aided in this
> way. As soon as anything is effected you shall be notified and your
> wishes consulted as far as practicable.[19]

At most of her stops Catharine was told that "many excellent
women in that vicinity who were unemployed would thankfully

engage in such service." Mary Lyon was the only person to point out that while Catharine promised a great deal, she guaranteed nothing. All Catharine Beecher offered was the opportunity "to spend a few weeks at Cincinnati in preparing for an unknown field with an unknown salary, and to be under obligation to an unknown donor," Mary Lyon wrote. Yet Catharine considered her tour a grand success, for she had obtained the names of over one hundred women who were willing to become "missionary teachers," and she had discovered that Easterners might be willing to finance the training of these women.[20]

Before Catharine's Cincinnati school failed in 1837, she had therefore already established herself as a traveling agent linking the East with the West. In the mid-1840s this role became an important aspect of her career. The summer of 1836 proved to her that traveling boosted her spirits, improved her health, and might be much more rewarding than her stationary life in Cincinnati. In 1843, when she revived her faltering career, she returned to the themes and the style of her tour of 1836.

Catharine could not immediately implement her educational plans begun in the summer of 1836 because the demise of her school a year later temporarily deprived her of an institutional base. The Western Female Institute, directed now by Mary Dutton although financially controlled by Catharine, had lost most of its students to other Cincinnati academies. Ever since 1835 Mary Dutton had been sending distress signals to Catharine, warning her of the school's declining fortunes. In the spring of 1837 the school was clearly on the road to failure, and in a long and bitter letter to Hammond's newspaper Catharine accused the city of educational backwardness and ingratitude.[21] Catharine claimed that her school had failed because Cincinnati was not interested in the education of its daughters, but the continued vitality of several other female academies disproved this claim.[22] Catharine's school failed because she alienated her constituency. Her school never included the daughters of families who were members of Joshua Wilson's old-school Presbyterian Church and had mainly drawn upon the daughters of the families in Beecher's Second Church. Since the ladder of social ascent in Cincinnati churches moved from Wilson's to Beecher's church, these families were the more socially ambitious ones, and they represented that combination of refinement and piety that Catharine had looked to as her main support in both Hartford and Cincinnati. Yet these were the very people Catharine had alienated by her social machinations.

❧❦

Just as Catharine's fortunes reached a low point in 1837, Angelina and Sarah Grimké presented her with an excellent opportunity to develop a new constituency and seize the cultural initiative on a set of issues having concrete relevance to the lives of many Americans. As female abolitionists, the Grimké sisters had in 1836 begun to raise their voices not only against slavery, but against the exclusion of women from the ranks of social activism.[23] In Catharine's tour of the East that summer she had counted Angelina Grimké among her chief competitors for the allegiance of a newly self-conscious generation of American women. Now early in 1837 Angelina Grimké announced that she planned to tour the North and form antislavery societies among northern women.[24] Catharine immediately challenged Angelina Grimké's leadership and defined her own counterproposal for the role of women in American society.

In her *Essay on Slavery and Abolitionism with Reference to the Duty of American Females* (1837) Catharine Beecher began the task that was to occupy her for the rest of her career — that of interpreting and shaping the collective consciousness of American women. Angelina and Sarah Grimké and Catharine Beecher engaged in a two-year printed debate, wherein the Grimké sisters linked the cause of women's rights with that of abolitionism, and Catharine Beecher urged the unification of American culture around a new image of politically transcendent womanhood.[25]

Whatever it later became in the Victorian 1870s and 1880s, Catharine's definition of female influence was originally designed to act as a unifying force in a disintegrating society. Catharine's vision of a world of morally superior women was forged against the reality of the failure of the male-operated system of political rights in Cincinnati in the 1830s.

In the summer of 1836 Cincinnati had experienced the worst race riots in the city's history. Two days of mob destruction in August of that year culminated antiblack sentiment that had been growing in Cincinnati and Ohio throughout the decade. In 1833 alone over a thousand free blacks who could not meet the requirements of newly enforced black codes were banished from

Ohio. From 1829 to 1834 there was a dramatic decline in Cincinnati's free black population because nearly two-thirds of these people left the hostile city.[26]

Of all the issues that most traumatized Cincinnati society and most agonized the Beecher family, abolition stood foremost. When James Birney's press was destroyed during the riot of August 1836 many people believed that the violence was condoned by some of Cincinnati's leading citizens. Clearly hostile to abolitionist sentiment, men like Nathaniel Wright and Judge Burnet winked at the mob action. The city was deeply divided by this incident, however, and some, like Samuel P. Chase and Charles Hammond, a local newspaper editor, supported Birney's right to free speech.[27] Here then was an opportunity for Catharine to show not only that she sought to conciliate opposing factions in the city, but that she proposed a new kind of moral authority to replace the troublesome rules of natural rights theory. By asserting the moral superiority of women Catharine could transcend the political issues of civil and natural rights that seemed to be destroying the harmony of the nation as well as that of the city.

The attitude of the Beecher family toward abolition was not fully clear when Catharine wrote her *Essay,* but her support of the recolonization of American blacks represented most of the Beecher family's opinion during the crisis of the 1830s. Harriet privately expressed her astonishment at the support given to the anti-Birney mob by some of Cincinnati's leading citizens, and Henry Ward, temporarily editor of a clerical journal in 1836, mildly reproved the mob, yet both of them then believed that abolitionism was an "ultra" position taken only by fanatics. Lyman Beecher wrote to William Beecher in 1835 that the abolitionists "are the offspring of the Oneida denunciatory revivals, and are made up of vinegar, aqua fortis, and oil of vitriol, with brimstone, saltpetre, and charcoal, to explode and scatter the corrosive matter." [28] The Beechers had certainly done little to deserve their reputation as abolitionists, but as antiabolitionist passions grew increasingly strong in Cincinnati, they found that they were nevertheless a popular target for these passions. Only Edward Beecher's courageous *Narrative of the Riots at Alton* broke through the family's hesitancy and firmly declared sympathy for the abolitionists in 1837. Yet not until a decade later when the issues had vastly altered from their context of the 1830s did Harriet and Henry Ward assume a leadership role in the abolitionist movement, and they did so only after they had left the tension-filled atmosphere of the border cities of the West.

Catharine had been present at the confrontation between James Birney and Judge Jacob Burnet when Burnet urged Birney to stop publishing his *Philanthropist* and warned that any mob sacking the press would include two-thirds of the city's property holders.[29] In proving that she stood solidly behind those who condemned the abolitionists for their socially disruptive measures, Catharine had everything to gain and little to lose. Yet her attitude toward abolitionism was not merely opportunistic. She was not merely joining the winning side of antiabolitionism but was searching for an alternative to the failed machinery of democratic politics. In the context of the increasing political violence she advocated that women exercise a new kind of political influence that would be only indirectly related to politics as it was then practiced.

Both Catharine Beecher and the Grimké sisters believed that women should play important social roles, and that women should not be isolated from the forces shaping American life. Their differences lay in the way in which they believed female influence should be exerted and the kind of society that would foster such influence.

Angelina and Sarah Grimké based their arguments on a natural rights platform, claiming that the influence of women should not be expressed differently from that of men since both sexes were morally responsible creatures endowed with inalienable natural rights. "Now I believe it is woman's right to have a voice in all the laws and regulations by which she is to be governed, whether in Church or State: and that the present arrangements of society, on these points, are a *violation of human rights, a rank usurpation of power,* a violent seizure and confiscation of what is sacredly and inalienably hers," Angelina Grimké wrote Catharine Beecher at the height of their published debates.[30]

Catharine countered that the influence of women should be asserted differently from that of men, and that their influence should be as different in kind as it was different in method. Whereas the Grimkés wanted to extend popular democracy to include women, Catharine wanted to restore hierarchical authority and give women a place within that hierarchy. "It is the grand feature of the Divine economy, that there should be different stations of superiority and subordination," Catharine insisted in her *Essay on Slavery and Abolitionism with Reference to the Duty of American Females* (1837), "and it is impossible to annihilate this beneficent and immutable law." Relations between parents and children, masters and servants, students and teachers, and men and women all exemplify the natural hierarchy of social relations, Catharine said. "Heaven has appointed to one sex the superior, and to the other the subordinate station," she continued, "but while woman holds a subordinate relation in society to the other sex, it is not because it was designed that her duties or her influence should be any the less important, or all-pervading." Rather, Catharine concluded, it was designed that the mode of gaining influence and of exercising power should be altogether different and peculiar to women. Whereas a man may engage in public issues, the woman's influence should remain within "the domestic and social circle"; whereas a man may act aggressive to achieve his goals, a woman must conquer by "kindly, generous, peaceful and benevolent principles," Catharine wrote.[31]

Yet while Catharine seemed to be arguing on behalf of the traditional view that limited women to their homes, her discussion on closer view was more subtle. For it politicized the traditional female sphere of the home. In this area, she said, the nation's ability to "weather the storms of democratic liberty" would be proven. Let the men argue in the political arena, she said, for political power as it is now exercised in the United States seems destined for self-destruction. The democratic process, Catharine said, was by itself not sufficient to promote either private or public happiness. While this process is going on, she asked, "must we be distracted and tortured by the baleful passions and wicked works that unrestrained party-spirit and ungoverned factions will bring upon us . . . ? Must we rush on to disunion, and civil wars, and servile wars, till all their train of horrors pass over us like a devouring fire?" The only viable alternative to such self-destruction, Catharine said, was to locate the nation's moral center in the home and to let its spirit through the activities of women "be infused into the mass of the nation, and then truth may be sought, defended, and propagated, and error detected, and its evils exposed." [32]

Catharine's *Essay* provided two specific proposals for the creation of a national ethic of domestic virtue. First the character of women

should be highly differentiated from the character of men in order
to allow women to exemplify domestic virtues; and second, women
should permeate the nation with their special character through
their influence as teachers in public schools. The character Catharine prescribed for women was not different from traditional
female virtues, but it was more highly codified and contrasted with
the character of men. In a typical passage Catharine wrote:

> Let every woman become so cultivated and refined in intellect, that
> her taste and judgment will be respected; so benevolent in feeling and
> action, that her motives will be reverenced; so unassuming and un-
> ambitious, that collision and competition will be banished; so "gentle
> and easy to be entreated," that every heart will repose in her presence;
> then, the fathers, the husbands, and the sons, will find an influence
> thrown around them, to which they will yield not only willingly but
> proudly.[33]

Men feel "dignified and ennobled in acknowledging" such female
influences, Catharine said, and there is a peculiar propriety in the
present democratic emergency of "looking for the especial agency
and assistance of females" since they "are shut out from the many
temptations that assail the other sex," since they mingle throughout
the community at all levels, and since they know well how to preserve "peace and goodwill among men" because their own comfort
and happiness depends on their ability to cultivate male goodwill.[34]

Catharine took the traditional submissive role of women and
turned it into a sign of superior moral sensibility. In suggesting
that the nation turn away from the turbulence of political democracy and emphasize the stabilizing influence of peaceable
womankind and the home, Catharine joined a growing American
tendency to glorify domesticity. In this volume Catharine merely
declared her interest in the topic, but through her *Treatise on
Domestic Economy*, which she began to write immediately after
completing her *Essay*, Catharine assumed national importance as a
person able to define and embellish the fine art of domestic virtue.
Now, in 1836 she defined three basic points: the present was a
time of rapid social change, when all past beliefs were being
questioned and new ones tested; abolitionists were part of this
contemporary pace of change but threatened to turn change into
destruction; and, finally, women were uniquely qualified to heal

social divisions and work as meliorative rather than destructive agents of social change.

She also defined the parlor as a cultural podium and described the home not as the place isolating women from political and social influence, but as the base from which their influence on the rest of the culture was launched. Angelina and Sarah Grimké offered American women political and social equality; Catharine Beecher offered them dominance in the domestic sphere where their lives were centered and promised them a moral effect on much that lay outside that sphere. In the two decades ahead, when Catharine Beecher's cultural influence was at its height, she elaborated this "pedestal" characterization of women's role.

Here in the 1830s the core of the feminist dilemma took shape — whether to assert female influence as a function of their difference from men, or on the basis of their human equality. Although Catharine Beecher chose the first and Angelina and Sarah Grimké the second, each was a feminist insofar as she was trying to shape American society to respond to the needs and talents of women. In the short run of the next fifty years, Catharine Beecher's tactics were the more successful, possibly because they prescribed less dramatic cultural changes, spoke to real American anxieties about the pace of change, and introduced important stabilizing factors into the national ideology. To attack the problem as straightforwardly as the Grimkés did was to push the eighteenth-century ideology of natural rights into an area where American men had never applied it. Angelina and Sarah Grimké did not think it was demanding too much from a democratic republic to eliminate the habitual prerogatives of the male as well as the traditional privileges of the aristocracy. In this time of great social and political ferment, Catharine Beecher deemed it more prudent to consolidate the culture around known female and male virtues and to mediate national differences of class and race by creating a new female caste identity embracing all races and classes. In the decades ahead, Americans moved far toward adopting the Grimkés' views of slavery, but they sided with Catharine Beecher's views on women.

℀ 10 ℀

Pretty Thoroughly
Metaphysicated, 1837–1843

In 1837 Catharine Beecher's increasing centrality within a developing national consensus was not so apparent as her continued isolation in Cincinnati, for in spite of the national publicity focused on Catharine Beecher's exchange with Angelina Grimké, Catharine's *Essay on Slavery* was virtually ignored in her adopted hometown. Having neither a local institutional identity nor the means to create an alternative one, a series of failures finally led her to a three-year career moratorium during which, her spirits depressed and her will paralyzed, Catharine reverted to a dependent role in her father's household.[1]

This was a critical period for Catharine. Nearly forty years old, she could easily have slipped permanently into the role of the spinster aunt whose basic needs were met by various members of her family in return for her assistance in operating the household. Catharine's own Aunt Esther had led a long and happy life in this capacity in the Beecher family, and Catharine now had six married siblings whose growing families provided ample opportunity for her to duplicate Aunt Esther's role. Catharine's only real competence was directing and operating female academies, but she was unwilling to begin another one. Ever since the crisis over Zilpah Grant in Hartford in 1829 Catharine had developed a strong distaste for the routine responsibilities and frustrations involved in running a school, and she had concluded early in the 1830s that "continuous labor or responsibility" was "hazardous" to her health.[2]

Catharine may have had psychological rather than physiological problems that prevented her from beginning a new school. Her life was not a pattern of steady achievement, but of accomplishment and withdrawal. She had difficulty committing herself to any one project over a substantial period of time. In the quarrels and recriminations among Mary Dutton, Harriet Beecher Stowe, and

Catharine after the Western Female Institute was dissolved, Harriet accused Catharine of lacking the ability to see any project through to its finish, tending instead to abandon it in midcourse. She did not have trouble committing herself to projects initially, Harriet concluded, but she did have trouble sustaining that commitment.[3]

Although Catharine found it impossible to continue teaching, she clearly needed the money her school had earned for her. In the disposition of the school's furnishings and in collecting the tuition still due, Catharine quite ruthlessly appropriated all the money for herself and left Mary Dutton and Harriet to bear the financial losses of the school.[4] Catharine needed money badly enough to quarrel with her sister over small amounts, but she apparently preferred the pleasures of a leisured life to the toil involved in sustaining her financial independence. While the argument over the sale of the school's property continued in 1837 Catharine left for a summer's excursion to visit relatives in Connecticut and, on her return, friends who lived along the route from Connecticut to Cincinnati. Catharine wrote to Mary Dutton, "I am now with Theodosia" — one of her favorite former Hartford pupils who now lived in Detroit. "Theodosia, after a long season of misfortune is in the midst of prosperity, has a talented, wealthy, refined, pious and most tender husband, a son of his about twelve years old, a lovely boy, a new spacious house, and every comfort and convenience."[5] Catharine had a gift for uncovering such prosperous homes where, welcomed as a former mentor, she often stayed for weeks at a time. The style of life to which Catharine aspired was not within the means of Lyman Beecher, for he and the other impecunious members of the Beecher family were continually plagued by financial difficulties. Even if her desire for personal autonomy had lessened, Catharine might have sought financial independence simply to equip herself with the symbols of upperclass respectability.

During the next four years Catharine attempted to promote a joint literary career with Harriet, wrote and tried to market her text of moral instruction designed for elementary schools, tried to sell her arithmetic texts, and began to compile a textbook on "domestic economy." Only with the last of these, published in Boston in 1841, did Catharine regain her financial independence. In the mid-1840s it gave her the means and the leisure to pursue her plans for a national system of female-led education. During the lean years of the late 1830s, however, her main goal was to publish wherever and whatever she could and not to fade out of the public consciousness. Yet even this modest goal was not achieved, and the end of the decade found her retired within the domestic life of the Beecher household at Walnut Hills, sharing the general decline of the family's spirits that preceded Lyman Beecher's dismissal from his church in 1843. The suicide of George punctuated the Beechers' malaise that year, yet at the same time it jarred Catharine into the second creative stage of her career.

Catharine Beecher's pyschological state and financial plight were exemplified in her first and major success in fiction writing, a story entitled "Fanny Moreland, or the Use and Abuse of the Risibles." She sold the story to *The Christian Keepsake and Missionary Annual,* part of the growing genre of "gift books" designed as Christmas and New Year presents for a public that was increasingly attracted to the romantic aura of traditional English holidays. *The Christian Keepsake* was, like many gift annuals, modeled after an English forerunner of the same name, and its avowed purpose of combining "all that is ornamental, sweet and graceful in the Fine Arts [with] the hallowing and sanctifying influence of Evangelical Religion," must have attracted Catharine's eye as the perfect receptacle for her own literary combination of refinement and religious rectitude.[6] The *Annual* subsequently published several of Catharine's poems (some composed fifteen to twenty years earlier) and a few of Harriet's stories as well.

"Fanny Moreland" was an interesting autobiographical account of a young girl whose high spirits and gaiety won everyone's affection, but who was constantly urged to control her spirits lest they lead her to "excessive levity and worldliness." Fanny, Catharine wrote, "was not handsome, she was not witty, she was not learned, she was not rich, nor was she particularly useful, yet she was a universal favorite." Drawing on her own reputation at Miss Pierce's school, Catharine described Fanny as "forever busy in doing nothing." In an idealized version of the 1822 encounter between Catharine and Lyman Beecher, Fanny and her father discuss her levity. Although Fanny fears it as a block to her piety, her father reassures her that it need not be such but is simply a part of her character that she must learn to live with; although it needs to be controlled, it can also be innocently enjoyed. Religion does not "change the particularities of character," Mr. Moreland told Fanny, and she could be both pious and happy. After a crisis was precipitated by the arrival of an eminently pious uncle whom Fanny's parents fear she will offend by her levity but to whom she is instead endeared by her merriment, Fanny wins the day in urging "the peculiarities of her natural temperament," over all who would have her exert more control over it.

Catharine's story embodied her belief that character was more important than abstract religious beliefs and that engaging wit and character traits could win the affection of those who upheld traditional cultural forms. Yet if Fanny Moreland's father and uncle characterized the two sides of Lyman Beecher, Catharine's story revealed that she was still caught up in the contradiction of enjoying his love and fearing his judgment. Not yet free of the constraining forms of her father's Calvinist personality, Catharine seems to have wanted to break loose and, like Fanny, be loved for her own sake regardless of how well she conformed to traditional roles.

Returning to live in her father's house, Catharine again faced the rather critical problem of defining her role as a person and as a member of the Beecher family. To satisfy their father all her brothers had become or were becoming ministers, and her sisters had assumed orderly married lives, usually as the wives of ministers. Harriet dutifully married her father's chief ministerial assistant, Calvin Stowe, in 1836, and although the marriage was filled with tension, it gave Harriet a definite status and a specific identity, whereas Catharine, unwilling to accept the role of spinster aunt, retained an unresolved and unspecified identity as an aging daughter and a sometimes educator and writer.[7]

Financial success as a writer might have helped her need for role definition, but Catharine's stories and poems were not as fiscally successful as they were psychologically revealing, and at the end of 1837 she had earned only thirty dollars while Harriet, with considerably greater literary skills, had earned over three hundred dollars. "*I do it for the pay,*" Harriet said of her writing in 1838,[8] and by adopting an equally professional attitude toward her own fiction, Catharine quickly concluded that she would have to seek elsewhere for the financial rewards, personal security, and social approbation that accompanied the discovery of one's "calling" and thereby clarified one's status.[9]

To resolve this middle-age crisis of role identity, Catharine returned, after a year of lost labor trying to promote her *Moral Instructor,* to the source of her difficulties — her relationship with her father. In 1839 she resumed on the one hand the theological debate that had characterized the earlier crisis in their relationship. Now as an acknowledgment of her reentry into the Beecher family rather than her departure from it, Catharine tried to establish her credentials as a bona fide Beecher with all the theological privileges granted to the male members of the family. On the other hand, she immersed herself in the domestic arts and sought to prove her skills equal or superior to any of the married Beecher women. Catharine tried to debate the men on their grounds, and outperform the women on theirs. She infuriated her brothers and, never deigning to invite the affection of her father's third wife, Lydia Jackson, a New Englander whom he had married in 1836, she alienated her stepmother and many of her female in-laws.[10] Indeed Catharine seemed to have been courting expulsion from the family at the same time that she claimed to be promoting its welfare.

This eager pursuit of status within the family, balanced by a desire to escape from its forms altogether, began in Hartford in the summer of 1839 where Catharine, stranded without money to travel further, wrote "An Essay on Cause and Effect in Connection with the Doctrines of Fatalism and Free Agency." [11] She submitted it anonymously for publication in *The American Biblical Repository,* a clerical journal patronized mainly by New Divinity Congregationalists, where it appeared in the October issue.

This article was the source of an apocryphal family story that belittled Catharine's achievement at the same time it acknowledged it. Calvin Stowe, the story began, told an eminent German theologian that his sister-in-law had written the ablest refutation of Edwards's treatise on the will. "Vat a voman," the German supposedly replied as he threw up his hands, "refute Edwards on de vill! God forgive Christopher Columbus for discovering such a country." [12]

This story, as well as the brief controversy the article created in the pages of the *Biblical Repository,* focused upon the overt issues

Catharine raised on free will and determinism. Both the story and the controversy missed Catharine's real point, however. For buried beneath her lengthy doctrinal arguments was a moral rather than a religious point. Free will was important to Catharine not as a religious doctrine, but as the moral basis for self-sacrifice and self-denial. The orthodox doctrine, or what Catharine called "fatalism," held that the mind chooses that which seems most agreeable or that which is regarded as the greatest good for it.[13] Volition inevitably follows from the strongest motive presented to the will. Catharine opposed this doctrine not only because it limited human freedom, but because it allowed for no distinction between self-indulgence and self-denial. If the greatest good or the most agreeable is always chosen, then even acts of self-denial are made because they are the most agreeable, and the element of self-sacrifice is lost or translated into self-satisfaction. In a long discussion of the nature of cause and effect, Catharine insisted that an act of self-denial is genuinely sacrificial because it is caused not by the strongest motive but by the weaker.

Leonard Woods, the most distinguished defender of orthodoxy in Massachusetts, replied to Catharine's article, though he felt uncomfortable commenting on an anonymous article since "the writer of the Essay may be one for whom I entertain a very sincere esteem and affection. I choose to think that he is so," Woods wrote, "[for he] has given such evidence of ability to write well, possesses also a sincere love of the truth, a full conviction of the narrow limits of human intelligence, humility, candor, reverence for the Scriptures, and every other quality which belongs to the Christian character." Woods, then, recognized that Catharine wrote within the orthodox tradition and only sought to revise rather than to destroy orthodox beliefs. Woods replied that he could not understand why the anonymous writer valued the privilege of choosing the weaker motive. It did not limit human freedom to choose the strongest motive, Woods said, for this was what made men "rational beings." "Can you think it a privilege to be influenced by a weaker, rather than a stronger motive?" Woods asked. "To be governed in your voluntary actions by reasons of *less* weight, those which *appear* to you of less weight rather than by those which are, or appear to be of greater weight?" [14]

Orthodoxy was certainly a clearer and more straightforward moral system than Catharine's. To Leonard Woods, evil was evil and good was good, and there was no special virtue attached to the act of overcoming a temptation to evil. Temptation itself was evil, and the Christian prayed to be freed of it just as he prayed to be freed of all vile and wicked feelings. Woods pointed to the moral confusion created by Catharine's theory of choosing the weaker motive. Every man disapproves of "his disorderly affections and desires, and condemns himself on account of them," Woods wrote, and if such desires become stronger than virtuous desires, then the man himself is "depraved and wicked." [15] The Christian however gives such disorderly desires no opportunity to grow to such strength, and no occasion arises when he chooses good and also chooses the weaker motive. The good is always the stronger motive.

In the context of Catharine's life in 1839 and under the illumination of Woods' criticism, her theory seems peculiarly appropriate to female experience as well as to the experience of a person who is alternately attracted to and disapproving of worldly pleasures. For, a woman who must surrender her stronger motive in order to accommodate a father or a husband or a male-oriented society is an example of a person who is governed in her voluntary actions by reasons of less weight, or which appear to her of less weight, than to those to which she originally and personally gave greater weight. She is also an example of a person who is granted social and moral approbation for acting upon the lesser of two motives and is often made to feel "depraved and wicked" for acting on the stronger of her motives because they do not suit male purposes. Under the cover of an anonymous male identity, Catharine had written a female commentary on evangelical morality. She did not openly rebel against its forms, but she did redesign its emphasis to suit her own experience. Ultimately it was a moral design that spoke for men as well as for women who felt their motivation subject to external forces. Americans became increasingly adept at making the best of this situation by equating "duty" with "morality."

Catharine's return to doctrinal disputation in 1839 brought the decade around to a full circle, for she returned to the issues that had engaged her in 1829, when she began to teach her first class in moral philosophy. A return to doctrinal disputation was for Catharine a return also to the Beecher home. In 1829 she had taken every opportunity to discuss her current reading and thinking with her father and family in Boston. "Catharine has been here and we have all been pretty thoroughly metaphysicated," Harriet had written from Boston during the time Catharine was composing her *Elements of Mental and Moral Philosophy.* "Let me give you an idea of our manner of life," Harriet had continued. "At breakfast we generally have the last evening's argument hashed through and warmed over, indeed they serve us with an occasional nibble through the whole day. One of Bishop Butler's arguments lasted us for nearly three meals, but I suppose the reason was that it was too rough for mastication." [16] In 1839 Catharine revived these domestic diversions not only with her father in Walnut Hills, but also with her brother Edward at his Illinois home and with her much younger brother, Charles, who was studying theology at Indianapolis. Catharine delved once more into fine theological distinctions and careful logical deductions. These discussions were not casual conversations to while away a family visit but rather were conducted with intense seriousness and with strong feelings by all the participants. A year after her *Biblical Repository* article Catharine's relish for such discussions had not diminished, though her brothers' energies were beginning to flag. Charles reported to Lyman Beecher in September 1840: "Having witnessed the discussion which took place between Cate and Edward and also noticed the representation she is disposed to make of it, I have considered it advisable to state for your consideration certain facts concerning subsequent discussions between her and myself." Catharine had claimed to have won an argument with Charles and Edward on the definition of "producing cause" and "fatalism," and Charles disputed her claim of victory in eight pages of a closely written letter to Lyman. Charles rendered a word-by-word account of their discussion, and he pleaded, "In quoting her language I have been exact — in respect to mine, I have corrected several places where my idea was obscure — I wish you now to judge." The anger aroused in Charles showed the heat with which these discussions were conducted.

> I have simply to say in respect to these controversies, that (1) with Edward I consider them as barren of wholesome fruit as the scholastic jargon of the middle ages, (2) As to Catharine's mind it is the last that should flatter itself with the hope of disentangling the subject, (3) That as to Edward, She neither does nor can comprehend him, by reason that his region of truth and thought is too far above her. (4) That the only source of truth is *slow* patient, comprehensive in-

duction and generalisation. I am reading the Bible through diligently
on three topics, slavery, predestination or free will and preexistence,
marking all passages as I go.

As a postscript Charles added that if Catharine published another
piece in the *Biblical Repository,* he would write a reply to it.[17]

This experience of 1839 and 1840 was similar to that of 1822
when Catharine had, in a time of personal disappointment, thrown
herself so wholeheartedly into a theological dispute that the dispute
assumed a life of its own, substituting in its vividness and intensity
for the life she had failed to lead. Catharine's religious disputa-
tions were signs of her return home, and there she stayed for the
next few years, arguing against traditional orthodox doctrines and
forwarding what she considered to be more valid ideas. The intensity of her family debate was fired by Catharine's belief that she
spoke for the common understanding and the public welfare against
the self-serving and unnecessarily obtuse reasoning of her brothers'
theology.

Lyman Beecher, extremely solicitous about Catharine's mental
health, was perceptive enough to see that Catharine acted from
psychological need as well as intellectual belief, and he defended
her against her brothers' expressions of annoyance and resentment.
He urged them to omit from their letters anything that might
"wound" Catharine "too deep," for, he said, "with her nervous
incapacities she feels deeply any appearances of light estimation in
the part of her family friends who she so sincerely loves." Lyman
added that Catharine's overbearing manner should be understood
as her defense against unhappiness. "In her trying situation it is
a happy knack of being always in the right demanding gratitude.
For shut out from her wanted active labour if she could not plan
and correspond and keep herself in the stream of interested action
for the public good she would be exceedingly unhappy." By the
end of 1842, however, Lyman admitted that Catharine's verbal
assaults upon the young and sensitive Charles were too aggressive
and that Lyman would "have to lead her off the track." [18]

In the summer of 1843, perhaps at Lyman Beecher's encouragement, Catharine set out for a vacation in the East, traveling for
the first time in her own buggy.[19] Her first stop was at the home of

her brother George in Chillicothe. The morning after Catharine's arrival George lay dead in his garden, killed by a self-inflicted gunshot wound in the head. Harriet's first thought upon learning the news was to fear the effect of George's death upon Catharine. The family suddenly seemed vulnerable to death and disaster, and Catharine's mental condition seemed to mark her as the next to fall. "Our circle has begun to break up," Harriet wrote. "Who shall say where it shall stop?" [20]

Indeed Catharine was deeply affected by George's death. Many of the psychological strains that had prompted his suicide were similar to those she had experienced. To please his father George had become a minister, a career for which he was sorely unsuited. His life had been plagued by mental and spiritual anxiety. Lyman Beecher's unrelenting ambition for the spiritual achievements of his sons only added to George's sense of spiritual anxiety, since he failed to rise either to his father's expectations or to those of his congregation. He exhausted himself in his spiritual labors and suffered at least three nervous breakdowns. Like Catharine, he had been unable to escape his father's influence and unable to succeed in a career that was modeled after his father's example.[21]

Almost immediately after his death, Catharine began to read through George's papers and letters, trying to interpret the meaning of his life. This experience marked a turning point in her own life. She never again lapsed into a state of psychological dependence upon her family, and the Beecher residence in Walnut Hills was no longer her permanent home. She left it to build a new career. Never again did she defend her father's prestige or beliefs as loyally as she had in the 1830s. Events of the next decade showed that she too felt her life had been ruined by her father, and she too was driven to extreme measures because she was not always able to cope with the nature of her father's influence on her life.

For the present, however, Catharine interpreted George's life in a mode fit for public presentation. She compiled a memorial volume that was published the next year as *The Biographical Remains of Rev. George Beecher*. The public lesson Catharine drew from George's life was not the finality of his failure, but the strength of his efforts to overcome his failings. Her memorial volume was presented, she said, "to awaken hope and encouragement in all who, amid similar embarrassments, are pressing forward to the mark for the prize of their high calling." [22] George's heroic efforts to overcome his self-doubts and dedicate himself to his small congregation greatly impressed Catharine. His efforts inspired her to press forward against her own psychic disabilities and professional disappointments. She resolved to attain the success that George had hoped for but failed to achieve. As in 1823, Catharine seemed to be better able to define or delineate her own life after immersing herself in and partially identifying with the personal papers of a life recently terminated. Through Alexander Fisher and George Beecher she vicariously explored the meaning of death and could thereafter better assess what life meant to her. On both occasions the experience fostered a kind of rebirth, as if, having survived so close a brush with death, she had won a claim on life.

Catharine continued her vacation dressed in mourning, but her spirits were more animated than they had been for three years. She traveled from July to October, frequently lodging in taverns and rarely remaining longer than a day in one place. She revived old friendships, made some new ones, heard Finney preach on perfectionism, stayed in a Shaker community, and by the end of September, having extensively and enthusiastically toured in upper New York and western Massachusetts, she left the vacation retreats of the Mohawk Valley and the Berkshire Mountains for a week in New York City.[23]

There Catharine's determination to begin a new career was fully demonstrated, for with the help of her hostess, Mrs. Cortlandt Van Rensselaer, she began to outline an ambitious educational program for the American West.

Part IV

NATION-BUILDING,
1843–1856

༄ 11 ༅

The Building of a Glorious Temple, 1843

Insofar as Catharine Beecher's career can be said to have had a widespread and immediate impact on her society, that effect was achieved through the publication of her *Treatise on Domestic Economy*. Even before Catharine Beecher set out for Chillicothe in 1843, her *Treatise* had entered its fourth printing since its publication by a small Boston firm in 1841. After polishing the text to solidify its confident, authoritative tone, Catharine had in 1842 negotiated a new contract with Harper and Brothers. Its system of national distribution was well designed to exploit the demonstrated public enthusiasm for her text, and thus she had at last found an effective means to disseminate her ideas on American women. The *Treatise* was reprinted nearly every year from 1841 to 1856. Together with her supplementary receipt book, first published in 1846 and reprinted fourteen times before the publication of her enlarged compendium *The American Woman's Home* in 1869, Catharine Beecher's *Treatise* established her as a national authority on the psychological state and the physical well-being of the American home. This reputation was fortified by her *Letters to Persons Who Are Engaged in Domestic Service* (1842) and her *Letters to the People on Health and Happiness* (1855).[1]

Catharine's *Treatise* explained every aspect of domestic life from the building of a house to the setting of a table. Students of technology have noted its crisp and effective designs, such as that for the plumbing system of a kitchen.[2] Describing the first servantless household, she supplied designs for the ingenious labor-saving devices she believed more pertinent to a democratic and "improving" age. In 1840, women who relied on written rather than oral instruction in domestic arts had to read separate books on health, child care, housebuilding, and cooking, or else rely on English compendiums that drew these topics together but were, in their extensive use of servants, inappropriate for American readers.[3] Catharine's was the first American volume to pull all the disparate domestic employments together and to describe their functions in the American environment.

In addition to its functional utility, the book devoted careful attention to the psychology of domesticity. This duality of purpose made her book unique when it was published and renders it historically significant for the twentieth century. Here for the first time was a text that standardized American domestic practices — prescribing one system that integrated psychological, physiological, economic, religious, social, and political factors, and in addition demonstrating how the specifics of the system should work. In the next three decades Catharine Beecher could enter virtually any community in the United States and expect to be received as the heroine who had simplified and made understandable the mysterious arts of household maintenance, child rearing, gardening, cooking, cleaning, doctoring, and the dozen other responsibilities middle class women assumed to keep their children and husbands alive and well.[4] Her *Treatise*, well worth its price of fifty cents, conveyed a sense of shared experience, but its purposeful tone prevented it from lapsing into sentimental intimacy. Catharine took her constituency seriously, and they rewarded her with their patronage.

A Treatise on Domestic Economy appeared at a time when there was a great need for such a standardized text. Many cultural indicators point to the heightened concern over the quality of domestic life in the 1840s — a concern that grew more emphatic when increasing geographic mobility removed many families from traditional sources of domestic knowledge.[5] Just when Americans began to expect more from their domestic lives than ever before, the ability of the average American woman to meet this expectation diminished as she moved away from communal and familial ties that might have fortified her skills. Scholars of the history of technology have confirmed the technological rigor of Catharine Beecher's household designs, and have credited her with the beginning of household automation. Her innovations were meant to fill the gap she perceived between the society's expectations of women and the resources at their disposal for fulfilling those expectations. She more than anyone else may have made domesticity workable.[6]

Catharine was acutely conscious of the trials to which women were put by being unprepared to assume their domestic burdens. Conditions were so bad, Catharine said, that "it would seem as if the primeval curse, which has written the doom of pain and sorrow on one period of a young mother's life, in this country had been extended over all." This was due to a lack of adequate information about how to fulfill domestic responsibilities. Tocqueville also noted the pioneer woman whose "delicate limbs appear shrunken; her features are drawn in; her eye is mild and melancholy; her whole physiognomy bears marks of a degree of religious resignation, a deep quiet of all passion," Catharine quoted him. "To look at [her children's] strength, and her languor, one might imagine that the life she had given them had exhausted her own." [7]

Even settled communities desired new definitions of and attributed greater importance to domestic duties. In Hartford a young preacher named Horace Bushnell agonized over his inability to arouse the interest of his congregation in the early 1840s, but in 1845 his career was rescued by a series of sermons declaring the careful nurture of children in the home as more important than conversion in shaping a Christian character. His parishioners eagerly adopted this doctrine, for it condoned the distinctive meanings they had already begun to attribute to the family group as an oasis of innocence amid the commercial acquisitiveness of American society.[8] To this emerging ideology of domesticity, Catharine Beecher's *Treatise* contributed both practical details and some basic building blocks of social theory.

Its major contribution was to define a new role for women within the household. Of her four major predecessors, three were men, and all assumed male control of the domestic environment. In *The Father's Book* (1834), Theodore Dwight assumed male hegemony in the household, as did Amherst College's President, Herman Humphrey in his *Domestic Education* (1840). William Alcott advocated a more open and mutual relationship between men and women in his *Young Housekeeper* (1838), but he, like Lydia Maria Child in *The American Frugal Housewife* (1832), assumed the continuance of traditional gender roles inherited from the eighteenth century. While overtly acknowledging male dominance, Catharine Beecher's *Treatise* also exaggerated and heightened gender differences and thereby altered and romanticized the emphasis given to women's domestic role. Subsequent domestic manuals described a significantly different role for women from that anticipated by Dwight, Humphrey, Alcott, and Child.[9] Horace Bushnell and Sarah Josepha Hale, the two chief representatives of this later style, diverged from Catharine Beecher on many points, as we shall see, but they shared essentially the same universe — one bifurcated into masculine and feminine dichotomies.

Quite apart from its ability to elucidate the new American ideology of the family, Catharine's book was, on a more utilitarian level, a badly needed modern compendium of the domestic arts relating to health, diet, hygiene, and general well-being. As a postrevolutionary generation bent on extracting practical benefits from their theoretical innovations, many Americans believed that elementary matters like diet and health should be as susceptible to improvement as anything else in the new age, and that wherever possible they should be made perfect. These expectations outreached the still rather crude abilities of professional medicine, however, and men and women turned to a variety of popular nostrums ranging from patent medicines to phrenology in their search for physiological betterment.[10] In this context Catharine Beecher offered to new and settled communities alike a scientific but personal guide to improved health and well-being. The contrast between Catharine's *Treatise* and its best-selling predecessor, Lydia Maria Child's *The American Frugal Housewife* (1832), was as great as that between medieval and modern medicine. Child's volume passed on traditional home remedies for a wide variety of ailments and injuries, but gave no causal explanation for the link between illness and treatment. Catharine, however, explained such physiological differences as that between arteries and veins, and she described the fundamentals of modern first aid.

She provided a solid basis for understanding how the body functioned and how to keep it functioning well. Complete with illustrations describing the bone, muscle, nerve, circulation, digestive, and respiratory systems, her discussions of the bodily functions were straightforward and informative, presenting the topic in ways that engendered self-confidence and self-understanding. Catharine did not reserve the role of expert for herself but readily acknowledged the medical sources she had used and implied that anyone could easily learn as much as she by mastering these basic physiological facts.[11] Like Dr. Benjamin Spock's *Baby and Child Care* of a century later, Catharine's manual provided simple rules to enable the reader to judge for herself how best to deal with an inevitably more complicated reality. Thus in a typical discussion of a point of infant care she explained:

Take particular care of the food of an infant. If it is nourished by the mother, her own diet should be simple, nourishing, and temperate. If the child be brought up by hand, the milk of a new-milch cow, mixed with one third water, and sweetened a little with *white* sugar, should be the only food given, until the teeth come. . . . If the food appear to distress the child, after eating, first ascertain if the milk be really from a new-milch cow, as it may otherwise be too old. Learn also whether the cow lives on proper food.

Perhaps as important as the simple rules were the frequent exceptions her manual pointed out. After a discussion of "the management of young children," in which she recommended government "by rewards more than penalties" and advised an intermediate path between too stern parental control and too weak, she concluded with a discussion of exceptions to that rule, the sensitivity of which was worthy of a twentieth-century child psychiatrist:

Children of active, heedless temperament, or those who are odd, awkward, or unsuitable, in their remarks and deportment, are often essentially injured by a want of patience and self-control in those who govern them. Such children often possess a morbid sensibility, which they strive to conceal, or a desire of love and approbation, which preys like a famine on the soul. And yet, they become objects of ridicule and rebuke, to almost every member of the family, until their sensibilities are tortured into obtuseness or misanthropy. Such children, above all others, need tenderness and sympathy. A thousand instances of mistake or forgetfulness should be passed over, in silence, while opportunities for commendation and encouragement should be diligently sought.[12]

The volume was like a good companion — knowledgeable but unpretentious, supportive without being intrusive, and above all, able to resolve self-doubts. Designed to reduce the anxiety of the reader, Catharine's discussions commiserated with her about the difficulties of her duties and supplied convincing resolutions of the ambiguities and contradictions involved in her everyday tasks.

※

The major ambiguity faced by American women in the 1830s and 1840s was not, however, whether they should govern their children with a light or heavy hand, but how, in an egalitarian society, the submission of one sex to the other could be justified. Women in America had always experienced such inequity, but they had never before needed to reconcile it with a growing ideology of popular democracy and equal rights.[13] Furthermore, this contradiction was heightened as the increased options available to white males in the first decades of the nineteenth century seemed to accompany a more sharply limited sphere designated for white women during the same period.[14] Catharine Beecher did not believe that the connection between these two phenomena was accidental. Like other writers of the period, most notably Sarah Josepha Hale and Horace Bushnell, Catharine Beecher tried to reconcile the inequality of women with an egalitarian democracy by emphasizing the importance of woman's sphere of domesticity.[15] But unlike Bushnell and Hale, Catharine Beecher did not try to obscure the fundamental assumption of inequality upon which this separation of spheres rested. Bushnell and Hale believed that women were "naturally" suited to domesticity, but Catharine Beecher explained to her readers that women were restricted to the domestic sphere as a political expedient necessary to the maintenance of democracy in America.

The greater the social, political, and economic expansiveness in the country at large, the greater the tensions, and the keener the need to discover ways to reduce conflict, Catharine believed. Otherwise the system might generate more self-destruction than coherence. In a democracy as agitated and tension-filled as the United States in the 1840s, some form of hierarchy was needed to avoid a war of all against all, she said. She led her readers to conclude that by removing half the population from the arena of competition and making it subservient to the other half, the amount of antagonism the society had to bear would be reduced to a tolerable limit. Moreover, by defining gender identity as more important than class, regional, or religious identity, and by ignoring altogether the imponderables of American racial divisions, she promoted the belief that the society's only basic division was that between men and women.

Catharine Beecher drew most of these ideas from her reading of Tocqueville's *Democracy in America,* and she frequently quoted at length from his study. "The Americans have applied to the sexes the great principle of political economy which governs the manufactories of our age," Catharine explained, "by carefully dividing the duties of man from those of woman, in order that the great work of society may be the better carried on." To support her remarks she cited Tocqueville's belief that "in no country has such constant care been taken, as in America, to trace two clearly distinct lines of action for the two sexes." Tocqueville noted, Catharine continued, that the American woman's centrality in the home did not subvert the power of the man in the family. Americans believe, Tocqueville concluded,

> that the natural head of the conjugal association is man. [Americans] do not, therefore, deny him the right of directing his partner; and they maintain, that, in the smaller association of husband and wife, as well as in the great social community, the object of democracy is, to regulate and legalize the powers which are necessary, not to subvert all power.[16]

Elaborating on Tocqueville's analysis, Catharine explained that this sharp division of sex roles arose from the tensions generated by democratic conditions. Unlike the females of "monarchical and aristocratic lands," where "all ranks and classes are fixed in a given position, and each person is educated for a particular sphere and style of living," Catharine wrote, American women live in a society where "every thing is moving and changing." The flow of wealth is constantly shifting, she added, and since the society lacks permanent definitions of status, it is in a constant state of agitation.

> Persons in poverty, are rising to opulence, and persons of wealth, are sinking to poverty. The children of common laborers, by their talents and enterprise, are becoming nobles in intellect, or wealth, or office; while the children of the wealthy, enervated by indulgence, are sinking to humbler stations. The sons of the wealthy are leaving the rich mansions of their fathers, to dwell in the log cabins of the forest, where very soon they shall bear away the daughters of ease and refinement, to share the privations of a new settlement. Meantime, even in the more stationary portions of the community, there is a mingling of all grades of wealth, intellect, and education. . . . Thus, persons of humble means are brought into contact with those of vast wealth, while all intervening grades are placed side by side. Thus too, there is a constant comparison of conditions, among equals, and a constant temptation presented to imitate the customs, and to strive for the enjoyments, of those who possess larger means.

In this democratic turmoil, Catharine said, in order to decrease hostilities and tensions, "a system of laws must be established, which

sustain certain relations and dependencies in social and civil life."
Chief among these was the subordination of the wife to the husband. Like the subordination of children to parents, employees to
employers, and citizens to magistrates, the subordination of women
to men was necessary if society was to "go forward harmoniously." [17]

The position of women in American culture was therefore an
example of how "superior and subordinate relations" contribute
to "the general good of all." Women "take a subordinate station"
not because they are naturally subordinate, or even because subordination suits them, but because it promotes the general good of
the society.[18] Catharine believed it was essential to tell women
that their submissive role had a social importance transcending their
own personal interests, for she thought that they would thereby be
better reconciled to it and more effective in implementing the
grander purposes of their role.

This was only one example, however, of the ways in which the
American domestic experience could promote the national good,
but it and other potential contributions to the general weal could
not be fully utilized as long as Americans remained confused about
the link between domesticity and nationality. In her *Treatise*
Catharine Beecher proceeded, often by indirection and implica-
tion, to shape a coherent ideology of domesticity that would answer
the needs of American democracy.

Catharine began with the premise that the home was a perfect
vehicle for national unity because it was a universally experienced
institution recognizing no economic, political, or regional boundaries. Even girls who worked in the mills made a small home for
themselves, Catharine said, and adopting Tocqueville's thesis that
the conditions of mobility and equality in America engendered a
loss of traditional social identities, she pointed to the domestic experience as a focus around which a new and unified national identity could be built. For the language of domesticity could more
easily be universalized than any single dialect of class or region or
age. At the beginning of the 1850s Harriet Beecher Stowe did much
to persuade Americans that white and black Americans obeyed the
same domestic impulses, and through *Uncle Tom's Cabin* she
helped unify a theretofore divided northern opinion. At the beginning of the decade Catharine Beecher set out to transcend social
divisions by emphasizing the universality and standardizing the
contours of domestic values. Her task was lightened by the fact

that she could build on the traditional American distinction between sex roles and the contemporary eagerness to reinforce them.[19]

To this principle of universality, Catharine added four corollary
concepts to round out her domestic ideology. By the end of her
Treatise the domestic sphere seemed not so much removed from as
central to the national life.

Catharine first paid ample homage to the role of women in shaping the future of the American experiment. After a long quotation
from Tocqueville testifying to the significance of the "social revolution" in America, Catharine agreed that the millennium seemed
to be coming in a social rather than a strictly religious form.
"Startled kings and sages, philosophers and statesmen, are watching
us with that interest which a career so illustrious, and so involving
their own destiny, is calculated to excite," Catharine wrote. "They
are studying our institutions, scrutinizing our experience, and watching for our mistakes," she said, "that they may learn whether 'a
social revolution, so irresistible, be advantageous or prejudicial to
mankind.' " The future of the United States was a global, not just
a national concern. "This is the Country," Catharine continued,

> which the Disposer of events designs shall go forth as the cynosure of
> nations, to guide them to the light and blessedness of that [millennial]
> day. To us is committed the grand, the responsible privilege, of
> exhibiting to the world, the beneficent influences of Christianity,
> when carried into every social, civil, and political institution. . . .

Since the future of the world depended on the United States, and
the future of the United States depended on "the intellectual and
moral character of the mass of the people," and the shaping of that
character was in turn "committed mainly to the female hand,"
Catharine concluded that "to American women, more than to any
others on earth, is committed the exalted privilege of extending
over the world those blessed influences, which are to renovate degraded man." [20]

Catharine insisted all American women were equally important
to the achievement of this task. Their class or regional differences
did not matter since they all worked within a shared system of
values and toward the same goal. "No American woman then has
any occasion for feeling that hers is an humble or insignificant lot,"
Catharine continued, for "the value of what an individual accom-
plishes, is to be estimated by the importance of the enterprise

achieved, and not by the particular position of the laborer." Women should not see themselves as "isolated" laborers, Catharine said, but should be "invigorated and cheered" by the fact that they are "indispensable portions of a grand result." The end of the first section of her *Treatise* rose to the pinnacle of rhetorical heights to extol the unified purposes of American womanhood:

> The woman who is rearing a family of children; the woman, who labors in the schoolroom; the woman who, in her retired chamber, earns, with her needle, the mite, which contributes to the intellectual and moral elevation of her Country; even the humble domestic, whose example and influence may be moulding and forming young minds, while her faithful services sustain a prosperous domestic state;— each and all may be animated by the consciousness, that they are agents in accomplishing the greatest work that ever was committed to human responsibility. It is the building of a glorious temple, whose base shall be coextensive with the bounds of the earth, whose summit shall pierce the skies, whose splendor shall beam on all lands; and those who hew the lowliest stone, as much as those who carve the highest capital, will be equally honored, when its top-stone shall be laid, with new rejoicings of the morning stars, and shoutings of the sons of God.[21]

This apotheosis of American national development was to be achieved by the united efforts of American women — exemplary in their ability to conform to the needs of their nation on the basis of their gender alone and to disregard their secondary identities of class and locale. Thus through their nurturing role women were bound to a common purpose and form. In contrast to most of American society, they formed a homogeneous group.

Employing Tocqueville again, Catharine noted further that most of American society acknowledged the homogeneous identity of women by generalizing the domestic relationship between men and women throughout the culture. Thus the whole culture was in a sense made "safe" for women, so that wherever they moved in it, the ideology of male protection and female dependence would be maintained. Thus, Tocqueville saw that "in America, a young unmarried woman may, alone, and without fear, undertake a long journey." For whatever her status all women are assumed by American men "to be virtuous and refined." "As if in compensation for [their subordination]," Catharine said, women "universally in this country, through every class of society [are given] precedence

. . . in all the comforts, conveniences and courtesies, of life." [22] Catharine did not articulate this argument fully, but she implied that since a woman's gender defined her completely, the culture could, be adding a middle-class bias to female identity, significantly enlarge the scope of middle-class values and behavior. For every woman then became a purveyor of middle-class culture. Thus what some historians have called the feminization of American culture can be seen as a means of promoting nationally homogeneous cultural forms, and the emphasis given to gender identity can be viewed as an attempt by a society laden with class and regional anxieties to compensate for these divisive factors. [23]

Besides the creation and extension of a homogeneous ethic, domesticity contributed two other stabilizing pillars to American democracy. These were, according to Catharine Beecher, the example women provided of voluntary and self-initiated submission to authority, and the compensatory role women played in counteracting commercial and acquisitive values. In their submission to men American women acted as an archetypal example of how to achieve social order in a democracy, Catharine said, for their marriage partner, being of their own choosing, is legitimized in his authority over her, just as the American government, being of the people's choosing, is justified in the assertion of its authority. [24] Again quoting Tocqueville, Catharine's *Treatise* concluded that women deem it an honor to act in this exemplary manner: "They attach a sort of pride to the voluntary surrender of their own will, and make it their boast to bend themselves to the yoke, not to shake it off." [25] A more far-reaching and immediately effective consequence of American domesticity, however, was to define an oasis of noncommercial values in an otherwise acquisitive society.

Like other writers of the period, including Sarah Josepha Hale and Horace Bushnell, Catharine Beecher believed that the values of the home stood in opposition to some other American values, but unlike Bushnell and Hale, she wanted the same set of values to apply to both spheres, and she was far more aggressive in applying domestic values to the rest of society. The success of Catharine Beecher's *Treatise* may have been due to its ability to combine a convincing domestic ideology with practical advice demonstrating how these ideals could be realized. Recognizing the practical fact that American women lived in a society as well as a home, she frequently noted the ways in which the values of the society necessarily impinged on the home. "The practice of early rising has a relation to the general interests of the social community, as well as to that of each distinct family," Catharine wrote in a typical passage. "Now if a small portion of the community establish very different hours," she continued, decrying the practices of some families, "it makes a kind of jostling, in all the concerns and interests of society." [26] In both theory and practice, Catharine's *Treatise* promoted congruence between domestic and social values. That goal remained unchanged by the fact that the spheres were not yet completely in harmony.

Horace Bushnell and Sarah Hale, however, described a basic and enduring opposition between the values of domesticity and much of American society. In *Christian Nurture* Bushnell described the home as a source of "permanent, consistent, singleness of aim," set apart from a too mobile and confusing outside world. In contrast to "the extreme individualism of our modern philosophy," Bushnell said, the family operated by an "organic law" by "associating children with the character and destiny of their parents." In what was perhaps the beginnings of the feminine mystique, Bushnell attributed to the mother powers of intuition and sentiment that play on the child's "emotions and sentiments, and work a character in him by virtue of an organic power." Nevertheless, Bushnell admonished the women who acted by this mystical romantic formula to recognize the occasions when "common sense and solid reality" are needed, when "no rhapsodies are wanted, or flights of feeling." [27]

While the mother was thus encouraged to use her powers of intuition, she was denied their full employment, and required to recognize the greater authority of the common sense world her sons were destined to enter after their character had been properly molded. Bushnell could more easily ignore the contradictions of this policy than could the women who tried to implement it. They were left to discover for themselves when to employ their "organic" powers and when to use their common sense. *Christian Nurture* may have closed the gap between parent and child, but it enlarged the gulf between the home and the outside world, and placing women firmly inside the walls of domesticity, it asked them to perform a kind of penance for the sins of a society they were not fully allowed to enter. Catharine Beecher's readers labored under no such handicap, for they were asked to eliminate rather than to endure the contradictions between general and domestic values.

Sarah Hale, editor for half a century of the influential magazine, *Godey's Lady's Book,* also adopted and promoted the ideology of domesticity as a compensating set of values in "a society given over without reservation to the pursuit of wealth." [28] The male and female spheres were separated to allow men to continue their acquisitive pursuits and to enable women to concentrate on their moral role. Without one the growth of the society would stop, and without the other the course of that growth might be morally objectionable. Together they gave the society an energized labor force and a free conscience. So long as women's labor was unsullied by the business mentality, so long as it was a labor of love and not for gain, the culture might retain its contact with primitive virtue and goodness.[29]

Catharine's analysis of domesticity does not differ in purpose from that of Bushnell or Hale. All agreed that the isolation of women in the home and away from full participation in the society decreased the tensions and anxieties that characterized American life. They agreed, moreover, that this was done "in order that the great work of society may be the better carried on." [30] But rather than seeing the home as a haven set apart from society to compensate for or counteract certain characteristics of American life, Catharine saw the home as an integral part of a national system, reflecting and promoting mainstream American values. The only requirement for a place on this cultural dais was that women reject aggression and embrace deference as a style of social interaction.

Three lifelong concerns of Catharine Beecher's were resolved in her ideology of domesticity. First, domesticity revived the Puritan notion of the subjection of the individual to the larger social welfare, yet it presented this notion in a form acceptable to the nineteenth century. In this democratic context the home was a much more effective agency of social authority than the clergy or aristocracy. For in the delineation of its own lines of authority the family relied on "natural" relationships of superiority and subordination. As a society in miniature, the family could therefore be used as a model for the extension of such relationships elsewhere in the society. Although the family located authority at a personal level, domesticity, as Catharine Beecher described it, confirmed the individual's obligation to recognize and conform to "a system of laws" that sustained "superior and subordinate relations" in the society as a whole.

Second, domesticity answered the dilemma over piety and morality that Catharine inherited from her father. Bushnell, a clergyman like Lyman Beecher, superimposed a romantic epistemology on a common-sense culture in order to maintain the importance of piety over morality. Catharine overcame this dichotomy by using the concept of self-denial to show how the impulses of the heart were related to external behavior. Self-denial was built into the very identity Catharine Beecher defined for women in the United States. Submission to the will and needs of others was, Catharine believed, automatically required of American women. Therefore their own personal promptings of the heart were necessarily related to their behavior since sacrifice was by definition an act that linked selflessness of heart with an external deed.

In her *Treatise* Catharine called on businessmen to imitate the self-denying ethic of the home and use their wealth "for the greatest good of those around them," rather than for "mere selfish indulgences." Fighting the spread of undomestic and "aristocratic" habits in the wealthy, Catharine decried the "great portion of the rich [who] seem to be acting on the principle, that the more God bestows on them, the less are they under obligation to practice any self-denial, in fulfilling his benevolent plan of raising our race to intelligence and holiness." [31]

In addition to treating the two important problems of leadership and morality, Catharine's brand of domesticity also addressed the problem of national unity — a concern Catharine inherited from her father but recast in a mold that gave centrality to women. Her *Treatise* promoted a practical as well as theoretical base for national unity, however, for throughout her rules for health care, her receipts, her formulas for household management, her description of proper manners, her prescriptions for infant care, Catharine sought above all to standardize and systematize American domestic practices.

This urge for regularity that marked nearly every page of Catharine's *Treatise* had both a personal and a social dimension. On a private level it tried to lift women out of the confusing morass of contradictory demands on their time and energies by establishing priorities or precise timetables and by adopting efficient work methods. "Without attempting any such systematic employment of time, and carrying it out, so far as they can control circumstances, most women are rather driven along, by the daily occurrences of life," Catharine wrote, "so that, instead of being the intelligent regulators of their own time, they are the mere sport of circumstances." There was nothing, she said, "which so distinctly marks the difference between weak and strong minds, as the fact, whether they control circumstances, or circumstances control them." [32] This private psychological regimen was further enhanced by the belief that these same priorities and practices were adopted by families throughout the country.

Deeming the standardization of public manners and attitudes as important as standardization of household routine, Catharine Beecher said that just as one set of management rules could apply to all households, so one code of manners applied to all Americans. "Now the principles of democracy require, that the same courtesy, which we accord to our own circle, shall be extended to every class and condition; and that distinction, of superiority and subordination, shall depend, not on accidents of birth, fortune, or occupation, but solely on those relations, which the good of all classes equally require," Catharine wrote. "The distinctions demanded, in a democratic state, are simply those, which result from relations, that are common to every class, and are for the benefit of all." Thus although class differences do admittedly exist, Catharine said that American manners should not reflect these differences, but rather acknowledge differences of status only where these are "common to every class." Manners may therefore recognize only differences such as those between men and women, children and elders, feeble and healthy. "The rules of good breeding, in a democratic state must be founded on these principles," Catharine concluded. "Otherwise there would be constant scrambling, among those of equal claims, and brute force must be the final resort." [33]

In a similar way she provided rules standardizing diet, food preparation, meal hours, health care, house and kitchen furnishings, size and number of rooms, charitable responsibilities, and recreation — here even suggesting that "serious and intelligent persons" patronize horseraces "in order to regulate them." [34]

In the history of writings on domestic management, *A Treatise on Domestic Economy* stood between traditional guides like Lydia Maria Child's *The American Frugal Housewife* of 1832 (for many years its chief competitor) and professional writings like Helen Campbell's *Household Economics* of 1898. Catharine Beecher marked the midpoint between Child's "general maxims" and Campbell's highly specialized lectures. This progression is perhaps best described by their respective attitudes toward the rooms of a house. Child nowhere mentioned differentiated rooms within the home; Catharine Beecher provided detailed drawings and instructions for the construction of an eight-room house, each room designed for an explicit use as a parlor, kitchen, bedroom, or nursery; and Helen Campbell further elaborated on these distinctions to claim that "a separate room is the right of every human being; a place where one can lock the door, be safe from intrusion, and in silence and freedom gather strength for the next thing to be done." [35] Catharine Beecher's concern was to subsume individual diversity in order to build a commonality of culture. By the end of the century this culture had passed through the crucible in which its identity was forged and had elaborated so ubiquitous a structure that isolation was more to be desired than heightened participation.

Catharine's several writings on domestic economy in the 1870s and her enlarged and partially revised *The American Woman's Home,* co-authored with Harriet Beecher Stowe in 1869, presented essentially the same ideology linking domestic life with the life of the nation, but two pairs of tensions that Catharine had tried to resolve in the 1840s appear by the 1870s to have stretched beyond the possibility of mutual accommodation. Neither the relationship between men and women nor that between upper and lower classes were by 1869 so easily resolved for Catharine. For each of these new problems Catharine devised new domestic forms.

Articulating a more complex argument in defense of "the unequal distribution of property," generally more conscious of the gulf between rich and poor, and citing Herbert Spencer rather than Tocqueville to justify the importance of the domestic sphere, Catharine advocated in 1869 the creation of settlement houses wherein "several ladies" should take up residence in areas of urban poverty and "from the vast accumulation of misery and sin at hand on every side, should select the orphans, the aged, the sick, and the sinful, and spend time and money for their temporal and spiritual elevation." [36] The last paragraph of *Miss Beecher's Housekeeper and Healthkeeper* of 1873 rejoiced "in the increasingly open avenues to useful and remunerating occupations for women, enabling them to establish *homes of their own,* where, if not as the natural mother, yet as a Christ-mother, they may take in neglected ones, and train future mothers, teachers, and missionaries for the world." [37] The family, although still a source of morality and virtue, seemed no longer a society in miniature to Catharine. It seemed to embody rather than to meliorate the tensions between social classes and between men and women. In her later works Catharine appended to the usual domestic forms an entirely female domesticity, in which a woman "who earns her own livelihood can institute the family state" by adopting children. "Then to her will appertain the authority and rights that belong to man as the head of a family," Catharine pointed out. She also reminded her readers "that the distinctive duty of obedience to man does not rest on women who do not enter the relations of married life." [38] Between 1841 and 1869 Catharine Beecher not only witnessed the development of an urban industrial society, but she also committed herself to the creation of a more autonomous female culture.

Thus her *Treatise* paradoxically provided Catharine with the framework whereby she could begin to explore alternatives to the American ethic of domesticity. Nevertheless she was too deeply immersed in its rituals to break away completely from domestic forms. In her *Treatise* she had articulated concepts central to her own life as well as to the life of her nation. For her the *Treatise* was both a summary and an exorcising of the domestic impulses she had known since childhood. It cleared the way for new personal and professional concerns. For the nation, domesticity may have been equally effective in easing the passage from turbulent youth to regulated maturity.

🌿 12 🌿

Education at the West, 1843–1847

In an atmosphere congenial to her from both past acquaintance and future strategy, Catharine began to outline an ambitious new educational program in the summer of 1843. She was staying in New York City with Mrs. Cortlandt Van Rensselaer, and if she had been wandering all summer in search of the best means of launching her new career, Catharine could not have picked a better means than the Van Rensselaer family. Cortlandt Van Rensselaer was a descendant of old Dutch aristocracy and still held considerable wealth and social prestige. Though he was an ordained Presbyterian minister, his talents were not wasted by the church on a congregation but were instead used for fund-raising. At the time of Catharine's visit he was leading a campaign for one hundred thousand dollars for Princeton Theological Seminary. In 1846 he became president of the Presbyterian board of education and devoted his energies to raising funds to endow parochial schools and colleges. Catharine gained access to his skills and influence through her close friendship with Van Rensselaer's wife, her former Hartford pupil, Catharine Cogswell.[1] She stayed at the Van Rennselaers' home for a week and succeeded in gaining their support for her plan to create a national organization for the training and placement of women teachers. Catharine's last act of the summer was to accept fifty dollars from the Van Rensselaers as the first contribution toward the funding of the proposed organization.[2]

For the next decade and a half Catharine Beecher maintained the pace of life that she began in the summer of 1843. She sought out people like the Van Rensselaers, who were either themselves wealthy or could open doors to the wealth of other evangelical individuals and groups. She toured constantly in both East and West, raising funds, seeking sites for schools and seminaries, and recruiting teachers to occupy them. Her *Treatise* made her nationally known, and her frequent speaking tours kept her immediately in the public view.

By the end of the 1840s she was one of the most widely known women in America.

Over the course of the decade, as she met with greater and greater success in promoting the primacy of women in American education, Catharine's public and private lives converged. Finally she had found a role commensurate with her personal needs and desires, and much of her achievement during this decade may have arisen from that congruence. As she traveled about the country advocating a special role for her sex, she became the living embodiment of that role. This new consistency in Catharine's life lent conviction to her activities and greatly enhanced her powers of persuasion.

The merger between Catharine's public activities and her private needs did not, however, resolve the deep psychological problems that lay beneath the surface of her personality. Although she championed a special role for women, she still felt the burden of her own life circumstances. Although she lectured to others on self-sacrifice, she remained unreconciled to the self-denial of her own life. From 1844 to 1850, as Catharine grew enormously in public stature, she also accumulated considerable psychological strain.

Catharine returned to Cincinnati in the fall of 1843, inspired by the support of the Van Rensselaers. She spent the winter striving to create a national organization to promote "the cause of popular education, and as intimately connected with it, the elevation of my sex by the opening of a profession for them as educators of the young." All that winter and spring she corresponded with prominent individuals in the East and West, soliciting their endorsement of such an organization.[3]

Meanwhile she insisted to Calvin Stowe that he act as the figurehead and official agent of the organization. Stowe was extremely reluctant to do so, but since Catharine was convinced that male leadership was needed to give the organization credibility, she found a way to overcome his initial refusal. She wrote to several men whom Stowe respected, describing her proposed organization and claiming that Stowe had agreed to lead it but that his role must be kept secret until his plans were "more matured." She then asked her correspondents, "Encourage Mr. Stowe in this effort," but "omit my name and all allusion to me in what you may write." [4] Letters poured in to Stowe from all quarters urging him to persevere in this benevolent enterprise, and that pressure combined with Harriet's and Catharine's was more than he had the power to resist. For three years, until Catharine found another man to act as a figurehead, Stowe was the captive leader of Catharine's organization. Making light of her husband's well-founded fear of Catharine's designs, Harriet wrote to Stowe: "As to Kate it is all a mere nervous fidget on your part. . . . You seem somehow to connect very terrible ideas with poor Katy as if she was going to carry you off bodily one of these days but I think on that point you may set your heart at ease." [5]

Catharine did indeed carry Stowe bodily to New England the following year, however, when she began her campaign in earnest. When she left Cincinnati in the spring of 1844, Catharine's original plan was to use whatever funds her nascent organization might raise to support a new seminary in Putnam, Ohio. Sarah Beecher, George's widow, was independently wealthy and had agreed to sponsor a new teachers' seminary near her family home at Putnam. Perhaps moved by gratitude for Catharine's memorial volume, perhaps by Lyman Beecher's appeal in Catharine's behalf, Sarah promised Lyman that "while she lived and possessed the means [Catharine] should never lack support and sympathy." This promise afforded him enormous "relief and pleasure," and it gave Catharine's activities a focus.[6] Yet after Catharine experienced very enthusiastic audiences that spring and summer, she concluded that she did not need to be connected with a school in order to raise funds. Not wanting to be tied to a seminary anyway, Catharine changed her tactic, and in the winter of 1845 she remained in the East to continue her speaking tours and organizing efforts. Accompanied by Calvin Stowe or her younger half-brother, Thomas Beecher, she visited almost every major city in the East, delivering a standard speech and organizing local groups of church women to collect and forward funds and proselytize her views.[7]

Catharine's addresses were subsequently published in three volumes by Harpers. The first was entitled *The Evils Suffered by American Women and American Children: The Causes and the Remedy*; it was followed by *The Duty of American Women to Their Coun-*

try; and lastly, by *An Address to the Protestant Clergy of the United States*. These addresses clarified the ideas Catharine had evolved over the course of the last two decades. Now however like a practiced evangelist she played expertly upon the feelings and fears of her audience and ultimately brought them to commit themselves to her vision of a nation redeemed by women. The full meaning of Catharine's exhortation was not revealed until halfway through her addresses. First she gained her audiences' sympathy for the sufferings of masses of American children under cruel teachers and in degenerate environments. She quoted from several reports to state legislatures that described "the comfortless and dilapidated buildings, the unhung doors, broken sashes, absent panes, stilted benches, gaping walls, yawning roofs, and muddy moldering floors," of contemporary schools and "the self-styled teachers, who lash and dogmatize in these miserable tenements of humanity." Many teachers were "low, vulgar, obscene, intemperate," according to one report to the New York State legislature, "and utterly incompetent to teach anything good." [8]

To remedy this situation Catharine then proposed a national benevolent movement, similar to the temperance movement or the missionary boards, to raise money for teachers and schoolrooms. Yet Catharine's plan went even beyond the contemporary benevolent models. Her chief goal was to "elevate and dignify" her sex, and this goal was inextricably bound to her vision of a more consolidated society. The united effort of women in the East, combined with the moral influence of women in the West, would create homogeneous national institutions, Catharine asserted. The family, the school, and the social morality upon which these institutions were based would everywhere be similar. Sectional and ethnic diversities would give way to national unity as the influence of women increased.

To make her image of a unified society more understandable to her audience, she explained that it was a Protestant parallel to the Catholic pattern of close interaction between social and religious forms. Protestant women should have the same social support for their religious and moral activities as Catholic nuns received from their society. She related the stories of many women she had known who were willing to sacrifice themselves to socially ameliorative efforts, but who had been rebuffed by public opinion and restricted to quiet domestic lives. "Had these ladies turned Catholic and offered their services to extend that church, they would instantly have found bishops, priests, Jesuits and all their subordinates at hand, to counsel and sustain; a strong *public sentiment* would have been created in their favor; while abundant funds would have been laid at their feet," she said.[9] Her plan envisioned a similar kind of cultural support for Protestant women. A web of interlocking social institutions, including the family, the school, and the church, would form a new cultural matrix within which women would assume a central role.

The ideological basis of Catharine's social theory was self-denial. The Catholic church's employment of self-denying women initially attracted Catharine to it as a model for her own plan. Yet Catharine emphasized that her notion of self-denial was different from the Catholic one. The Catholics had "a selfish and ascetic self-denial, aiming mainly to save *self* by inflictions and losses," Catharine said, whereas she advocated self-denial not as the means of personal salvation, but as the means of social cohesion. The self was given over to the society. Expanding on the definition of virtue that she had evolved over the course of the last two decades, Catharine said that "a universe of finite free agents" is held together only by acts of self-denial and that *"all* good" was created "immediately or remotely by *self-denial and self-sacrifice.*"[10] Self-denial was an inclusive virtue that could be practiced by wealthy and poor, converted and unconverted, by persons of all ages and both sexes. As the ideological basis of a national morality it was especially congenial to Catharine since women could be both the embodiment and the chief instructors of self-denial. It made possible an expanded cultural role for women as the exemplars and the teachers of a national morality.

To support this cultural role for women Catharine advocated three corollary ideas, each of which pointed toward a more consolidated American society. First, she said, women should abolish class distinctions among themselves and form one united social group. Catharine Beecher had earlier defended class distinctions as a part of the natural order of God's universe, but such divisions were no longer endorsed in her public writings. This change in her views was prompted in part by a visit she made to Lowell, Massachusetts, where she went to look for teachers. Catharine did not believe the Lowell owners' claims that factory work was a means of self-improvement for the women operatives. She concluded that at Lowell and in New York City women were deliberately exploited. "Work of all kinds is got from poor women, at prices that will not keep soul and body together," Catharine wrote, "and then the articles thus made are sold for prices that give monstrous profits to the capitalist, who thus grows rich on the hard labors of our sex." [11] Rather than participate in this kind of class exploitation, Catharine suggested women should donate their services to the cause of education. Although they might still be poor, their economic sacrifice would transcend class lines and benefit the whole nation instead of a self-interested class of businessmen.

While economic factors oppressed working-class women, social custom suppressed upper-class women. "The customs and prejudices of society forbid" educated young women from engaging in socially useful employments. Their sufferings were just as keen as those of working-class women, Catharine said, the only difference being that their spirits were starved instead of their bodies. "A little working of muslin and worsted, a little light reading, a little calling and shopping, and a great deal of the high stimulus of fashionable amusement, are all the ailment their starving spirits find," Catharine wrote. "The influence and the principle of *caste*," she maintained, must cease to operate on both these groups. Her solution was to secure "a proper education for all classes, and make productive labor honorable, by having all classes engage in it." [12]

The specific labor Catharine endorsed for both groups was teaching. Working class women should leave the factories and seize the opportunity to go to the West as missionary teachers. Their places in the factories should be taken by men. Upper-class women, Catharine said, should do whatever they could to contribute to the "proper education" of American children. Whether by teaching themselves, or by raising funds, or by supervising schools in their community, all well-to-do women could do some productive labor for education. By their efforts, moreover, the public attitude toward the teaching profession could be changed. Teaching is regarded "as the most wearying drudgery, and few resort to it except from necessity," Catharine said, but by elevating the teaching profession into a "true and noble" one, and by making it the special "profession of a woman," women would be freed from the caste principles that suppressed them and enter into a new casteless, but elevated condition.[13] In effect Catharine would eliminate the extremes of class identity and fortify a middle-class social order.

The second corollary to the new social role Catharine described for women was that of fostering the nation's social conscience. Young women teachers in the West would be in the vanguard of settlement, and from them the character of the place would take its shape. "Soon, in all parts of our country, in each neglected village, or new settlement, the Christian female teacher will quietly take her station, collecting the ignorant children around her, teaching them habits of neatness, order and thrift; opening the book of knowledge, inspiring the principles of morality, and awakening the hope of immortality," she said.

> Soon her influence in the village will create a demand for new laborers, and then she will summon from among her friends at home, the nurse for the young and sick, the seamstress and the mantuamaker; and these will prove her auxiliaries in good moral influence, and in sabbath school training. And often as the result of these labors, the Church will arise, and the minister of Christ be summoned to fill up the complement of domestic, moral and religious blessing.[14]

Catharine cited several examples of western settlement where the female teacher preceded the minister. Thus she asserted that a woman could be chiefly responsible for setting the moral tone of the community. A community could coalesce around women rather than the church.

The promotion of national unity was a third aspect of the new social role Catharine was defining for women. The special esteem in which American women were held meant that their united actions would have a nationwide effect. "It is the pride and honour of our country," she said, "that woman holds a commanding influence in the domestic and social circle, which is accorded to the sex in no other nation, and such as will make her wishes and efforts, if united for a benevolent and patriotic object, almost omnipotent." Women thus had the power to shape the character of the whole nation, and that character, Catharine said, would be one of a united nation rather than a collection of sections. "It is to be lamented that the principle of *national* patriotism has had very little nourishment in our country, and, instead, has given place to *sectional* or *state* partialities," she said. "What more promising method for remedying this defect than uniting American women of every state and every section in a common effort for *our whole country*." The moral education thus promoted would also serve as an agent for national unity since it would train "the whole rising generation in common moral principles." Catharine took special

Catharine Beecher at age 57. Wisconsin State
Historical Society.

Beecher family portrait, 1855. *From left to right, top row:* Thomas K., William, Edward, Charles,
Henry Ward; *bottom row:* Mrs. Hooker, Catharine, Lyman, Mrs. Perkins, Mrs. Stowe, James.
Courtesy of Stowe–Day Foundation, Hartford.

Beecher house in East Hampton, New York. From *The Autobiography of Lyman Beecher,* ed. Barbara Cross (Cambridge, Mass., 1961).

Beecher house in Litchfield, Connecticut. Courtesy of Stowe–Day Foundation, Hartford.

Facade of Hartford Female Seminary, taken from the school's diploma. Connecticut Historical Society, Hartford.

"A small church, a school-house, and a comfortable family dwelling may all be united in one building, and for a very moderate sum. . . ." Illustration and accompanying text from *The American Woman's Home,* pp. 454–56.

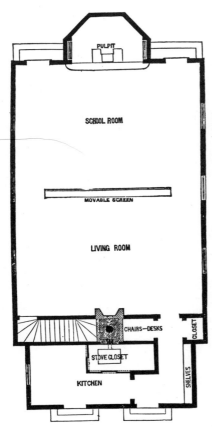

Thus, through the week, the school can be in one division, and the other still a sizable room, and the kitchen be used for teaching domestic economy and also for the eating-room. On Sunday, if there is a movable screen, it can be moved back to the fireplace; or otherwise, the sliding-doors may be opened, giving the whole space to the congregation. The chimney is finished off outside as a steeple. It incloses a cast-iron or terra cotta pipe, which receives the stove-pipe of the kitchen and also pipes connecting the two fire-places with the large pipe, and finds exit above the slats of the steeple at the projections. Thus the chimney is made an exhaust-shaft for carrying off vitiated air from all the rooms both above and below, which have openings into it made for the purpose.

The poor young girl whom the mother is dressing for a

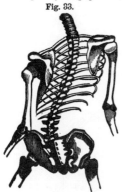

Fig. 33.

sacrifice to this horrid fashion, remorselessly girds the waist just where the bones have least internal support and yield the easiest. The small floating ribs are pressed unequally and laterally against the spine, because the intestines can not yield the equal support required. The result is a distortion of this kind. Fig. 33.

Any mother can discover when this deformity is secured by examining these drawings— Fig. 34 showing the external appearance of the back as Nature designed it should be, and

Fig. 35 the deformity caused by tight dress. These views are presented, because in many cases this evil, if discovered soon enough, can be remedied by methods to be hereafter indicated.

Fig. 34.

Fig. 85.

Illustration and caption from *Letters to the People on Health and Happiness,* pp. 178–79.

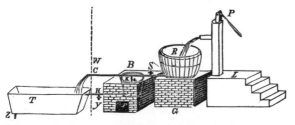

Illustration and caption from *A Treatise on Domestic Economy,* p. 275.

P, Pump. L, Steps to use when pumping. R, Reservoir. G, Brickwork to raise the Reservoir. B, A large Boiler. F, Furnace, beneath the Boiler. C, Conductor of cold water. H, Conductor of hot water. K, Cock for letting cold water into the Boiler. S, Pipe to conduct cold water to a cock over the kitchen sink. T, Bathing-tub, which receives cold water from the Conductor, C, and hot water from the Conductor, H. W, Partition separating the Bathing-room from the Wash-room. Y, Cock to draw off hot water. Z, Plug to let off the water from the Bathing-tub into a drain.

pains to present in detail the moral principles upon which "all sects
are agreed." [15]

※.※

At the end of each address Catharine presented to her audience
her plan for practical action. A committee of clergymen led by Stowe
would, as soon as sufficient funds were raised for a salary, "appoint
one man who shall act as an agent," giving his full time to the
organization. The committee would also appoint "a Board of
Managers, consisting of men from each of the principal Protestant
denominations from each of the different sections of the country."
In addition, local committees of women would raise funds "to aid in
educating and locating missionary teachers." In the West such committees could aid in providing schools for those sent out. In both
places the committees could publicize the cause. Lastly Catharine
revealed how "every woman who feels an interest in the effort can
contribute at least a small sum to promote it" by immediately pur-
chasing Catharine's *Treatise on Domestic Economy* and her *Domestic Receipt Book,* since half the profits from the sale of these books
was to be given to the cause.[16]

Catharine Beecher apparently misled her audience when she
claimed that "the copyright interest in these two works is held by
a board of gentlemen appointed for the purpose." Her original
contract with Harper & Brothers, still preserved by Harper & Row,
gave Catharine full control of the profits and did not mention a
"board of gentlemen." Catharine's contract gave her 50 percent of
the net profits, so she was correct in representing to her audience
the fact that only half the price went to the publisher. But when
she said that "Half the profits (after paying a moderate compensation to the author for the time and labour of preparing them, the
amount to be decided by the above gentlemen) will be devoted to
this object," she misrepresented the flow of power and profit between
herself and the "gentlemen." For neither Stowe nor any of the
other named Cincinnati clergymen would have been capable of
questioning Catharine's use of the money that came to her from
Harpers. Catharine had a reputation in her family of being "clever"
to deal with financially, and it was extremely unlikely that Calvin
Stowe would have crossed swords with his sister-in-law on financial
issues. Later, when a salaried agent was found for the organization,

he received his funds from the money he himself raised, not from the profits of Catharine's books.

Catharine's tactics in presenting herself and her cause to the public made her an enormously successful publicist. She sent circulars signed by Calvin Stowe to county newspapers and small-town clergymen throughout the East and West, asking for the names of women who might be willing to serve as missionary teachers and for the names of towns and villages where such teachers would be welcomed. The Catholic analogy and the ideology of self-denial made her efforts newsworthy, and to make the work of county editors easier she dispatched articles, such as the one entitled "Education at the West — Sisters of Charity," for newspapers to print alongside Stowe's circular.[17] The primary targets for Catharine's fund-raising efforts were the local groups of church women she organized in every city and town she visited.[18] She asked each group to make at least a hundred-dollar donation, this being the amount necessary to train and locate one teacher.

Catharine's efforts gained the endorsement of the most prominent American educators. Horace Mann, Henry Barnard, Thomas Burrowes, Samuel Lewis, and Gorham Abbot lent their support, and with each new endorsement by a national figure, Catharine's local fund-raising became more successful.[19] Catharine's tactic in each city was to plead her cause with the town's most eminent personage and, having gained his or her endorsement, to use it to build a substantial and active local committee. In this way she even drew into her cause those who traditionally opposed evangelical projects and especially opposed the Beecher family.

For example, Catharine Sedgwick, as a member of Brahmin Society and a Unitarian in Boston, believed (correctly) that she and Catharine Beecher stood on opposite sides of political, social, and religious issues. She was initially not sympathetic to Catharine's plan, seeing it as merely the most recent evangelical scheme of the Beecher family. Yet when Catharine asked Catharine Sedgwick in the name of Horace Mann to join her cause, Miss Sedgwick found it difficult to withhold her aid. Perplexed, Catharine Sedgwick wrote to Horace Mann: "I found a letter awaiting me here from Miss

Beecher requesting me to act as one of a Committee with Mrs. Mann to advance her (Miss B's) philanthropic project for saving the country." There were "obvious difficulties attending acting in concert with Miss B." and becoming one of her "collaborateurs," Catharine Sedgwick continued, but on the other hand, she said, "[I do] not feel at liberty to decline rendering any service in my power in so great a cause," especially since Horace Mann endorsed it. "To relieve my perplexity I throw myself on your dictation," Miss Sedgwick concluded, and at Mann's advice she agreed to add her name to the growing list of luminaries that Catharine had collected for her cause.[20]

By the spring of 1846 Catharine had delivered her addresses in most of the major cities of the East. Everywhere she called upon women to "save" their country from ignorance and immorality, and everywhere women responded. In Boston the Ladies Society for Promoting Education at the West donated several thousand dollars over the course of the decade to Catharine Beecher and her cause, and in other cities similar groups of women were organized by her into active proponents of her ideas on women and education. She corresponded with these groups constantly, relating her recent advances in other cities and exhorting her followers on to greater efforts. In a typical five-week period early in 1846 Catharine spoke in Pittsburgh, Baltimore, Washington, D.C., Philadelphia, New York City, Troy, Albany, and Hartford. She retraced her steps often, sometimes staying only one night in a place — long enough to deliver a public speech, encourage her old supporters, and welcome new ones. She traveled like a candidate for political office, moving quickly from one city to another, thereby promoting a large amount of newspaper coverage of her arrivals and departures.[21]

By the summer of 1846 Catharine's fund-raising efforts had proved that her cause could provide the salary of a full-time agent, and Calvin Stowe, extremely eager to be relieved of his duties in behalf of his sister-in-law, helped her search for a suitable substitute. They found their man in the governor of Vermont, William Slade, who, after considerable pressure from Stowe and encouragement from Horace Mann, accepted the position in July 1846. When his term expired in October, he was to go to Cincinnati as the Secretary and General Agent of the Central Committee for Promoting National Education. His main duties were to travel in the West, find locations for teachers, organize committees to support them there, and aid Catharine's publicizing efforts in the East.[22]

In August 1846 Catharine returned to Cincinnati for the first period of complete relaxation she had known since she began her campaign in the winter of 1843. Her journal, marked every day with correspondence, travel plans, and public meetings for two and a half years, was blank for a whole month. With Slade's acceptance Catharine's career had reached another turning point, but its implications were not yet clear in the summer of 1846. In October she returned East to conduct a series of public meetings with Slade. Together they rallied their forces in Hartford, New Haven, Albany, New York, and Boston. Early in 1847 while Slade went on to Cincinnati, Catharine stayed behind to organize the first groups of missionary teachers.[23]

In Albany in the spring of 1847 and in Hartford in the fall Catharine collected two groups of thirty-five young women for one month's training before they were sent to locations Slade had found for them in the West. The local women's committees provided room and board for Catharine and her young women. Catharine lectured the prospective teachers on how to meet all the difficulties that were to face them in the West: how to overcome the lack of books and proper schoolrooms; how to train children to good moral habits "when all domestic and social influences tend to weaken such habits"; how to impart spiritual training "without giving occasion for sectarian jealousy and alarm"; and how to preserve their health "from the risks of climate and the dangers of overexertion and excessive care." Catharine also lectured on the ways in which they could influence the community outside the schoolroom. They learned how to teach "the laws of health by the aid of simple drawings on the blackboard so that the children could copy them on slates to take home and explain to their parents," and how to teach certain branches of "domestic economy" so that parents would "be willing to adopt these improvements." Most of all they learned how to be moral examples that the rest of the community could imitate.[24]

Most of the seventy young women were New Englanders; only three came from New York and one from Pennsylvania. More than half of them went to Illinois and Indiana, seven crossed the Mississippi into Iowa, and a few went to Wisconsin, Michigan, Kentucky, and Tennessee. Each of them was expected to act as "a new source of moral power" in her community, and the reports they made at the end of the year revealed how seriously they took this charge. "The Lord has seen fit to crown my feeble efforts with unexpected success. There have been a series of evening meetings here and ten of my scholars are rejoicing in their Savior," reported one of the most successful young women. Twenty-three of the group also reported modest successes in instituting Sunday schools, instructing even their most rebellious students in religion and the Bible, and leading community prayer meetings. Most of them lived in primitive surroundings and faced daily obstacles, not the least of which was local hostility to religion in public schools. Several teachers said they circumvented this objection by agreeing not to begin the school day with prayer and by teaching moral precepts rather than religious beliefs. All of the teachers were obliged to repay the hundred dollars "lent" to them by the organization, and although few were able to do so in full, most of them returned some part of their very small salaries to William Slade or Catharine Beecher.[25]

The letters Catharine received from these teachers testified to the effectiveness of her training and to the tenacity of purpose she instilled. One woman went West to join a constituency that had migrated from North Carolina, Tennessee, and Germany and was met with a log cabin classroom holding forty-five pupils ranging in age from six to eighteen, and a community of hostile parents. "They seem desirous to have their children educated, but they differed so much about almost every thing, that they could not build a schoolhouse," she wrote Catharine.

> I was told, when I came, that they would not pay a teacher for more than three months in a year. At first, they were very suspicious, and watched me narrowly; but, through the blessing of my heavenly Father, I have gained their good will and confidence, so that they have provided me a good frame schoolhouse, with writing-desks and a blackboard, and they promise to support me all the year around.

Having proved herself in their eyes, she succeeded next in drawing both parents and children to a Sunday school. Then, because the nearest church was seven miles away and the people did not go to it, she persuaded them "to invite the nearest clergyman to preach" in her schoolhouse the next Sunday. This New England woman, though unused to frontier conditions, decided to stay on in the place even though she had to board "where there are eight children and the parents and only two rooms in the house," and she went without simple amenities such as candles and a place to bathe.[26]

Most of Catharine's correspondents dwelled on the memory of "those seasons of social communion and prayer at Hartford" preparatory to their departure. These memories returned, they said, "like balm to the spirit when oppressed with care." [27] The real privations and disappointments experienced by these women did not lessen their loyalty to Catharine and her cause. Their human commitment was as important in effecting her goals as was the financial support of the eastern public.

Developments shaping the teaching profession at this precise moment made the field especially receptive to Catharine Beecher's view that it properly belonged to women. Although female teachers began to replace men in some eastern states in the 1830s, the utility of that shift was not apparent to most state and local boards of education until 1840. What had begun as an improvised economy measure had by then proved to be a pedagogic as well as a fiscal improvement, and as these obvious benefits were discovered by state and local boards of education from 1840 to 1880, women gradually replaced their male predecessors in the teaching profession. By 1888 63 percent of American teachers were women, and in cities women constituted 90 percent of the teaching force.[28]

Although it is impossible to measure completely Catharine Beecher's impact on the profession, her publicizing in behalf of women did at least facilitate an otherwise confused transition period in the nation's schools. For the traditionally higher value attached to male labor blinded many communities to the advantages of female teachers, and as late as 1850 the state of Indiana viewed the female teacher as the exception rather than the rule.[29] The West was, on the whole, slower to employ women as teachers, perhaps because it attracted ample numbers of ambitious men who, typically, would teach for a brief period or even a few years before locating more lucrative commercial employment.[30] These male teachers were usually paid twice as much as female teachers, and a male teacher frequently brought fewer pedagogic talents to the job than a woman. In

New York, one of the earliest states to shift to women teachers, the state board of regents in 1838 still assumed that teachers should be male, and they failed to approve the governor's request that normal schools be attached to female academies because they concluded that men, rather than women, needed the normal training.[31] Therefore it was far from obvious to the American public that teaching was a woman's profession.

On the other hand the shift to women teachers was well enough along by 1843 to provide a solid factual basis for Catharine Beecher's claims on their behalf. In Massachusetts, the first state to promote the employment of women as teachers, women outnumbered men three to two in 1837 and two to one in 1842.[32] Many school districts had since the 1820s routinely employed women to teach the summer session, although they believed men were needed to "manage" the older boys present at the winter school session. Some New York districts learned in the 1820s that they could, with the state subsidy of half a teacher's salary, employ a woman to teach full-time and thus not have to bear any of the cost themselves.[33] As a leading educator pointed out later in the century, "the effective reason" women were employed in schools was that they were "cheaper than men." If they had not been cheaper, "they would not have replaced nine-tenths of the men in American public schools." [34]

The need for such educational economies became more critical in the 1830s and 1840s, when immigration and internal migration increased the population of many areas, but did not immediately increase the tax base. By reducing the school costs by hiring women, a district could accommodate its larger numbers of children without taxing itself at a higher rate.[35]

Three basic assumptions were used to justify these lower salaries for women: women, unlike men, did not have to support a family; women were only working temporarily until they married; and the free workings of the economic marketplace determined cheaper salaries for women. Women do not "expect to accumulate much property by this occupation; if it affords them a respectable support and a situation where they can be useful, it is as much as they demand," wrote the state superintendent of Ohio in 1839. He therefore urged "those counties who are in the habit of paying men for instructing little children" to hire women since "females would do it for less than half the sum and generally much better than men can." [36]

Catharine chose to exploit the short-term gains that these discriminatory practices brought to women, and her publicity on behalf of female teachers emphasized their willingness to work for less money. "To make education universal, it must be moderate in expense," Catharine wrote in a petition to Congress in 1853 for free normal schools for female teachers, "and women can afford to teach for one-half, or even less, the salary which men would ask, because the female teacher has only to sustain herself; she does not look forward to the duty of supporting a family, should she marry; nor has she the ambition to amass a fortune." Catharine also insisted that women's employment as teachers would not create a "celibate class" of women, but that their employment was only temporary, and would in fact prepare them to be better wives and mothers. By defining teaching as an extension of the duties of the home, Catharine presented her idea in a form most likely to gain widespread public support. "It is ordained by infinite wisdom, that, as in the family, so in the social state, the interests of young children and of women are one and the same," Catharine insisted.[37]

Since the profession had lower pay and status than most men qualified to teach could get elsewhere, since the economics of education called for even lower pay in the 1830s and 1840s, and since the schoolroom could be seen as functionally akin to the home, both public sentiment and economic facts supported Catharine Beecher's efforts to redefine the gender of the American teacher.

※※

In 1847 Catharine Beecher saw her work of the last four years coming to fruition. The organization that she founded and Slade led would, in the course of the decade ahead, send four hundred and fifty teachers to the West.[38] Yet Catharine became almost immediately dissatisfied with the organization, and in 1848 she broke with Slade and began to form a new one. Slade's leadership had rendered Catharine's public efforts superfluous. There was no longer any need for her to write public speeches or address large gatherings. The organization was successfully formed, and all Catharine had to do was to receive the funds sent her by local committees and to arrange for a brief training period for the groups of young women. There was no lack of funds, women, or locations for them, and Catharine was reduced to the role of a secretary who saw that these connections were smoothly made. After her dramatic public role Catharine was not content to play this secondary one.

From the beginning of his tenure as general agent of the Central Committee for Promoting National Education, William Slade demonstrated his intention to remain independent of Catharine's control. When he arrived in Cincinnati early in 1847 he discovered that the city was not sympathetic to his or Catharine's efforts and that Catharine had misled him by claiming strong local support. Although she had organized a group of Cincinnati clergymen under Stowe's leadership, this was merely a paper unit, and the men who held real power in the city had already told Catharine that they opposed her plan to locate her agent in Cincinnati. Nathaniel Wright tried to warn her against such a step and said that in his opinion a paid agent of a benevolent organization developed "a sort of monomania not perceptible to his friends who participate in his enthusiasm, but apparent to the world at large." [39] Finding that "the world at large" in Cincinnati did not welcome him, Slade left the city after three months and settled in Cleveland, where he dropped Catharine's title of Central Committee and renamed the organization The National Board of Popular Education. Under Slade's leadership it flourished for five years but began to fade in the mid-1850s. Slade's move to Cleveland revealed to Catharine that he was a man who would exercise real rather than nominal leadership and, unlike Stowe, would not allow her to maintain control of the organization. In the summer of 1847 Catharine had to decide whether to follow Slade's leadership or to strike out on a new course of action.

She retired to a health retreat in Vermont, where she nursed her psychic as well as her physical ailments. There she cultivated the friendship of a woman upon whom she could rely as a secretary — Catharine's original idea of Slade's role — but who would not think of challenging Catharine's authority. There she also focused her attention on Delia Bacon, a former pupil who was at that time burdened with personal sorrow. Catharine wove her fate and Delia's together from 1847 to 1850 while she broke with Slade and entered a new period of personal crisis. This relationship was almost an act of symbolic self-annihilation out of which Catharine once again harbored the hope of creating a new life.

❧ 13 ❧

An Outgoing of Heart, 1847–1850

During her last three years of public activity Catharine had periodically retreated to Brattleboro, a fashionable health resort in Vermont. She patronized an establishment there that put its patients through a program of baths designed to alleviate any and all kinds of nervous and physical disabilities. In the summer of 1845 Harriet Beecher Stowe had joined Catharine at Brattleboro, and she remained seven months longer attempting to restore her health while her children and Calvin Stowe managed as best they could in Walnut Hills. Brattleboro was not entirely a woman's world, but it was a world apart where women were freed of the demands otherwise made upon them by their family or society. It was the closest American equivalent to the European spa, where one's mental or physical ailments were assets rather than liabilities, where symptoms were closely watched by sympathetic nurses, and where one was encouraged to think mainly about one's self rather than one's duties to others. For Catharine Beecher it was an oasis of self-interest in the world of self-denial she had created for herself in her public writings and public personality. There, where illness justified self-indulgence, Catharine spent at least two months out of every year from 1843 through the 1850s.[1]

Since the time of her nervous collapse in Hartford in 1829, when she "could neither read, write, or converse, nor even bear to hear conversation," Catharine had periodically suffered from nervous prostration. During the 1830s and 1840s her "nervous excitability" centered "in one limb" — usually a foot. Knowing that the origin of her foot "paralysis" was "nervous" or psychological, Catharine had in the 1840s sought the "remedial agency" of hypnosis. In Boston in 1845 she underwent a series of mesmerizings — an early and primitive form of psychoanalysis that was then much in vogue. Within a period of ten days she was hypnotized eight times. This experience, Catharine said, "brought out new and yet consistent combinations of the materials [of] my past experience." During the winter of 1845

Catharine also visited a clairvoyant in New York, through whom she attempted to reach the spirits of "departed friends." In the mid-1840s she was struggling to sort out the meaning of her "past experience" and thereby free herself of her current nervous distress. Yet mesmerizing failed to cure her, for she recorded in her journal a week later that her "trouble" still disturbed her sleep.[2]

After "psychology" had failed to cure her, Catharine turned to the water cure and, with renewed vigor, tried to purge her "trouble of the nerves." She later described her treatment at Brattleboro:

> At four in the morning packed in a wet sheet; kept in it from two to three hours; then up, and in a reeking perspiration immersed in the coldest plunge-bath. Then a walk as far as strength would allow, and drink five or six tumblers of the coldest water. At eleven A.M. stand under a douche of the coldest water falling *eighteen feet, for ten minutes.* Then walk, and drink three or four tumblers of water. At three P.M. sit half an hour in a *sitz*-bath (i.e. sitting bath) of the coldest water. Then walk and drink again. At nine P.M. sit half an hour with the feet in the coldest water, then rub them till warm. Then cover the weak limb and a third of the body in wet bandages and *retire to rest.* This same wet bandage to be worn all day, and kept constantly wet.[3]

Catharine enjoyed the treatment for its own sake, but her nervous condition remained the same.

Catharine's spirit was a troubled one during the 1840s. Her life was a pattern of incessant, almost frenzied activity, broken by occasional seasons at Brattleboro, where she collapsed as soon as she arrived. Early in 1847 she closed the journal she had kept for four years with a poem that was full of self-pity and described her own psychological distress during these years:

> Oh deem not they are blest alone
> Whose lives a peaceful tenor keep,
> For God, who pities man has shown
> A blessing for the eyes that weep.
>
> The light of joy again shall fill
> The eyes that overflow with tears.
> And weary hours of woe and pain
> *Are promises of brighter years.*
>
> For God hath marked each sorrowing day,
> And numbered every bitter tear

> And Heaven's long years of bliss shall pay
> For all his children suffer here.[4]

It seems incongruous that at the height of her public success Catharine should have become increasingly conscious of her personal problems. Yet both her private retreats to Brattleboro and her public activities elsewhere may have sprung from the same source — her desire to transcend the life she was living and create a different one. Her poem stated this desire in religious terms, but Catharine had since 1822 dedicated herself to creating a purely worldly life for herself. Her father believed and her own actions proved that worldly activities were essential to her happiness. Yet as soon as the dimensions of her success were clear, Catharine turned away from it, perhaps revealing her inability to carry any project through to its finish, perhaps expressing her disappointment at discovering that this too had failed to fulfill her life or embody her desires.

Although she was approaching the age of fifty, Catharine Beecher had not been able fully to transcend the complex of personal problems that had taken form in the 1820s. She had tried to turn Fisher's death into a "blessing" and see it as an event that opened new alternatives and opportunities for her. Yet this expanded spectrum of choices seems to have created more confusion than clarity in Catharine Beecher's life. By 1847 her life was a bundle of contradictions. She was an expert on domestic economy, but had no home of her own; she was a writer on the moral education of children, but had no children herself; she was a competent religious writer, but had never experienced conversion; and she urged young women to become teachers, but was herself not willing to teach. The only consistent element in Catharine's life was her role as a publicist of self-sacrifice since she believed that her personal life was one of self-denial and self-sacrifice.

At Brattleboro that summer, concentrating on her personal problems, Catharine drew to her two women who in various ways mirrowed or objectified her own frustrations. She invited Delia Bacon, the younger sister of a leading Connecticut clergyman who herself had just experienced a disastrous end to a love affair, to join her there and subsequently to speak to her prospective teachers in Albany. Catharine also invited Nancy Johnson, a lively young woman whose life circumstances had drawn her into teaching, to stay with her at Brattleboro at Catharine's expense. Catharine fastened a claim to the friendship of both these women, and through them she expressed the psychological tensions that had been forming inside her at least since she left Cincinnati in 1843 and possibly since she had entered teaching in 1822. Through Delia Bacon she expressed her resentments and hostilities. Through Nancy Johnson she expressed her desire for a new life.

Catharine was involved simultaneously with these women from 1847 to 1849. Although her relationship with Delia continued until 1850 (a year after her friendship with Nancy ended), the totality of her experience at the end of the 1840s is best understood by first analyzing the events connected with Delia, and then resuming a chronological account of Catharine's life with Nancy from 1847.

The parallels between Catharine Beecher and Delia Bacon were remarkable and numerous. Both were related to prominent Connecticut clergymen and experienced a dramatic reversal of their plans for marriage. Both made their living in intellectual pursuits, both had strong personalities, and both were vulnerable to ridicule. Each of them in different ways felt the harsh force of the Congregational church as a sequel to an interrupted courtship.

Delia Bacon had been one of Catharine's outstanding pupils in Hartford in the 1820s, and she had since launched a successful career as a writer of historical fiction and a popular lecturer on Shakespeare and other literary topics. She had conducted classes in New York, Boston, New Haven, and Hartford, subscribed to by women of all ages, but particularly by young women, married or unmarried, who had the leisure to engage in such activities after their formal schooling had ended. Like Margaret Fuller, Delia Bacon's exuberant and slightly unorthodox behavior had earned her the title of "The American Corinne." From 1845 to 1847 she had engaged in a prolonged flirtation with a wealthy young minister nearly ten years her junior, Alexander MacWhorter. He had been recently ordained after studying at Yale with Nathaniel William Taylor.[5]

In 1846 Catharine Beecher had observed the friendship between Delia Bacon and Alexander MacWhorter and asked a friend of MacWhorter's whether this meant they were engaged. His friend scoffed at the idea that MacWhorter would marry a woman of Delia's age and character. Catharine's subsequent inquiries set off a chain of events that led to MacWhorter's public statement denouncing Delia for initiating their relationship and shamelessly pursuing him. Delia then tried to defend herself by proving that he had proposed to her. Two of the most powerful clergymen in Connecticut — Nathaniel Taylor, who took MacWhorter's side, and Leonard Bacon, who defended his sister — were soon arrayed against each other in a case of honor in which the Bacon family decided that Delia's name could be cleared only by a clerical trial of MacWhorter. Her career would be ruined, they believed, if MacWhorter's charges were not disproved. Yet Taylor was determined to prevent the case from coming to trial.[6]

Disaster hung like a cloud over Delia Bacon in the spring and summer of 1847, and Catharine Beecher was very strongly attracted by it. In April she visited Taylor to learn more of the case. Nathaniel Taylor was one of her father's closest friends and the only man besides Lyman and Joel Hawes who had spoken with her at length during her personal and religious crisis of 1822. While she was writing her *Elements of Mental and Moral Philosophy* Catharine had spent several weeks in the Taylor home. Just as Lyman considered Taylor a brother, so Catharine viewed him as a second father. While visiting Taylor in 1847 the parallels between her own and Delia's experience became strikingly clear to Catharine. She wrote Leonard Bacon:

> It was one of the most painful interviews of [my] whole life. It seemed as if the whole being, of a . . . surpassing intellect, of iron will, and of impetuous feeling, of ripened skill and acuteness, and of almost unbounded power of influence over other minds, was now firmly grappled in a struggle to overthrow those principles of truth and justice that are the pillars of human society.[7]

Taylor and the power of the church were pressing Delia to drop her charges against MacWhorter just as Lyman Beecher had pressed Catharine with the doctrine of the church to abandon her claims to worldly happiness. Catharine's description of Taylor's iron will, ripened skill, and power over other minds could have been an exact description of Lyman Beecher in 1822. After this interview with Taylor Catharine was never far from Delia's side. She immediately invited Delia to spend the month of May with her in Albany, and together they received the news from Leonard Bacon that the New Haven West Association had passed his motion to bring MacWhorter to trial on the charges of calumny, falsehood, and disgraceful conduct.

Catharine's interview with Taylor marked an important turning point in her life. Taylor represented the religious and cultural heritage that she had alternately denounced and supported but had never transcended. For a quarter of a century she had tried to find her place within and define her relationship to this heritage. Her ambivalent attitude toward it was closely bound up with her ambivalent attitude toward her father. For this heritage and for her father, Catharine came to believe, she had renounced her claim to personal happiness and had taken up a life of public service. Catharine now felt the burden of society's refusal to permit a woman to combine a career with personal happiness. Catharine did not resent choosing a career, but she was angered by the need to abstain from private happiness. Men like Taylor were not forced to make such a choice, but women like herself and Delia Bacon were. By 1847 it was too late to reconstruct an alternative set of life choices, but it was not too late to gain revenge. Through Delia Bacon she launched a bitter attack upon Taylor and the church, and in Delia Bacon she re-created and dramatized her own personal sacrifice.

Catharine remained close to Delia before the trial began and prepared her for it as if she were preparing her for a ritual of martyrdom. They entered the courtroom together. "Her friends," Catharine later wrote, "prepared her for the sacrifice and attended her to it, with some such feelings as those of old might have experienced when they accompanied their martyr friends to their 'tortures strange and fiery wheels.' " For more than two weeks of eight-hour sittings Catharine attended the trial, spoke frequently as a witness, and recorded all the proceedings in a notebook. The experience was excruciating for Delia Bacon, since she sought not martyrdom but only the restoration of her reputation. When the committee of clergymen who heard the case finally judged MacWhorter "imprudent," but not guilty of the charges brought against him, Catharine reacted as if she were reliving her own crisis of 1822. "This decision, adopted by men who from early life had been regarded as the central agency of a great and powerful system of influences, came like desolation," she said. "During the sleepless night that followed, the waking visions that haunted the hours of rest seemed like some of these troubled dreams of the sick bed, when the sun seems moving from his centre, and all the heavenly bodies are rushing from their courses in confusion and dismay." [8]

Although Catharine was engaged in other activities with Nancy

Johnson during the next year, she returned to Delia's case in 1849 and wrote a book based on her notes of the trial. By publishing it Catherine completed Delia Bacon's martyrdom. The book, *Truth Stranger than Fiction: A Narrative of Recent Transactions Involving Inquiries in Regard to the Principles of Honor, Truth and Justice Which Obtain in a Distinguished American University*, attacked Yale, Nathaniel Taylor, and the whole institutional structure of the Congregational church. The story Catharine revealed was indeed one of sordid clerical behavior: MacWhorter was a fop and a cad who was protected by those, like Taylor, who believed that the clergy should be above public remonstrance. Delia Bacon was a member of Joel Hawes's congregation and had gone to him for spiritual aid in her distress and told him the history of her romance with MacWhorter. Hawes, learning things that could help Mac-Whorter's and Taylor's side, had passed on the information to Taylor, who then called Hawes to testify in MacWhorter's defense at the trial. Hawes had then refused to be cross-examined by Leonard Bacon. Mrs. Taylor had developed a strong liking for MacWhorter and an antipathy for Delia, and she was behind a whisper campaign among the wives of Connecticut clergymen to smear Delia's reputation and bias the judges against her.[9]

Catharine's book revealed all this and more, but it was mainly a paean to Delia's sacrifice on the altar of the Congregational church. Catharine had never succeeded as a writer of fiction, but here in this true story with which she so closely identified, she believed she had material for a tale that would rival anything her sister had written. Delia was shocked to learn that Catharine intended to revive the episode, and after reading the manuscript she implored Catharine not to publish it. "I am tired of being 'a victim!' " she told Catharine. "I do not wish to be 'a heroine.' " The strain of her unhappy romance and its ensuing trial had already cost Delia her peace of mind, and she and her friends and family had begun to fear for her sanity. In 1849 she urged Catharine to realize that the publication of this book might cost her her life. "I cannot purchase anything but heaven at this cost," Delia said. "So you see beforehand some of the fiery garlands and sacrificial ornaments of this new kind of martyrdom to which, without my own consent, you wish to dedicate me." [10]

Lyman Beecher was appalled by Catharine's attack on Taylor, and he and her brothers did all they could to gain possession of the manuscript and destroy it. "My various brothers [were] in full pursuit, some of them fancying an insane hospital my only proper residence," Catharine said, but her family's hostility only fortified Catharine's will. For she saw it as another reason why she, as one who was persecuted and misused, should take up Delia's cause. "The blame and outcry of those who would still 'hush up' this monstrous outrage," Catharine wrote, "will all be turned on me. Let it come. I cannot suffer in a better cause." If Delia was reluctant to be the sacrificial heroine, Catharine was not. "The Almighty hand which has erased this purpose from your mind, has written it, as with living fire, upon mine," she wrote Delia, "and if all the human voices on this vast globe should come up in one roar of rebuke and defiance, it would not move me." She said that forces she did not fully understand were leading her on:

> A hand that I could not relinquish has led me on, a voice that I would not disobey had bade me go forward. I do assure you that if an angel with a drawn sword had barred my advance in any other path, and if, as of old, His majestic voice had commanded "thus saith the Lord, write all these words in a book," my mind would have been no more strongly bound, than it now is, to the fulfillment of this undertaking.[11]

Catharine was determined to complete Delia's martyrdom. Her own and Delia's suffering had merged into one, and, Catharine believed, "[my] destiny is now united with hers."

The force of Catharine's conviction finally overcame Delia's power to resist, and in 1849 she accepted Catharine's invitation to spend a month as her guest at the Round Hill Water Cure in Northampton, Massachusetts, the health resort to which Catharine had recently shifted her patronage. They shared a room and both underwent the treatment of baths, packing, and showers.[12]

Truth Stranger than Fiction was published at Catharine's expense in 1850. In her preface she appealed to the public and all right-thinking clergymen to vindicate Delia's honor and to condemn the clerical elite to whose interests she had been sacrificed. Catharine sent copies of the book to each of the Congregational associations of New England and to several leading religious and intellectual journals. She wrote a letter to all the ladies' committees that supported her educational activities, urging them to buy the book, speak to their clergymen, and write to newspapers about it.[13]

Catharine's public and personal experience had become so inter-mingled that she could not distinguish between them. She inserted in the book a note publicizing her recent educational activities and used the book to enhance her "moral" stature within her con-stituency. As a postscript she claimed that Delia was about to join her educational efforts, and that the book had been a necessary step toward clearing Delia's name before she joined Catharine's organization.

Catharine had become an expert publicist, and she managed to get the book reviewed in the *New York Tribune,* the *North Ameri-can Review,* and *The Literary World.* Horace Greeley called Cath-arine's publication of the book "a deed of noble self-sacrifice and moral heroism," but the other two journals were less sympathetic and said that they only condescended to review the book at the urging of the author. Although Catharine may have hoped for wide critical acclaim, she did not receive it, and with Delia's de-parture to England, the case fell from public view.[14] As soon as Catharine's book was published Delia escaped to England, where she devoted seven years of fruitful scholarship to her theory that Sir Francis Bacon had written Shakespeare's plays. Yet her mental distress steadily grew, and in 1858 her family brought her back to America and placed her in an insane asylum, where she died the next year.[15]

Through Delia Bacon Catharine had tried to resolve her rela-tionship with her Connecticut heritage. She henceforth openly op-posed her father's Calvinist religion and the social matrix that supported it. Two books written by her in the 1850s called upon Americans to disavow the beliefs and the leadership that dominated their religious life and adopt her own precepts of social morality. Henceforth her educational projects were devoted not to imposing the authority of a missionary elite upon ignorant masses, but to aiding those groups — particularly women — who already embodied her notions of social virtue.

Catharine Beecher's life crisis at midcentury arose from uniquely personal factors, yet in three important ways it also embodied and exemplified tensions experienced by many other women of the period. In her readiness to take offense at what she perceived as a loss of female status, in her attack on male cultural prerogatives, and in her failure to develop substantial ego strengths she may have expressed more antagonism and revealed more internal weaknesses than most of her female contemporaries, yet because of its archetypal qualities her outburst can do much to illuminate the shadowy and shifting contours of nineteenth-century female experience.

Although Catharine flamboyantly overreacted to Delia's potential loss of status in the MacWhorter affair, she may also have been responding to deeper currents of female status loss in nineteenth-century culture. Gerda Lerner has analyzed the 1840s as a decade during which American women became aware of their relative loss in political and economic status compared to men. Although in absolute terms women's political activities steadily increased during the first five decades of the nineteenth century, in relative terms the gap between men and women widened tremendously as the franchise was extended to greater and greater numbers of white males, including larger groups of recent immigrants.[16] Catharine Beecher was then one of a large class of educated and active American women who felt this relative loss of political status. Although she opposed Elizabeth Cady Stanton's agitation for equal political rights, she clearly resented and tried to overcome (in a way that would have been quite uncharacteristic of her mother's generation) the gap that separated her from political power within the Evangelical structure of authority. This was the political arena she knew best, and her exclusion from it was surely made more bitter by the raised expectations she brought to it by virtue of being as well versed in its nuances as most male contemporaries.

Much of Catharine Beecher's lifework can be seen as a bridge across the growing gap that separated the rising expectations of early nineteenth-century women from the social, political, and economic realities of their culture. In many ways her ideology of domesticity was an effort to overcome the relative deterioration in the status of women that occurred when economic production was transferred from the household to the factory. Until the effects of industrialization on the status of women have been more fully explored, Alice Clark's conclusion still stands: the small gains made in factory employment opportunities did not compensate for the high status losses incurred by the shift away from the household as the basic unit of economic production.[17] Women had played a large and obvious role there and recent scholarship demonstrates that society esteemed this contribution and rewarded it by granting women more sense of personal autonomy in the eighteenth century than they experienced in the nineteenth.[18] The dependency roles to which women were increasingly reduced in the nineteenth century had a direct and deleterious effect on their own sense of self. Although men too suffered potential status loss in this transition, which removed them from the means of production, for women the displacement was more complete. For they were treated as marginal members of the industrial work force and were gradually perceived as separated not only from the means of production, but from economic activity itself. An ideology of self-sacrifice could mask some of the losses women felt about their status in the first half of the nineteenth century, but it supplied inadequate nourishment for their crippled sense of self-esteem.

Along with an absolute loss of economic status, and a relative loss of political status, women also experienced an absolute loss of personal autonomy during the middle decades of the nineteenth century. Recent scholarship by Daniel Smith has measured the extent to which the personal identities of women were attached to the family into which they were born in the eighteenth century but were cut off from that root in the nineteenth century and more completely appended to their husbands.[19] The necessity for maintaining the dependent status of women grew more apparent as women during this period explored possible avenues of escape from it. In the minds of many, dependency was the natural state of womanhood and to throw off these ties was to commit an antisocial and unnatural act. Such charges were leveled against Angelina and Sarah Grimké by the Massachusetts Congregational Clergy in 1838 when that group insisted that men should actively oppose any woman who thinks male "care and protection of her seem unnecessary. . . ." [20]

The struggle to achieve autonomy was often misperceived as an attack on male prerogatives, but sometimes it was exactly that. Catharine Beecher's assault on Nathaniel Taylor was more atypical in its intensity than in its motivational origins. In addition to the more overt movement for women's rights and the subtle subversion of male authority contained in female literature, small groups of otherwise anonymous mid-nineteenth-century women could and did openly challenge male hegemony though the risk of social censure was high and costly.[21] Catharine Beecher was not the only woman who paid homage to the cult of "true womanhood" but regularly broke out of its constraints.

In addition to the external pressures of social disapproval, the internal psychic resources of mid-nineteenth-century women inhibited their assertion of autonomous selfhood. As Carroll Smith Rosenberg has suggested, the rigid dependency roles for women during this period enclosed them in a circle of paralyzed potentiality. The psychic breakdown of many women can thus be directly attributed to their inability to develop substantial ego strength.[22] Catharine Beecher's lapse into near hysteria in the late 1840s reflected the difficulty she had in maintaining her psychic equilibrium during her challenge to Taylor's authority. When faced with personal or vicarious (as in the case of Delia Bacon) reversal, she had little ego strength on which to draw. She grew increasingly disoriented and all but abandoned the effort to integrate her internal world with that of her surroundings. Hysteria was in this sense a form of dysfunctional resistance to her social roles of dependency and submission. Yet her case and Delia's indicate that the strains and costs of self-assertion and of overt opposition to male authority were often more than an ego unpracticed in autonomy could accommodate.

Catharine's life during these years was not given completely to hostility and renunciation. A countercurrent of affirmation had begun to form during the summer in which Catharine shared Delia's sacrifice at the New Haven trial. The summer of 1847 she had also cultivated the friendship of Nancy Johnson, and in the following year in Nancy's company she struck out on a new path that was to carry her through the 1850s. Female friendship was the nineteenth-century antidote to the wounds inflicted by the inequities of gender.

Nancy Johnson was a young woman from Vermont who had been recommended to Catharine by Governor Slade as someone who could aid her with secretarial details during the two months before the Albany training session. Nancy had worn an artificial foot since her childhood, and she and her family believed that her handicap precluded any other life but teaching. She was a remarkably spirited person, however, and her love of adventure later led her into quite a different career. In the 1850s and 1860s she lived among and wrote about the Iroquois, and as "Minnie Myrtle" she became a popular free-lance European correspondent for American newspapers.[23] Catharine was immediately attracted by Nancy's vigor and enthusiasm, and Nancy was openly impressed by the power of Catharine's personality and the elegance that surrounded her at Brattleboro. The paths of the two women crossed just when they most needed each other.

Nancy Johnson described the scene at Brattleboro as one peopled by the "rich and accomplished" in an environment of "wealth and comfort." Catharine was one of the forty patients who were under the care of a team of doctors and private nurses and some "twenty German servants" who trotted about "loaded with tubs of water, pitchers of water, blankets, beds, etc." [24] In Nancy, Catharine had found a very companionable young woman whom she could easily impress. She quickly gained Nancy's indebtedness. Extremely solicitous for the care of Nancy's "lame" foot, Catharine urged her "to become a hydropathist" and to take the water cure at Catharine's expense. Whether she was moved by Catharine's interest in her or simply overpowered by Catharine's personality, Nancy found almost immediately that she was under more obligations to Catharine than she had initially expected. She was free of Catharine's influence for only a few months during the next two years.

Catharine spent the winter of 1847 at Henry Ward Beecher's new home in Brooklyn, where she began a book on the religious training of children.[25] Catharine's attitudes toward the topic were in flux, however, after her encounter with Taylor and Delia Bacon's trial, and the book was not published until several years later when she had thought through the implications of her break with the church. In February 1848 she put aside her manuscript and began to plot a new course of action.

Slade's independence and Taylor's enmity precipitated Catharine's plan for a spring trip to the far West, where she meant to challenge Slade's leadership and assert new cultural goals for her educational efforts. After deciding this, Catharine immediately wrote Nancy Johnson and urged her to come along on a tour of Philadelphia, Baltimore, and Washington, and then proceed on to Cincinnati.[26] Catharine did not disclose that she planned to travel much farther west than Cincinnati, but she held out the promise of an exciting trip and more of the elegant company to which she had introduced Nancy at Brattleboro. As Catharine's private secretary, Nancy assured her father, "I should see much of the world and be introduced to the very best society, religious and literary, that these cities offer." Since Catharine was also "an invalid" and therefore always required "good quarters," they would always stay in the best homes, Nancy said. "I always find," she concluded, "that to have been with her is enough to recommend me to the attention of all the great and good." [27]

The parallels between Nancy Johnson and Catharine were not as extensive as those between Delia Bacon and Catharine, but they were nevertheless striking. They were both teachers who came to the career by necessity rather than by choice, both had experienced an accident that circumscribed their opportunities to marry (for Nancy believed that her amputated foot had rendered her unmarriageable), and both were eager to escape the routine of teaching and the constraints of the lives they had been leading. Catharine made a great deal of Nancy's "crippled foot" and emphasized the fact that they were, each in her own way, invalids. Catharine was aware of the parallels between herself and Nancy, and through them she asserted her claim on Nancy's loyalty and tightened her hold on her friendship. She had converted Nancy to her own belief in the water cure, and Nancy believed that she owed her current good health to this treatment and Catharine's advice.

Nancy was flattered that such an eminent woman as Catharine Beecher should single her out for friendship. "To be her good friend is as high a compliment as could be paid me," Nancy wrote her father. "That she took a great fancy to me and is my true friend is certainly true. I love her too." [28] Late in February Catharine and Nancy met in Philadelphia, where Catharine revealed her plans for an extended western tour, her intention to break with Slade, and her hope to found women's colleges of a new kind in the West.

At Philadelphia and Baltimore Catharine read to the local women's committees the letters she had received from teachers sent out in 1847. Many of them were in need of immediate aid, but William Slade refused to accept any responsibility for their care beyond providing them with the means to reach their destination, Catharine said.[29] She insisted that Slade was remiss in his duty and called upon the women of Philadelphia and Baltimore to provide her with funds to travel west and care for the needs of stranded teachers. Her appeal was answered with several hundred dollars. Catharine claimed further that Slade was a narrow-minded Congregationalist who overemphasized the role of the church and ignored Catharine's efforts to include teachers of all varieties of religious belief. Catharine believed this of Slade because she wanted to, not because it was true.

This suited the picture she was beginning to form in her own mind of a man who resembled Lyman Beecher more than William Slade. She described Slade as a man who was hardened against the appeals of the women who looked to him for aid, and who against her will imposed the constraints of Congregational beliefs and attitudes upon the organization she had created. Like Taylor, Slade appeared to Catharine as another version of Lyman Beecher. He oppressed the women in his charge with his religious beliefs and he refused to respond adequately to the suffering he had created in the first place by placing the women wrongly. Around Slade Catharine created another situation in which she was forced by the hardness of a man to sacrifice her peace of mind and face a frightening future. Of her preparations for her western tour Catharine wrote:

> I had heard terrific accounts of the winter journey across the mountains — of frightful precipices, which there was no way of escaping but to put the stage horses on a full run over a glare of ice, down a curving and fearful descent! There was no other way than this now open. So I made my will, had my daguerreotype taken for father, and made all other proper arrangements, for a roll down the Alleghenies.[30]

Catharine had been away from her father and his Walnut Hills home for a year and a half when she returned there with Nancy Johnson in late February 1848. During her absence from Lyman, Catharine had expressed considerable hostility toward men who seemed to resemble him, but for Lyman himself she displayed only love and devotion. From Henry's home in Brooklyn she had written her father: "Your picture given to Henry stands on the mantle and every time I come in the room I feel an outgoing of heart." It was nevertheless impossible for her to live with Lyman in Walnut Hills. Sometime in the mid-1840s she had initiated a quarrel with Lyman's third wife that was so bitter and intense as to preclude any but the briefest visits to the Beecher home. Therefore Nancy

Johnson and Catharine stayed only one night in Walnut Hills and then moved into Samuel Foote's home, where they spent the remainder of their stay in Cincinnati.[31] Catharine had managed to keep her distance from her father and yet continue to profess her love for him. She had not resolved the complex emotions of love and hostility she felt for him, and she directed her animus more toward the tradition he represented than toward Lyman himself.

In this period, when Catharine was feeling the strains of the cultural and psychological bonds that tied her to her father and his evangelical tradition, her discomfort was eased by the companionship of Nancy Johnson. In her Catharine had found a kind of alter ego whose dedicated loyalty reassured Catharine of the correctness of the actions she was taking. Nancy Johnson resembled Catharine in many ways, but differed from her in one important respect — she was not deeply affected by the religious life of her native New England. In her company Catharine's desire to break out of that religious heritage was reinforced.

The exhilarated tone of Catharine's tour in the spring of 1848 showed how heartily she welcomed this escape from the evangelical activities that had engaged her in the past. She claimed that she went West to aid her missionary teachers, but in fact she was exploring sites upon which she could build a new female seminary and include a home for herself within it. Her enthusiasm and high spirits rose from her hopes for the future and her momentary release from the burden of her evangelical past. Her commitment for the present was primarily to her own happiness.

Catharine's tour of 1848 set the standard for her activities during the next several years. She was responsible to no one but herself. Her success in fund-raising financed the extensive traveling she enjoyed so much, and she alone controlled the use of whatever surplus money she raised.[32] Her eastern connections made her far more successful in fund-raising than the westerners who tried to finance seminaries for their daughters by selling bonds in the East. She was therefore received in the West as a powerful and important person. Wherever she traveled she stayed in the finest homes, and her income of nearly a thousand dollars a year provided her with the trappings of elegance to match the style of life in the homes where she stayed.

Catharine and Nancy Johnson were highly conscious that they were envied and censured by those who thought that "all the honors

as well as all the privileges of life belong to those who *marry*," and
this set the tone for their new life style. They were deliberately
proving that they had "no religion or philosophy that teaches the
doctrine" that if a woman does not marry "it is her duty to stay
forever at home, to find there all her means of pleasure and improvement." Far from being tours of duty and sacrifice, Catharine's travels
were gay and adventurous. "Miss Beecher is the most agreeable of
travelling companions — always in good spirits and full of humor
and life," Nancy Johnson wrote her father. "We are never *out of
talk,* and often get into a frolic day and *night*." [33]

Catharine's tour was typical of many of her subsequent ones.
The first portion of their journey took them to Indianapolis, Louisville, St. Louis, and Keokuk and Burlington, Iowa. "We stop in
some pleasant family and all other pleasant families call upon us
and invite us to spend a day or dine at their houses, so we see all
the richest and most intelligent people and learn all the best things
as well as all the worst about the country and people," Nancy wrote.
In Louisville they stayed at the "beautiful residence of Bishop
Smith," he and Bishop Potter of Philadelphia being Catharine's
chief Episcopal supporters. On the second swing of their trip from
Burlington to Galesburg, Peoria, Jacksonville, Springfield, St. Louis,
and back to Burlington, they stayed at the home of Mr. Gale, who
founded and owned most of the town named after him; in the
"elegantly furnished" home of the mayor of Peoria, where they were
served from silver dishes and Catharine played the rosewood piano
in the parlor; at the home of the president of Illinois College at
Jacksonville, which was "thronged with callers" during their week's
stay; and at the "richly furnished" Mather home in Springfield.[34]

They traveled by stage, private carriage, and riverboat, across the
prairie and on the Ohio, Mississippi, and Illinois rivers. Their life
aboard riverboats was as adventurous as their life on land was elegant. In each of their three river trips they received special attention from the ship's captain. On the first voyage from Louisville to
St. Louis, "the Captain was a polite, dignified, intelligent, companionable man and very polite to us particularly," Nancy wrote.
"So we sat on the hurricane deck all day, me reading to him and
Miss B. or he talking much to our edification." From St. Louis to
Burlington they met "another pleasant captain who played the
guitar and violin and was in every way agreeable." On their third
voyage the "gentlemanly captain" made a special stop by the

ruins of the Mormon temple at Nauvoo so that they could visit it. On shipboard they met men like "Mr. Taylor, the richest man in Kentucky, a lawyer and a cousin of the old general who was very attentive to us and by his wit and information wild [*sic*] many a weary hour." [35]

Catharine and Nancy were eager for adventure, and when their boat hit a snag or stuck on a sand bar in the area of the Mississippi known as "the boats graveyard" they did not feel "a shadow of fear" but "slept soundly all night and laughed gayly all day." Catharine stayed on deck at night when they passed such high points in their trip as the wild merging of the Missouri and Mississippi rivers. By moonlight "we could even distinguish [the Missouri's] dark waters pouring over the crystal luxury of the Mississippi," Nancy wrote. Catharine deliberately routed their trip so they could "see much more of the country" than her business needs required. They traveled by stage "through dense forest over almost impassable roads where we were kept in a carriage only by two men holding it up on one side," and through "spreading prairies," where it was "a grand sight to look ahead on such an expanse," and where "to see at night a hundred fires running over that limitless field [was] beyond conception glorious." [36]

In this mood of high adventure and new freedom, Catharine explored each of their stopping places as a possible site for a female college. Burlington seemed at first the most rewarding prospect, since during her first stop there in March she had gained the support of the town's leading citizens. "Miss Beecher whose name has long since become a household divinity is now in Burlington," the local newspaper had announced. "She submitted to a meeting of gentlemen on Monday evening interested in female education, a plan of a school for this purpose, which seems to meet with general approbation." [37] When she returned in May, Catharine found that the local citizens had failed to proceed with the school as they had promised. For the first time since 1831 Catharine resumed the labors of a school principal. She rented and furnished a building into which she moved two teachers whom she had sent to Burlington from Albany, and she established in the building a school "for thirty pupils" and a boarding house for the teachers. She had written Slade asking for at least two more teachers, but a variety of mishaps prevented them from reaching Burlington.[38]

Catharine, feeling certain that Slade was deliberately sabotaging her efforts, went into a swift mental and physical decline. "Miss Beecher was confined to her bed for a fortnight," Nancy wrote, "and was taken from her bed and carried to the boat." [39] She urged Nancy to stay on and keep the school alive until she could return with more teachers. Nancy Johnson was left in the relatively primitive building in Burlington while Catharine returned to her water cure in the East. Catharine had succeeded in creating a new seminary, but perhaps foreseeing the work involved in operating it, perhaps disappointed with the lack of local initiative in aiding the school, perhaps desiring to confront Slade face to face, she was not willing to stay on and nurture the school.

For seven months Nancy Johnson remained there, acting, with little money, as the principal, cook, housekeeper, financier, and one of the three teachers in the school. "You would laugh to see me and hear me bargaining for wood and coal and flour and meat in the morning directing affairs in the kitchen and then in the School Room teaching and lecturing," Nancy wrote home, describing the tasks that Catharine had avoided through her sudden illness. After repeatedly appealing to Catharine for aid, she closed the school down in December because the winter conditions made it impossible to continue without money or assistance and retreated to St. Louis, where she spent the winter with relatives.[40]

With Nancy Johnson Catharine had affirmed her desire for a new life in the West. As her sudden illness suggested, her capacity for affirmation was limited, but it was not exhausted. She returned to St. Louis in the spring of 1849 to rescue Nancy Johnson, and when Nancy announced she was leaving the "cause" and returning home to Vermont, Catharine did not try to dissuade her.[41] By that time she had found another teacher and another site for her projected model seminary. This one, Milwaukee-Downer College in Milwaukee, occupied her for the next ten years and lasted until midway through the twentieth century, when it merged with the University of Wisconsin.

In the course of the 1840s Catharine had revived her faltering career and had become a public personage. She had sounded the depths of her personal problems, and although she had not resolved them but only deflected them onto another, she had, unlike her brother, survived the experience. Her public role became her major strength, and she proved her ability to sustain that role even if she had to shift stages and alter the supporting players. For several years in the 1840s she worked within the evangelical framework provided for her by her father. Her plan to educate the children of the West with missionary teachers was directly modeled upon her father's efforts to train ministers for the West. Yet it was not the plight of children but the fate of women that primarily interested her. Within the evangelical framework inherited from her father she developed a focus upon women and in New Haven in 1847 she suddenly concluded that this evangelical structure was more oppressive than beneficial for women.

Catharine's work henceforth assumed what might be called a Victorian cast. Her western tour of 1848 marked a brief hiatus between two cultural modalities. In the late 1840s the evangelical emphasis fell away from Catharine's work, and she was left with a single focus upon women — a more secular, distinctively urban perspective that envisioned special professional roles for women. The sweeping social and moral roles she had built for her sex in earlier decades lost priority in a society where urban life and secular institutions were becoming increasingly important. If her earlier call for women to save their country was colored by millennialist exaggeration, it nevertheless envisioned a place for women at the forefront of American life and within the sweep of historical change. Professional competence replaced evangelical fervor in Catharine's framework for women in the 1850s, and what her work lost in expansiveness, it gained in solidity and specificity.

❦ 14 ❦

Protective Customs, 1855

It was probably not coincidental that Catharine Beecher began to write about widespread female invalidism in American society just at the time she saw and articulated the opposition between herself and male-dominated evangelical culture. Catharine had, however, been interested in the state of health among American women since she first explored the topic in her *Treatise on Domestic Economy,* and from the time she resumed a public career in 1843 she had persistently noted and inquired about the health of the women she encountered. While frequenting water-cure establishments, visiting female seminaries, or organizing women to support western teachers during the 1840s, Catharine collected evidence to confirm her belief that women were more often ill than well, and that chronic disabilities were widespread among the female population. By 1854, when she wrote *Letters to the People on Health and Happiness,* her basic assumption was that female debility was a sign of some fundamental opposition between the needs of women and many of the conditions of American society.

In a chapter entitled "Statistics of Female Health," Catharine presented the results of a personal poll to show the extent of female invalidism. Sampling a total of seventy-nine communities and over one thousand women, she found that the sick outnumbered the healthy by a ratio of three to one. In a typical community profile (Batavia, Illinois) she recorded:

> Mrs. H. an invalid. Mrs. G. scrofula. Mrs. W. liver complaint. Mrs. K. pelvic disorders. Mrs. S. pelvic diseases. Mrs. B. pelvic diseases very badly. Mrs. B. not healthy. Mrs. T. very feeble. Mrs. G. cancer. Mrs. N. liver complaint. Do not know one healthy woman in the place.

Surveying the health of her personal acquaintances, she concluded, "I am not able to recall, in my immense circle of friends and acquaintances all over the Union so many as *ten* married ladies born in this century and country, who are perfectly sound, healthy, and vigorous." [1] Although Catharine Beecher's casually gathered statistics provide impressionistic rather than conclusive measurements of the health of her generation, they do show that great numbers of women perceived their health as precarious, and they demonstrate the ubiquity of the image that linked women with infirmity in the middle decades of the nineteenth century.

The pattern of recurrent illness she disclosed in others was also true of Catharine Beecher's own life. She consistently responded to external rebuffs by becoming unwell. Beginning in 1829 with the refusal of Zilpah Grant to join her school, and most recently in 1842 during her quarrelsome year in the Beecher home, Catharine translated her psychological discontent into corporeal illness. On these occasions, while searching for sympathy in an apparently uncongenial world, Catharine found illness more rewarding than health. "I am most concerned about Catharine," Harriet had written in 1842. "The nervous instability of her system is so great that she seems to me in danger of paralysis." [2] Several purposes were simultaneously served by such a tactic. The tension between her assertive public role and the society's preference for passive women was momentarily eliminated since she could sink into a socially accepted dependent role without actually renouncing her desire for independence. Illness was also an escape from Catharine's own contradictory definition of women as submissive and weak but nevertheless radiant with self-denying strength. Since self-indulgence was required of a convalescent, she could enjoy a rare respite from the ideology that enjoined women to serve others. Perhaps most importantly, invalidism was a way of marking her exclusion from the culture's dominant values of competition, achievement, strength, and self-assertion. Women were not allowed full participation in these values anyway, and through illness Catharine and others like her could express covert opposition to a society that omitted them from the activities it valued most. If their sex disqualified them from full social usefulness, then it could also disable them for the performance of their unrewarding routine duties.

Women like Catharine who experienced recurrent debilities could find institutional support in the dozens of new water-cure establishments that sprang up to serve them in the 1840s. These centers of female-oriented culture made it possible for women to escape the confines of their sick rooms and commune with sympathetic peers. From the 1840s to the 1880s 213 water-cure centers emerged to treat a predominantly female clientele, and Catharine Beecher was among their most enthusiastic patrons. In her *Letters to the People on Health and Happiness* Catharine praised the "inestimable benefits" of the water cure, and highly recommended its restorative powers. In her search for mental and physical well-being, Catharine took up temporary residence at thirteen spas, and even after she ceased to take the water treatment itself, she continued to visit the places because she found them so congenial. When her strength was fading before her death in 1878, she went to live with her brother, Thomas Beecher, at Elmira, New York, in order to be near the Elmira water cure.[3]

There was something profoundly comforting about these cure centers to Catharine Beecher, and like other women, she patronized them because they offered services available nowhere else in American society. There female communality replaced the characteristic isolation of American domestic life, bodily sensuality could be freely indulged, and an unwanted pregnancy might even be terminated. Most importantly, at a time when orthodox medicine offered women little more than biblical admonitions on the inevitability of pain, hydropathy sympathetically sought to meliorate the wide variety of ailments and diseases associated with female reproductive processes.

Hydropathy was based on the belief that water was the natural sustainer of life, and its basic tenets were bathing, wet compresses, steam, massage, exercise, the drinking of cold water, and a spare diet. From the time of its founding in 1845 through the 1890s, the *Water Cure Journal* — its motto, "Wash and Be Healed" — popularized the cure, listed new establishments, presented exemplary case histories, and promoted many corollary doctrines, such as temperance, women's rights, and abolitionism, that arose from its premise that all human beings are created equal and that their natural goodness should not be adulterated.[4] As a system hydropathy was less successful and less organized than other contemporary medical cults, notably Thomsonianism and homeopathy, but the particular female needs that hydropathy served were not met through any other form of medicine.[5]

At water-cure establishments women were encouraged to break

the cultural taboo against open discussion of their bodies. "The experience of each individual gradually becomes known to most of his fellow patients," Catharine wrote in praise of the cure in the *New York Observer* in 1851, and this communal aspect of the treatment could provide women with the psychologically reassuring knowledge that their problems were shared by others.[6] The opportunity to speak openly of one's symptoms and fears was itself therapeutic, but when these related to female generative organs it was usually impossible to do so in one's normal home environment.

The strong emphasis on exercise, massage, bathing, and general attention to the body also provided women with an opportunity to experience sensual pleasure. Under the guise of restoring their health, women could indulge their otherwise forbidden desires for physical sensuality, and some descriptions of water-cure treatments seem to express covert sexual feelings. Nudity and exhilaration were, in any case, frequent experiences during a water-cure treatment. Since more sexual feeling was attributed to men than to women in this period, hydropathy centers were therefore unique in providing a socially approved sensual experience for women.[7]

Many water-cure establishments devoted their primary attention to women's diseases. The most frequently mentioned ailment was that of the fallen womb (*prolapsis uteri*), but other illnesses connected with menstruation, childbirth, and the generative organs were also prominent topics of discussion and treatment.[8] Women may have chosen the water cure to treat these ailments because it provided a supportive female environment and frequently employed women doctors, but in so doing they were probably also choosing the best medical treatment available to them at that time.[9] In comparison with orthodox medicine, the water cure at least provided the fundamentals of exercise, cleanliness, good diet, and a reassuring environment, rather than leeches, injections, and strong drugs in the isolation of one's normal domestic circumstances. One outstanding specialist in uterine diseases in 1858 still taught medical students to insert leeches into the womb even though he admitted that this could "induce a paroxysm of almost intolerable suffering." [10]

A major tenet of the water cure was that it treated the whole person, not just single symptoms, so it tried to discover what combination of causes in a woman's life was producing the ailment and helped her organize her life to avoid its continuance. This practice was far in advance of allopathic medicine and may have been especially pertinent to the treatment of ailments relating to female generative processes.

Water-cure specialists also developed a significantly different attitude toward childbirth than that held by orthodox medicine. Their concern for the life of the mother led them to such innovations as the cold hip bath to retard hemorrhages after childbirth, and their view on abortion was significantly more sympathetic to the needs of women than that of nascent gynecological specialists. Voluntary abortion was made illegal by state laws that prohibited "the administration of any noxious drug, or destructive substance, or the use of any instrument" to interrupt a pregnancy. Nearly every newspaper of the period, however, carried advertisements for abortive pills — disguised as potions to "begin the monthly cycle." [11] Clearly women in the mid-nineteenth century were seeking contraceptive and abortive remedies, and water-cure centers constituted one of their few sources of information and treatment.

The best example of such sympathetic treatment was that provided by Russell Trall, one of the initial popularizers and leaders of hydropathy. In his *Hydropathic Encyclopedia* of 1853, he mentioned "the safe period" and other contraceptive methods. Trall believed, Norman Himes noted in his *Medical History of Contraception,* "that a woman had an absolute right to determine when she should, and when she should not conceive." Himes concluded that some of Trall's treatments were "abortifacient," and although the distribution of contraceptive information was illegal, Trall's overall tone of piety and respectability protected him from prosecution.[12]

Orthodox medicine, by contrast, emphatically denied that women had any right to control the birth of their children. "The dread of suffering, fears respecting their own health and strength, the trouble and expense of large families, and professedly, also, the responsibility incurred in the education of children, these and other reasons equally futile and trifling . . . induce them to destroy the product of that conjugal union for which marriage was instituted," Dr. Hugh Hodge asserted in lectures delivered at the University of Pennsylvania medical school in 1839.[13] Given the hostility of orthodox medicine to the "trifling" needs of women, the ban on contraceptive information, and the contrasting sympathetic leanings of many hydropathists, hydropathy seems to have offered a third alternative to the nineteenth-century woman's choice between celibacy and painful annual childbearing.

Catharine was not unaware of the sexually therapeutic practices of some water-cure establishments, and although it was only while taking the cure that she allowed herself to experience and speculate about sensual pleasure, she roundly condemned any overt expression of such feelings. She severely criticized those who believed "that no perfectly-developed man or woman is possible, so long as any of the functions and propensities are held in habitual constraint." Doctors who "maintain that the exercise of all the functions of body and mind is *necessary to health*," were especially pernicious, Catharine said, for women patients had no protection against their advances. "A terrific feature of these developments," she said, "has been the entire *helplessness* of my sex, amidst present customs and feelings, as to any *redress* for such wrongs, and the reckless and conscious impunity felt by the wrong-doers on this account." [14] Although women may have been assaulted as well as treated at some of these centers, and although Catharine may have patronized only the most irreproachable establishments, it nevertheless seems clear that women went to these centers to cure ailments connected with sexuality, and that Catharine Beecher's favorite spas differed from the disreputable ones mainly in their superior techniques for sublimination rather than their elimination of a sexually charged atmosphere.

Although in *Letters to the People on Health and Happiness* Catharine Beecher devoted a chapter of special praise to hydropathy, it was only one of several remedies she suggested to improve the health of American men, women, and children. Most of her recommendations were embedded in detailed discussions of the body and its functions. With even more extensive illustrations and explanations than in her *Treatise on Domestic Economy*, she analyzed human physiology in scientific terms but easily understandable prose. Her basic emphases were placed on adequate exercise, proper diet and clothing, cleanliness and fresh air. She repeatedly and strongly criticized tightly laced corsets as the source of a wide variety of female illnesses, including the displacement of the internal organs. Much of Catharine's scientific knowledge was drawn from Elizabeth Blackwell's *The Laws of Life,* originally delivered as a series of lectures in New York in 1852 and devoted primarily to the health of women.[15] In this book, as in her *Treatise,* Catharine skillfully bridged the gap between technical knowledge and popular practice. She again drew heavily from other sources, but once more her personal experience and her own cultural judgments formed the core around which the book was shaped.

One important new cultural consideration introduced in Catharine's *Letters to the People on Health and Happiness* was a remarkable chapter insisting on "the necessity for protective customs" to regulate relations between the sexes. This Victorian note was a new one for Catharine, possibly caused by her recent conflict with the male world, but apparently also arising from her new estimate of city life. Whereas the tone of her *Treatise* was addressed to a mobile population, this volume seemed written for settled, urban readers. In it men and women were no longer bound together by a shared millennial vision. Earlier the basic differences between men and women had meshed in a harmonious division of labor. Now these differences clashed and made the sexes adversaries. The submissiveness of women made them prey to men who "in this highly-stimulating age, are not to be regulated in their outbursting passions by theories of morals educed by the genius of man and the light of reason." The city's "unnatural confinement" upset the natural disparity of strength between men and women.[16]

The urban environment impaired the health of men and women alike, Catharine said. "As wealth and luxury have increased, houses have been made tight, windows have been corked, fire-places have been shut up, and close stoves and furnaces introduced." For the unventilated rooms, heavy diet, and lack of exercise that characterized urban life, Catharine prescribed fresh air, nourishing meals, and calisthenics. And for the social conditions of the city she advocated new "protective customs" to regulate relationships between the sexes. Young people especially needed protection against "outbursting of sensibilities that they have not learned to control," Catharine said, and "the freedoms that have been tolerated in the associations of the young of both sexes require new restraints and customs." [17]

"*The whole of our adult population* should be appraised of certain dangers as yet but little known," she said, "and should be thus induced to institute protective customs and precautions, which at former periods were not so much demanded." Whereas innocence had been sufficient to protect the young from sin at an

earlier time, they now needed *"the protection of knowledge."* Just
as Catharine believed women should know how their bodies functioned and recognize symptoms of very personal disorders, so she
insisted that women needed to be warned against evil and given
knowledge of it in order to resist it effectively. Yet just as she was
not willing to present "the facts and details" of women's diseases
(which if known, she said, "would send a groan of terror and horror
all over the land,") so she could not fully specify what "knowledge"
she now deemed necessary. Catharine suddenly inhabited a world
where alarming new forces, as yet not fully identified, replaced the
order she had known. In these circumstances one could see evil
everywhere, and the best protection against it was a generalized
armor of social regulations. The need was greater because the threat
was still inchoate. "The truth should be plainly set forth," Catharine concluded, "that the snares, temptations, and dangers that
will assail the young at this and the coming period, are altogether
beyond any thing known in our past history, or any thing which
is now imagined." [18]

Although Catharine's growing antipathy to male prerogatives in
the 1850s may explain why she was among the first to adopt this
Victorian attitude toward relations between the sexes, the full
causal pattern shaping this change was as complex as that shaping
the preceding ideology of domesticity. Catharine's Victorianism was
a break with the style of domesticity but a continuance of its goals.
The main difference introduced by the 1850s was the need Catharine felt to discover new ways to maintain the boundaries between
men and women in an urban environment where both sexes might
be performing similar functions. Victorianism was for Catharine
an effort to restore the distinctions or boundaries between the
sexes by finding new criteria to replace the obsolescent "natural"
ones of domesticity. Catharine Beecher's own life was a testimonial
to the fact that some women were not behaving "naturally" — not
devoting their lives to the nurture of small children and homemaking. The inclusion of women alongside men in the class of
industrial workers was but one example of the ways in which an
increasingly complex urban society blurred the lines that separated
men from women. Victorianism was an effort to retain the old
ideological goal of domesticity by continuing the belief that society's
fundamental social divisions were the "natural" ones of sex, rather
than the pernicious ones of class.

In this sense Catharine Beecher's emerging Victorian attitudes may be seen as a continuation rather than a rejection of her earlier beliefs. Catharine herself in *Letters to the People on Health and Happiness* decried the abandonment of the sexual division of labor and its replacement with a class system. "Now the labor appointed to man in cultivating the earth, in preparing its fruits, and in many mechanical pursuits, will be found to be that which exercises all the muscles of the body appropriately and healthfully," she said. "So also the labor appointed to woman in the family state, involves just that variety of employment, which, if wisely adjusted, would be exactly what is best calculated to develop every muscle most perfectly, while in the performance of these duties the mind has healthful occupation." But the increasing division of labor along class lines had disrupted this natural order, she said, and to it much of the ill health of Americans could be attributed. "Every man who can do so, avoids these healthful pursuits as less honorable," she said, "and seeks in preference those that shut him up in study, office, or store, to overwork his brain and leave his muscular system to run down for want of vigorous exercise and fresh air." [19]

The same effect of class was debilitating women. "And so almost every woman, who has it in her power, turns off the work that would make herself and her daughters beautiful, graceful and healthful, to hirelings." A society that divided "the labor of life" by this method, Catharine said, created one group with weakened muscles and another with overworked bodies and neglected brains. This division, she said, was entirely inappropriate for a society that claims "to take the lead in guiding all others to the most perfect state of social, civil, and moral development." Those countries "whose customs are founded on the assumption that one class of people are to do the work and another class are to appropriate the best fruits of this labor," she continued, "have instituted social customs on the plan of making every possible barrier of separation between these two classes." For the United States to follow this system would mean the abandonment of its pride in the belief "that all men are equal in rights and privileges, and that no aristocracy can flourish here." [20]

Catharine Beecher's conscience and her social fears were aroused by the increasing signs of class divisions in American life, but there was very little she was able to do to assuage her fears beyond insisting on the maintenance of gender boundaries rather than class boundaries to mark the basic divisions in American society. As these gender boundaries became more and more dysfunctional, she and others like her became more and more resourceful in the distinctions they could draw between men and women.

Gender differences could be emphasized through fashionable clothes as well as Victorian manners, and while Catharine Beecher became a strong advocate of the latter, she bitterly opposed the tightly laced corsets that constricted women's midsections to the willowy dimensions so admired by the era. She and others concerned with women's health in the period attributed a great variety of serious internal disorders to the displacement of ribs, lungs, stomach, intestines, bladder, liver, and uterus by these corsets. "The protracted agonies that I have seen and known to be endured as the result of such deformities and displacements," she said, were worse than "the horrible torments inflicted by savage Indians or cruel inquisitors on their victims." She believed that much of female invalidism, especially urinary and uterine difficulties, was related to these efforts to achieve exaggeratedly narrow waists. The health of all American women was thus impaired, she said, "for it is not one class, or one section" but an entire gender that is encouraged to follow this fashion. Catharine provided several diagrams to show how "this horrid fashion remorselessly girds the waist just where the bones have least internal support and yield the easiest." [21]

If these practices produced a higher than normal incidence of disorders related to the bladder and uterus, the air of concealment and innuendo that surrounded female invalidism and the delicacy and fragility attributed to female physiology may be more understandable. During this time women seem to have become conscious of illnesses related to their sexuality, but, while unwilling to suffer silently as they had in the past, they nevertheless received little sympathy or curative aid from the American medical profession. No longer willing to take a heavenly reward instead of a worldly cure, they were born a generation too late to be mollified by Roxana Beecher's attitude of religious resignation, but too early to benefit from the medical advances — especially germ theory — that transformed gynecological medicine at the end of the nineteenth century.[22]

Made conscious of the special nature of the bodies they inhabited, women became newly aware of the hazards as well as the virtues of their sex. Although the society acknowledged their virtues with a pedestal, women had to confirm their own sense of the hazards since neither clergyman nor physician was adequate to the task. Women did this by elaborating invalidism into a set of social formulas that objectified and institutionalized anxieties too widely and deeply felt to be borne alone. The "decline," convalescence, and recovery rituals of the female sick room allowed women to communicate with one another about these fears. In her *Treatise on Domestic Economy* as well as her *Letters to the People on Health and Happiness* Catharine Beecher articulated these private apprehensions, especially those connected with childbirth. She said she had "repeatedly heard mothers say, that they had wept tears of bitterness over their infant daughters, at the thought of the sufferings which they were destined to undergo; while they cherished the decided wish, that these daughters should never marry." [23] The possibilities of companionship and consolation provided by the rituals of invalidism may have made it easier to acquiesce in the difficulties of marriage and child-bearing roles, thereby forestalling such a total rejection as this woman voiced.

Through invalidism women could also express affection for one another. Whether acting as nurse or patient, the usual taboos against intimacy between women were suspended when they cared for each others' illnesses. Much of the companionship and love in Catharine Beecher's life originated at water-cure centers, where the ties of a casual friendship could, through mutual health concerns, be easily transformed into bonds of intimacy. With Nancy Johnson, Delia Bacon, and others, Catharine overcame the isolation that characterized much of her emotional life by expressing her interest in their health. Without such an emotional outlet as that provided by the mores of invalidism, the human warmth in Catharine Beecher's life would have been significantly reduced. It was a guise under which she could express her desire for human contact. Catharine's and Harriet's relationship was strained in the late 1830s, but Catharine reestablished her intimacy with her during a long stay together at Brattleboro in the mid-1840s. When Calvin Stowe began to believe that Catharine was wooing Harriet away from him and wrote to protest their prolonged cure, both sisters used the protection that invalidism provided and successfully defended their need to stay on together.[24]

Harriet used this time to assess her marriage, and in the first in a series of letters to Calvin she recalled the "sickness, pain, perplexity, constant discouragement, wearing, wasting days and nights" of her early marriage when Calvin was often absent raising funds for Lane Seminary and of little help when he was present. "Ah, how little comfort had I in being a mother — how was all that I proposed met and crossed and my way ever hedged up! In short God would teach me," Harriet concluded, "that I should make no family be my chief good and portion, and bitter as the lesson has been, I thank Him for it from my very soul." [25]

Catharine saw healthier and more productive alternatives for women than invalidism, however, and as an antidote to it she prescribed proper physiological knowledge, healthy diet, exercise, and, above all, some kind of worthy and engaging labor. Foremost among her recommendations, of course, was teaching. Her book ended with a plea for the support of and participation in the work of the American Woman's Educational Association. The object of the association, she reminded her readers, was "to aid in securing to American women a liberal education, honorable position, and remunerative employment *in their appropriate profession*," being "the training of the human mind, the care of the human body in infancy and sickness, and the conservation of the family state." She particularly urged her readers to support the current effort of the association to endow a college at Milwaukee "to furnish the salaries of three superior teachers who "shall take charge of the three departments set forth as constituting *the profession of woman.*" [26]

Catharine's *Letters to the People on Health and Happiness* was quickly followed by the publication of *Physiology and Calisthenics for Schools and Families,* and in the winter of 1855 she set out on a tour of the Midwest to promote the sale of her health books. This tour was a great success. She visited Chicago, Galesburg, Indianapolis, Cincinnati, and Columbus, where she urged that her health books be adopted for use in the local schools. Her greatest success was in Cincinnati. "There I had a grand time," Catharine wrote in a family circular letter. "The Superintendent of the City Public Schools was greatly interested. He got an order from the Board of Trustees to have all the schools dismissed one half day that the teachers might meet me." Five hundred teachers and "persons otherwise interested" heard Catharine's uncle, John Foote, read from her book. Then she addressed the gathering. "The meeting went off in great style," Catharine said, "and they all say the thing shall go. If it does go, then it will go all over the West and East too, and will make a marvelous sale of the book." [27]

Catharine continued to meet enthusiastic audiences in promoting her books that summer and fall, and by October she concluded that she had enough money to build a home on the site of the new college she had been promoting in Milwaukee.

☙ 15 ☙

A Kind of Lady Abbess, 1849–1856

In the last fully active decade of her career Catharine Beecher continued to travel, raise funds, promote her books, and publicize the cause of women's education. Toward the end of the 1850s, she also resumed her interest in moral philosophy. Although her activities in this decade were not new, they were different in tone from her earlier work and writings. For the dominant tenor of her efforts in the 1850s was not evangelical, but secular, urban, and professional. Until 1857 most of her labors were devoted to the women's college she founded in Milwaukee. There she defined a more restrained social role for women. No longer calling upon women to save their country, she urged instead that they create professional roles out of their domestic duties as mothers, nurses, and teachers. This shift of emphasis in Catharine's educational activities was prompted by her own desire to lead a domestic life and still retain her professional role. She attempted to incorporate a home of her own within the college at Milwaukee. When the trustees rebuffed this plan in 1856, Catharine turned away from the college to resume her writings on moral philosophy.

On her tour with Nancy Johnson in 1848 Catharine had organized in Jacksonville, Illinois, an "auxiliary committee" to Slade's board in Cleveland and had selected a less assertive man to act as this committee's paid agent. After a confrontation with Slade the following year, Catharine ended her connection with the National Board of Popular Education. The committee at Jacksonville was her temporary organizational base until she founded a new society in New York in 1852 called The American Woman's Educational Association. In 1849 Catharine issued a circular declaring her break with Slade and defining the differences between his and her organizations: "All those who choose to furnish funds simply to prepare and transfer teachers to the west can contribute directly to the funds of the Board [in Cleveland]," she said, "while those who prefer to provide for a more enlarged mode of operation, can place their contributions under the control of this auxiliary committee at Jacksonville." Catharine's "enlarged mode of operation" consisted of founding colleges in the West to train women for their threefold profession as teachers, healthkeepers, and homemakers.[1]

On her way to rescue Nancy Johnson in St. Louis in the summer of 1849, Catharine had met in Le Roy, New York, another young woman who appeared a likely companion for her new efforts in the West. She invited Mary Mortimer to spend the autumn with her at the Round Hill Water Cure where they would talk over Catharine's plans. "Miss B. professes to have taken a liking to me," Mary wrote a friend, "and builds an 'air castle' as she calls it, in which she puts me as a 'leading spirit.'" Like Nancy Johnson, Mary Mortimer suffered from a lame foot, and Catharine won her affection by supervising her cure through hydrotherapy. By the winter her "crippled condition" was cured. "I think I never felt more deeply under obligations to friends than now," Mary wrote. "Miss Beecher has been so kind, so benevolent, so thoughtful." [2] Mary Mortimer was to spend the rest of her life in Milwaukee. For six years she nurtured the institution where Catharine hoped to retire and remained there long after Catharine abandoned it.

While Mary took the water cure, Catharine raised money in the East and negotiated with Milwaukee business leaders the way in which it would be spent. On a tour that took her through Providence, Philadelphia, Norwich, and New London, Catharine raised over thirteen hundred dollars for the cause of women's education in the West. From various other sources that winter she received donations amounting to another thousand dollars.[3] Catharine's ability to raise money made her a woman of considerable importance to any group of western citizens who desired to build a school for their daughters. Catharine learned of such a group in Milwaukee and dispatched her Jacksonville agent to the city to reach an understanding with them. Catharine would provide a teacher and one thousand dollars for equipment for the school if the local citizens would erect a building and allow her to shape the school's policy. The Milwaukee citizens instantly agreed to her proposal.[4]

Catharine Beecher's school filled a real cultural need in Milwaukee. The town was not two decades old when she arrived there with Mary Mortimer in 1850, and cultural and social patterns had not yet been set. The group with which Catharine allied herself was attempting to establish itself as the city's cultural elite, but its preeminence was challenged by the local "democracy" and by a continuous flow of immigrants from the "refined circles" of the East. The men who sent their daughters to Catharine's school and acted as its trustees were businessmen who controlled the city's finances but not its politics. They were Whigs and the town consistently voted Democratic. From 1846 to 1860 Milwaukee had only one non-Democratic mayor, and "the democracy" considered itself the sworn enemy of Milwaukee's "privileged few." [5] The families with whom Catharine associated set themselves above the masses by adopting eastern aristocratic styles of life. Yet the provinciality of their culture was repeatedly revealed to them by the manners of every new family that emigrated from the "upper circles" of the East to Milwaukee. To maintain the social status of their daughters they had previously sent them to be educated in the East. This was an expensive and a self-defeating exercise, however, for it did not train young women to lead the culture of a frontier city.[6]

The leading member of Milwaukee's social elite was Increase Lapham, a self-taught geologist and botanist who had helped plan the city's canals and streets in 1836 and was subsequently instrumental in promoting a variety of civil projects, including the town's educational institutions.[7] In 1848 he declared to a group of prominent citizens that if Milwaukee did not establish local colleges for its sons and daughters, "the inevitable result will be that we shall have the mortification of seeing our sons and daughters rank second rate in the society of our own city! Those who come in from the east, where better institutions exist, will have a superior education and they will assuredly take the lead and outshine us entirely!" Soon after this speech Lapham traveled to the East to try to raise funds for Milwaukee schools, but his trip was a complete failure.[8] Catharine Beecher's proposal to establish a college for women in Milwaukee could not, therefore, have come at a better time. The Milwaukee elite needed her as much as she needed them. It was a site with as much potential as Cincinnati had had two decades before.

Part of Catharine's dedication in Milwaukee Female College between 1850 and 1856 arose from her hope to create a home there for herself. From the beginning her labors in Milwaukee had a domestic flavor. "I found it necessary, on account of my health," she wrote in 1851, ". . . to go to housekeeping in the school-building. In doing this, I had the whole responsibility of making all the purchases, and directing every detail, just as every housekeeper does in going to housekeeping, and for those two months [in the fall of 1850] I had the same family care as other housekeepers have." [9] Catharine had "very comfortable arrangements made for our accommodations in the way of rooms," Mary Mortimer wrote. She planned to have the schoolrooms "carpeted and furnished as nicely as if they were 'down east,' — our yard to be set out with flowers, etc." [10]

In Milwaukee Catharine had found the place where she could fulfill the role she had defined in her writings of the 1840s. Like a Catholic nun or Mother Superior she could pursue her self-denying labors in comfort, secure in her position, and conscious of the support of her community. Fredrika Bremer met Catharine in Milwaukee in 1851 and described her as "a kind of lady-abbess in educational matters." Outside the walls of her institution Catharine received as much respect as she did inside. She was treated as an honored guest of the city and the socially ambitious vied with one another for her company.[11] Catharine Beecher was fifty years old, and she felt the need to prepare a home where she could retire in the near future. She stayed long enough in Milwaukee to give the school her personal imprint, and then returned to the East to raise funds for it.

In Hartford in the spring of 1851, where she was writing a book to promote contributions to the college, Catharine's desire for a domestic life overcame even her standing quarrel with her stepmother. Lyman and Lydia Beecher had left Cincinnati that spring and retired in Boston, where they rented a house near the Edward Beecher family. Lyman was seventy-six years old. Catharine hoped that she would be able to keep house for him in Boston as she had done in Litchfield in 1816. She wrote Lydia Beecher: "I wish it could be so arranged that I could keep house, and you and he board with me. I could do twice as much *head* work if I could have the gentle exercise and the *amusement* of housekeeping. . . . I have funds enough to provide what furniture we should need." Perhaps anticipating her stepmother's rebuff, Catharine added: "If this is not done, and I am to help father, I must take board wherever you and he are domesticated. I hold myself in readiness to do all I can for *his* comfort and *yours*." Lydia Beecher adamantly refused to consent to either of these arrangements, and until Lyman Beecher's death in 1862 she made it impossible for Catharine to live in the same house with her father.[12]

For the next five years Catharine worked to establish in Milwaukee a substitute home for the one she could not create with her father in Boston. She toured the East raising funds for Milwaukee and returned there at least twice a year to see that the college was developing along the lines she desired. In Catharine's absence Mary Mortimer loyally represented her interests. When she was not traveling or visiting in Milwaukee, Catharine lived with Harriet or boarded at health retreats in Ohio, Massachusetts, and New York.

With both local support and Catharine's careful nurture, Milwaukee Female College grew steadily during the early 1850s. In the summer of 1851 Catharine designed an ambitiously large and handsome building for the college, and construction began on it immediately. A normal department was added to the college when it moved into its new Gothic structure in the fall of 1852. The school then had 120 pupils and, including Mary Mortimer, a staff of 4 teachers.[13]

When the trustees concluded that they could not raise the money to repay the college's construction loan, Catharine founded the American Woman's Educational Association. This group was ostensibly dedicated to promoting Catharine's new educational ideas, but it was also designed to finance Catharine's dream of a perfect retirement home.[14]

Catharine's new educational ideas as she presented them in her book of 1851, *The True Remedy for the Wrongs of Women,* and in the "Annual Reports" of the American Woman's Educational Association, were based on three principles. First, women's colleges should be founded in "large towns and cities," where they would create urban centers of female influence. The woman's college in the city replaced the rural missionary teacher as the chief agency by which Catharine sought to have women exert their social influence.[15] Catharine herself was an urban personality. She thrived amid social gatherings, public meetings, controversy and debate. She was happiest when she was moving among "influential" people and seeking to swing the weight of their influence behind her projects. Her constituency had always been one of lawyers, judges, businessmen, eminent clergymen, and their wives. Catharine's career had been built upon the culture and wealth of American cities, and it was there that she finally decided the most important future influence of American women lay.

Second, Catharine emphasized that the faculty of these colleges should be organized "on the college plan of co-equal responsibility" rather than the seminary plan of a principal and subordinate teachers, and that part of the faculty should be paid by an endowed fund rather than by students' tuition. This arrangement, Catharine believed, would lend dignity to the teachers in women's colleges equal to that enjoyed by professors in male colleges. It would also prevent the burden of the institution from falling on the shoulders of one person. Under the college plan, Catharine wrote, teachers would be insured "liberal and permanent support, posts of high honor, the means of self-improvement and only such an amount of labor as is consistent with such improvement." [16] Catharine thus returned to the notions that had originally brought her into teaching in 1822. She had then been inspired by the example of her fiancé's career and had hoped to lead an intellectual life similar to his. Teaching had been an alternative to marriage for Catharine, and she had hoped to find in this career the same social prestige and financial security that she would have enjoyed had she married Fisher. During this final effort in the 1850s to shape her life after her desires, Catharine therefore sought the prestige, security, and leisure that had eluded her throughout her teaching career.

Third, Catharine said that the purpose of a woman's college was to prepare women for their "true profession" as educators and homemakers. In addition to a literary or general education, the college should therefore have two other divisions — a normal department and a department of domestic economy. The head of each of the three divisions, Catharine said, should be supported by an endowed fund, while the remainder of the teachers would be paid by students' tuition. The normal department, she said, should give women the opportunity to remain single and be self-supporting. The head of that department should "aggressively" seek out teaching positions for its graduates.

The ability to secure an independent livelihood and honorable employ suited to her education and capacities is the only true foundation of the social elevation of woman, even in the very highest classes of society. While she continues to be educated only to be somebody's wife, and is left without any aim in life till that somebody, either in love, or in pity, or in selfish regard at last grants her the opportunity, she can never be truly independent.

She went on to say that teaching should become a "profession for women, a profession as honorable and as lucrative for her as the legal, medical and theological professions are for men." While Catharine meant to provide for the single woman, she did not herself identify so strongly with the normal department of Milwaukee College as she did with that of domestic economy. Mary Mortimer began to head the normal department in 1852, and Catharine planned to have her continue in this capacity. She herself preferred to take the endowed teachership in domestic economy. The person occupying this chair, Catharine said, would "attend to the *health* and the *domestic habits* of the pupils. It would be her express aim to see that every one was *trained* to be *perfectly healthy* and to be thoroughly qualified to fulfil all the *domestic duties* of a woman in all her possible future relations." [17]

The goals of Catharine's educational efforts in the 1850s were therefore congruent with her personal desires. When realized, they would allow her to enjoy the pleasures of urban life, promote the prestige of the teaching profession, establish the financial independence of single women, and yet daily occupy herself with domestic concerns.

Catharine succeeded in drawing people of wealth and prestige into the American Woman's Educational Association, and for four years the organization raised almost two thousand dollars annually to pay the salaries of the teachers in Milwaukee and to finance Catharine's traveling expenses. The main purpose of the association, however, was to raise an endowment of twenty thousand dollars for the heads of the three departments in Milwaukee and this it failed to do.[18]

The membership of the American Woman's Educational Association encompassed three kinds of people: businessmen, educators, and popular writers. Yet most of them were in some way identified with American religious life. Cyrus Field, for example, was a New York entrepreneur who probably agreed to serve as a member of the association's board of directors because Catharine appealed to him in his capacity as the son of a Connecticut Congregational clergyman. Benjamin Bonney was another successful businessman who served on Catharine's board and had also founded a society of laymen attached to the Presbyterian church. Charles Tracy, similarly, was a prominent New York lawyer who was active in the Episcopal church. In addition to these businessmen, Catharine's association included the wives of many of the leading educators in New York. "Mrs. Professor D. C. Van Norman" was the wife of the principal of Rutgers Female Institute in New York, and she and her husband were active in church affairs. The wife of the principal of the Free Academy in New York, later the City College of New York, was an important member of Catharine's organization. Her husband was an ordained Congregational minister. The third group in the association were women writers and editors such as Sarah Josepha Hale, Caroline Kirkland, and, of course, Harriet Beecher Stowe. The Cortlandt Van Rensselaers were also active supporters of the association.[19]

Although all of these people contributed respectable amounts annually to the association, their primary service to Catharine was to lend their prestige to her fund-raising efforts in New York and throughout the East. Catharine continued to visit the same groups that had supported her in the 1840s and from them the association received about half its income. The other half Catharine raised locally in New York.[20]

After two years of fund-raising efforts with the American Woman's Educational Association, Catharine Beecher was no closer to endowing the three teaching chairs in Milwaukee than she had been in 1852. It seemed highly unlikely that she would raise twenty thousand dollars in this way, and she began to think of ways to endow only the domestic-education chair or at least to finance a home in Milwaukee from which she could direct the department of domestic economy. The citizens of Milwaukee had in the meantime raised ten thousand dollars in 1854 to clear the college's construction debt,[21] and Catharine imagined that if she could raise only part of the money needed to build a home in Milwaukee, the rest of the costs might be furnished by the trustees. At this juncture Catharine wrote her two books on health and hoped they would be as lucrative for her in the 1850s as her book on domestic economy had been in the 1840s. After their completion and before her pro-

motional tour of Illinois and Ohio, she went to Milwaukee to ask
the trustees to select a site for a "cottage" to house the department
of domestic economy; the trustees tentatively agreed to build a
house following her specifications.[22]

Following her successful promotion of her health books, Catharine concluded that her royalties from Harpers "will enable me
to put up a house of my own on land adjacent to the institution
at Milwaukee." She was looking forward to retirement there since
she would at last be able to enjoy domestic comforts and at the
same time continue to engage in her professional activities. "There I
hope to complete the plan so many years aimed at and so little
understood," she wrote Lyman. Although she regretted that she
would be so far away from her father, she took comfort in the
fact that her brothers would be nearby. "Thus Edward will be in
Illinois and I only a few hours ride from him in Wisconsin. I
think William and Charles will probably follow. This is as I
hoped would come. I always lamented our emigration from the
West and hoped for a return to it again." She planned to spend
her last eastern winter in Boston, she continued to Lyman, "so I
can then come in and see you every day." [23]

From Boston that November Catharine sent her design for a
house to Increase Lapham and urged him to begin construction
immediately. "I am very anxious to have the building erected so
that I can come out and organize the Domestic Department in the
spring if possible — say early in May." She wanted a house "so
built and arranged that two teachers shall have the quiet and comforts of an independent home — shall not be forced to have a room
mate . . . and shall not be crowded into a great family of boarding scholars." She promised to contribute three thousand dollars
toward the building and assumed that the trustees would finance
the rest of the cost. From Columbus that February Catharine wrote
Lapham that she had found an architect for the house and intended
to send him to Milwaukee to supervise the construction.[24]

Lapham's reply destroyed Catharine's hopes for a home of her
own. "I hardly know what reply to make to your letter," Lapham
began. The trustees would not agree to finance half the cost of a
home that would be used primarily for herself. "It is thought by
some members of the board that for you to purchase a lot and
erect the building entirely on your own account would be the better course," Lapham wrote, "both for your own interest and to

avoid any trouble that might arise from joint ownership." [25] This Catharine Beecher could not afford to do.

Bitterly disappointed, she ended her relationship with Milwaukee Female College and resigned from the American Woman's Educational Association. To Lapham she wrote that the college would now have to proceed "without further aid from our Association," and "without further cooperation on my part." At the annual meeting of the American Woman's Educational Association in May, Catharine announced her withdrawal but added that "should a time arrive when such an amount is held by your Board as warrants the full organization of the Health and Domestic departments" at Milwaukee or elsewhere "it would give me pleasure to render any personal services which your Agent and Committee might seek." Catharine's actions destroyed the effectiveness of the association, however, and having lost the allegiance of its New York membership, it was subsequently unable to finance a domestic department for Catharine. Milwaukee Female College did complete a building to house the department of domestic economy in 1861, and Increase Lapham asked Catharine to head it. By then it was too late for Catharine to leave her home with the Stowes in Hartford, and the Milwaukee building, in any case, was more of a dormitory than a private home. "A suitable building was indispensable to my fulfilling my part of the agreement," Catharine said, and "the building as now progressing is not suitable." [26]

The spring of 1856 marked the end of Catharine Beecher's career as an educator. As she had done on many past occasions of disappointment, she turned that summer to religious and moral writing. Although she might have hoped to resume her educational activities after her spate of writing on moral topics, she never thereafter succeeded in reviving her career. The Civil War prevented her from reentering public life when she had completed her volumes on moral philosophy, and by the end of the war she was too old to begin anew once more. In 1870 she came out of retirement to act for a few years as principal of the Hartford Female Seminary, but this effort, like most of her correspondence and writings from 1861 till her death in 1878, was an attempt to recapture her past rather than to forge a new future.

Part V

RESOLUTION AND RETIREMENT,
1850–1878

16

The Intimacy and Familiarity
of Sisterhood, 1850–1857

Personal autonomy came slowly and painfully to Lyman Beecher's children, and most of them did not fully measure the meaning of adult independence until Lyman himself grew incapacitated by senility in the 1850s. That decade was as crucial for the Beecher family as it was for the nation. Both were dominated by a sense of impending change. Beginning with the Fugitive Slave Act of 1850 and ending with Lincoln's election, the events of these ten years transformed a buoyant republic into a nation on the brink of civil war. For the Beechers it was similarly a decade of fundamental reorientation. The family abandoned its western ambitions and returned to the old centers of eastern culture. Henry Ward moved first, at the end of the 1840s, to Plymouth Church in Brooklyn. Harriet began setting up house for the Stowes in Brunswick, Maine, in 1850, enormously relieved that Calvin's professorship at Bowdoin College allowed them to escape from a Cincinnati she had grown to loathe. About the same time, William left his Ohio congregation for a church in rural Massachusetts, and seven years later Charles resigned from a professorship at Knox College in Illinois, for a church in Massachusetts. Mary, who married Thomas Perkins in the early 1830s, had not participated in the family's westward migration and remained all her adult life in Hartford. Although Edward spent a decade in Boston, he left it in 1855 and was the only Beecher to remain in the West long after midcentury. When he retired in 1871, however, Edward moved from Galesburg, Illinois, to Brooklyn to be nearer his siblings.[1] Catharine's retirement plans for Milwaukee were initially designed to include proximity to several of her brothers' western churches, and the only consolation to emerge from the collapse of those plans was the great comfort she took during the last two decades of her life in being near her family in the East.

Yet while she reestablished her kinship ties during this period, Catharine seemed to inhabit a vague area between her father's and her siblings' generations. While Harriet, Henry, and, to some extent, Edward spoke for a new generation opposed to orthodoxy in religion and compromise in politics, Catharine tried to resolve the concerns of a generation past. Her half brothers, Thomas and James, and her half sister, Isabella — children born to Harriet Porter Beecher between 1822 and 1828 — were shaped even more than Harriet and Henry by war and postwar concerns, and they further accentuated the fundamental antebellum cast to Catharine's life and work.[2] Nevertheless during the 1850s and 1860s she did struggle to draw out the full implications of her work, and she was still engrossed in it when she died at the age of seventy-eight in 1878.

By 1851 Catharine saw that Lyman Beecher's usefulness in the West was clearly at an end. "As for father he is beating about to find places to preach so as to save souls," Catharine wrote to Henry's wife, Eunice. "I think I never heard him preach better, and it grieves me to see how little he is appreciated and that half of his energies are out of employ," she continued. "There are small minds at helm now in these parts and the sooner father is put where he can have full scope and fair appreciation the better for him and the cause he is serving. It will," she concluded, "add years to his life to put him in the right place and that *now* is not *at the West*."[3]

Lyman's move to Boston later that year did not, however, provide the tonic that Catharine had hoped. His spirits, in fact, declined rapidly once the dependency relationship between himself and his children was reversed, and during 1853, after devoting two years to the compilation of his writings, "his mind was gradually retreating and hiding itself as in some deep mysterious cave."[4] Charles Beecher assumed responsibility for completing the autobiography Lyman could no longer write, and the family reverberated with the effort of Lyman's grown children to come to terms with the meaning of their personal and intellectual independence. For Catharine more than for the others this meant resolving issues already developed. Life palled a little when Lyman's creative antagonism was removed, and the last two decades before her death were no longer a series of new beginnings. Catharine's life developed into a predictable coda. She completed her opposition to evangelical dogma while affirming her commitment to its basic thrust and continued to evolve a female culture within the constraints of the domesticity she had earlier outlined. Yet before she began her final works, Catharine established a reassuring intimacy with her sister Harriet. For like others in the family, Catharine could not, in isolation, face the demise of its patriarch.

Charles, laboring on the *Autobiography* through the 1850s, stated most eloquently the dilemma shared by most of Lyman's children: how could they continue the vitality of his commitment to life, if they did not share the motivating source of his energy — a confirmed belief in eternal afterlife. Catharine almost alone among the children did not allow herself to question this belief so fundamental to her father's work. Yet Charles spoke for her as well as for the others when he sensed the opening of a void with the passing of his father's faith. In one of the most moving letters of the Beecher family correspondence Charles summed up Lyman's relationship to his children, dwelling on Catharine's life as a symbol of the family's former unity.

Compiling the autobiographical material of the 1820s was "deeply affecting," Charles wrote Henry in 1857. "It is really one of the most solemn things I have attended to for a long time." Charles' first thoughts were for his own children and his inability to manifest a concern for them analogous to Lyman's. Lacking both Lyman's faith and his familial commitment, Charles nevertheless continued to seek personal meaning in a world drained of significance. "Is eternal punishment a reality? Father thought so. He never doubted. Strike that idea out of his mind, and his whole career would be changed, his whole influence on us modified," Charles wrote. "Yet Isabella and Mary, I fear reject father's belief on this point, and Hatty's mind is I fear shaken — do you believe in it? Do you really believe that the wicked will exist forever, and continue forever in sin?" Charles pleaded with Henry for an answer. "Do you believe this? How can we affect our children as Father did us, if we have not the same concern for them, the same sense of their awful danger?" Charles lamented that he had "no real communion with God" and yet had "no life to struggle for any." His soul seemed "cold as death," yet he felt "a kind of settled resolution" not to waste his life.[5]

One answer to Charles's existential dilemma was to restore "the early unity of the family." If he could not recapture Lyman's sense of commitment and meaning, he could at least establish better contact with the survivors of that world, Catharine being its primary representative. Charles wrote to Henry:

> I have been deeply touched for *Catharine* in reading over her early letters. I wish you could read them. All before and after her engagement with Fisher, and his Death. All her deep and painful struggles in religious matters for years. How she has suffered! How she has been tried! And yet the character she shows is a very interesting one — I mean in her letters. Now I know she has peculiarities that repel some from her. And yet it seems sad to me to see her cast out as it were from the family circle by Mary and Hatty and you — not that she is really cast out — but something *virtually* pretty near it. Yet she is sincere and kind, and benevolent. That is she seems to have been so, both by natural impulse and on principle. Cannot she be made to feel more of the warm sympathy of fraternal affection in her loneliness? [6]

In one sense Catharine Beecher's concern with domesticity was an effort to capture and objectify the personal meaning that her own family had for her. Yet in another sense, just as Lyman did not confuse God's judgment with his own hopes for his children, so Catharine never blurred the distinction between her own family and the ideal state she believed domesticity could be. This made it easier for her to accept the marginal status she acquired in the Beecher clan, but it did not reduce her primary commitment to it. The last twenty years of Catharine Beecher's life were both a return to and a renewal of the struggle with her family. It was through Harriet in particular that Catharine reconfirmed her familial ties.

Lyman had feared for many years that after his death his other children would not adequately care for Catharine. In 1844 he expressed the deepest gratitude to George's widow, Sarah, when she offered to provide a permanent home for Catharine. "I spoke to her of my sympathy for Catharine more than for all the rest of my children when I should be called away and herself without support of her own and without health in the decline of life," Lyman had written Lydia about his interview with Sarah. "When in health and prosperity," Lyman said, Catharine had "cast her bread upon the waters. None of her age and with her means have been more public spirited and liberal than she," and he hoped others in the family would remember this later.[7] The success of Catharine's *Treatise* rendered Sarah's protection unnecessary then, and when Catharine did have a demonstrated need for familial support and sympathy after Lyman could no longer provide it, she turned to Harriet.

Throughout the 1850s — both before and after her Milwaukee effort — Catharine's fierce loyalty to Harriet was an important dimension in her life. The two sisters had been close since 1845, when Harriet expressed her enthusiasm for Catharine's *Duty of American Women*. "It is a stroke well aimed, well struck and must do good; well done Katy!" Harriet had written then. Catharine's role in effecting Harriet's release from her domestic trauma in Cincinnati may have forged a closer bond between them. Catharine moved into the Stowe house in Brunswick even before Calvin arrived there, and she ran the house while Harriet wrote *Uncle Tom's Cabin*. To pay for the refurbishing of the rambling Brunswick house, Catharine organized a boarding school of Beecher nieces and nephews, and arranged for the purchase of a new furnace, fixtures, furniture, carpets, wood, and coal. The only way she could make Calvin comfortable about these improvements was "by taking all the task myself and agreeing to foot all the bills that were not by the salary and income from the pupils," Catharine wrote Mary. Describing their daily routine, Catharine said she was "trying to get Uncle Tom out of the way" before the winter began. "At eight o'clock we are through with breakfast and prayers and then we send off Mr. Stowe and Harriet both to his room in the college. There was no other way to keep her out of family cares and quietly at work and since this plan is adopted she goes ahead finely," Catharine said. "I look forward with the greatest interest to our winter's work," Catharine concluded. "My only anxiety is in regard to that Milwaukee operation."[8]

Harriet's and Catharine's concerns were closely intertwined in this period. The week before Catharine's letter to Mary, Harriet had written Lyman and Henry: "I am going to write to you in relation to Catharine's affairs — as they have now become in a measure interwoven with mine. She has agreed to give me a year of her time to act conjointly with me and my own children," Harriet explained.[9] Catharine's help in Brunswick was essential, Harriet continued, yet it meant that her sister had to leave her work on behalf of women teachers. Harriet hoped that Lyman and Henry would by their enthusiastic public support for Catharine's

work, make it possible for her to take some time away from it, or
even better, permanently retire.

Harriet urged them to read *True Remedy for the Wrongs of
Women* — "I beg you will not let another day pass without reading
it as an act of justice to yourselves and to the public," — and she
launched into a complete analysis of Catharine's lifework. Until
she read *True Remedy,* Harriet said,

> I had no proper appreciation of her character and motives of action
> for this eight or ten years past. I considered her strange, nervous,
> visionary and to a certain extent unstable. I see now that she has
> been busy for eight years about one thing: a thing first conceived upon
> a sick bed when she was so sick and frail that most women would have
> felt that all they could hope for was to lie still and be nursed for the
> rest of their lives, then she conceived this plan of educating our coun-
> try by means of its women and this she has steadily pursued in weari-
> ness and painfulness, in journey in peril of life and health, in watch-
> ing and in prayer.

Her work was so spread out "from Maine to Georgia and from
Massachusetts to Iowa" that many of her own family had not seen
that it formed "a great *whole,*" Harriet continued, "and have
supposed that she was constantly attempting and constantly failing."
Catharine had earned and spent for the cause nearly five thousand
dollars in the last few years, Harriet said, "and she has worked as
yet almost *against* even her own family, for hitherto you know that
we have not had full confidence in her plans, but the time has come
when in my judgment there is ground and full ground for such
confidence and when to neglect them any longer would be unwise
and inexcusable," Harriet insisted. Although several of the details
and fragments of Catharine's work had failed, Harriet admitted,
she believed the "movement as a whole" was "a sublime specimen
of that force of character which God gives to an individual now
and then when he has a purpose to carry by them and which may
almost be regarded as an inspiration." [10]

Broaching a theme that reemerged in Catharine's work at the
end of the decade, Harriet concluded: "Furthermore this thing
has *got to go,* and it will go either in your hands and under your
influence or it will go by the aid of such men as Horace Mann,
Horace Greeley and all that modern reform party who all stand
waiting for the moment when Catharine will come on their side."

If Henry and Lyman failed to uphold Catharine's work, Harriet warned, "it will be instantly referred to them [the reformers] and go with acclamation, but it will take the impress of their sentiments, not of yours. And which is best, judge ye." While Henry and Lyman were "lukewarm and full of other things [the reformers] . . . meet Catharine with the warmest of zeal with offers of time, money, influence, everything. They are noble men, noble minded, noble hearted, energetic, and yet I would rather they came into the movement as accessories than as leaders, that thus they might have their sentiments modified by you," Harriet ended on a note of family loyalty, "for they need it." [11]

Catharine and Harriet were in sisterly agreement throughout that decade about the "low worldly" stance of many clergymen in the evangelical tradition and the more attractive attitudes of secular leaders like Mann and Greeley. "I have been mortified and astonished to see men of piety and men I thought *clear headed* as befogged as I found them all over the country," Catharine wrote about the clerical response to the Fugitive Slave Act. "I was not surprised at that!" Catharine said of Nathaniel Taylor's hedging on the issue, and she felt vindicated in her earlier attack on his character in *Truth Stranger than Fiction*. After reading Greeley's *Hints Toward Reforms,* Catharine explained, "When worldly men take such high Gospel ground and our leading ministers take such low worldly ground, how will the problem work out?" Catharine praised Henry's "pieces on slavery" in *The Independent* and said that his views on "that Fugitive Slave Bill (which I hope is yet to be whipped off to the ends of the Universe) suit me exactly." [12] As with much of the rest of the country, Catharine and Harriet grew considerably more radical in their attitudes toward slavery after the Fugitive Slave Bill. And their discovery of the clergy's widespread fallibility on the slavery issue heightened their sensitivity to its attitudes toward women.

During their closeness of the early 1850s Catharine and Harriet reinforced one another's opposition to the male dominance of evangelical protestantism. Harriet, like Catharine before her, focused on a specific clerical target, the Reverend Joel Parker, whom she attacked in *Uncle Tom's Cabin*; and Catharine's quarrel assumed majestic proportions with the publication of two volumes later in the decade. In her novel, which sold 300,000 copies in its first year, Harriet quoted Parker, a widely known Philadelphia Presbyterian minister, as justifying slavery because it had "no evils but such as are inseparable from any other relations in social and domestic life." Parker threatened a lawsuit, but Harriet stood her ground firmly, and in a letter to the *New York Observer* declared, "I grant I am a woman, but withall a woman well reputed," and in the stance of Cato's daughter, she continued,

> Think you I am no stronger than my sex
> Being so fathered.[13]

Lyman Beecher's daughters had learned from him how to fight in the evangelical cause, and as his days of battle drew to an end, they adopted his verbal arsenal for their own purposes. Although Calvin and Henry Ward negotiated a settlement with Joel Parker, and Harriet withdrew the quotation in later editions, her general indictment of the American clergy remained clear in *Uncle Tom* and in her public statements.[14] The main thrust of her remarks was that the clergy was not worthy of the trust the people placed in it as the nation's moral arbiters, and that they violated rather than upheld natural human virtues, the chief of these being associated with the domestic state. Women and Negroes, rather than the clergy, she believed, were the repository of moral virtue.

Catharine extended her sister's contentious mood with a thoroughgoing attack on John P. Jewett, the publisher of *Uncle Tom's Cabin,* who reaped 90 percent of the profits on the enormously successful book. Initially Jewett had offered Harriet a choice between sharing evenly the profits and losses of publication and a 10 percent royalty on every copy sold. Not wishing to take the risk involved in the first option, Harriet had chosen the second. Yet the immediate and astonishing success of the novel aroused Catharine's desire for a reconsideration of the contract terms, and, thinking that Jewett's profits were inordinate, she waged a spectacular personal campaign to force him to alter the terms of his contract with Harriet. This effort, beginning in 1852 and lasting through 1855, distressed most of the Beecher family, who viewed it as another of Catharine's disreputable antics, but Harriet recognized the impulses of sisterhood and loyalty that inspired Catharine's campaign. Fresh from her own attack on Joel Parker, Harriet understood Catharine's animus against men she believed unworthy of their positions of power and influence.[15]

The relationship between Catharine and Harriet in this period went much deeper than a mutual respect for and defense of each other's work, however. Both sisters took their Beecher identity very seriously, but both, because of their gender, were denied the usual acknowledgment of that identity through a ministerial career. Nevertheless, they were unable to follow Mary Beecher Perkins's example and lead completely private lives. Sharing the same commitment to their Beecher identity and its accompanying New England heritage, and also sharing the same ambiguity of status within that tradition because of their sex, Harriet and Catharine established a special relationship in which they acknowledged the peculiarities of their predicament. In 1843 Catharine had lent her more well-known name to Harriet's first volume of fiction, *The Mayflower, or Sketches of the Descendents of the Pilgrims,* a series of stories Catharine had collected, prepared for publication, and for which she had written an introduction. She praised good fiction in general and Harriet's in particular for its ability

> to improve the manners by an acquaintance with the refinements of polished society, to increase a knowledge of the world by vivid pictures of men and things, to cultivate the taste by exhibitions of the beautiful, correct, and pure, to elevate the sentiments, to expand the generous and benevolent sympathies, and to cherish religious principles and pious aspirations.

And Catharine identified Harriet as a sister "trained from childhood under her care." Catharine may have also arranged for Harpers to publish the volume. Catharine's enthusiasm for and support of Harriet's literary career continued through the 1840s, and it was to Catharine that Harriet first confided her plan to write a novel about slavery.[16]

Although Catharine may have had no more influence on *Uncle Tom's Cabin* than freeing Harriet from her domestic obligations, the novel did nevertheless exemplify the kind of female influence Catharine prescribed in her *Essay on Slavery and Abolitionism* in opposition to the Grimkés' active abolitionism. In her *Essay* Catharine urged women to "appeal to the kindly, generous, peaceful and benevolent principles" of those whom they opposed and to assert their influence through "the domestic and social circle." Harriet did believe she was appealing to the compassion of slaveholders by depicting the domestic plight of slaves, and she exemplified Catharine's belief that women should transcend regional loyal-

ties through her characterization of Northern complicity and
hypocrisy in Simon Legree.[17]

More significant for their personal relationship, Harriet began in
1853 to review material for inclusion in Lyman's autobiography,
and she read, perhaps for the first time, the family letters pertaining
to Catharine's crisis of 1822. She was also reminded of the maternal
sympathy Catharine had expressed during Harriet's own difficult
and introspective adolescence. After the family had left Litchfield
in 1827 and Harriet was adrift in unfamiliar Boston, she had
written Catharine: "I don't know as I am fit for anything and I
have thought that I would wish to die young and let the remember-
ance of me and my faults perish in the grave rather than live, as
I fear I do, a trouble to everyone. Mamma often tells me that I
am a strange inconsistent being. Sometimes I could not sleep and
have groaned and cried till midnight while in the daytime I tried
to appear cheerful." Catharine had immediately arranged for
Harriet to leave Boston and join her in Hartford. There Harriet's
spirits assumed buoyancy, and she developed the self-respect that
characterized most of her life. Research into the family past initiated by the autobiography reminded Catharine and Harriet of
their youthful closeness, and Catharine frequently referred after
1853 to the ways in which she had acted as a mother to Harriet
from 1816 until her marriage to Stowe in 1836 and to the "intimacy
and familiarity of sisterhood" that continued to characterize their
relationship.[18]

In 1855, very soon after Lyman Beecher's eightieth birthday,
Catharine organized a grand family reunion, and Lyman posed with
his children for a first and final family portrait. Catharine remarked
at the time that she felt more closely identified with the past than
the present, and more with Lyman's experience than that of her
younger brothers and sisters. "The last two or three years I have
felt more and more of that 'peace that passeth all understanding,' "
she wrote him. "As every year brings me nearer to departed friends,
the veil that separates us seems to grow thinner so that I feel almost
as near and present with those who are with the Lord as with those
who are still prisoned in these earthly tabernacles." [19] In the picture
Catharine sat on Lyman's right, holding his arm, her expression
projecting the solemnity of the occasion. Lyman alone, by now only
dimly aware of what was happening around him, seemed unwilling
to share the poignant mood and bear the burden of past remem-

brances that was evident on everyone else's face. The children were more aware than he was that the event marked the passing of an era. (Portrait reproduced in illustration section.)

Two years after this picture was taken, Harriet began to write one of the most significant descriptions of life in New England when it was dedicated to pleasing a jealous and angry God. *The Minister's Wooing* was written to commemorate that era, to pay tribute to Catharine's place in it, and, above all, to reconcile the author to the death of an unconverted son.

In July 1857 Harriet's eldest son and favorite child, Henry, had drowned at the age of nineteen in the Connecticut River by Dartmouth College, where he was a freshman. One of Harriet's first responses was to send a long letter to Catharine, her thoughts bearing the mark of ideas in Catharine's publication of that year, *Common Sense Applied to Religion, or the Bible and the People*.[20] In this work, Catharine summarized her quarrel with the New England tradition and, among other things, insisted that God saved those who seemed to want to be saved, not merely those who had passed through a conversion experience. Harriet wrote that she had been at first completely bereft:

> If ever I was conscious of an attack of the Devil trying to separate me from the love of Christ, it was for some weeks after the terrible news came. I was in a state of great physical weakness, most agonizing, and unable to control my thoughts. Distressing doubts as to Henry's spiritual state were rudely thrust upon my soul. . . . It was as if a voice had said to me: . . . You had perfect confidence that he would never take your child till the work of grace was mature! Now He has hurried him into eternity without a moment's warning, without preparation, and where is he?

Upon reflection, however, Harriet came to the same conclusions reached in Catharine's *Common Sense* and agreed that "it is our duty to assume that a thing which would be in its very nature unkind, ungenerous, and unfair has not been done," and that Henry was surely in Heaven.[21]

During the course of the next year, however, the tensions between Harriet's own belief and disbelief in Henry's redemption, the obvious parallels between her own present anguish and Catharine's of 1822, and her recent exposure to the full panorama of Calvinist New England in Lyman's autobiographical papers, prompted her to try to resolve through her writing what she could not in any other way achieve: a full analysis of the human condition as it existed and continued to exist in the harsh environment of New England Calvinism.

The Minister's Wooing was set in the eighteenth century and had many fascinating dimensions, but the light it threw on Catharine's character was especially revealing. Casting Catharine as a combination of Mrs. Marvyn and Mary Scudder of the novel, Harriet paid tribute to her strength of character and intellectual independence — neither quality auguring well for an easy passage through the rites of Calvinism. Harriet was closer to Catharine than any other person and certainly the most perceptive of those who knew her. Her characterization of Catharine's personality was as apt as her definition of Catharine's intellectual dilemma.

"Mary was only a recast in feminine form of her father's nature," the novel established at an early point. "The elixir of the spirit that sparkled within her was of that quality of which the souls of poets and artists are made; but the keen New England air crystallizes into ideas, and restricts many a poetic soul to the necessity of expressing itself only in practical living." It was easy enough, Harriet continued, "for Mary to believe in *self*-renunciation, for she was one with a born vocation for martyrdom; and so, when the idea was put to her of suffering eternal pains for the glory of God and the good of being in general, she responded to it with a sort of sublime thrill, such as it is given to some natures to feel in view of uttermost sacrifice." In a plot that might have applied to either Catharine or Harriet, the heroine was asked to marry a stiff but much revered gentleman and to accept marriage as a kind of self-renunciation. Fisher, transformed into a dashingly handsome sailor named James Marvyn, was the one Mary secretly loved. When he was lost at sea, both Mrs. Marvyn and Mary became disconsolate, but all ended happily when James miraculously returned and Mary married him instead of the esteemed, but unloved, gentleman.[22]

The chief drama of the novel centered on Mrs. Marvyn's dilemma when confronted with the death of her unconverted son. Here the character was drawn entirely from Catharine Beecher's experience. Although Mrs. Marvyn once had a woman's instinctive desire to inhabit a world of feeling, she had learned to repress emotion and sublimate her desires in intellectual activities. For long periods of time she was absorbed in "mathematical or metaphysical studies," and her fascination with theology acted like a "slow poison" to her instincts for life. Faced with the death of her son at sea, Mrs. Marvyn plunged to the heart of the Calvinist dilemma: although she rejected the theological argument that condemned her son, she saw all around her a world whose laws confirmed the truth of sacrifice and self-denial. "I have thought, in desperate moments, of giving up the Bible itself," Mrs. Marvyn declared, "but what do I gain?"

> Do I not see the same difficulty in nature? I see everywhere a Being whose main ends seem to be beneficent, but whose good purposes are worked out at terrible expense of suffering, and apparently by the total sacrifice of myriads of sensitive creatures. I see unflinching order, general good-will, but no sympathy, no mercy. Storms, earthquakes, volcanoes, sickness, death, go on without regarding us. Everywhere I see the most hopeless, unrelieved suffering—and for aught I see, it may be eternal. . . . We see a Being who gives himself for us,—and more than that, harder than that, a Being who consents to the suffering of a dearer than self.[23]

As one whose mind pursued a course of logic to its final conclusion, Mrs. Marvyn was crushed by "abstract certainties" of Calvinist logic. Her mind, Harriet wrote, was "enchained by glacial reasonings, in regions where spiritual intuitions are as necessary as wings to birds." She could not transcend the limits of the logical system that entrapped her.[24] She was too honest and too serious to accept a less compelling explanation for the evil she saw around her than that offered by Calvinism. The most she could do was to admit that evil was inherent in life, but that it was compensated for by the good that was achieved through sacrifice. This embraced and explained her own experience, and it reconciled her to an existence that was far removed from the joyous life she would have designed had she been the Creator. Harriet portrayed this predicament as one of high seriousness and significance, certainly meriting respect. Here was the New England tradition cast in its most majestic yet most uncompromising form.

Unlike Harriet, Catharine lacked the wings of spiritual intuition that might have lifted her above the grinding gears of Calvinist logic. Yet Harriet's success in both grasping and transcending the terms of her New England culture marked her as a woman of extraordinary insight and imaginative power. Catharine was first, last, and always a woman sensitive to the power of, and seeking to modulate the circumstances around her. She developed a great skill in reshaping and orchestrating the given elements of her culture, but precisely because of her concentration on this task, she could not extricate herself from its fundamentally uncongenial structure. On the contrary, the greater the distance between herself and purposeful workings of that structure, the greater her debilitation.

In another sense, however, regardless of their disparate methods, Catharine and Harriet did work toward the same goal — that of translating Calvinism into a social rather than a religious system. Harriet's novels, *Uncle Tom's Cabin* being a prime example, placed the self in a profoundly social context. Breaking with much of the romantic tradition in American fiction, Harriet's characters occupied neither the ideological terrain of Hawthorne, the natural setting of Cooper, nor the moral landscape of Melville. Rather, Harriet's primary interest was focused on the interaction between the malleable human being and the social milieu. The place where human motivation and social context met was also Catharine's lifelong concern. Both Harriet and Catharine were fascinated with the social workings of Calvinist culture, and just as some Enlightenment figures of the eighteenth century were more interested in the clocklike workings of the universe than in the creator who had set it working, so Harriet and Catharine became more interested in the social dynamics of the Calvinist system than in the original religious purpose it was designed to serve.

This much, at least, was true of Catharine's final significant work, *Common Sense Applied to Religion, or the Bible and the People.* Retaining the basic structural elements of redemption and damnation, she translated these into completely social terms, and God grew so remote as to be irrelevant to the workings of the system. It was to this work that Catharine turned when she began to anticipate the failure of her Milwaukee plans. Written in various Beecher homes during 1856 and 1857, the task still seemed incomplete to her after *Common Sense* was published, and she labored another two years on a sequel entitled *An Appeal to the People on Behalf of Their Rights as Authorized Interpreters of the Bible.* Although all these writings bore a theological guise, their real import was social. "As to this theological question it is to me now not a *theory* alone, it is practical," Catharine wrote Leonard Bacon as she began work on her second volume. She explained that she could not proceed with her educational plans until her basic theological stance was resolved. "The whole operation I have been carrying on the last seven years is stopping to have this question settled," she concluded. "After you have read my book you will understand this better." [25]

Although Catharine may have come to a standstill in her educational work with the successful but independent Milwaukee venture and the failure of her institutions elsewhere, educational organizing in any case was henceforth not her primary concern. Like others in the Beecher family during the 1850s, Catharine wanted permanently to establish her place in, her attitude toward, and her interpretation of her Calvinist heritage. Edward Beecher's *The Conflict of Ages* (Boston, 1852) had early in the decade defined his eccentric accommodation with Calvinism by asserting a preexisting state in which all souls were granted the opportunity to do right, but some chose to do wrong. Thus Edward retained his belief in the fundamental division between the saved and the damned, but he was no longer tortured by those whose perdition seemed to be shaped more by their worldly circumstances than by their sinful hearts. The world in the second half of the nineteenth century was not what it was at the century's beginning, and old systems of belief were dissolving even in the hands of those who still served them. Catharine's open attack on the old system actually saved the kernel of its faith, and her *Common Sense* and *Appeal to the People,* part ratiocination, part deep conviction, were entirely worthy of her status as the one Beecher who struggled a lifetime to ease the grip of her paternity.

☙ 17 ☙

The Grand Law of the System, 1857–1864

Puritanism's demand for an intense personal commitment served well the seventeenth-century need to overcome the old authorities of aristocracy and court. It established fervent new personal loyalties in place of the old and encouraged a new kind of group solidarity to supplant the traditional ones based on caste or locale. The same motivations that facilitated the transition to a modern society in England also nourished an early sense of purpose and distinctive identity in the American colonies. By the middle of the nineteenth century this mode of thought had exhausted its remarkable, but not unlimited, ability to energize and motivate large numbers of people. The power of the machine was fully as awesome a God to worship as Calvin's, and one no longer needed a wrathful deity to explain the widespread human suffering caused by the passing of the traditional order. What Puritanism had explained during the passing of the medieval order, Darwinism explained to the emerging industrial order. The fittest survive. God seemed less necessary to a culture that proceeded according to a clearly delineated course of evolutionary development. Optimistic "Victorian" credos resounded from pulpits as well as soapboxes and permeated Anglo-American culture without regard to class, just as its Puritan antecedent had done.[1]

What Catharine Beecher and a host of others realized, however, was that optimism wears thin on an empty stomach, and no culture can afford to let large numbers of people conclude they are "unfit" just because they are not on the top of the heap. The culture needed a system of belief that embraced these people and cemented their loyalties to the emerging social structure. Catharine meant to contribute to such a belief system. By emphasizing the importance of suffering, she tried to design a faith appropriate for the comfortable as well as for the miserable. Catharine recognized the essential similarity of needs shared by her contemporary nineteenth-century culture and by the earlier society that Puritanism served. Each revolved around two simple, but indispensable, ideas: what one does on earth affects how one prospers later; and the distribution of rewards and punishments rests not in human hands, but is accomplished through a more extensive system in which humans are but a small part.[2]

When Catharine Beecher came to record her final assessment of New England theology, she bore it such a cosmic grudge that only these two essential elements escaped scathing criticism. *Common Sense Applied to Religion, or the Bible and the People* was dedicated "To the People as the safest and truest interpreters of the Bible and To Woman as The Heaven-appointed educator of Mind." Her second volume, *An Appeal to the People on Behalf of Their Rights as Authorized Interpreters of the Bible* was dedicated "To the Editors of the Secular Press, True Tribunes of the People, Called of God in behalf of the Commonwealth to defend Liberty of Conscience, Freedom of Speech and the Right of all to Interpret the Bible for Themselves, Unrestrained by any Ecclesiastical Power." [3] Catharine Beecher's brash endorsement of this triumvirate — the people, women, and the press — was overstated, but it characterized her desire to break old molds of thought and formulate new ones. Much in Catharine's books was new for her, yet the books' significance lies not in their originality, but in their capacity to present old ideas in new forms. Although she seemed an innovator, Catharine actually endorsed as much as she rejected of the New England tradition.

Nevertheless the earlier vitality, exhortation, and breadth of import were gone from her writings. Her ideas now oscillated along a series of narrow axes between poles like temptation and rectitude or self and social system. If her later writings demonstrate the tenacity of the New England tradition, they also reveal the barrenness of the "realist's" universe when compared to the passion of the evangelical's. The specifics of Catharine Beecher's own experience had reduced her life from an orchestration of possibilities to a series of polarities, and so it was with the general contours of her thought. Whereas her earlier style emphasized the way in which interlocking hierarchies and social networks could forge the creation of a new social order, those hierarchies and networks were for her discredited or dissolved, and the emerging social order of the latter half of the nineteenth century seemed justified for her not by any specific qualities or goals, but simply by the fact of its existence. Adaptation replaced authority as the chief modality of her thought.

As Walter Houghton has suggested, the key to Victorianism may lay not in propriety alone, but in a variety of dualisms, each pole of which is conceived in absolute terms. Whereas ambition and conscience were, for example, welded together in the service of a higher goal in evangelical thought, they later easily separated into polarities. The self then achieves orientation between them by the intensity of moral energy — such as that manifested through qualities of ardor or endeavor or self sacrifice — with which one addresses each pole, rather than by the resolution of the polarity.[4]

Believing she could define religious and moral beliefs more appropriate for the mid-nineteenth century than those currently advocated by Protestant theology, Catharine asked rhetorically, "Is it to be supposed that theology alone, of all departments of science, has reached its culminating point, so that there is no possibility of improvement?" [5] She attacked the Calvinist notions of original sin, conversion, and God's grace. These were perversions introduced into the Christian religion by Augustine, Catharine said, drawing on her vast knowledge of church history, and they were still sustained by prominent American theologians. Catharine analyzed the theology of several leading clergymen, including Horace Bushnell and her brothers Edward and Henry Ward Beecher, to prove that even their revised forms of Calvinism maintained the basic premises of "Augustinian" religion.[6]

Catharine attacked the institution of the church as well as its doctrines and allied herself with the secular elements in American society. The "vast array of wealth, position, influence, and elclesiastical power" of American Protestant churches "is actually combined to sustain these theological theories," she said, and she called upon her readers to supplant church authority and dogma with their own common sense beliefs. Secular leaders, Catharine said, were already beginning to replace the moral leadership of the clergy and the church. "The press and public lectures are extensively supplanting the pulpit as organs of moral and religious influence," she commented, and declared her belief that "the leaders of the secular press" would prove "the most effective leaders in the intellectual and moral advance of humanity." "The great masses" of American men and women were no longer willing to submit to the church's doctrines, Catharine said. They were no longer able to believe that they were born with corrupt natures and needed to be reborn through God's grace in a conversion experience. They no longer fully believed that the fate of the regenerate and the wicked were predestined and that all actions before conversion were worthless in the eyes of God because they were those of an unregenerated soul.[7]

Catharine recapitulated the psychological principles from her *Elements of Mental and Moral Philosophy* to show that "the mind" acts according to its own laws, and she restated her corollary belief that "our minds" exist "in a social system" in which "each mind is made dependent for happiness on those around him." Happiness, Catharine said, can only be found by linking our personal mental laws with the mental and social laws that govern "the vast system in which we are placed." The chief law that governed mental development was, Catharine said, the principle of progression from lower to higher mental activity. "In the commencement of existence pleasure is secured mainly through the senses. Then come the higher social and domestic pleasures; then follow the intellectual enjoyments, the various gratifications of taste, and all the multitudinous resources open to a highly-cultivated, virtuous, and religious man." To accomplish this progression, she said, the lower pleasures must always be sacrificed to the higher. "Thus life commences with desires that are to be *controlled* and *denied*," and the process of denial continues throughout life. In a world of interdependent minds, self-sacrifice was also a social principle whereby one avoided injuring others and escaped personal injury. "The lesser good of the individual," Catharine said, "is always to be sacrificed to the greater good of the many." [8]

In Catharine's earlier writings the law of God was roughly congruent with the laws of man. There was no inherent conflict between human institutions and heavenly proscriptions. Yet now in the 1850s Catharine saw a clear difference and possible conflict between heavenly and earthly justice and between religious benevolence and social rectitude. In all cases she maintained that the best rule for men to follow was a worldly rather than a heavenly one.

In 1830 Catharine had equated self-sacrifice, benevolence, and rectitude, but now in her more secular mood she made a careful distinction between benevolence and rectitude. Benevolence was merely willingness to act in sacrificial ways, but rectitude went beyond this and included a consideration of the social circumstances surrounding the act. "It is important to discriminate more exactly in regard to the principle of *benevolence* and the principle of *rectitude*," she now wrote. "The principle of rectitude is more comprehensive in its nature," she said, "[because] it relates to all the laws of the system of the universe." Mere benevolence alone might omit important worldly considerations like propriety or duty. One "must not only choose to promote the greatest possible happiness, but must choose the right way of doing it," Catharine emphasized. The rules of rectitude were essentially social, and they could conceivably conflict with religious benevolence. When faced with such a conflict, one was to choose the rule of rectitude over that of benevolence. "It may be the case that benevolence acts contrary to the true rules of rectitude," Catharine said, "and thus may mar rather than promote happiness." [9]

Catharine thus transferred her moral philosophy from religious to secular grounds. The duty of men should be performed with reference to their social surroundings, and they should cease to trouble themselves with God's plan, for "the great system of the universe" would operate without their aid. They need not act in perfect accord with God's laws, but only exhibit "*tendencies* that *fit* to that great system of things in which men find themselves." In comparison with "the infinite and eternal" moral standard, the mind's action "may be very imperfect," Catharine said, "but in shorter terms every human mind is *perfect* when it is aiming to know what is right and to do it." [10]

Catharine's argument that the individual should take his moral guidelines from his society rather than from God was the basis of her morality. If social influences were so important a part of human morality, then it was essential that these influences be salutary. Each individual should strive to establish "a community" around himself, Catharine said, "where every social influence shall repress vice and encourage virtue." All moral people should freely expose and protest "against all that they believe wrong in the opinion or conduct of others," for in a community of moral and self-denying people, "no fear could intrude, where every mind was conscious that its own happiness was the constant care of every one around." This community was especially important where children were "being trained to virtue," Catharine said. "Where all around are practicing virtuous conduct — where all admire and praise only what is good and right — it is far easier to secure obedience to the rules of rectitude, than where the example and sympathy of surrounding minds are opposed to virtue." [11]

Popular evolutionary phrases like "the history of man," "the progress of mankind," and "the system of things" replaced religious concepts like "the will of God," "Providence," and "the laws of God," in her last writings. In this developmental, nonreligious scheme of thought, Catharine found an intellectual framework for her moral philosophy that was even better suited to her central idea of self-sacrifice than evangelical religion had been. For self-sacrifice in a purely religious context was not the only path toward redemption or the only manifestation of one's love to God. However, in the social context in which Catharine now placed it, self-sacrifice did constitute the only means of individual salvation and cultural regeneration. "The history of an individual is the history of self-conquest," Catharine wrote in this new secular mode. "It is a history of the self-denial and suffering involved in subjecting the physical to the intellectual, and both to the moral nature." The history of an individual and the history of a society were based on the same principle of suffering and self-sacrifice. "In like manner," Catharine continued, "the history of the race, from infancy through its stages of barbarism, heathenism, civilization, and Christianity, is a process of *suffering*, as the lower principles of humanity are gradually subjected to the higher." [12]

Catharine's notion of self-sacrifice was well-suited to a society that believed in the principles of progress and civilization but was increasingly aware of the hazards that accompanied progress. Wealth and luxury were desirable but could also be debilitating. Urban life was a mark of advancement but could also foster social infirmities. An increasingly complex culture was a sign of national maturity, but it could also be a harbinger of old age and cultural decay. Catharine explicitly recognized that both hope and fear were expressed in American attitudes toward progress, and she offered her principle of self-sacrifice as an answer to the dilemma of progress.

"The higher pleasures of the intellect and of the moral nature are dependent on culture," Catharine said, and the more developed a culture is, the higher are the mental and moral achievements of its people. Yet a highly developed culture presents dangers as well as advantages. "We find," Catharine said, "that abundance of ease and prosperity enervates mental power." The United States seemed to her a nation poised either to profit from or decline because of its cultural advances. "The last twenty-five years has exhibited a career of prosperity and self-indulgence that has alarmed every reflecting mind; and the question has often been pressed in private and in public. Are we too, like Greece and Rome, to be debilitated and demoralized by civilization and prosperity, and be supplanted by races less civilized but more vigorous?" Advancing civilization made higher intellectual and moral achievements possible, but it also created moral complications. "The higher a civilization advances," Catharine said, "and the more the modes of enjoyment, the more complicated become the questions of right and the more frequent the temptation to wrong." [13]

The answer to the perplexities created by the increasing worldliness of American society was not, Catharine said, to retire from the world or to seek an escape in an other-worldly religion. The Puritan solution of being *in* the world but not *of* it was an unacceptable one for Catharine because she believed that the fate of an individual was in a sense culturally determined, and to separate oneself from one's culture was to arrest one's moral and intellectual development. In her *Religious Training of Children in the School, the Family, and the Church,* published in 1864 but composed in part during the 1850s, Catharine elaborated this point further. Worldly experience and experiment were the only ways to fulfill one's moral nature, Catharine said, "for no one, however right the motive or intention may be, can discover what will cause more or less good or evil but by experiments in which the evil as well as the good is detected by experience." The Revelation of God was no aid in an advanced civilization, Catharine said, for "to learn what is right and wrong in all the thousand and million complications of life by revelation, would involve the necessity of a direct revelation every hour of every day, to every individual of the race." In simpler times, Catharine said, "one act of renunciation of the world placed a man out of range of its temptation," but the challenge to mid-nineteenth-century man was "to live in the world, to receive its prosperity, wealth, and all their involved temptations," and still remain virtuous. *"This,"* she said, was "a far higher elevation of moral and religious excellence." [14]

Yet Catharine's moral theory did not leave the individual without a guide through the "thousand and million" moral complications of a prosperous civilization. Although God's revelation could not supply a guiding principle, the secular history of man, and the developmental system that encompassed that history, could. In the 1850s Catharine introduced her law of self-sacrifice with a fanfare that had never accompanied it in her earlier moral and religious writings:

> We now come to the *grand law* of the system in which we are placed, as it has been developed by the experience of our race, and that, in one word, is
>
> SACRIFICE! [15]

If self-sacrifice and suffering were adopted as an antidote to ease and prosperity, then America would not follow the fate of Rome, Catharine said, for although prosperity was debilitating, "the effects of suffering are salutary and tonic." If it could be proved, moreover, that the truest happiness was gained through suffering, then earthly happiness would not be purchased at the price of cultural decline. Catharine's books were attempts to prove just this. One of the major themes of her moral philosophy was "that happiness is to be gained only by more or less suffering." [16]

Each of Catharine's three books was a treatise on self-sacrifice. This *"grand law"* was more than a guide to individual virtue and cultural survival. For upon it Catharine also built theological doctrines to justify the ultimate separation of the vicious from the virtuous and to explain evil. It was a law that permitted Catharine to break with the religious form in which her father's ideas were cast and yet to reaffirm them in another form. In addition to sustaining her father's belief in the "fearful sanctions of eternity" and the immutability of evil, Catharine's law of self-sacrifice upheld his hope for a consolidated society. "We are now going through a period of demolition," Catharine said. "In morals, in social life, in politics, in medicine, and in religion there is a universal upturning of foundations. But the day of reconstruction seems to be looming, and now the grand question is: Are there any sure and universal principles that will evolve a harmonious system in which we shall all agree?" [17] Catharine's books were her effort to evolve the social and moral "principles of reconstruction."

Because the mechanisms of human intelligence and motivation were everywhere the same, and because they functioned everywhere in a social context, Catharine believed there could be a set of principles around which the whole society could consolidate. A pluralist universe was outside her ken.

The single most important psychological mechanism in Catharine's writings was what she called "generic purpose." It was, however, almost entirely a social creation. "Experience has proved," Catharine said, "that such a generic purpose will not either be originated or sustained except by the social influences of surrounding minds." [18]

Generic purpose was important because it defined motives as well as conduct. It was for Catharine the equivalent of the conversion experience. "The commencement of 'a new life,' " Catharine said, "consists, not in the change of the nature of man, but in the commencement of a *ruling purpose*." It "may be an unconscious, gradual process by educational training, or it may be an instantaneous and conscious act," she wrote, but in either case it defined "the chief end or grand object" of an individual's existence.[19]

Governing or generic purpose was important to Catharine's moral philosophy in three ways. It gave direction and meaning to the vagaries of individual experience; it provided the motivating force that struggled against other internal motives not congruent with the generic purpose; and it determined every individual's ultimate destiny in the present life and hereafter.

The generic purpose, whether it is to gain wealth or political power, to be honorable or to do good, will, Catharine said, "determine the nature and the succession of the mind's conceptions. . . . If a man has chosen to find his chief happiness in securing power and honor, then those conceptions will be the most interesting to his mind that best fall in with his object." Thus human experience is not a series of disconnected particles but flows according to a plan. The governing purpose can control "our emotions, our desires and our thoughts," Catharine said, and "we have the power to regulate our emotions and thoughts through the discriminating agency of the governing purpose." [20]

The generic purpose was more than a selective agency, however; it was also an adjunct of the will and struggled against other powerful desires that ran counter to it. Here Catharine introduced suffering and self-denial as a major part of human experience. For the governing purpose was never so strong as to override other desires without a struggle. The highest kind of generic purpose in

Catharine's moral philosophy was to promote the happiness of others. But this purpose continually encountered struggles against other self-serving desires. Catharine Beecher was far more interested in these peripheral struggles than in the easier decisions made by the governing purpose. "When the strongest desire is for that which is best," she wrote, "the choice is *easy,* and the mind always chooses the best good." These kinds of choices were right, she said, but not meritorious. Only "when there is a struggle between a sense of what is right and best, and [a stronger] desire, and a choice is made which involves self-denial and self-sacrifice, [do] we feel that the act is one which is meritorious and deserving of reward and praise." For to choose without a struggle is not to choose what is right, but merely what is most desired. "To choose what we desire most," Catharine said, "even when it chances that our choice is that which is *best* and thus right, does not meet our idea of a meritorious and praiseworthy act." [21]

Suffering itself was for Catharine the only truly moral act. "Voluntary suffering," she said, "is discerned to be the highest kind of good and right conduct." The only happiness worth gaining is earned through suffering, she said, and in many cases the emotions are mixed together. "The most elevated and ecstatic happiness is combined with the keenest suffering," she said, "and suffering is the chief cause of the happiness thus secured." [22]

In terms very similar to her father's justification of evil on the grounds that without it God would have no means of showing His forgiveness and mercy, Catharine concluded that evil was a necessary element in human experience, for without its temptations, no act of self-sacrifice or self-denial would be possible. Happiness would not be created through suffering, and there would be no way to tell whether one was motivated to perform a virtuous act for the benefit of others or for the benefit of oneself. Just as Lyman had argued that evil was a necessary background to show the beauty of God's goodness, so Catharine said that the highest good was only revealed by its encounter with evil. "Thus," she said, "good will constantly be educed from evil." [23]

In addition to acting as the guide through daily experience and providing the stage for the performance of self-sacrifice, the generic purpose determined the ultimate destiny of individuals. For while those whose generic purposes are leading them into greater obedience "to the great system of things," will continue to grow in virtue, those with self-serving generic purposes will become steadily more vicious. "Mankind as a race are to continue to progress until at some period a certain portion will arrive at the entire and perfect obedience to the law which, at the present state of being no one has ever yet attained," Catharine said. "But on the other hand this progress will be attended with the hopeless and perpetual ruin of multitudes who, as individuals, take a retrograde course and grow more and more guilty and miserable." Catharine used evolutionary rhetoric, but the conclusions she reached were close to those asserted by her father's evangelical beliefs. Some were to be saved and others damned, not only on the basis of their conduct, but according to the nature of their internal motives. This separation of the vicious from the virtuous had a cultural advantage, Catharine said, for it "will purify the commonwealth" and "contribute to the improvement of the race." [24]

Catharine Beecher's grand law of self-sacrifice was designed for a society troubled by its dedication to worldly pursuits. The financial panic of 1857 caused many people to question this dedication, and the revival that quickly followed in 1858 demonstrated that many were searching for ways to restore their confidence in themselves and their world.[25] Although Catharine's first book was written a year before this urban revival, she addressed the concerns of those people who later participated in it. Worldly pursuits, she assured them, could be safely enjoyed provided they were seen as duties, rather than pleasures. "In this light, music, drawing, painting, sculpture, architecture, the drama, poetry, laughter, all things that import enjoyment to any mind are *right*," she wrote, "and may become positive duties," for they are pursuits to which the lower emotions have been sacrificed. The moral complications created by worldliness were enormously simplified by the law of self-sacrifice. "Every attempt to develop any faculty of enjoyment . . . every effort to provide ailment for such developed capacities is right," she said, "provided it is done according to the great law of sacrifice, viz., that individual enjoyment be made subordinate to the general good, and that no greater good be sacrificed for a less, either for self or for the commonwealth." Even financial failure could be read not as a warning against worldliness, but as an "ennobling" experience of suffering.[26]

Catharine Beecher's midcentury moral philosophy portrayed the ways an individual or a culture could learn to survive within "the great system of the universe." The individual was caught up in a "system" he had neither designed nor desired, but if he did not obey its laws, it would destroy him. The only alternative to destruction was to join "the system" and try to eliminate any qualities that marked one as an opponent of the higher laws that governed it. "The history of an individual is a history of self-conquest," Catharine Beecher said, and the highest achievement of an individual's life is to sacrifice it for others and for "the universal system of which all men are a part." This moral view was not unique to Catharine Beecher, for it spoke for the mood of many people before, during, and after the Civil War. Oliver Wendell Holmes, Jr., was perhaps the most prominent advocate of this view, and his belief in it was shaped by his Civil War experience.[27] In 1864 Catharine Beecher wrote as one who had seen her prophecy fulfilled. "In this grand emergency," she wrote, "what deeds of self-sacrifice . . . have evolved!" The Union army seemed to her the embodiment of the principles of her moral philosophy:

> Enrolled in ranks, each with its subordinate and superior officers, who exact unquestioning, unfailing faith and obedience, till at last the whole vast body is moved by one controlling mind as its head — one who decides for all and each which shall have the post of comparative ease and honor, and on which, as unknown privates, shall fall the forlorn hope and certain death.[28]

This was not a heroic sacrifice, distinguished by deeds of individual courage and carried out for the sake of a God who watched over the fate of every human soul. It was a fatalistic sacrifice marked by obedience and performed blindly because "one controlling mind" demanded it.

Catharine Beecher struggled most of her life against the "fatalism" of her father's religion, but in this passage that marked the close of her last book of moral philosophy she returned to the spirit if not to the letter of his belief. This passage resembled the note she had written more than forty years before to her father. There she had described herself as a helpless soul adrift in a swift current that bore her toward destruction while God watched on but refused His aid. The "one controlling mind" of 1864 was as cold as God had seemed to her in 1822. The only difference between the two passages is that Catharine had come to glorify a world view and a personal experience she had once protested. The effects of suffering in Catharine's own life were far from "salutary and tonic." Yet she recommended that others voluntarily adopt a philosophy she herself had followed out of necessity rather than choice.

Catharine still had not discovered an explanation or justification for a "system" that demanded unquestioning obedience but was unresponsive to the suffering that accompanied obedience. Cultural progress was the justification she adopted, but it has the ring of expediency rather than conviction in her prose. "The system of things" was a phrase that appeared often in Catharine's three books, yet its vagueness demonstrated her lack of interest in the specific nature of or the rationale behind the system. After a lifetime of real and imagined suffering she emphatically believed she had experienced constraints imposed upon her by some outside force, and she was more interested in analyzing that experience than she was in investigating the nature of the outside force. She had experienced suffering and self-sacrifice, but the act of ordering that experience was for her more "salutory" than suffering itself had been. Throughout Catharine's career she had tried to order her own experience by objectifying it. In Hartford she had transferred her analysis of her own character into an analysis of the character of her students. Now at the end of her career she engaged in the same kind of exercise and reconciled herself to sacrifice by studying it objectively.

A review of all three of Catharine's works in the *Christian Examiner* praised their "earnestness and vigor." The reviewer remarked that he was "glad all the more the writer is a woman. It is some guarantee that the discussion will not proceed in the ruts of tradition, and that the theology of the pulpit, the divinity schools, and the ministerial conventions is to be ventilated and humanized." Catharine's personal narration of enduring "perplexities and agonies . . . under Calvinistic theories" impressed her readers, for they could sympathize with her righteous indignation at "the effect of these doctrines on the young, and especially young women." [29] Fewer reviewers noted, however, that she had constructed a new system equally as oppressive, perhaps especially so to women, who were to act as its prime exemplars.

"This work is offered, not as one of metaphysics and theology, to exercise the intellect alone," Catharine wrote in *Common Sense Applied to Religion.* "It presents the grand practical question of life to *woman,* as the mother, the educator, the nurse, and the fountain of home sympathies for the race." For women were to do the work of national redemption under the new dispensation Catharine had described. "The great want of our race is *perfect educators* to train new-born minds, who are *infallible teachers of what is right and true,*" she exclaimed. Theories of morality and religion, moreover, "are especially to be examined and decided on by *woman,* as the heaven-appointed educator of infancy and childhood." Women were rebelling against the theology of their ministers, Catharine concluded, and she meant to supply them with a viable substitute.[30]

Although the writing of *The Religious Training of Children in the School, the Family, and the Church* carried Catharine's theological wrestlings into the 1860s, her work thereafter, especially on women, took a much more practical turn. True to her pattern of seeking consolation in theological and philosophical speculation, Catharine became engrossed in these works of 1857, 1860, and 1864 after her Milwaukee disappointment. She began the last decade of her life by reopening the Hartford Female Seminary. Under the prosaic influence of operating a school again, her heart lightened, and her subsequent writings on women, emphatically conservative though they occasionally were, raised many issues not yet resolved a century later than she wrote.

❧ 18 ❧

A Trunk without a Label, 1864–1878

Much of the fabric of Catharine Beecher's life was woven by the interplay between her own sense of self and the stereotypes through which American society viewed her. Although on many occasions she exaggerated her self-importance and earned a well-deserved rebuke, the tension between her refusal to compromise her dignity and the nineteenth-century prejudice against independent unmarried women shaped her life in significant ways. Since 1822 she had instinctively opposed the subtle self-abasement her society asked of women, and she increasingly resisted its ridicule of unmarried women. Since she took both social opinion and her own self so seriously, she spent much of her energies on the trauma of choosing between them, or on laboriously reconciling them. She respected her culture, and she never accommodated herself to the fact that the feeling was often not reciprocal.

Like many other women of her time, and before and after, her life was a series of exploratory ventures, sounding out one prospect, suffering excruciating rebuke, retrenching, and searching for another. In her older years, however, Catharine finally learned to take the world less seriously, and she rested secure in her own sense of worth. She was able to joke about her public personality, and when she received less than what she considered her due, she learned to ignore her detractors. In 1860, responding to a public attack on Henry Ward Beecher, she sympathized with his predicament and humorously asked him to reserve a place near by in the ranks of the derogated. "I am sure father meant to *entail* me as well as you with some of his tares," she said.[1] When she discovered in her seventies a course at Cornell she had long wished to study, Catharine took up residence in Ithaca and reported her presence and purpose to Andrew D. White, Cornell's president. "I regret to say, Miss Beecher, that as yet we have no courses open to women," White replied. "Oh that is quite all right, Doctor White, in fact I prefer to take it with men," Catharine answered, and registered her intention to reside in a local dormitory. "But, Miss Beecher, that is a dormitory for young men," White explained. "It has no accommodations for ladies!" Holding her ground, Catharine retorted, "I have inspected the accommodations and find them entirely satisfactory, and as for those young men, who are of appropriates ages to be my grandsons, they will not trouble me in the least." [2] She enjoyed the course, and Cornell survived the encounter.

Catharine continued throughout the 1860s to travel, organize, and proselytize in behalf of women teachers, and although the Board of Managers of the American Woman's Educational Association voted to disband in 1862 since "no effort with the public could be wisely attempted in the present state of our public affairs," Catharine ignored the decision, and continued its activities without the managers' aid.[3] In 1878 — long after the association had ceased to function in either its fund-raising or its institution-founding capacity — she was still keeping its records. Undaunted by an attendance of only three members in 1870 — herself, Mary Mortimer, and the woman in whose home the meeting was scheduled — Catharine drew up an ecumenical list of potential recruits including Catholics, Jews, Unitarians, Universalists, Swedenborgians, Quakers, and Baptists, along with the usual Episcopalians, Congregationalists, Presbyterians, and Methodists.[4] Catharine had not learned to accept defeat. Neither had she ceased to enlarge her definition of the virtuous.

In her usual style Catharine's travels in the late 1850s and early 1860s included self-initiated invitations to the homes of acquaintances along her route. "My health and nervous excitability are such that I can talk only a short time at once on any subject in which I feel any deep interest," she wrote Nathaniel Wright in prelude to her visit to Cincinnati in 1859. "I am still so lame that I could not come easily to see you — nor should I wish to tax you with repeated calls. For this reason I shall ask the privilege of the hospitalities of your house for two or three days," Catharine ingeniously concluded. Retaining her taste for travel, Catharine was less perturbed by its frequent inconveniences than were the friends and relatives who were called upon to assist her. Henry described to Eunice in telegraphic style an encounter with Catharine in one of her irresponsible moods. "Cate and Hattie at Susan's from Elmira — go home today. Cate lost pocketbook — in your way — couldn't get trunks, go over to see, very likely the rascal sent checks and got *trunks too* — lively times and good morals!"

Although she began in the early 1860s to return the free rail passes she had wheedled out of major railroad companies in the 1840s, Catharine's last trip to Milwaukee was as late as 1864, and the year before her grand nieces marveled at her fearless undertaking of an all-night journey from Hartford to Brooklyn. By her sixty-seventh year, however, Catharine adopted tamer habits, and took pleasure in, she said, "a delightful house where I board in the city [New York], where I can see friends every day, ride in cabs, etc. So I am spending a very pleasant winter. My health perfectly good and no walking needed." [5]

Lyman Beecher died in January 1863 after a decade of senility broken only by brief flashes of comprehension. A "solemn, joyful" family reunion and memorial service took place a week later in Henry's church. "The air around us in the church seemed . . . full of bright visionary faces of those *called* dead, but who live more truly than we do," Harriet wrote of the occasion. [6]

Even before her father's death Catharine had become an Episcopal convert. Her spiritual pilgrimage ended in the church that emphasized the institutional and social aspects of faith. "I have more and more realized how much we are dependent for truth not on God alone, but also on our fellow men," Catharine had written Leonard Bacon prior to her change of church membership. She took the decision very seriously and continued in a subsequent letter, "I write again because I do not suppose you fully comprehended my aim. I really feel the need of counsel." In working on her volume about the religious training of children, Catharine had concluded that only the Episcopal church treated children decently. "For they, by baptism, *do* [erase] the evil done by Adam's sin, so that the child can be successfully *trained* by a *religious growth.*" Other Protestant churches, continuing the Calvinist tradition, prefer a testimonial of rebirth to gradual training during childhood, Catharine said, and by so doing they treat children as aliens. "Now what I am to say [in response to this]," Catharine continued, "is to go into the Episcopal Church and you will be free — more free than in any other denomination. Strange as it may seem, you will find it to be the fact." [7] Half pleading with Bacon to prove her wrong, Catharine found his final reply to her unsatisfactory, and she completed her *Religious Training of Children* a confirmed Episcopalian.

Catharine Beecher's *Religious Training of Children* was a lucid example of the way nineteenth-century American religious thought reversed the sequence of innocence and evil in life's stages. Calvinism viewed children as corrupt, their inherent evil being later redeemed by a conversion of spiritual rebirth. Since rebirth usually occurred in early adulthood, there was a basic congruence between the individual's natural physical growth and the culture's view of his appropriate spiritual growth. The life progression was from corruption to purity, and knowledge fostered and accompanied that progression. During the nineteenth century popular thought turned this progression on its head, and by the time Catharine wrote her book in 1864, children were deemed innocent at birth but gradually corrupted by the world around them. Their education was therefore given over to the preservation of their innocence rather than to the eradication of their sin. Yet it was precisely at this point that a great difficulty emerged, for, as Catharine pointed out in *Letters to the People on Health and Happiness,* innocence could not be preserved by ignorance. One had to know evil in order to resist it successfully. "Victorian" parents therefore set for themselves the impossible task of preserving natural innocence and yet acknowledging that exposure to evil was virtually inevitable and even necessary, thus polluting innocence through experience and adulthood.

An extremely popular etiquette book published in the year of Catharine's death wrestled with the dilemma. "There are some careful and conscientious mothers, who, watching the gradual change from infancy and childhood to youth and maturity, and who, marking how often additional knowledge is accompanied by additional sin, wish that their children's ignorance of evil might be prolonged," Mrs. H. O. Ward declared in *Sensible Etiquette.* "Innocence is lovely in the child, because in harmony with its nature; but our path in life is not backward but onward, and virtue can never be the offspring of mere innocence," she continued. "If we are to progress in the knowledge of good, we must also progress in the knowledge of evil," she explained. "Every experience of evil brings its own temptation and according to the degree in which the evil is recognized and the temptations resisted, will be the value of the character into which the individual will develop." [8]

Catharine Beecher had foreseen the development of this moral formula in the 1830s, long before the culture boxed itself completely into the predicament. If good is natural but knowledge pollutes it, then morality consists of either ignorance or a tantalizing involvement with and a painful exorcising of evil. In neither case is morality an affirmation of the good. Although Horace Bushnell, Catharine Beecher, and the mainstream of American culture had rejected the Calvinist explanation of the origin of evil, they did not modify their vision of a world divided sharply between good and evil. Personal evil was to Calvinist an inevitable and natural sign of corrupt human nature; a nature transcended only by death and until then to be borne with as good grace as possible. To the generation that rejected this view of human nature, the slightest blemish was viewed as an unnatural sign of weakness to be purged as thoroughly as possible. The rejection of natural human evil and the purgation of evil through suffering went hand in hand in the nineteenth century. Mrs. Ward's *Sensible Etiquette* continued: "Though suffering be the price of such a character, welcome be the suffering. . . . As Bushnell says: 'There are no fires that will melt out our drossy and corrupt particles like God's refining fires of duty and trial. . . .' "

The Victorian period thus can be seen as a brief era in modern Western history lacking an explanation for evil. It fell between Calvinism and Freudianism — two systems of belief viewing human evil as an inevitable and understandable aspect of human nature. Catharine Beecher's *Religious Training of Children* presented both the origin, the logical expansion, and the full development of this Victorian dilemma. The book can be seen as equally divided into three parts: a discussion of her early rejection of the doctrine of natural depravity; an insistence on the continued reality of evil and the dangers it posed to human innocence; and a resolution of the relationship between innocence and evil through self-sacrifice and suffering as a purgation of evil. "As liberty and intelligence have increased the people have more and more revolted against theological dogmas that contradict common sense and wound the tenderest sensibilities of the soul," Catharine wrote. But "the dangers of the future life" remained, she insisted, and the purpose of this life was to separate the virtuous from that "portion of our race [who] will exist forever sinful and consequently miserable." Therefore the human race cannot simply relax and enjoy its inherent goodness, but must guard against defiling it. The highest virtue that one can develop, then, is the ability to deny oneself the pleasures that might pollute. The child should be "taught . . . self-control of its own appetites and passions," and to meet "all the involved temptations" of the world with self-sacrifice, doing "not what we like to do, but those things which are contrary to our tastes." [9]

The evolution of this ethic in Catharine Beecher's life and thought was shaped by her inability to abandon Calvinism in its entirety, although she greatly needed to reject its central view of human nature. Retaining, as did most of her generation, a belief in the sharp separation of good from evil — manifested both in this world and in the next — she remained loyal to the outer shell of the belief system that she had robbed of its explanatory power. Catharine believed she was taking great risks in asserting the basic goodness of human nature. The fact that she could assert human goodness but not at the same time advocate a life devoted to enjoying it meant only that she was struggling within, not blindly disregarding, her historical circumstances.

During the hectic war years when the family correspondence was filled with heated debate about the efficacy of Lincoln's management of the northern strategy, the demands on Harriet as a world-famous author increased, and she drifted away from her former intimacy with Catharine. Their intimacy was restored, however, by their collaboration on *The American Woman's Home* in 1869. For almost a year Catharine lived with the Stowes in their modest home that was part of Hartford's famous Nook Farm literary colony, with the mansions of the Samuel Clemens and the Charles Dudley Warners forming the two other points on a triangular piece of shared suburban land.[10] For three years thereafter Catharine's spirits and energies revived, and she revitalized the Hartford Female Seminary, played an active role in the debate on women's suffrage, and clarified her assessment of the needs of American women. It was not until 1875 that her focus on events became less acute, and she lapsed into nominal charity work.

The American Woman's Home, a formidable sequel to Catharine's compact *Treatise,* contained little new besides Harriet's elaborate designs ranging from shoe bags to entryways and Catharine's increasing support of a female-headed household. Some modern improvements in stoves, "earth closets" and the like were graphically illustrated, and except for Harriet's four new utilitarian chapters on decorating and gardening, the bulk of the volume was drawn from Catharine's *Treatise*. One theme, however, was significantly heightened by both illustrations and text — the character of the Christian household, which was usually depicted as a combination of home, school, and church. This was Catharine's final vision of a unified institutional matrix. "A small church, a schoolhouse, and a comfortable family dwelling may all be united in one building, and for a very moderate sum," Catharine wrote, "as will be illustrated by the following example." Elaborate drawings and explanations then showed how the room devoted to school during the week could be transformed into a church on Sunday by the removal of a screen in front of the pulpit. "During the week, the family work is to be done in the kitchen, and the room adjacent be used for both a school and an eating-room," Catharine explained. "Here the aim will be, during the week, to collect the children of the neighborhood, to be taught not only to read, write, and cipher, but to perform in the best manner all the practical duties of the family state. Two ladies residing in this building can make an illustration of the highest kind of 'Christian family,' " Catharine continued, by adopting orphans, caring for the aged, and employing "boys and girls in various kinds of floriculture, horticulture, bee-raising, and other out-door employments, by which an income could be received and young men and women trained to industry and thrift. . . ." Catharine called for the establishment of such home–school–churches by "Christian women in unhealthful factories, offices, and shops; and many, also, living in refined leisure, who yet are pining for an opportunity to aid in carrying the Gospel to the destitute." [11] The need for women to "earn an *independent livelihood,* especially in employments that can be pursued in sunlight and the open air," was very great, she concluded, and she urged her readers to support the work of the American Woman's Educational Association toward that end.[12]

By 1869 the cultural matrix Catharine had promoted all of her adult life was close to confirming its national authority. The family, no longer needed as an agency for facilitating such a unified culture, emerged in *The American Woman's Home* in a new idealized state as the epitome of harmonious social interdependence. Catharine's lengthy analysis of the needs of an expanding democracy were replaced by a description of the family as a small-scale model of how the society as a whole should function. "The distinctive feature of the family is self-sacrificing labor of the stronger and wiser members to raise the weaker and more ignorant to equal advantages," Catharine began. "The father undergoes toil and self-denial to provide a home, and then the mother becomes a self-sacrificing laborer to train its inmates," she wrote. "The useless, troublesome infant is served in the humblest offices; while both parents unite in training it to an equality with themselves in every advantage. Soon the older children become helpers to raise the younger to a level with their own," Catharine continued. "When any are sick, those who are well become self-sacrificing ministers. When the parents are old and useless, the children become their self-sacrificing servants." [13]

The ideology of domesticity had been raised from a millennial experiment to an accepted model of social organization. Catharine wrote as though she assumed her reader's agreement. "The family state then, is the aptest earthly illustration of the heavenly kingdom, and in it woman is its chief minister," Catharine rather briefly stated in comparison with her earlier lengthy justification in the *Treatise.* "To man is appointed the out-door labor — to till the earth, dig the mines, toil in the foundries, traverse the ocean, transport merchandise, labor in manufactories, construct houses, conduct civil, municipal, and state affairs, and all the heavy work, which, most of the day, excludes him from the comforts of a home," Catharine added in a new description of the varieties of modern male labor. "But the great stimulus to all these toils, implanted in the heart of every true man," she continued, "is the desire for a home of his own, and the hopes of paternity." [14] The male was truly now as deeply implicated in the ideology of domesticity as the woman. In the 1840s the burden of stability had fallen primarily and nearly exclusively on the woman, and it may have been a sign of the success of the national ethic that both men and women were assumed to respond to the same image of personal happiness.

During the year Catharine and Harriet collaborated at Nook Farm Catharine fully reentered the Hartford social milieu, recapturing the sense of belonging that had characterized her life there nearly fifty years earlier. Her friends were likely to receive elaborate invitations to such pleasantries as "a door-step concert at Nook Farm with Miss Beecher at the guitar," or an evening of sermons in parody form such as that featuring Catharine in an oration against tobacco, or charades at a tea party with Horace Bushnell and other older Hartford luminaries in attendance.[15]

It was out of such a re-creation of the Hartford environment of the 1820s that Harriet and Catharine agreed to reopen the Hartford Female Seminary. With the advent of public high schools for girls, the seminary had become an economically and pedagogically marginal institution, and they hoped their names would restore its prestige. As principal, Catharine moved into the house where the other teachers and twenty students boarded. One of the young teachers recalled, "[Catharine] often invited me into her bedroom which was a South-east corner one, in a large white house, surrounded by fine trees and stood on a small elevation which we approached by eight or ten steps." At the boardinghouse Catharine arranged frequent "little parlor dances" in the evening, and it was "a very happy and home-like place." Catharine still made her own shoes with soft soles, and her favorite dress was of black lace over pink linen.

Catharine organized the curriculum to make the most of Harriet's skills in composition and Calvin's in biblical history. Classes occasionally met in the Stowes's home.[16] At the end of the year a young cousin, Katy Foote, assumed responsibility for the seminary, and although Catharine had put one thousand dollars of her own money into refurbishing the building, the seminary remained more a relic than a functioning institution during the latter decades of the nineteenth century.[17]

What new vitality Catharine failed to generate in her seminary she succeeded in arousing in her own life, however, and the next two years were filled with correspondence, organizing efforts, and fund-raising for new women's universities, one of which eventually became Simmons College in Boston. Although the American Woman's Educational Association was little more than a paper organization, she used it as an umbrella for her activities.

Catharine's work during these two years, well summarized in her *Woman's Profession as Mother and Educator with Views in Opposition to Woman Suffrage* (1872), curiously combined both conservative and radical proposals for the future of women in America. Catharine identified her attitude as "conservative," and, as an outspoken opponent of female suffrage, she reverted to her class bias against placing political power in the hands of women who did not share her middle-class political views. She was in favor of suffrage for women who through wealth or economic independence were on the tax rolls. Yet Catharine's heart was never engaged at this level of the suffrage discussion, and she gave it only a passing reference. Her writings and speeches moved quickly on to an exhortation in favor of an educational system that would provide all women with economic independence, and a full criticism of the American denigration of women's work. Speaking in Boston in 1870, Catharine declared her complete support for the right of women to "happiness and usefulness" equal in value to that of men, and she emphasized her agreement with the suffrage movement's claim that women in America have "never been allowed such equal advantages and that multiplied wrongs and suffering have resulted from this injustice." Finally, Catharine said, she agreed "that it is the right and duty of every woman to employ the power of organization and agitation, in order to gain those advantages which are given to the one sex, and unjustly withheld from the other." Nevertheless she believed that suffrage would not solve the problems faced by women in America, and "that the evils it is hoped to cure by the ballot would continue and increase for a long period." [18] Instead of concentrating on suffrage, Catharine argued, women should unite to establish their economic independence and insist that their domestic labor be granted the dignity and respect accorded to male labor outside the home.

In her writings twenty years earlier Catharine had made both these points, insisting that the "real wrongs" of women were that their domestic "profession" was "dishonored." Although they were encouraged to pursue a variety of academic studies, they were in fact "now only educated to be somebody's wife" and could only rarely put their education to use in some gainful employment. In 1898 Catharine's grandniece, Charlotte Perkins Gilman, granddaughter of Mary Beecher Perkins, would elaborate this argument into one of the most important feminist treatises of the nineteenth century, *Women and Economics*.[19] The avowed aim of the American Woman's Educational Association had always been to establish teaching positions for women so they could become financially independent. It also wished to create institutions to instruct young women in domestic duties, especially the moral and religious training of children, so that women's work could develop a professional status equivalent to that of medicine, law, and business for men.[20] In one of their last collaborative works, Catharine and Harriet composed a pamphlet urging that women be trained as "home physicians [who would] be as liberally educated and paid as men for curing diseases." These women would focus on preventive medicine and public health, areas ignored, the authors said, by the current tendency of the medical profession to follow only their own "pecuniary interest." [21] In 1871 Catharine and Harriet distributed a circular advertising their intention to begin such medical training in a summer institute under the auspices of the American Woman's Educational Association, but they received little response.[22]

To the public who knew her, then, Catharine's alternatives to women's suffrage were no surprise. On at least one occasion she shared a platform with Elizabeth Cady Stanton, and since her half-sister, Isabella Beecher Hooker, was a prominent suffragist and Henry Ward Beecher was President of the American Woman Suffrage Association, Catharine was on excellent personal terms with members of the more conservative wing of the suffragist movement.[23] Catharine attacked the education of wealthy girls as leaving them "no opening — no promotion — no career, except that of marriage, and for this they . . . [must] wait to be sought. Trained to believe marriage their highest boon, they are disgraced for seeking it, and must affect indifference," Catharine exclaimed. For poor women the same economic dependence on men prevailed. Catharine sympathized with factory women, and other working women, including prostitutes, who could not find work at a living wage. "Multitudes of these unfortunates have only two alternatives — on the one hand, poor lodgings, shabby dresses, poor food, and ceaseless daily toil from eight to ten or fifteen hours"; on the other hand, she could succumb to a life of prostitution, Catharine said, which provided for all her needs and released her from a life of inadequately rewarded toil. "Where is the strength of virtue in those who despise and avoid these outcasts," Catharine concluded, who "might not fail in such perilous assaults?" [24]

Although Catharine could not offer full solutions to the problems created by a rapidly industrializing and urbanizing society, she did advocate "the importance of educating every young girl with some practical aim, by which, in case of poverty, she might support herself." Recommending teaching as a primary instance of such economic independence, Catharine now criticized the fact that women teachers were "unjustly denied equal compensation" for equal work, and she now insisted that women should fill civil service and professional positions. "Still more unjust is the custom which gives superior advantages to men for the scientific and practical training for a profession by which an honorable independence may be secured and almost none at all are provided for women," Catharine concluded near the end of a speech. "So also in the distribution of public offices of trust and emolument which secure an income from the civil state, there are several in which women can perform the duties as well or better than men," she said.[25]

Returning in each speech to her work in founding women's educational institutions, Catharine reiterated her belief that "when institutions are endowed to train women for all departments connected with the family state, domestic labor, now so shunned and disgraced, will become honorable, will gain liberal compensation, and will enable every woman to secure an independence in employments suited to her sex." Catharine's image of women's work, once illuminated by a millennial glow, now bore a highly professional hue. Her new message was addressed not to a culture defined by the broad strokes of romanticism and evangelicism, but by the sharp lines of the realist, where every element could be carefully placed in its specified niche. Her present concern was that women were being left out of society's increasingly specialized work roles, and she saw both the need to include them in new areas of employment and to specialize, professionalize, and thereby raise the status of women's domestic work.[26]

Summarizing her labor of the last few years, Catharine said she gained great pleasure from it although it produced no tangible results. Her companionship with Harriet and her acceptance of the fact that she could not afford a home of her own may have contributed to the softened and more benign outline of Catharine's visage during this last decade of her life. She viewed her failures with equanimity and seemed genuinely grateful for her continued ability to play a public role and be well received by audiences. "I have been for many years a wanderer without a home, in delicate health, and often baffled in favorite plans of usefulness," she said. "And yet my life has been a very happy one, with more enjoyments and fewer trials than most of my friends experience who are surrounded by the largest share of earthly gratifications." Her health was restored, she said, thanks to hydropathy, and although "in early life, at its most favored period," she was "happy chiefly by anticipations that were not realized," she now had "that satisfying, peaceful enjoyment of the present," and took pleasure in whatever work she was doing.[27] Catharine Beecher seemed to have come full circle to the kind of tranquillity she had known as a child but with an added mildness of manner that came from knowing she was an autonomous person, answerable to neither a dominating father nor an ambivalent God.

Although Catharine's belated sense of achievement was slightly ruffled by the writing of her memoirs and the remembrance of past indignities in 1874, she continued her role as a distinguished personage whenever the opportunity presented itself. In attendance with Emma Willard at teachers' conventions, at a congress of academic women in 1875, and later as an esteemed member of the Twenty-third Ward Charity Association of New York City, Catharine retained just as authoritative a manner as she brought to organizations of her own founding.[28]

She was intent during these last years on establishing her integrity of purpose and her professional commitment to the cause of women. To this end Catharine presented a carefully drawn image of herself in her *Educational Reminiscences and Suggestions*, emphasizing the consistency of her life and work. This was not difficult since the bulk of her narration dealt with events after 1844.[29] But Catharine did take the liberty of redefining two important aspects of her early life: she redrew the outlines of her relationship with Roxana, and she completely omitted any reference to Alexander Fisher. For a woman who advocated strong female-role identity passed from mother to daughter within the domestic context, Catharine's own early family life was not as exemplary as she might have wished. Therefore, although she did full justice to Lyman's role in her upbringing, she slightly exaggerated her debt "to certain traits in [her] mother's character and their influence on [her] early training." [30] By excluding Fisher from her memoirs Catharine established her consistency of purpose in her dedication to public service and in her later espousal of the cause of independent, unmarried women. Her brush with dependency and Fisher was thus best forgotten. Perhaps in all honesty Catharine viewed the courtship as an aberration beyond her control in a life otherwise devoted to exploring its own possibilities. In any case, Catharine visited the

Fisher farmstead in Franklin soon after the completion of her memoirs, and in front of the old-fashioned fireplace of the guest room, she slowly reread and then deliberately committed to the flames her correspondence with Fisher.[31]

Catharine's life had been a rich mixture of affirmation and denial. Her own attitude toward her abilities alternated between a desire to succeed and a will to fail. Her talents were profoundly modified by the channels of self-doubt they passed through and the restricted openings she permitted them. The lack of strong models of female achievement in her culture impaired her capacity to believe in herself. Often losing touch with the source of her motivations, she sometimes drove herself in contradictory directions. Yet her self-affirmation was strong enough to lead her through a life full of ambiguities and unaided by a ready-made identity chart. Throughout her life Catharine Beecher enjoyed herself more than she liked to admit, and she maintained secret resources of self-respect.

The struggle between the given elements of her culture and her own individuality was lifelong but creative as well as costly. Raised to assert a strong personality and shaped by commitment instead of passivity, Catharine contained elements of her culture that were not routinely assigned to women. She never fully agreed that male and female traits were "natural," and she was always highly conscious of their social origins. With reference to Roxana in her *Reminiscences* Catharine concluded: "I think that my mother's natural and acquired traits tend to prove that there is in mind no distinction of sex, and that much that passes for natural talent is mainly the result of culture." [32] Enculturation in Catharine's case provided her with a dilemma rather than a narrowly hewn path. Yet she persistently fought her culture's effort to deny her in adulthood the potential it had built within her in childhood.

Catharine projected many of these personal and cultural dilemmas onto her work in the cause of women. Alternating between the poles of submission and independence, Catharine's images of women were designed to serve the purposes of both cultural stability and personal fulfillment. Although not inherently in opposition, the historical circumstances of women in nineteenth-century America did render these purposes contradictory. Seeing this contradiction, Catharine tried to resolve it through the notion of self-sacrifice. But her work on behalf of women extended beyond that notion, and she explored a full range of possibilities along the axis between selflessness and autonomy. She worked within the given elements of her culture, but she tried to make the most of them.

In 1877 Catharine sought out the comfort of the Thomas Beecher home in Elmira and its neighboring water cure. Thomas was the most generous Beecher personality besides Harriet, and Harriet traveled too frequently for Catharine to depend on her presence should she be in great and urgent need. Moreover, in Julia Beecher, Thomas had married a woman whose instinctive goodwill distinguished her from most Beechers. In reply to Thomas's hesitant request that they provide a final home for Catharine, Julia wrote, "I think there are worse afflictions in the world than the care of an old Christian woman who has at least tried to do good all her life and needs someone's kind attentions till the Lord calls her home. I am not going to worry about *that*." [33]

Catharine had chosen her retirement home well, but she complained to Harriet of boredom and restlessness. Harriet replied with characteristic cheer that Catharine had "more talents for making life agreeable than most women" her age, that she had "an agreeable vein of humor" was "good natured and cheerful" and should "visit and cheer some sick people at the cure and make life brighter" around her. "Meanwhile the government of the world will not be going on a whit worse that *you* are not doing it," Harriet said. "I am relieved and glad to think of you at home at last with Brother Tom," she continued. "Too many years have passed over your head for you to be wandering like a trunk without a label." [34]

During her year in Elmira Catharine did as Harriet advised. She visited and encouraged the cure residents, offered "a course of lectures at the female college of Elmira, going over every morning before eight o'clock and speaking to the young ladies before their lessons began," and established a close friendship with a woman at the water cure. Exchanging confidences one day, Catharine told this friend of her visits long ago with Kate Fox and another celebrated medium. Catharine said "They cut up all sorts of capers, and used to try to mystify [me] in all sorts of ways. Once they told [me] they had seen a vision of [my] father, who appeared to be kneeling before [me] offering [me] a rose as the emblem of [my] purity." To this Catharine replied, " 'Such nonsense! When my father never in his life praised me, although he used to say that I was the best boy he had.' " [35]

Catharine died of a stroke in her sleep a year after she came to Elmira. A few days before she died she began a new round of correspondence with publishers and educators. "My plan is to consult the heads of women's institutions and superintendents of common schools this summer. . . . and I am going to Philadelphia and am forming women's committees to cooperate." She said, "[I am] stronger than for years, but take up no new responsibilities." Thomas described her last days as "like a mirror fractured, each piece like the whole." "She was," he said, "incessantly, yet incoherently active," moving from sewing to letter writing, to piano playing, to metaphysics.[36]

Obituary notices generally pointed out that "she inherited from her father great directness and positiveness of manner, and made it always apparent that her mission in this world was not to entertain but to instruct and improve." Edward, however, conducted a memorial service in Thomas Beecher's church a few days after her death and spoke of her as she would have wished him to — with personal memories of her as a sister and a Beecher.[37]

NOTES

Introduction

1 Andrew Jackson Downing, *Cottage Residences; or, A series of designs for rural cottages and cottage–villas, and their gardens and grounds* (New York, 1842) codified American domestic architecture in such a way as to relate it to both the European grand style and the nineteenth-century American vision of nature as the source of moral authority. Catharine Beecher did not have the benefit of his work when she put forward her own very similar set of house designs in 1842. Harriet Beecher Stowe initially constructed an expensive and dysfunctional mansion in Hartford in 1863 that she abandoned in 1873 for the more modestly orthodox structure described here.

2 See Yehudi A. Cohen, "Social Boundary Systems," *Current Anthropology* 10, no. 1 (February 1969): 103–26, for a discussion of the ways boundary systems operate at the community and national level as well as around the family group. Such boundaries may either form networks that interact or compete, Cohen maintains, and the less completely the community boundaries are defined, the more fully the family will emerge as a socially distinct entity.

3 Historians owe a great deal to Philippe Aries's *Centuries of Childhood: A social history of family life* (New York, 1965) for reminding them that the family is as deeply involved in the currents of historical change as any other human institution. One classic speculation on the origin of the patriarchical household, the type within which Catharine was raised, is Thorstein Veblen's "The Barbarian Status of Women," *The American Journal of Sociology* 4, no. 4 (January 1899): 503–14. The change from this family form to one giving more power to women has been analyzed by Daniel Scott Smith in "Family Limitation, Sexual Control and Domestic Feminism in Victorian America: Towards a History of the Average American Woman" (Paper prepared for the Berkshire Conference of Women Historians, Douglass College, New Brunswick, N.J., March 2–3, 1973). The greater looseness of nineteenth-century domestic forms can be exaggerated, however, since they were designed to consolidate "character" and cement one to social norms, not to launch one on a voyage of self-discovery.

4 For two examples of the ways women subverted traditional forms while appearing to conform to them, see William Taylor and Christopher Lasch, "Two 'Kindred Spirits': Sorority and Family in New England, 1825–1846," *New England Quarterly* 36 (March 1963): 23–41, and Keith Melder, "Ladies Bountiful," *New York History* 48, no. 3 (July 1967): 231–54.

Chapter 1

1 Catharine Beecher, "My Autobiography for the Entertainment of Family Friends," Katherine Day Collection, Stowe–Day Foundation, p. 1 (hereafter cited as CB, "Autobiography").

2   See Charles Ray Keller, *The Second Great Awakening in Connecticut,*
    pp. 142–53 for Beecher's role in moral reform during this period. See
    also Samuel Buell, *A Faithful Narrative of the Remarkable Revival
    . . . 1764,* p. 25.

3   Lyman Beecher, *The Autobiography of Lyman Beecher,* ed. Barbara
    Cross, 1 : 34 (hereafter cited as LB, *Autobiography*).

4   Ibid., pp. 34–39.

5   Ibid., pp. 11–13, 32, 46.

6   Ibid., p. 85.

7   Ibid., pp. 44–81, 82, 86; Roxana Beecher to Harriet Foote, 15 Novem-
    ber 1799, LB, *Autobiography,* 1 : 84.

8   CB, "Autobiography," p. 1.

9   Ibid., p. 2.

10 The two bound girls "did all of the work of the family except the
    washing till the year mother died in Litchfield. Then they went back
    to Long Island" (ibid., p. 9).
        CB described the following labor by Roxana to produce a carpet:
    "She carded and spun the cotton, hired it wove, cut and sewed it to
    fit the parlor, stretched and nailed it to the garret floor, and brushed
    it over with thin paste. Then she sent to her New York brother for oil
    paints, learned how to prepare them from an encyclopedia, and then
    adorned the carpet with groups of flowers, imitating those in her
    small yard and garden" (*Educational Reminiscences and Suggestions,*
    p. 11 [hereafter cited as CB, *Reminiscences*]).

11 Roxana had nine children, six of whom were born in East Hampton:
    CB, 1800; William, 1802; Edward, 1803; Mary, 1805; Harriet, 1808
    (died in infancy); and George, 1809. In Litchfield Roxana bore three
    more children: Harriet, 1811; Henry, 1813; and Charles, 1815.

12 CB, *Reminiscences,* p. 15.

13 CB continued to say: "In due time, even in childhood, I was com-
    forted by finding that my uninteresting toils . . . could be made
    available to amusement." CB made elaborate dolls and constructed
    horses and chariots and other "droll contrivances" from scraps left over
    from her sewing. "When all was completed, I was amply rewarded by
    the surprise and hearty laugh of my father" (ibid., p. 13).

14 CB, "Autobiography," p. 10.

15 LB, *Autobiography,* 1 : 101. CB's contribution.

16 CB, "Autobiography," p. 10.

17 LB, *Autobiography,* 1 : 101. CB's contribution.

18 Mary Hubbard to LB, [1811], LB, *Autobiography,* 1 : 173.

19 LB, *Autobiography,* 1 : 104. CB's contribution.

20 Roxana Beecher to Harriet Foote, 15 November 1799, LB, *Auto-
    biography,* 1 : 84.

21 LB, *Autobiography*, 1 : 103, CB's contribution; CB, "Autobiography," p. 6.

22 LB recalled his whaling excursions: "Once we came near the whale. 'Pull! Pull!! pull!!!' and the harpooner stood in the bow, almost near enough — I saw over my shoulder a boiling pot a little ahead. I longed he should strike the whale" (LB, *Autobiography*, 1 : 88); CB, "Autobiography," p. 6.

23 LB, *Autobiography*, 1 : 102–03. CB's contribution.

24 Ibid., p. 104. CB's contribution.

25 Keller, *The Second Great Awakening,* analyzes the profound changes wrought by the revival in the church and the culture, as deism retreated and organized benevolence replaced both eighteenth-century rationalism and seventeenth-century orthodoxy. Keller emphasizes the close relationship between Dwight and LB.

26 LB, *Autobiography*, 1 : 49. Harriet Beecher Stowe's description of her father's revivalism.

27 Ibid., 1 : 143, an extract from LB's farewell sermon.

28 See Keller, *The Second Great Awakening,* pp. 145–54.

29 LB, *The Practicality of Suppressing Vice by Means of Societies Instituted for That Purpose,* pp. 8–9.

30 LB, *The Bible a Code of Laws.*

31 LB, *The Practicality of Suppressing Vice,* p. 17.

32 LB, *The Bible a Code of Laws,* p. 41.

33 For the best interpretation of LB's theological innovations, see Sidney Earl Mead, *Nathaniel William Taylor 1786–1858.* The quotation here is from LB's sermon of 1807, "The Government of God Desirable," an excerpt printed in LB, *Autobiography*, 1 : 117.

34 LB, *Autobiography*, 1 : 119.

35 See H. Shelton Smith, *Changing Conceptions of Original Sin,* pp. 60–133 for the challenge to LB and his response.

36 LB said of Nathaniel Emmons, the most distinguished contemporary Edwardean: "*He* ought to be ashamed for putting [the doctrines of original sin and election by grace] in such a shape that ninety-nine in a hundred would be sure to misunderstand what he meant" (LB, *Autobiography*, 1 : 117–18). LB felt only scorn for the idea that men should be willing to be damned for the glory of God.

37 Ibid., p. 46.

38 Horace Mann was one example of this. See Raymond B. Culver, *Horace Mann and Religion in the Massachusetts Public Schools,* p. 5.

Chapter 2

1 LB, *Autobiography*, 1 : 108–09.

2 Richard J. Purcell, *Connecticut in Transition : 1775–1818.* Purcell called Litchfield "the citadel of conservatism" (p. 175).

3   See Richard L. Bushman, *From Puritan to Yankee,* pp. 215–16, 238, 259.

4   "Colonel Tallmadge is a man of wealth and influence, and is also foremost in conference meetings. The first people here are decidedly the most religious" (Harriet Beecher Porter to ———, 4 December 1817, LB, *Autobiography,* 1 : 271). For the history of the Litchfield church, see also LB, *Autobiography,* 1 : 153.

5   For pictures of Litchfield houses see C. Matlack Price, "Historic Houses of Litchfield," *The White Pine Series of Architectural Monographs* 5, no. 3 (June 1919). For other information on Litchfield, see Alden C. White, *The History of the Town of Litchfield, Connecticut, 1720–1920.*

6   Purcell, *Connecticut in Transition,* p. 193.

7   Emily Noyes Vanderpoel, *Chronicles of a Pioneer School from 1792 to 1833, Being the History of Miss Sarah Pierce and Her Litchfield School,* pp. 402–04.

8   E. D. Mansfield, *Personal Memories,* pp. 122–40.

9   LB, *Autobiography,* 1 : 165. CB's contribution.

10 Ibid., p. 159; Mansfield, *Personal Memories,* p. 127.

11 The private journal of Mr. John P. Brace in Emily Noyes Vanderpoel, *More Chronicles of a Pioneer School, from 1792 to 1833,* p. 94 cites CB's journal as a prizewinning one. The bulk of Vanderpoel's two volumes on the school consists of these journals.

12 CB, *Reminiscences,* p. 25.

13 See the journal of Eliza Ogden, 1816–1818, in Vanderpoel, *Chronicles,* pp. 160–74.

14 Vanderpoel, *More Chronicles,* p. 94.

15 Vanderpoel, *Chronicles,* p. 168.

16 CB, *Reminiscences,* p. 26.

17 Vanderpoel, *More Chronicles,* p. 94.

18 CB, *Reminiscences,* p. 26.

19 Ibid.

20 Vanderpoel, *Chronicles,* p. 122; LB, *Autobiography,* 1 : 166. CB's contribution.

21 Ibid., 1 : 159. CB's contribution.

22 While the Beechers were at East Hampton and when Mary Foote was only eighteen, she married "a rich merchant from the Island of Jamaica who was a distant relative" (CB, "Autobiography," p. 10). She was unhappy living in a slave society and left her husband and returned to live with the Beechers. Mary Foote Hubbard wrote in 1811 when CB was away from Litchfield visiting the Foote home in Nutplains, Connecticut: "I miss [CB] in my room, in the house, in my walks, and when I ride" (Mary Hubbard to Esther ———, 11 Septem-

ber 1811, LB, *Autobiography*, 1 : 169). For a description of the Beecher family in Litchfield, see CB's contribution to LB, *Autobiography*, 1 : 159–67. CB "making fun for everybody," is from Mary Beecher to Edward Beecher, 4 February 1819, LB, *Autobiography*, 1 : 301. For Roxana's social timidity, see Harriet Beecher Stowe's contribution to LB, *Autobiography*, 1 : 225, and CB, *Reminiscences*, p. 16.

23 LB, *Autobiography*, 1 : 215. Roxana's emphasis. (All subsequent emphasis comes from original author unless otherwise noted.)

24 CB, *Reminiscences*, pp. 19–20.

25 "Saturday after the rolls were called Miss Pierce went for Mr. Beecher. She said she wished us to pay particular attention to what he said as he was not going to be here but two or three Saturdays more; he was going [on] a long journey again, at which all the girls joined in a laugh. I suppose it was because he was going to Boston to buy him a wife" (from the journal of Eliza Ogden for the summer of 1817, in Vanderpoel, *Chronicles*, p. 171); LB [quoting CB] to Harriet Porter, September 1817, Day Collection.

26 LB to Harriet Porter, September 1817, Day Collection.

27 CB's entire letter to Harriet Porter is printed in LB, *Autobiography*, 1 : 264–65.

28 CB to ———, 21 November 1817, LB, *Autobiography*, 1 : 270.

29 LB, *Autobiography*, 1 : 261–62; CB, *Reminiscences*, pp. 24–25.

30 Harriet Beecher to ———, 4 December 1817, LB, *Autobiography*, 1 : 273.

31 Most of CB's poems are collected in a bound MS, Day Collection, inscribed, "Revd. Lyman Beecher, D.D. To a dear father these little pieces are inscribed by his grateful and affectionate daughter." An example of her humorous poetry are the lines she wrote when her younger sister Harriet requested an epitaph for the gravestone of the parsonage cat:

> Here died our kit
> Who had a fit,
>   And acted queer.
> Shot with a gun,
> Her race is run,
>   And she lies here.

32 For the social life of Litchfield's young people, see Mansfield, *Personal Memories*, p. 136. CB names her Litchfield beau as "John P." in a letter to Louisa Wait, [May 1819], Beecher–Stowe Collection, folder 14. Schlesinger Library. Radcliffe College. Quotation is from CB to Harriet Porter, [September 1817], LB, *Autobiography*, 1 : 265.

33 CB to Louisa Wait, 11 May 1819, Beecher–Stowe Collection, folder 14.

34 CB to Louisa Wait, [1819], Beecher–Stowe Collection, folder 14.

35 CB to Louisa Wait, 4 June 1819, Beecher–Stowe Collection, folder 14.

36 LB to CB, 26 May 1819, Beecher–Stowe Collection, folder 2.

37 "Your father and Catharine had a pleasant visit at Northampton, and returned safe, having passed the Sabbath at Hartford" (Mrs. Beecher to Edward Beecher, 1 November 1818, LB, *Autobiography*, 1 : 277).

38 Lucy ——— to Louisa Wait, [1816], Beecher–Stowe Collection, folder 19; LB to CB, 26 May 1819, Beecher–Stowe Collection, folder 2.

39 The most thorough analysis of LB's social aims is in Keller, *The Second Great Awakening*, pp. 47–62, 105–64, 221–22. See also Barbara M. Cross, Introduction to LB, *Autobiography*.

40 CB's bound music MS is in the Beecher–Stowe Collection. For her dedication to music at this time, see Mrs. Beecher to Harriet Foote, 7 June 1820, LB, *Autobiography*, 1 : 316.

41 Harriet Beecher Stowe's reminiscences in LB, *Autobiography*, 1 : 397. (Harriet hereafter referred to as HB or HBS.)

42 CB's most ambitious poem was a long Indian ballad, "Yala," dealing with the adventures and tragedies of the Bantam Indians who lived around Litchfield before the white settlement. See her bound MS, Day Collection; *The Christian Spectator,* founded by Beecher, Taylor, and others around 1815, to carry the messages of the "New Divinity" against Old Calvinists, Episcopalians, and Unitarians. See LB, *Autobiography*, 1 : 241.

43 LB to CB, 26 May 1819, Beecher–Stowe Collection, folder 2.

44 LB to CB, 8 June 1819 and April 1821, Beecher–Stowe Collection, folder 2.

Chapter 3

1 Horace Mann to Lydia Mann, [April] 1822, Horace Mann Papers, box 3, Massachusetts Historical Society.

2 Alexander Metcalf Fisher Collection, Beinecke Library, Yale University, preserves many of Fisher's private papers from which this analysis of Fisher is partly drawn. For other accounts of Fisher's life, see William Chauncey Fowler, *Essays,* pp. 141–51, and Edwards A. Park, *Memoir of Nathaniel Emmons,* pp. 234–37.

3 CB, "The Evening Cloud," *The Christian Spectator* 2, no. 1 (January 1820) : 81. CB signed her poem "C.B."

4 Alexander Fisher, "Review of Dr. Brown's Essay on the Existence of a Supreme Creator," *The Christian Spectator* 1, no. 7 (July 1819) : 414–21; Lyman Beecher Stowe, *Saints, Sinners and Beechers,* p. 81.

5 L. B. Stowe, *Saints, Sinners and Beechers,* p. 81.

6 On the relationship between marriage and conversion see *The Christian Spectator* 1, nos. 8 and 9 (August and September 1819) : 412, 514, 568.

7 The best summary of LB's theological position on conversion is in Sidney Earl Mead, *Nathaniel William Taylor, 1786–1858,* pp. 68, 120.

8 LB to William Beecher, 6 February 1819, LB, *Autobiography,* 1 : 288.

9 Ibid; LB to Edward Beecher, 22 June 1820, LB, *Autobiography,* 1 : 317. (Edward hereafter referred to as EB.)

10 For a general analysis of Doddridge, see Geoffrey F. Nuttall, *Philip Doddridge 1702–51.* For the wide influence of Doddridge upon young people in CB's circumstances, see CB, *The Religious Training of Children in the School, the Family, and the Church* (New York, 1864), p. 131. The American Tract Society was still reprinting Doddridge's *Rise and Progress* in the 1840s.

11 Philip Doddridge, *The Rise and Progress of Religion* . . . Chapter, pp. 41, 93, 132, 164.

12 CB (statement of religious resolutions), 29 March 1821, Beecher–Stowe Collection, folder 315. CB's resolutions began: "I will devote one hour each day to reading the Bible and religious books with prayer and meditation and also a portion of time before I sleep. On the Sabbath I will endeavor to devote the whole day to public worship, reading and serious reflection, and at other times I will attend religious meetings whenever it is in my power."

13 Ibid.

14 LB to EB, 7 April 1821, LB, *Autobiography,* 1 : 341.

15 EB to CB, 29 March 1822, Beecher–Stowe Collection, folder 2.

16 LB to EB, 1 April 1822, LB, *Autobiography,* 1 : 353.

17 CB to Louisa Wait, 18 May 1821, Beecher–Stowe Collection, folder 14.

18 CB to LB, 5 June 1821, Beecher–Stowe Collection, folder 13.

19 Ibid.

20 CB to Louisa Wait, 18 May 1821, Beecher–Stowe Collection, folder 14.

21 Postscript by EB in a letter from LB to CB, April 1821, Beecher–Stowe Collection, folder 2; CB to Louisa Wait, [1820], Beecher–Stowe Collection, folder 14.

22 LB to CB, 26 July 1821, Beecher–Stowe Collection, folder 2.

23 CB to Louisa Wait, 18 May 1821, Beecher–Stowe Collection, folder 13.

24 LB to CB, 26 July 1821, Beecher–Stowe Collection, folder 2.

25 LB to CB, 20 October 1821, Beecher–Stowe Collection, folder 2.

26 CB's first letter from Litchfield indicating her permanent return home was written to her Grandmother Foote, 23 November 1821, in LB, *Autobiography,* 1 : 346.

27 CB to Louisa Wait, January 1822, Beecher–Stowe Collection, folder 14.

28 LB to George Foote, 24 January 1822, LB, *Autobiography,* 1 : 351. At home that winter and spring, CB was busy with the domestic affairs of the Beecher household. She took charge of the housekeep-

ing when all the adults except her became ill. Since the boarders and children had filled the house beyond its capacity — perhaps due to her unexpected arrival — she arranged for her sister Harriet to spend several months with the Foote family. (CB to Mrs. Foote, 23 November 1821, LB, *Autobiography*, 1 : 346.) In February Mrs. Beecher gave birth to a daughter, and CB took charge of their care. Even though HB was away from home, CB still included her among her numerous charges and wrote her letters of sisterly admonition. "We all want you home very much, but hope you are now where you will learn to stand and sit straight, and hear what people say to you, and sit still in your chair, and learn to sew and knit well, and be a good girl in every particular" (CB to Harriet Beecher, 25 February 1822, LB, *Autobiography*, 1 : 352).

29   Not until the fall of 1822 was EB able to piece together the details of the shipwreck from the two survivors who returned to the United States. The results of his interviews with these two men, on CB's behalf, are found in EB to CB, 23 August 1822 and 22 October 1822, Beecher–Stowe Collection, folder 2.

30   LB to CB, 30 May 1822, LB, *Autobiography*, 1 : 355–56. In a poem Catharine expressed the belief that her personal loss was less important than her religious distress:

> I weep not that my youthful hopes
>   All wrecked beneath the billows rest,
> Nor that the heavy hand of Death
>   Has stilled the heart that loved me best.

> But ah! I mourn the moral night
>   That Shrouds my eyes in deepest gloom;
> I mourn that, tempest-toss'd on earth,
>   I have in heaven no peaceful home.

(CB to EB, 4 June 1822, LB, *Autobiography*, 1 : 357.)

31   EB to CB, 30 May 1822, Beecher–Stowe Collection, folder 2.

32   CB to EB, July 1822, LB, *Autobiography*, 1 : 359. CB's sense of the unalterable effect of her past experience was further revealed in the same letter: "I have gone on indulging this propensity year after year and time has only added new strength to it. . . . I feel that I am guilty, but not guilty as if I had received a nature pure and uncontaminated. I can not feel this; I never shall by any mental exertion of my own." William James, *The Varieties of Religious Experience*, pp. 189–259, eloquently analyzes the subconscious and conscious processes at work during conversion and the regenerative effect of these processes. He concludes that there is "an admirable congruity of Protestant theology with the structure of the mind" in allowing the subconscious desire for self-surrender to wash over the conscious mind

and rid it of the worldly and spiritual failures associated with past conscious experience.

33 Recollection of Henry Ward Beecher, quoted in L. B. Stowe, *Saints, Sinners and Beechers,* p. 91.

34 CB to EB, 4 June 1822, LB, *Autobiography,* 1 : 356.

35 LB to EB, 2 August 1822, LB, *Autobiography,* 1 : 360.

36 The best description of the decline from piety to morality in the Calvinist tradition is Joseph Haroutunian, *Piety Versus Moralism.*

37 EB to CB, August 1822, Beecher–Stowe Collection, folder 2.

38 LB, *Autobiography,* 1 : 360.

39 Ibid., p. 361; CB to EB, July 1822, LB, *Autobiography,* 1 : 360.

Chapter 4

1 EB to CB, 21 June and 18 July 1822, Beecher–Stowe Collection, folder 2.

2 CB to EB, 22 October 1822, Beecher–Stowe Collection, folder 2.

3 Ibid; Catharine M. Sedgwick, *A New England Tale.*

4 EB to CB, 27 October 1822, Beecher–Stowe Collection, folder 2.

5 LB to CB, 27 October 1822, LB, *Autobiography,* 1 : 365–66.

6 LB to CB, 27 October 1822, LB, *Autobiography,* 1 : 364.

7 CB to EB, 9 October 1822, Beecher Family Papers, Williston Memorial Library, Holyoke College, and CB to LB, New Year, 1823, LB, *Autobiography,* 1 : 374.

8 The Alexander Metcalf Fisher Collection, contains Fisher's religious diaries, his personal correspondence, his notebook memoir describing his temporary insanity, notebooks filled during his insanity, and his scientific papers.

9 Bound notebook relating his mental derangement, 24 May 1817, A. M. Fisher Collection, pp. 1, 20.

10 Bound religious diary, 15 February 1817, 12 July 1818, and 1 August 1819, A. M. Fisher Collection.

11 CB to LB, New Year, 1823, LB, *Autobiography,* 1 : 373; ibid., p. 369.

12 LB to CB, 29 January 1823, Beecher–Stowe Collection, folder 2.

13 CB's argument for the Newtonian view of God is best rendered in her letter to LB, New Year, 1823, LB, *Autobiography,* 1 : 368–74.

14 LB to CB, 29 January 1823, Beecher–Stowe Collection, folder 2; LB to CB, 2 March 1823, LB, *Autobiography,* 1 : 383.

15 CB to LB, 15 February 1823, LB, *Autobiography,* 1 : 377.

16 CB to LB, New Year, 1823, LB, *Autobiography,* 1 : 368.

17 CB to Louisa Wait, 22 January 1823. Beecher–Stowe Collection, folder 14.

18 The controversy between CB and Yale is discussed in EB's letters to
    CB, 11 December 1822 and 13 January 1823, Beecher–Stowe Collec-
    tion, folder 2. CB's epitaph reads:

> Thy grave O Fisher, is the rolling flood
> Thy urn, the rock eternal reared by God!
> Yet near thy home raised by affections hand
> To speak thy name, this simple stone shall stand.
> How dark the scene, till Faith directs on high
> Beyond those orbs that charmed thy youthful eye
> There now thy noble mind expanding glows
> In floods of light nor pain nor darkness knows.
> Youth, Genius, Knowledge, Virtue, past away
> From Earth's dim shores, to Heaven's eternal day!

(CB to Louisa Wait, 22 January 1823, Beecher–Stowe Collection,
folder 14.)

19 Fisher's portrait is reproduced in L. B. Stowe's, *Saints, Sinners and
    Beechers,* p. 90. For ceremonies honoring Fisher, see accounts in *The
    Christian Spectator* 4, no. 7 (July 1822): 389–92; *New Englander* 1
    (1843): 457–68; James Luce Kingsley, *Yale College,* pp. 229–31;
    Fowler, *Essays,* pp. 141–51; Park, *Memoir of Nathanael Emmons,*
    pp. 234–37.
20 EB to CB, 28 August 1822, Beecher–Stowe Collection, folder 2.
21 EB to CB, 13 November 1822; EB to CB, 11 December 1822; EB to
    CB, 13 January 1823; all in Beecher–Stowe Collection, folder 2.
22 EB to CB, 11 December 1822, Beecher–Stowe Collection, folder 2.
23 CB, *Reminiscences,* p. 29; CB to Louisa Wait, 22 January 1823,
    Beecher–Stowe Collection, folder 14.
24 CB to LB, 15 February 1823, LB, *Autobiography,* 1 : 378.
25 Ibid.
26 LB to CB, 21 March 1823, Beecher–Stowe Collection, folder 3. Ex-
    cerpts from this letter are reprinted in LB, *Autobiography,* 1 : 384.
    Lyman continued, "[I] should be ashamed to have you open, and
    keep only a common-place, middling sort of school." He said, "[Your
    school] is expected to be of a higher order; and unless you are will-
    ing to put your talents and strength into it, it would be best not to
    begin." Lyman hoped she would see the propriety of his remarks,
    and that he made them for her own sake as well as for Mary's and
    his own and the public good. "All say the school will rise past a
    doubt if made in point of accuracy, solidity, efficiency and ornament
    such as they need."
27 Ibid. MS copy of LB's letter.
28 Ibid.
29 Ibid.

Chapter 5

1 For a description of the reputation of CB's school see Thomas Woody, *A History of Women's Education in the United States,* 1 : 320–22.

2 CB, *Reminiscences,* p. 31.

3 LB to CB, 3 December 1823, Beecher–Stowe Collection, folder 11.

4 LB to Catharine, Edward, Mary, and George Beecher, July 1823, and LB to CB, 3 December 1823, LB, *Autobiography,* 1 : 404–05.

5 CB to Louisa Wait, 23 August 1824, Beecher–Stowe Collection, folder 14. The identity of this suitor remains obscure. CB to Louisa Wait, 30 September 1824, Beecher–Stowe Collection, folder 14.

6 "We have established a system of classification and mutual instruction," she wrote Louisa, "and we are confined only half the day" (CB to Louisa Wait, 7 June 1824, Beecher–Stowe Collection, folder 14).

7 Ibid.

8 "I visited Mrs. Sigourney that evening. We had for gentlemen Professor Hale the grammar school master, Mr. Blanc the deaf and dumb teacher, G——— the lecturer, and a Roman Catholic Priest. The Priest came home with Mary and the deaf and dumb with me" (CB to Louisa Wait, 6 August 1824, Beecher–Stowe Collection, folder 14).

9 A good biographical account of Lydia Sigourney is Gordon S. Haight, *Mrs. Sigourney, the Sweet Singer of Hartford.*

10 CB to Louisa Wait, 22 May 1825, Beecher–Stowe Collection, folder 14.

11 CB to Louisa Wait, 7 December 1824, Beecher–Stowe Collection, folder 14.

12 LB to CB, 26 December 1825, Beecher–Stowe Collection, folder 3.

13 Ibid.

14 Mary Beecher to EB, 5 April 1826, Beecher Family Papers, Williston Memorial Library.

15 Ibid.

16 CB to John MacAlister and Son, 6 June 1826, Dreer Collection, Historical Society of Pennsylvania.

17 CB, "An Address Written for the Young Ladies of Miss Beecher's School," 18 October 1823, Beecher–Stowe Collection, folder 314.

18 CB to Mrs. Harriet Porter Beecher, [Fall 1823], Day Collection; CB to LB, New Year, 1823, LB, *Autobiography,* 1 : 370.

19 CB to EB, 18 July 1824, LB, *Autobiography,* 2 : 7–8; LB to CB, 3 March 1824, LB, *Autobiography,* 1 : 409.

20 See Keller, *The Second Great Awakening,* p. 237.

21 CB to EB, 8 January 1825, LB, *Autobiography,* 2 : 9; CB to EB, 20 April 1825, LB, *Autobiography,* 2 : 16; ibid.

22 CB to EB, 25 April 1826, Beecher Family Papers, Williston Memorial Library; LB to EB, 5 September 1826, LB, *Autobiography,* 2 : 48.

23 LB to EB, 4 September 1826, LB, *Autobiography,* 2 : 47; HBS's recollection in LB, *Autobiography,* 2 : 85.

24 "It is not the most fashionable part of the community" (Edward Bradley to Harriet Bradley, 18 June 1827, Bradley–Hyde Papers, folder 3, Schlesinger Library).

25 LB to CB, 8 September 1826, LB, *Autobiography,* 2 : 49–50.

26 LB to William Beecher, 13 April 1826, LB, *Autobiography,* 2 : 42; CB to EB, 25 April 1826, Beecher Family Papers, Williston Memorial Library.

27 CB to EB, 1 June 1826, Beecher Family Papers, Williston Memorial Library; CB to EB, 9 June 1826, in ibid.

28 CB to EB, 1 June 1826, in ibid.

29 CB to EB, 9 June 1826, in ibid.

30 Ibid.

31 LB to CB, 30 June 1826, LB, *Autobiography,* 2 : 44–45.

32 Ibid.

33 LB to CB, 8 September 1826, LB, *Autobiography,* 2 : 49–50.

34 CB, "To those who profess, or have the hope of Piety in Miss Beecher's School," bound MS, Day Collection. "Remember you are 'the called' of Jesus Christ. A holy nation. A peculiar people. That ye should show forth the glory of him who called you from darkness into marvellous light. Remember the church of God is set for a light in the world. It is the salt of the earth, to preserve and redeem it by labours and prayers, a beacon to guide by its blessed light the children of this lost world to glory and to God." She urged them to stand this week as beacons to the rest of the town and she concluded:

> I beseech you by the pangs you felt when your own feet were in the horrid pit and miry clay, by the hopes of peace ye have tasted in communion with God and the hope of Heaven; by the great love of him who hath washed you in his own blood and sent you forth as his dear children, by the ineffable blessedness of the heavenly mansions you hope to inhabit, by the weeping and woe of that hell from which you are redeemed, by all that is glorious in our hopes and dreadful in our fears for the future destinies of the dear immortals around us—*be faithful in interest, in labours and prayers* . . . and those so redeemed by your faithfulness shall rejoice with you to enter the joy of our Lord.

35 Edward A. Lawrence, *The Life of Rev. Joel Hawes, D.D.,* p. 106.

36 Ibid., p. 116; Joel Hawes, *Lectures Addressed to the Young Men of Hartford and New Haven.*

37 Barbara Cross, *Horace Bushnell, Minister to a Changing America,* p. 34.

38 CB to Sarah Terry, a series of six undated letters, [1826], Day Collection.

39 CB, *Reminiscences,* p. 48.

40 "Hartford Female Seminary Reunion" (Hartford, 1892) in Hartford Female Seminary Papers, Connecticut Historical Society.

41 George Leon Walker, *Address at the Two Hundred and Fiftieth Anniversary of the First Church of Christ, Hartford,* p. 376.

42 Ibid., appendix 12, pp. 462–63, 466–67. This appendix lists the amounts paid for pews and slips when the church was built in 1809 together with the name of the purchaser. On pp. 466–67 is a ground plan of the church showing the placement of pews. Altogether Daniel Wadsworth paid $2,737 for all the pews he bought in 1809. For a sketch of Wadsworth, see Florence Crofut, *Guide to the History and Historical Sites of Connecticut,* 1 : 238.

43 CB, *Reminiscences,* p. 33. There is an engraving of the Hartford Female Seminary on a Hartford Female Seminary diploma in the MSS Collection, Connecticut State Library.

44 CB, *Reminiscences,* p. 33; Walker, *Address,* pp. 462–63. All of these men were large donors with pews in the front of the church.

45 *Catalogue of the Officers, Teachers, and Pupils of the Hartford Female Seminary* (Hartford, 1827), p. 2.

46 Walker, *Address,* p. 467; Cross, *Horace Bushnell,* p. 34.

47 *Catalogue,* 1827, p. 2; ibid.

48 *Appleton's Cyclopaedia of American Biography,* ed. James Grant Wilson and John Fiske, s.v. "Day, Thomas (1777–1855)"; *Dictionary of American Biography,* ed. Allen Johnson, s.v. "Ellsworth, William Wolcott (1791–1868)."

49 CB, *Reminiscences,* p. 33; ibid.

50 CB to Louisa Wait, 30 September 1824, Beecher–Stowe Collection, folder 14.

51 CB, *Reminiscences,* p. 33; CB to LB, 16 February 1827, in Charles E. Stowe, *Life of Harriet Beecher Stowe Compiled from Her Letters and Journals,* p. 37.

52 CB, "Female Education," *American Journal of Education* [Boston] 2, nos. 4 and 5 (April and May 1827) : 219–23, 264–69.

53 Mrs. Pilkington [Mary Hopkins], *A Mirror for the Female Sex,* "printed by Hudson and Goodwin for Oliver and I. Cooke." Oliver Cooke was a stationery and book seller and printed school texts.

54 Haight, *Mrs. Sigourney,* p. 87.

55 CB, "Female Education," p. 221.

56 Other like-minded educators included Miss Zilpah Grant at Ipswich, Mary Lyon at Mt. Holyoke, and Emma Willard at Troy. Woody, *A History of Women's Education,* 1 : 301.

57 CB, "Female Education," p. 221.

58 Ibid., pp. 219, 220, 222, 264–69.

59 Ibid., p. 219.

Chapter 6

1 CB, *Reminiscences,* p. 51.
2 John Higham's essay *From Boundlessness to Consolidation* draws attention to the different cultural contexts of the early and late century and reveals the early emergence of Victorian cultural forms. William G. McLoughlin's *The Meaning of Henry Ward Beecher* traces the contribution of another member of the Beecher family to the Victorian cultural matrix. Henry was born thirteen years after Catharine and thereby entered fully and easily into the Victorian mental set. Two outstanding examples of late Victorian spokesmen are James Thompson Bixby, *The Ethics of Evolution* and Charles William Eliot, *American Contributions to Civilization,* esp. pp. 87, 267, 283.
3 Other figures mentioned by Higham are Frederick Law Olmsted, Henry C. Carey, and Oliver Wendell Holmes.
4 CB, *Reminiscences,* pp. 51, 54.
5 *Catalogue of the Officers, Teachers, and Pupils of the Hartford Female Seminary, 1828* (Hartford, 1828); *The Annual Catalogue of Hartford Female Seminary* (Hartford, 1831). These catalogues list the hometown of each pupil. The families belonging to the First Church are listed in Walker, *Address.*
6 CB to EB, 23 August 1828, Beecher Family Papers, Williston Memorial Library.
7 HB to Georgiana May, May 1833, in Charles E. Stowe, *Life of Harriet Beecher Stowe,* p. 67.
8 See Herbert W. Schneider, *A History of American Philosophy,* pp. 202–12 for a good, compact analysis of the shift in American philosophy from Enlightenment rationalism to Scottish Common Sense. Joseph Haroutunian, *Piety Versus Moralism,* focuses on the role of the "New Divinity" and is an excellent source for understanding how the ground was readied for the introduction of Common Sense. The best study of the Scottish school is S. A. Grave, *The Scottish Philosophy of Common Sense.* A useful analysis of the school's effect on American colleges and universities is G. Stanley Hall's "On the History of American College Textbooks and Teaching in Logic, Ethics, Psychology, and Allied Subjects," American Antiquarian Society, *Proceedings* 9 (1895) : 137–74. Daniel Walker Howe, *The Unitarian Conscience, Harvard Moral Philosophy, 1805–1861,* is a superb study of the liberal wing of Common Sense philosophy. Before writing her book CB read "Locke, Reid, Steward, Brown and other works in English" (*Reminiscences,* p. 52).

CB wrote at the very beginning of philosophical mode, and she had to feel her way without the benefit of many previous American examples. Because she shared many of the concerns common to those who followed her, her book was in many ways similar to subsequent works of moral philosophy. Since, however, there was no accepted system of moral philosophy until Francis Wayland's *Elements of Moral Science* established one in 1835, CB's work does not exactly fit the mold cast later. Only one text of moral philosophy predated CB's. This was Thomas C. Upham, *Elements of Intellectual Philosophy.* Yet Upham's work was not widely circulated until it was republished in 1831 as *Elements of Mental Philosophy, Intellect, and Sensibilities.* In 1832 Jacob Abbott, a leading popularizer of evangelical beliefs, edited John Abercrombie's *Inquiry into the Intellectual Powers,* and this Scottish work was subsequently taught in many seminaries and academies. Upham's book differs significantly from CB's, and she was apparently unaware of its existence in 1828 when she began her own. See Hall's article, "On the History of American College Textbooks," for a complete bibliography of moral philosophy texts. CB's is not included, presumably since it was not published commercially and was never widely circulated.

9 Francis Wayland, *Elements of Moral Science with Questions for Examinations,* p. iv.
10 Howe, *The Unitarian Conscience,* pp. 139–40.
11 Ibid., p. 140. For another discussion of the emergence of a new academic national leadership inspired by the Common Sense philosophical perspective, see Wilson Smith, *Professors and Public Ethics.*
12 CB, *The Elements of Mental and Moral Philosophy, Founded upon Experience, Reason and the Bible,* p. 250.
13 Wayland, *Elements of Moral Philosophy,* p. 298.
14 Sidney Mead, *Nathaniel William Taylor, 1786–1858,* pp. 101–34 analyzes the way the "New Divinity" tried to combine both piety and morality in the self-initiated conversion experience Taylor urged upon his listeners, but the distinction remains one of the fundamental dividing lines between religious experience of the seventeenth and eighteenth centuries and that of the nineteenth century. Upham, Abercrombie, and Wayland adopted from Scottish works the view that behavior was the key to morality. See especially Dugald Stewart, *Elements of the Philosophy of the Human Mind,* esp. 2 : 243. Jonathan Edwards, the dedicated defender of piety against morality was, however, not entirely free of sexually differentiated modes of piety. In his "Character of a Truly Virtuous Person" (1723) he describes the piety of a young woman as characterized by "a strange sweetness in her mind, and singular purity in her affections; is most just and conscientious in all her conduct." The same attributes could, however, apply to a man, and Edwards does not conclude that the

piety of the young woman causes her to be a better housewife or mother, but draws her instead into a self-centered fulfillment. "She loves to be alone, walking in the fields and groves, and seems to have someone invisible always conversing with her" (from Sereno E. Dwight, ed., *The Works of President Edwards,* 1 : 114–15).

15 Wayland, *Elements of Moral Science,* p. 298.
16 Ibid.
17 Howe, *The Unitarian Conscience,* p. 128.
18 CB, *Elements,* pp. 56–57.
19 Ibid., p. 250.
20 Ibid., p. 430. See Sydney Ahlstrom, "The Scottish Philosophers and American Theology," *Church History* 25 (September 1955): 257–72, for the way in which Scottish philosophy viewed benevolence and selfishness, and the alteration it wrought in American religious thought.
21 See Jonathan Edwards, *The Nature of True Virtue,* pp. 85–97.
22 CB, *Elements,* p. 57.
23 The Hartford Convention of 1816, at which the secession of New England from the federal union was discussed, demonstrates Connecticut's willingness to lead conservative dissent against national policies. The organizing force of the Second Great Awakening may have contributed to supraregional thinking in Connecticut, however, and led many conservatives to believe in the cause of a homogeneous, New England-led national culture. By 1830 CB was certainly not alone in her vision of a unified society. See Donald G. Mathews, "The Second Great Awakening as an Organizing Process, 1780–1830: An Hypothesis," *American Quarterly* 21, no. 1 (Spring 1969) : 23–44.
24 Wayland, *Elements of Moral Science,* p. 58.
25 CB, *Elements,* p. 386.
26 Ibid., p. 263.
27 Ibid., pp. 385–406.
28 Ibid., pp. 238–39.

Chapter 7

1 CB to EB, 28 August 1828, Beecher Family Papers, Williston Memorial Library.
2 CB, *Suggestions Respecting Improvements in Education, Presented to the Trustees.*
3 CB, *Suggestions,* p. 68.
4 James McLachlan, *American Boarding Schools,* p. 94.
5 Emma Willard, *An Address to the Public.* Emma Willard was one woman with ideas ahead of CB, and she established a boarding facility within her school by 1831. Yet as a married woman with a family she may have been viewed as a more stable model than CB by both

parents and donors to her academy. For further details see Alma Lutz, *Emma Willard, Daughter of Democracy* and Woody, *A History of Women's Education*, 1 : 344–48. McLachlan, *American Boarding Schools*, pp. 41–48, drew the distinction between boarding with local families, the norm for male and female boarding schools until the 1830s, and boarding in a facility on school grounds, an innovation used only by male students during the 1830s.

6 LB to CB, 3 February 1827, Beecher–Stowe Collection, folder 4.

7 HB to Cornelia Baldwin, [1830], Beecher–Stowe Collection, folder 235.

8 Linda Thayer Guilford, *The Use of a Life*, p. 87.

9 Ibid., p. 143.

10 Ibid., p. 144.

11 LB to Zilpah Grant, 23 November 1829, in Guilford, *The Use of a Life*, pp. 145–46; ibid., p. 149. Miss Grant supported a plan for boarding facilities and worked with Mary Lyon to create one at Ipswich in 1834, but she did not succeed before her health failed and she resigned in 1839. Woody, *A History of Women's Education*, pp. 349–50.

12 CB, *Reminiscences*, p. 65.

13 Woody, *A History of Women's Education*, pp. 317, 345–46, 358–59. It is interesting to note that the only exception to boarding with families before 1830 was the convent of the Ursuline Sisters, established in New Orleans in 1727 (Woody, p. 329) and continuing for over a century to provide for Catholic girls an institutional alternative to the family both as a source of socialization and as an alternative to marriage. Protestant women had no such alternative until teaching gave them one in the 1830s.

14 McLachlan, *American Boarding Schools*, p. 117.

15 *Connecticut Courant*, 16 November 1830.

16 LB to CB, 1 December 1826, Beecher–Stowe Collection, folder 4.

17 LB to CB, 3 February 1827, Beecher–Stowe Collection, folder 4.

18 CB, *Reminiscences*, pp. 67–75.

19 CB to Mary Dutton, 8 February 1830, Collection of American Literature, Beinecke Library. Emma Willard had been training teachers for years at Troy but not with the ideological perspective introduced by CB.

20 CB, *Suggestion*, pp. 46, 44–52.

21 CB to Mary Dutton, 8 February 1830, Collection of American Literature.

22 CB, *Suggestions*, p. 46.

23 Michael Katz, *The Irony of Early School Reform*, p. 60. Katz links the "feminization" of education with the dual processes of expanding institutional needs and rationalized institutional structure, and he

compares it to the widespread use of female labor in industry in the mid-nineteenth century: "School committees were faced with a rapid increase in numbers of children because of immigration, a scarcity of men because of industrial and commercial opportunities, and a consequent probably enormous rise in school costs. In this situation schoolmen, like industrialists, sought to increase the 'marginal productivity' of labor through training, feminization, innovation, and reorganization."

24 For a more detailed discussion of these processes, see chaps. 9–12.

25 Diary of Angelina Grimké, unpaginated vol. covering 17 November 1829–18 May 1833, Weld–Grimké Papers, Clements Library. Refer to same for all Angelina Grimké quotes in this chapter.

26 CB, *Reminiscences,* pp. 62–65.

27 CB, *Elements,* pp. 70–79.

28 HBS, "Catharine E. Beecher," in HBS et al., *Our Famous Women,* p. 89.

29 CB to Mary Dutton, 8 February 1830, Collection of American Literature.

30 CB, *Reminiscences,* p. 75.

31 LB to CB, 8 July 1830, LB, *Autobiography,* 2 : 167–68.

32 CB, *Reminiscences,* p. 52.

33 Letter from Henry Ware quoted in part in CB, *Reminiscences,* p. 53. Ware's emphasis.

34 CB to Archibald Alexander, 18 October 1831, American Prose Writers Collection, case 5, box 38, Historical Society of Pennsylvania.

35 CB, *Reminiscences,* pp. 52–53.

Chapter 8

1 LB to Messrs. Mahan, Vail, and Blanchard, 17 March 1832, LB, *Autobiography,* 2 : 191; CB, "Almanack and Journal," Beecher–Stowe Collection, folder 315.

2 Photograph of Cincinnati in the 1840s in *American Album,* comp. by eds. of *American Heritage,* p. 47.

3 John P. Foote, *Memoirs of the Life of Samuel F. Foote, by His Brother, John P. Foote,* p. 78 passim.

4 CB to HB, 17 April 1832, LB, *Autobiography,* 2 : 199–201; Richard C. Wade, *The Urban Frontier,* p. 244, describes Cincinnati as having the best educational facilities in the West in 1830, ranging from the primary grades to college. Cincinnati was also the driving force behind tax-supported free schools in Ohio. There were few cities in the whole nation so conscious of educational needs. CB had emigrated to a place superior to Hartford as far as the potential advancement of her own career was concerned.

5   CB to HB, 17 April 1832, LB, *Autobiography,* 2 : 199–201.

6   Daniel Aaron, "Cincinnati, 1818–1838: A Study of Attitudes in the Urban West," p. 210. Aaron discusses in anti-Turnerian terms the social, political, economic, and regional tensions that existed in Cincinnati in the 1830s, concluding: "Cincinnati certainly was no crucible where 'identity peculiarities melted away.' " For a study analyzing the nature of the Cincinnati leadership, see Walter Glazer, "Cincinnati in the 1840's: A Community Profile," p. 196.

7   Nathaniel Wright Papers, boxes 19 and 24, Library of Congress.

8   Robert Ernst, *Rufus King, American Federalist,* pp. 340, 358; Charles T. Greve, *Centennial History of Cincinnati,* 1 : 567.

9   Foote, *Memoirs of Samuel F. Foote,* pp. 52–98.

10 Semi-Colon Club Papers, Cincinnati Historical Society; Nathaniel Wright Papers, box 40.

11 Sketch by CB, Beecher–Stowe Collection, folder 315.

12 On Drake, see W. H. Venable, *Beginnings of Literary Culture in the Ohio Valley,* pp. 299–322; quotations are from Mansfield, *Personal Memories,* p. 262.

13 CB, "Almanack and Journal"; for a sketch of Burnet, see Mansfield, *Personal Memories,* pp. 155–57.

14 CB, "Almanack and Journal."

15 HB to Georgiana May, [1833] quoted in Charles E. Stowe, *Life of Harriet Beecher Stowe,* p. 69.

16 Randolph C. Randall, *James Hall, Spokesman of the New West,* p. 205. For a description of the *Western Monthly Magazine,* see pp. 221–54.

17 Venable, *Beginnings of Literary Culture,* pp. 421–22; Allen Oscar Hansen, *Early Educational Leadership in the Ohio Valley.*

18 *Western Monthly Magazine* 1 (October 1833) : 470.

19 CB to Mary Dutton, 3 February 1833, Collection of American Literature.

20 Ibid., 15 February 1833.

21 *American Annals of Education and Instruction,* ed. William Woodbridge, 3 (August 1833) : 380.

22 CB, "Almanack and Journal."

23 Mrs. William Beecher to Mary and Thomas Perkins, 4 November 1834. Typewritten copy in Beecher-Perkins Letters, Cincinnati Historical Society.

24 Ellen Kemper to her parents, 12 November 1834, Kemper Family Letters, box 2, Cincinnati Historical Society. For a description of Cincinnati schools, see John P. Foote, *The Schools of Cincinnati and Its Vicinity,* p. 64.

25 Western Literary Institute, *Transactions* 3 (October 1836) : 61–67.

26 See Gerda Lerner, *The Grimké Sisters from South Carolina,* pp. 126–64 for the entry of the Grimkés onto the national scene from 1835 to 1837.

27 William R. Taylor, *Cavalier and Yankee,* first noted this bargain: "In such a family, the woman supplied the moral force while the man was kept busy with material concerns and with politics" (pp. 118–19). Barbara Welter, "The Cult of True Womanhood, 1820–1860," *American Quarterly* 18 (1966) : 151–74, demonstrated the widespread popularity of this bargain by the 1840s and the image identifying women with domestic virtue.

28 CB, *An Essay on the Education of Female Teachers,* pp. 14–18. CB referred specifically to the Catholic religion of many immigrants. This reference may have been based on the prosperous Catholic cathedral that had been built in Cincinnati during the 1820s, and could accommodate 1,000 communicants—probably primarily of German origin. Wade, *The Urban Frontier,* p. 263.

29 CB, *Essay on Education,* p. 18.

30 CB to Mr. Wright and Mr. Guilford, 29 June 1835, Nathaniel Wright Papers, box 19.

31 CB, *Reminiscences,* p. 83; for Thomas Gallaudet, see Henry Barnard, *A Tribute to Gallaudet.*

32 LB, *Autobiography,* 2 : 244.

33 W. R. Keagy, "The Lane Seminary Rebellion," *Bulletin of the Historical and Philosophical Society of Ohio* 9 (April 1951) : 141–60.

34 Randall, *James Hall,* p. 245.

35 Ibid.

36 David Donald, "The Autobiography of James Hall, Western Literary Pioneer," *Ohio State Archaeological and Historical Quarterly* 56, no. 3 (July 1947) : 295–304.

37 Edward King to Sarah King, 24 December 1834, King Family Papers, Cincinnati Historical Society.

38 Ibid.

39 Ibid.

40 Edward King to Sarah King, 12 August 1835, King Family Papers.

41 Ibid.

42 Ibid.

Chapter 9

1 See Edwin C. Rozwenc, *Ideology and Power in the Age of Jackson* for a collection of documents pertinent to this theme, especially pp. 33–44, Daniel Webster's speech of 1836, before the Society for the Diffusion of Useful Knowledge in Boston. See also Alexis de Tocque-

ville's classic commentary on this period, *Democracy in America*. For a summary of the present historiography of the Jacksonian period, see John W. Ward, "The Age of the Common Man," in *The Reconstruction of American History*, ed. John Higham.

2   Rozwenc, *Ideology and Power*, pp. 86–87, presents a brief analysis of Cole's paintings. See also David Huntington, *Thomas Cole, Poet–Painter*, forthcoming. Outstanding among political radicals at this time was Orestes A. Brownson. See his "The Laboring Classes," from the *Boston Quarterly Review* 3 (July 1840) : 366–95. William Lloyd Garrison, of course, led the forces of radical abolitionism and began in the 1830s to combine this with political radicalism. See Aileen Kraditor, *Means and Ends in American Abolitionism*, pp. 78–141.

3   See, e.g., Daniel Webster in Rozwenc, *Ideology and Power* and Richard N. Current's *Daniel Webster and the Rise of National Conservatism*.

4   LB to Nathaniel Wright, 4 January 1840, Nathaniel Wright Papers, box 24.

5   Nathaniel Wright to LB, 14 January 1840, Nathaniel Wright Papers, box 24.

6   Barbara Cross, Introduction to *The Autobiography of Lyman Beecher*, 1 : xxxiii.

7   LB, *Autobiography*, 2 : 282–308; the entire text of Beecher's trial before the Presbytery of Cincinnati was published in New York: Arthur Joseph Stansbury, *Trial of the Reverend Lyman Beecher Before the Presbytery of Cincinnati on the Charge of Heresy, Reported for the "New-York Observer."* Wilson was a Southerner who strongly resented the fact that the trustees of Lane had chosen a New Englander as president. In 1848 a group from Wilson's church continued his struggle against Beecher by instituting a civil lawsuit claiming that the original benefactor of Lane, a Southerner, had intended tht the institution be run by the Southern branch of the church. See *History of the Foundation and Endowment of the Lane Theological Seminary*.

8   CB, *Letters on the Difficulties of Religion*, pp. 332–50; Elizabeth Blackwell "Diary," 24 June 1838, Blackwell Family Papers, box 55, Library of Congress. Elizabeth Blackwell's diary tells of Wilson's pamphlet attacking CB. Another reception of CB's book was printed in the Cincinnati *Western Messenger* 2, no. 2 (September 1836) : 111–20. "Her remarks on Infidelity show that she has had considerable experience in the world . . . and that she has studied and reflected well upon the subject, and although not original in any of her views has given us the arguments of Bishop Butler and others in an agreeable and taking dress. The book shows, that she is her father's daughter, that she has one more cell in the heart and one less in the brain

than he has. But this according to Fontanelle is only making the proper allowance for the difference of sex."

9 The best collection of primary documents relating to these changes is Joseph Blau, ed., *Social Theories of Jacksonian Democracy*; other pertinent studies are: Marvin Meyers, *The Jacksonian Persuasion*, for the conservative goals behind many Jacksonian innovations; Henry Nash Smith, *Virgin Land*, for the relation between "success" and other American beliefs; and Arthur Ekirch, Jr., *The Idea of Progress in America, 1815–1860*.

10 CB, *The Moral Instructor for Schools and Families*, p. 129.

11 William G. McLoughlin, *The Meaning of Henry Ward Beecher*, p. 235, discusses the preeminence of guilt as a theme in Henry Ward Beecher's writings of the 1880s. Both CB and Henry pursued the dynamic so well described by McLoughlin as: "To externalize it [guilt], to understand it, was to forgive it." Catharine's fascination with guilt for its own sake began much earlier than Henry's, however.

12 CB, *Letters on the Difficulties of Religion*, p. 13.

13 For examples of writings similar to and contemporary with CB's *Moral Education* see Almira Phelps, *The Female Student*; Lydia Sigourney, *Letters to Mothers*; Rev. John S. C. Abbott, *The School Boy* and *The Mother at Home*; and T. H. Gallaudet, *The Youth's Book on Natural Theology*. Moral education proceeded along the same lines of "character formation" in both the home and the school, and in both institutions women gradually replaced men as the major molders of moral character. Some major secondary sources treating this tradition are: Anne Kuhn, *The Mother's Role in Childhood Education*; Bernard Wishy, *The Child and the Republic*; Ruth Elson, *Guardians of Tradition*; American Schoolbooks of the Nineteenth Century; and Mary Patricia Ryan, "American Society and the Cult of Domesticity, 1830–1860."

14 CB to Mrs. Cogswell and Mary Weld, 29 May 1837, Beecher–Stowe Collection, folder 15. CB added, "I do wish that people would feel a little more respect for me and my works."

15 CB, *Reminiscences*, p. 91.

16 CB, "Almanack and Journal."

17 CB to Mary Dutton, 12 April 1836, Collection of American Literature.

18 CB, "Almanack and Journal."

19 CB, 15 July 1836, Strong Family Papers, additional box 4, Sterling Memorial Library.

20 CB, *Reminiscences*, p. 96; Mary Lyon to CB, n.d., quoted in CB, *Reminiscences*, p. 98; CB, *Reminiscences*, pp. 94–95.

21 *The Cincinnati Gazette*, 21 February 1837. CB had begun a subscription fund to raise an endowment for her school, but it had died

before it had fairly begun in 1835. In 1836 she discovered a new possible source of funds in a legacy left to the city but not then permanently allocated. She tried to channel this fund into female education and an endowment for the Western Female Institute and invited the fund's trustees together with all the former Litchfield and New England acquaintances she could muster to a meeting at Samuel Foote's mansion. There they consulted "relative to a plan proposed for securing a Female Institution in this city" (CB to Judge Torrence, Friday morning [1836], Torrence Family Papers, box 2, Cincinnati Historical Society). For a full year thereafter CB labored in vain to gain the allocation of the Hughes fund.

22 See Foote, *Schools of Cincinnati*, p. 64.

23 Lerner, *The Grimké Sisters*, pp. 127–242; Keith Melder, "Forerunners of Freedom: The Grimké Sisters in Massachusetts," *Essex Institute Historical Collections* 3, no. 3 (July 1967) : 223–50.

24 Lerner, *The Grimké Sisters*, p. 130, notes the growing reputation of Angelina Grimké in the prominent eastern circles where CB was also traveling in the summer of 1836. Angelina Grimké's organization speeches were later published as *An Appeal to the Women of the Nominally Free States*.

25 The exchange was initiated with Angelina Grimké's *Appeal to the Christian Women of the Southern States*, challenged by CB in *An Essay on Slavery and Abolitionism with Reference to the Duty of American Females*, and culminated with Angelina's *Letters to Catharine Beecher, in Reply to an Essay on Slavery and Abolitionism, Addressed to A. E. Grimké*.

26 Aaron, "Cincinnati, 1818–1838," p. 458; Greve, *Centennial History of Cincinnati*, p. 593.

27 One of the best descriptions of the response of Cincinnati's leadership is in HBS's letters of that period, in Charles E. Stowe's *Life of Harriet Beecher Stowe*, pp. 81–87.

28 Ibid., p. 83; LB to William Beecher, 15 July 1835, LB, *Autobiography*, 2 : 259–60.

29 CB, *Essay on Slavery*, p. 33; Aaron, "Cincinnati, 1818–1838," p. 458.

30 A. Grimké, *Letters to Catharine Beecher*, p. 113. Grimké's emphasis.

31 CB, *Essay on Slavery*, pp. 98–101.

32 Ibid., p. 106, 127–28.

33 Ibid., p. 101.

34 Ibid., p. 128.

Chapter 10

1 Although Angelina Grimké led a counterattack against CB's book in the pages of the *Liberator*, the Cincinnati newspapers made no men-

tion of her books on slavery or on religion. This silence is all the more remarkable since CB's *Essay on the Education of Female Teachers* (1835) received warm praise and extensive coverage in the *Cincinnati Gazette*, 9 June 1835.

2 CB, *Reminiscences*, p. 82.

3 HBS to Dear Sister Katy, [1838], Beecher–Stowe Collection, folder 235. In this letter HBS reminded CB that in 1833, "[I] had very serious doubts of your ability to carry it [the school] through and stated then often and fully and I told you often and fully, if you felt the least hesitation, to draw back before we committed ourselves."

4 Ibid. "My estimation of the matter is that I shall pay out for this concern $200 beyond what I receive," HBS said. Mary Dutton wrote CB that she had lost $500 of her own money in the school, but CB reproved her, saying that Mary exaggerated and that her loss amounted only to $100. Although CB had not worked as hard as either Mary or HBS, she felt justified in being the only one who made any financial profit from the school. The school was subscribed and furnished at her solicitation, CB said, and therefore the money raised by the sale of school property should go to her. CB defended her claim to even the smallest sums, and in arguing over the dispensation of $15, HBS reproved her: "What is that between thee and me?" CB to Mary Dutton, 10 August 1838, 21 May 1838, and 13 February 1839, all in Collection of American Literature. HBS to CB [1838], Beecher–Stowe Collection, folder 235.

5 CB to Mary Dutton, 10 August 1838, Collection of American Literature.

6 Rev. John A. Clark, ed., *The Christian Keepsake and Missionary Annual*, pp. 107–22. CB published another short story in *The Gift, A Christmas and New Year's Present for 1842* (Philadelphia, [1841]), pp. 209–42.

7 CB's siblings married and/or entered the ministry on the following dates: William, ministry — c. 1830, marriage — 1830, Catherine Edes; Edward, ministry — 1826, marriage — [1820s], Isabella Jones; Mary, marriage — late 1820s, Thomas Perkins; George, ministry — 1832, marriage — 1832, Sarah Buckingham; Harriet, marriage — 1836, Calvin Stowe; Henry Ward, ministry — 1837, marriage — 1837, Eunice Bullard; and Charles, ministry — 1844, marriage — 1840, Sarah Coffin. For the best discussion of the marital relationship of HBS and Calvin Stowe, see Edmund Wilson, *Patriotic Gore* (New York, 1962), pp. 15–31.

8 CB to Revd. Mr. Clarke, 22 November 1837, American Literary Duplicates, case 6, box 27, Historical Society of Philadelphia; HBS to Mary Dutton, 13 December 1838, Collection of American Literature; Ibid., 13 December 1838.

9 Some discussion of the means **CB** used to promote her books may reveal the kinds of bridges nineteenth-century authors constructed to reach their reading public. CB's efforts to promote her *Moral Instructor* were quite skillful and drew on nearly a decade of her experience in such matters. She had since 1831 considered school texts a possible source of income, and although she did not succeed in getting her *Elements of Mental and Moral Philosophy* published commercially, she had succeeded with two arithmetic texts, these the fruits of her first intellectual growth after reading Alexander Fisher's papers. In 1832 her *Arithmetic Simplified* had been published in Hartford, and a revised version, *The Lyceum Arithmetic,* had been published in 1835 in Boston. The Hartford text had proved unprofitable — CB claimed the publisher wouldn't promote it because it "was written by a woman," and he also set the price too high. To promote the 1835 edition CB had written her friends in education asking them "to exert themselves in promoting its introduction." She had urged its adoption on the grounds that "at least six per cent (probably more) of all that are sold are to be devoted to promoting the moral and religious education of this country." CB had been deliberately vague about where the educational fund ended and her own personal bank account began. "By the way I do not wish to make public the manner of employing the profits," she had written to Mary Lyon. "There are many reasons why it should only be communicated confidentially to the leading friends of education through the country," she added. "I am willing to employ my time in making school books and to devote the profits (of course reserving my own maintenance) to the cause of education. . . . I am desirous that no public mention be made of this plan either in print or in public meetings. It would be an ostentatious display from which I shrink and would in some way operate unfavorably to the plan proposed" (CB to Mary Lyon, 15 October 1834, Mt. Holyoke College Archives). CB did not usually shrink from publicity, and her reasons for concealment may have included the fact that she did not want anyone to hold her accountable for the uses she made of the profits. The amount necessary for her "own maintenance" was after all a matter for her alone to decide. In any case this *Arithmetic* had proved equally unprofitable. Her *Moral Instructor* got a better start, being published by Truman and Smith, the largest of Cincinnati's many publishing firms and the publisher of McGuffey's Eclectic Readers. When CB first came to Cincinnati, Truman and Smith, who dealt mainly in school texts, asked her to edit a series of eclectic readers. These readers (eclectic meaning that the materials were chosen from many sources) were extremely popular with grammar school educators, but since CB at

the time had been interested primarily in higher seminary education, she had recommended William McGuffey, who in 1833 began to compile his famous series. For a study of McGuffey's moral attitudes in his *Readers*, see Richard David Mosier, *Making the American Mind*; for CB's role in the McGuffey series, see Harvey Minnich, *Wm. Holmes McGuffey and His Readers*, p. 31.

By 1838 CB was eager to tap the lucrative common-school market and duplicate the financial success of McGuffey's readers. Statewide systems of publicity financed common schools had begun in a few states in the mid-1830s, and CB gained entrance to the common-school movement through her brother-in-law Calvin Stowe. In 1836 Calvin Stowe had gone to Europe to buy books for Lane Seminary. Because he was an active participant in the Western Literary Institute and College of Professional Teachers, he was also commissioned by the Ohio state legislature to write a report on elementary public education in Europe. Stowe's *Report on Elementary Instruction in Europe* (Columbus, Ohio, 1837), emphasized the Prussian integration of religious and secular instruction, and the Prussian view that the school was the servant of the state rather than of the individual. Stowe advocated teacher-training institutions, adequate pay, and comfortable schools, but he offered no solution to the quarrel then preoccupying the Ohio legislature as to how this common-school system could be financed. (Charles G. Miller, "The Background of Calvin E. Stowe's 'Report on Elementary Public Instruction in Europe,'" *Ohio State Archeological and Historical Quarterly* 49, no. 2 [April 1940].) CB agreed with Calvin Stowe's educational ideas, and she assumed that his name would provide an excellent introduction to others involved in common-school education elsewhere. As soon as her *Moral Instructor* was published she wrote Thomas Burrowes, state superintendent of schools in Pennsylvania, and Horace Mann, secretary of the board of education in Massachusetts, two men who were struggling to implement newly passed legislation for common schools in their states, and one of whom had shown considerable interest in Stowe's report. (Robert Landis Mohr, *Thomas Henry Burrowes, 1805–1871*, p. 60.) Burrowes had several hundred copies of Stowe's *Report* printed, and he distributed it widely throughout Pennsylvania and the East.

CB's letters to the two men were fundamentally alike. "On the advice of my brother-in-law, Professor Stowe," she said, she had sent them copies of her *Moral Instructor,* a book "designed to meet that great desideratum in education, a system of moral instruction for children, prepared for a regular study in schools." CB concluded that she had been led to believe that these men were interested in acquiring texts of moral instruction for their state systems, and she asked their aid in having hers adopted for such use. (CB to Thomas H. Burrowes, 2 April 1838, Stauffer Collection, New York Public Library. CB to Horace Mann, Esq., [1838], Horace Mann Papers, box 4.)

Both Burrowes and Mann had indicated that they favored some kind of moral education in the common schools. In a new law written by Burrowes in 1837 to amend the common-school system, he incorporated attitudes on moral instruction that were very similar to those of CB. Nonsectarian training of Christian character was advocated "to restrain vicious propensities, stimulate virtuous sentiments, purify the character and regulate the conduct of the pupil in subsequent life" (Mohr, *Thomas Henry Burrowes*, p. 70). Horace Mann was also not opposed to religious or moral training in public schools, for in his *First Report* to the Massachusetts legislature he stated his regret that the law of 1827, forbidding all sectarian teaching, had had the unfortunate consequence of eliminating religious and moral instruction altogether from the public schools, and he called for a text that would comply with the nonsectarian requirements of the law and yet portray "the beautiful and sublime truths of ethics and natural religion" (Raymond B. Culver, *Horace Mann and Religion in the Massachusetts Public Schools*, pp. 41–42). CB was aware of Mann's *First Report* and recommended her book as the text that would meet the needs of the Massachusetts schools. Yet moral instruction was a difficult commodity to sell since almost no text was completely free of sectarian bias. Even before CB's letter reached him, Burrowes had retired from his post in the midst of a controversy over religious instruction in the public schools, and CB's letter reached Horace Mann just as he had become involved in a public debate over his refusal to include a popular, but religiously orthodox, children's book in his approved list of books for the Massachusetts schools. This controversy raged for almost a decade and was the source of Mann's reputation as an opponent of religious teaching in the schools. Although CB's *Moral Instructor* was decidedly less orthodox than the book Mann opposed (Jacob Abbott's *Child at Home*), the grounds of Mann's objection to it would also have excluded her work from the Massachusetts schools. For Mann objected to Abbott's book on the grounds that it portrayed a system of moral laws. Unitarians and Universalists would regard such "laws of moral nature" as "mechanical and arbitrary," Mann said. (Culver, *Horace Mann*, p. 58.) CB's book was certainly rife with such laws, for the idea that the individual was accountable to an external moral law lay at the heart of her moral system. She believed that her book would offend no sectarian interest, and she included testimonials from Methodists, Baptists, Presbyterians, and Episcopalians and claimed that she also had a "complimentary" letter on her book by a Catholic priest. (CB to Thomas H. Burrowes, 2 April 1838, Stauffer Collection.) But her moral ideas were fundamentally grounded in New England Calvinism, and the wave of opposition to those ideas was then at its height in Unitarian Boston.

CB tried another tactic in promoting her book and asked Lydia Sigourney to advertise it in a ladies' magazine she edited. (CB to Mrs. Sigourney, 24 April 1838, Connecticut Historical Society.) "With this I send my winter's work, — a humble affair as to matter and manner, but dignified by the importance of the object at which it aims," CB began. "Cannot you help forward the introduction of such a work into schools, by a little notice of it in the Mothers Magazine — for if mothers will interest themselves to have moral instruction in schools the thing will be done." Catharine added that she hoped to expand her own role in such magazines and, by becoming a more prominent literary figure, gain wider patronage for her moral and religious books for children. She planned to write a sequel to the *Moral Instructor* entitled, "Religious Instruction for Schools and Families." For magazines and annuals, she said, "I intend to write several pieces of the lighter kind, and I wish when you write you would tell me which you would advise me to write for." Her object: "to make myself known, and as popular as I can, with all classes of readers — I need not tell you that this may be aimed at without any craving for fame or notoriety, but as one means of increasing the sphere of usefulness." CB wanted her "books for children to become extensively used, and the more I can gain public favor the more likely I am to secure it." In spite of these extensive efforts on behalf of her text it earned less than forty dollars during 1838 (CB to Mary Dutton, 11 March 1838, Collection of American Literature), and this failure coupled with her inability to publish widely in women's literary magazines or gift annuals, brought CB in the summer of 1839 to a professional dead end.

10   HBS summarized the relationship: "She [Lydia] has never loved or trusted us" (HBS to CB, 27 August 1858. Beecher–Stowe Collection, folder 97).

11   CB to Nathaniel Wright, 14 June 1839, Nathaniel Wright Papers, box 24. She wrote Nathaniel Wright for legal advice in forcing Truman and Smith to interpret their *Moral Instructor* contract with her more generously and asked him to take his fee out of the money he obtained for her from the publishing company. "As I have no other money due to me until November," she wrote, "and as all my friends *everywhere* find it almost impossible to get money for their own wants, unless I can receive this in July I shall be much embarrassed for means to travel."

12 This story appears in many places. See Lyman Beecher Stowe, *Saints, Sinners and Beechers,* p. 97.

13 [CB], "An Essay on Cause and Effect in Connection with the Doctrines of Fatalism and Free Will," *American Biblical Repository* 2, no. 4 (October 1839) : 381–408.

14 Leonard Woods, "Inquiries Respecting Free Agency," *American Biblical Repository* 5, no. 37 (January 1840) : 174–93.

15 Ibid., p. 181.

16 HB to Elizabeth Phoenix, 21 August [1830], Phoenix Family Papers, Sterling Memorial Library.

17 Charles Beecher to LB, 27 September 1840, Beecher–Stowe Collection, folder 217.

18 LB to Henry Ward Beecher, 8 December 1842, Beecher Family Papers, Sterling Memorial Library.

19 CB, "Memoranda, 1843–6," Beecher–Stowe Collection, folder 317.

20 HBS to Henry and Charles Beecher, 4 July [1843], Beecher Family Papers, Sterling Memorial Library.

21 CB, *The Biographical Remains of Rev. George Beecher,* pp. 6–13, *passim.* No member of the Beecher family admitted that George's death was a suicide. The coroner pronounced George's death accidental, and the official report stated that the gun had probably misfired when George put it to his face to see why it would not fire. Since the bullet entered his mouth, however, suicide seems a more likely explanation.

22 Ibid., pp. 10, 341.

23 CB, "Memoranda," 26 June–12 September 1843.

Chapter 11

1 Eugene Exman, *The Brothers Harper,* pp. 323–26, describes Harpers' distribution network during this period. CB's *Treatise on Domestic Economy for the Use of Young Ladies at Home and at School* was also adopted by Massachusetts for use in the public schools (Introduction to 1843 ed. of *Treatise*). It was reprinted in 1841 (Marsh, Capen, Lyon & Webb, Boston), 1842 (rev. ed., T. H. Webb, Boston), and in 1842, 1843 (new rev. ed.), 1845, 1846 (3rd rev. ed.), 1847, 1848, 1849, 1850, 1851, 1852, 1854, 1855, and 1856 by Harper & Bros., New York.
      The 1869 work, *The American Woman's Home, or Principles of Domestic Science,* was done jointly with HBS, presumably to capitalize on her national fame after the publication of *Uncle Tom's Cabin* in 1852. This was reprinted in 1873 as *The New Housekeeper's Manual: Embracing a New Revised Edition of the American Woman's Home; or, Principles of Domestic Science. Being a Guide to Economical,*

Healthful, Beautiful and Christian Homes. Other domestic economy publications by CB and HBS include: CB, *Miss Beecher's House-keeper and Healthkeeper* (1873), reprinted in 1874 and 1876; CB, *Physiology and Calisthenics for Schools and Families* (1856), reprinted in 1860, 1862, and 1867; CB and HBS, *Principles of Domestic Science; As Applied to the Duties and Pleasures of the Home. A Text Book for the Use of Young Ladies in Schools, Seminaries, and Colleges* (1870), reprinted in 1871 and 1873. HBS also published separately *House and Home Papers* (Boston, 1869) under the pseudonym Christopher Crow-field.

2 CB's architectural designs were executed by Daniel Wadsworth. She apparently did the other household designs herself. Jacques Ellul, *The Technological Society*, p. 326.

3 The most popular English work in America was Thomas Webster and Mrs. Parkes, *An Encyclopaedia of Domestic Economy*. The American edition was published by Harper. CB's *Treatise* (pp. 44–52) warned upper class American women against imitating English aristo-cratic languor and urged them to adopt a new model of American self-denying benevolent activity. The liability of American women to "melancholy, hysteria, hypochondriasis and other varieties of mental distress" was due to their inability to find activities commensurate with their aspirations, she said. If they could feel they were acting "for the good of society," their mental distress would cease. Lacking a social norm that was appropriate for American circumstances, and imitating the English example was disasterous for both middle and upper class American women, CB said. The "middle rank" of women suffered nervous exhaustion in trying to imitate a model that was economically beyond them, and upper class American women needed more moral nourishment than the English model provided.

4 When she entered Burlington, Iowa, in 1848, e.g., *The Iowa State Gazette* hailed CB's arrival: "Miss Beecher whose name has long since become a household divinity is now in Burlington" (29 March 1848). This widespread need is typically expressed in *Godey's Lady's Book* 23 (July 1841) : 41, by a letter from a mother: "I want more particu-lar directions. I want a daily course of conduct pointed out, by which I can make my daughters healthy as well as intelligent, and happy as well as good."

5 These themes are explored further in William R. Taylor, *Cavalier and Yankee,* esp. chap. 3; Bernard Wishy, *The Child and the Republic*; Barbara Cross, *Horace Bushnell, Minister to a Changing America,* esp. chap. 5; Helen Papashvily, *All the Happy Endings*; Arthur W. Calhoun, *A Social History of the American Family*, vol. 2, *From Inde-pendence through the Civil War,* esp. chaps. 5 and 6; and Glenda

Gates Riley, "The Subtle Subversion: Changes in the Traditionalist Image of the American Woman," *Historian* 32 no. 2, (February 1970).

One contributing cause to the disorientation of domestic life during these years might have been the beginnings of the shift to a consumer society. Not fully complete, this shift might have been far enough along to compel people to be conscious of keeping up appearances, but not sure enough of the mechanisms for doing it. CB at least presages this shift in her *Treatise* (p. 172) encouraging the consumption of goods as a means of promoting the national economy:

Suppose that two millions of the people in the United States were conscientious persons, and relinquished the use of every thing not absolutely necessary to life and health. It would instantly throw out of employment one half of the whole community. The manufacturers, mechanics, merchants, agriculturists, and all the agencies they employ, would be beggared, and one half of those not reduced to poverty, would be obliged to spend all their extra means, in simply supplying necessaries to the other half. The use of superfluities, therefore. to a certain extent, is as indispensable to promote industry, virtue, and religion, as any direct giving of money or time.

6 Ellul, *The Technological Society,* p. 326. Siegfried Giedion, *Mechanization Takes Command,* p. 614, pays tribute to CB's "classic proposals" for domestic efficiency.

7 CB, *Treatise,* p. 47.

8 Cross, *Horace Bushnell,* pp. 58–63.

9 Theodore Dwight, *The Father's Book,* pp. 187–99; Herman Humphrey, *Domestic Education*; William Alcott, *The Young Housekeeper*; Lydia Maria Child, *The American Frugal Housewife.* Although the first of this new literature of the 1840s, CB's *Treatise* generally embodied attitudes toward women found in such later works as: Margaret Coxe, *Claims of the Country on American Females*; Margaret Graves, *Women in America*; and Sarah Josepha Hale, *Housekeeping and Keeping House.* Harriet Martineau's *Household Education* is the only work of the 1840s that employs the less exaggerated gender roles of the eighteenth century. For more complete bibliographies of domestic manuals see Wishy, *The Child and the Republic* and Ryan, "American Society and the Cult of Domesticity, 1830–1860," (Ph.D. diss., University of California of Santa Barbara, 1971).

10 See Alice Felt Tyler, *Freedom's Ferment,* esp. chap. 16; and Joseph F. Kett, *The Formation of the American Medical Profession,* esp. chap. 5.

11 CB, *Treatise,* chap. 5.

12 Ibid., pp. 216–17, 231.

13 For an adequate summary of the position of women in late eighteenth- and early nineteenth-century America and the contrasts wrought by

Jacksonian Democracy, see Calhoun, *Social History of the American Family*, 2 : 79–131.

14 William Taylor touches on this dynamic in *Cavalier and Yankee*, pp. 166–76. Oscar Handlin has pointed out the same dynamic between white men and black men in seventeenth-century Virginia in *Race and Nationality in American Life*, chap. 1. The Seneca Falls Declaration of 1848 pointed to the manifest contradiction between democratic theory and democratic practices with reference to women. See Elizabeth Cady Stanton, *Eighty Years and More*, pp. 143–54.

15 For further discussion of Bushnell and Hale, see pp. 161–63. See also Riley, "Subtle Subversion," and Welter, "True Womanhood."

16 CB, *Treatise*, pp. 28–29, 40.

17 Ibid., pp. 25–26. Marriage across class lines was taken as proof that democracy was working and was a favorite theme of other domestic economy books besides CB's. See, e.g., Solon Robinson, *How to Live*, pp. 34–68. Intermarriage in this fashion could be seen in anthropological terms as similar to the exchange of women described by Claude Levi-Strauss in *The Elementary Structure of Kinship*: "The total relationship of exchange which constitutes marriage," Levi-Strauss suggests, "is not established between a man and a woman, where each owes and receives something, but between two groups of men, and the woman figures only as one of the objects in the exchange, not as one of the partners between whom the exchange takes place" (p. 115). Thus in the United States as well as in "primitive" tribes women may have been exchanged between otherwise hostile groups to promote amity between them. The general submission of women to men is a necessary precondition to such an exchange.

18 CB, *Treatise*, p. 26.

19 Ibid., pp. 25–38. For the domestic influence on *Uncle Tom's Cabin*, see Edmund Wilson, *Patriotic Gore*, pp. 11–35. Recent quantitative research by Kenneth Lockridge, "Literacy in Colonial New England: A Summary of Preliminary Researches," (paper written at the University of Michigan, 1973), indicates that gender identity became increasingly functional in New England society in the seventeenth and eighteenth centuries while class identity grew less functional. Literacy, Lockridge found, was related to class in the seventeenth century. Both men and women of upper income levels were literate, while both genders of lower income groups were generally not literate. This class-based distribution of seventeenth-century literacy gave way by the end of the eighteenth century to a gender-based distribution. Thus literacy became virtually universal among males of all classes, while fewer than 50 percent of women — regardless of class — were literate. "The imperviousness of women's illiteracy was the result of deliberate intention on the part of this culture," Lockridge concluded. "Women

were discriminated against because they were women, not because they were poor" (pp. 25–26). Nineteenth-century gender distinctions therefore began on a cultural foundation well established in the previous century. Similarly, the inverse relationship between class and gender identity and the tendency of the latter to replace the former as a basic building block of social structure was not an invention of the nineteenth century, but it was first given ideological articulation during that period.

20 CB, *Treatise,* pp. 35–37.

21 Ibid., pp. 37–38.

22 Ibid., pp. 32–33.

23 Fred Lewis Pattee, *The Feminine Fifties* (New York, 1940). Peter Stearns has pointed to the relationship between the accentuated gender identity of nineteenth-century English working class culture and the way that tended to obscure strong class identity in the same group. See his "Working Class Women in Britain, 1890–1914," in Martha Vicinus, ed., *Suffer and Be Still,* pp. 100–20.

24 CB, *Treatise,* p. 25.

25 Ibid., p. 29. Women who did not behave in this way, Tocqueville continued, foolishly exempt themselves from the only role the society defines as honorable, and praiseworthy for them.

26 Ibid., p. 127.

27 Horace Bushnell, *Christian Nurture,* pp. 36, 402, 30, and 388. Although Bushnell did not exclude fathers from nurturing responsibilities, he obviously expected them to bridge both the domestic and outside worlds, while mothers were to dwell only in "a place of quiet" and have "quiet minds which the din of our public war never embroils" (Bushnell, "American Politics," *The American National Preacher* 14 [New York, 1840] : 199).

28 Taylor, *Cavalier and Yankee,* p. 115.

29 Two typical passages from the "Editor's Table" of *Godey's Lady's Book* illustrate this ideology: "The destiny of the human race is thus dependent on the condition and conduct of woman. And now, when her condition is so greatly improved, her standard of conduct must be proportionately elevated. We do not mean by this, that she is to emulate man, or strive to do his work. She has a wide, a noble sphere of her own" (vol. 23 [August 1841], pp. 93–94). "And all in-door pursuits she should be encouraged to learn and undertake, because these harmonize with her natural love of home and its duties, from which she should never, in idea, be divorced" (vol. 47 [July 1853], pp. 84–85).

One of the best examples of Sarah Josepha Hale's way of thinking was manifested by Professor J. H. Agnew of the University of Michigan, writing in *Harper's New Monthly Magazine* 3, (October 1851): "Another office of woman is, *to check the utilitarianism, the money-*

loving spirit of the day," he said in a typical passage. [Agnew's emphasis.] "Women's office is *also to soften political asperities in the other sex, and themselves to shun political publicity."* Agnew concluded: "Another evident office of women is, *to regulate the forms, and control the habits of social life.* . . . Let man, then, exercise power; woman exert influence."

30 CB, *Treatise,* p. 28, quote from Tocqueville.

31 Ibid., p. 193.

32 Ibid., p. 160.

33 Ibid., p. 140.

34 Ibid., p. 246.

35 Lydia Maria Child, *The American Frugal Housewife,* went through thirty-three editions until it was last reprinted in 1870. A much smaller and somewhat cheaper volume than CB's *Treatise,* Child's *Housewife* was a compendium of general hints for economical housekeeping and cooking. Three-fourths of it were receipts. For the economic success of Child's volume (a fact which CB must have known about and which possibly inspired her to write her own domestic work) see Milton Meltzer, *Tongue of Flame,* p. 27. CB, *Treatise,* pp. 262–72 for drawings on house construction. Helen Campbell, *Household Economics,* p. 28.

36 CB and HBS, *American Woman's Home,* p. 447. The chapters written by HBS are clearly distinguishable from those written by CB. HBS's portions are not long and, unlike most of the rest of the book, deviate from the original topical scheme of the 1841 *Treatise.*

37 CB, *Miss Beecher's Housekeeper and Healthkeeper,* p. 465.

38 CB and HBS, *The American Woman's Home,* p. 204.

Chapter 12

1 *Dictionary of American Biography,* s.v. "Van Rensselaer, Cortlandt."

2 CB, "Memoranda," 15 September to 2 October 1843, Beecher–Stowe Collection, folder 316.

3 CB, *Reminiscences,* p. 101; CB, "Memoranda" lists correspondence for this period with Henry Barnard, William McGuffey (who had moved to the University of Virginia), John Quincy Adams, and several other leading Americans.

4 CB to Thomas Burrowes, December 1843, Stauffer Collection. This letter is typical of several others CB wrote to pressure Stowe.

5 HBS to Calvin Stowe, 4 December [1846], Beecher–Stowe Collection, folder 71.

6 LB to Lydia Beecher, 3 July 1844, White Collection, Stowe–Day Foundation. LB married Lydia Jackson in 1837, a year after the death of Harriet Porter Beecher.

7 CB, "Memoranda," 3 October 1844 to 7 June 1845.

8   CB, *The Evils Suffered by American Women and American Children,* p. 29.

9   CB, *An Address to the Protestant Clergy of the United States,* p. 29.

10 Ibid., pp. 22–23; CB, *The Evils Suffered,* p. 16.

11 CB, "Memoranda," 29 November to 4 December 1844; CB, *The Evils Suffered,* pp. 6–9.

12 CB, *The Evils Suffered,* pp. 11–14.

13 Ibid., p. 11.

14 Ibid., pp. 9–10.

15 Ibid., p. 11.

16 CB, *The Duty of American Women to Their Country,* pp. 112–31.

17 CB to Judge Lane, 26 July 1845, Ebenezer Lane Papers, Rutherford B. Hayes Library, Fremont, Ohio. CB undoubtedly knew that Elizabeth Seton had founded the first American religious community for women called "The Sisters of Charity" in 1810 and had soon thereafter opened the first parochial school free to children of all classes. Edward James et al., *Notable American Women, 1607–1950,* 3 : 265.

18 CB, *Reminiscences,* p. 115.

19 Samuel Lewis was the state superintendent of schools for Ohio; Gorham Abbot, the brother of Jacob Abbot, was the director of a fashionable school for girls in New York City. CB also appealed to Rufus Choate, then the director of the Smithsonian Institution, and Mrs. James K. Polk, the nation's first lady, for their endorsements. See CB to The Hon. Rufus Choate, 29 August 1846, HBS Collection, Clifton Waller Barrett Library, University of Virginia; CB to Mrs. James K. Polk, [1847], Hillhouse Family Papers, box 27, Sterling Memorial Library.

20 Catharine Sedgwick to Horace Mann, 31 January [1846], Horace Mann Papers, box 7.

21 CB, "Memoranda," 21 March to 27 April 1846. Charles Foster, *An Errand of Mercy,* p. 136, describes the traditional support New England women gave to education. The first female organizations in the country were formed for such a purpose — specifically to support men studying for the ministry. Early in the nineteenth century these female "cent societies" maintained 20 per cent of the ministerial students in New England. CB therefore drew on an organizational structure and a charitable predisposition that had existed among New England women for at least a generation.

22 CB, "Memoranda," 14 July 1846; CB, *Reminiscences,* pp. 114–15.

23 CB, "Memoranda," August to December 1846; CB, *Reminiscences,* p. 120.

24 William Slade, "Circular to the Friends of Popular Education in the United States," 15 May 1847, Increase Lapham Papers, State Historical Society of Wisconsin, Madison.

25 *First Annual Report of the General Agent of the Board of National Popular Education* (Hartford, 1848), pp. 15, 22–26.

26 CB, *The True Remedy for the Wrongs of Women,* pp. 163, 167.

27 Ibid., pp. 169–72.

28 Woody, *History of Women's Education,* 1 : 499.

29 Richard G. Boone, *A History of Education in Indiana,* p. 142.

30 Katz, *Irony of Early School Reform,* pp. 57–58. Katz's evidence disproves the stereotype of the antebellum male teacher as a vacationing college student. His data suggests that teachers shifted to the ministry, commerce, and medicine. He concludes that "others may well have looked on teaching as a way both to stay alive and to establish a local reputation while waiting for the right business opportunity to appear." Paul Monroe, *Founding of the American Public School System,* 1 : 487: "In the newer settled regions of the Middle West men still predominated in the teaching profession throughout this period."

31 Elsie Garland Hobson, "Educational Legislation and Administration in the State of New York from 1772 to 1850," *Supplementary Educational Monographs* 3, no. 1 (Chicago, 1918) : 75.

32 Woody, *History of Women's Education,* 1 : 497.

33 Hobson, "Educational Legislation," p. 66.

34 A comparison of salary rates for a three- to four-month period near the end of the 1840s compiled from the above sources reveals these differentials:

State	Year	Men	Women
Michigan	1847	$12.87	$5.74
Indiana	1850	12.00	6.00
Massachusetts	1848	24.51	8.07
Maine	c. 1848	15.40	4.80
New York	c. 1848	15.95	6.99
Ohio	c. 1848	15.42	8.73

Henry Barnard was practically alone in protesting this discriminatory practice. See "Report to the Secretary of the Board," *Connecticut Common School Journal* 1, no. 13 (1839) : 163–64. Charles William Eliot, "Wise and Unwise Economy in Schools," *Atlantic Monthly,* no. 35 (June 1875) : 715, quoted in Katz, *Irony of Early School Reform,* p. 58.

35 Katz, *Irony of Early School Reform,* pp. 56–58.

36 Woody, *History of Women's Education,* 1 : 491.

37 Petition appeared in *Godey's Lady's Book* (January 1853), pp. 176–77. CB wrote Horace Mann: "The great purpose of a woman's life — the happy superintendence of a family — is accomplished all the better and easier by preliminary teaching in school. All the power she may

develop here will come in use there" (CB to Horace Mann, in *Common School Journal* 5 [Boston, 1843] : 353.

38 *Annual Reports of the General Agent of the Board of National Popular Education* Hartford, 1848–1857).

39 Nathaniel Wright to CB, 4 April 1844, Nathaniel Wright Papers, box 25.

Chapter 13

1 For background on Brattleboro, see *Annals of Brattleboro, 1681–1895*, ed. Mary R. Cabot, 2 vols. (Brattleboro, 1921); and Charles Stowe, *The Life of Harriet Beecher Stowe,* pp. 112–19.

2 CB, "Memoranda," 10–20 January 1845; CB, *Letters on Health and Happiness,* n. 4, pp. 18–27, pp. 112–20.

3 CB, *Letters on Health and Happiness,* p. 117.

4 CB, "Memoranda," [1847], last page.

5 Vivian C. Hopkins, *Prodigal Puritan,* pp. 29–71.

6 Ibid., pp. 71–121. Vivian Hopkins' vivid account of these events drew heavily from CB's *Truth Stranger than Fiction.*

7 CB, *Truth Stranger than Fiction,* pp. 216–17.

8 Ibid., pp. 205–06, 237.

9 Ibid., pp. 93, 105–27, 227, passim. The independent evidence cited by Vivian Hopkins supports CB's allegations.

10 Delia Bacon to CB, quoted in CB, *Truth Stranger than Fiction,* pp. 272, 274.

11 Ibid., pp. 282–84. CB claimed in a letter to the *New York Tribune* in October 1850 that she had the support of her father and brothers, and in response to this Nathaniel Taylor wrote LB, "[I am] confident that there is some mistake here." Taylor suggested that LB make a public expression of his confidence in Taylor and Yale College, but LB, saying that the conflict was marked on the "interstices of my heart," made no public statement. (Nathaniel Taylor to LB, 12 October 1850, Collection). LB's comments are annotated on Taylor's letter. Mary Beecher Perkins, who had a social position of some eminence in Hartford, was mortified by CB's behavior and sent Thomas Beecher and Henry Ward Beecher in pursuit of her. "Now she has gone off to New York, without letting any one know where she is to be — saying that she will send word to her publishers how she can be communicated with thro' her *lawyer*," Mary wrote HBS. Mary considered but then decided against obtaining a court injunction against CB's publication. She anticipated that the book "will be like

throwing fire brands, arrows and death into the midst of the community here." On the other hand she anticipated "the most disastrous consequences to *her* . . . if she is stopped."

CB thought, Mary said, "she has a divine commission. She seems to feel all a martyr's spirit, so far as self-sacrifice is concerned. To me she seems a real fanatic and if she had lived in olden times would have been one who had a divine commission to kill the oppressors of the church." She urged HBS to send LB to New York to dissuade CB. "Her great object is to attack Yale College and the ministry of such men as Dr. Taylor, Professor Porter, Fitch, etc., and she really believes there will be such an uprising of public sentiment as will oblige these men to give up their places," Mary continued. "Henry's last advice to my girls was, girls get married — don't live to be old maids. It is well to derive improvement from all events," Mary concluded (Mary Beecher Perkins to HBS, 10 March [1850], White Collection).

12 Hopkins, *Prodigal Puritan*, p. 125. It may have been coincidental that CB's nervous condition improved dramatically after she published *Truth Stranger than Fiction*. She attributed her cure to a course of exercises, and thereafter went to health retreats to exercise as well as to take the water cure.

13 CB to Rev. Sir, 26 May 1850 (circular letter to Congregational ministers); CB to Dear Madam, 20 June 1850 (circular letter to supporters of CB's educational enterprises, Mt. Holyoke).

14 *New York Tribune,* 6 November 1850; *The North American Review* 72 (January 1851) : 151–53; *The Literary World* 7 (17 August 1850) : 133–. 34.

15 Hopkins, *Prodigal Puritans,* pp. 173–266.

16 Gerda Lerner, "The Lady and the Mill Girl: Changes in the Status of Women in the Age of Jackson," *Mid-Continent American Studies Journal* 10 (1969) : 5–15.

17 Alice Clark, *Working Life of Women in the Seventeenth Century,* pp. 286–96.

18 Daniel Scott Smith, "Child-Naming Patterns and Family Structure Change: Hingham, Massachusetts, 1640–1880" (Paper prepared for the Clark University Conference on the Family and Social Structure, 27–29 April 1972), p. 29.

19 Ibid.

20 "Pastoral Letter of the General Association of Congregational Churches of Massachusetts," cited in Lerner, *The Grimké Sisters,* pp. 189–94.

21 For the subversive ideas in contemporary literature by women, see Papashvily, *All the Happy Endings,* and Ann Douglas Wood, "The 'Scribbling Women' and Fanny Fern: Why Women Wrote," *American Quarterly* 23, no. 1 (Spring 1971) : 3–24. For an example of anony-

mous women see Carroll Smith Rosenberg, *Religion and the Rise of The American City; The New York City Mission Movement, 1812–1870* (Ithaca, 1971), pp. 97–125, on the New York Female Moral Reform Society.

22 For a description of life as paralyzed potential see Ann Douglas Wood, "Mrs. Sigourney and the Sensibility of the Inner Space," *New England Quarterly* 45, no. 2, (June 1972), and Barbara Welter, "Anti-Intellectualism and the American Woman: 1800–1860," *Mid-America* 48 (October 1966) : 258–70; Carroll Smith Rosenberg, "The Hysterical Woman: Sex Roles and Role Conflict in 19th Century America," *Social Research* 39, no. 4 (Winter 1972), pp. 652–78.

23 Biographical sketch, "Nancy Cummins Johnson," David Johnson Papers, Connecticut Historical Society.

24 Nancy Johnson to David Johnson, 13 March 1847, Johnson Family Papers. (Hereafter referred to as NJ to DJ; all are from David Johnson Papers.)

25 Henry Ward Beecher to LB, 4 December 1847, Beecher–Stowe Collection, folder 41.

26 NJ to DJ, 9 February 1848.

27 Ibid.

28 NJ to DJ, [February 1848].

29 CB, *True Remedy*, pp. 111–15. In this book CB announced her break with Slade and revealed the nature of her new educational enterprise of the 1850s. Her actions in Philadelphia and Baltimore are described.

30 Ibid., p. 116.

31 CB to LB, 28 December 1847, Beecher–Stowe Collection, folder 5; Lydia Beecher to CB, [1842–1845], White Collection; CB to Lydia Beecher, [1842–1845], White Collection; NJ to DJ, 25 February 1848.

32 CB to HBS, 28 December 1847, Beecher–Stowe Collection, folder 5. "I have the funds to use for their [the teachers'] comfort given to me and not to the Society," CB wrote, revealing that henceforth she intended to keep the money she collected rather than to turn it over to the society.

33 NJ to DJ, 25 March 1848; ibid.

34 NJ to DJ, Cincinnati, 25 February 1848; NJ to DJ, 25 March 1848; NJ to DJ, 17 April 1848; NJ to DJ, 8 June 1848; NJ to DJ, 7 August 1848.

35 NJ to DJ, 17 April 1848; NJ to DJ, 8 June 1848.

36 Ibid.

37 *The Iowa State Gazette,* 29 March 1848.

38 CB, *Reminiscences,* pp. 145, 149; *True Remedy,* pp. 118–31.

39 NJ to DJ, 7 August 1848.

40 NJ to DJ, 19 December 1848.

41 NJ to DJ, 9 April 1849.

Chapter 14

1 CB, *Letters on Health and Happiness,* p. 129. Donald Meyer provided
an interesting suggestion about female invalidism in *The Positive
Thinkers;* pp. 46–59, seeing it as a combined protest against and
filling the void of domesticity. William Wasserstrom's *Heiress of All
the Ages,* pp. 12–14, hinted that a "radical disharmony in sexual
relations" and women's unfulfilled sexual desires were responsible for
their invalidism and hostility to men. Wasserstrom quoted Victoria
Woodhull very effectively to support this idea, and showed that single
women also suffer from the effects of a society that denies their sexual
needs.

2 HBS to Calvin Stowe, 29 June 1842. Beecher–Stowe Collection, folder
69. Chap. 17 of CB's *Letters on Health and Happiness* related her
personal health experience. Although she could "not recall the memory of a single day of sickness from infancy to the age of twenty," CB
said her ill health began when "womanhood came." Fatigue and
nervous strain produced, she said, "a singular susceptibility of the
nervous system to any slight wound, bruise, or sprain. Such slight
accidents would bring on an affection in the injured part, which was
a semi-paralysis of the nerves of motion, attended by an extreme
sensitiveness of the whole nervous system, while the injured limb
remained weak and nearly useless for from two to twelve months."
These attacks, she continued, became "a sort of barometer of health,"
increasing as her health sank and decreasing as it rose. She concluded
that the water-cure principles of exercise, fresh air, proper diet, and
bathing would have eliminated this kind of invalidism from her life
from the late 1820s to the early 1840s (pp. 113–15).

3 Harry B. Weiss and Howard R. Kemble, *The Great American Water-
Cure Craze,* pp. 19–32, describes the growth of the water cure in the
United States; p. 217 cites its high proportion of women patients. CB,
Letters on Health and Happiness, pp. 120, 144; "Catharine Beecher
at Elmira" a MS sketch signed "R" in the Beecher Family Papers,
Williston Memorial Library.

4 David Campbell and Joel Shew, *Water Cure Journal* no. 1 (New York,
1845) : 2–7. The *Water Cure Journal* was published intermittently
from 1845 to 1913; Dr. Wesselhoeft et al., *The Water Cure in
America,* pp. 72–74.

5 Kett, *American Medical Profession,* pp. 32, 108, 185.

6 CB's *Observer* article cited in Wesselhoeft, *Water Cure in America,*
p. 6; *Water Cure Journal* confirmed CB's experience: "The hydropathic treatment differs from all others, inasmuch as it is adminis-
tered to hundreds of persons congregated in one place, who are in
the constant habit of meeting and discussing its merits, so that there

is nothing important that is not known to the whole body. Whilst under the allopathian and homeopathian treatment, patients are treated at their own homes, so that none but their own families know the results of either mode of treatment" (1, no. 5 [1 February 1846] : 67).

7 One description in the *Water Cure Journal* points to the sensuality of the treatment:

A large coarse blanket is spread upon a mattress. The patient lies down upon it, as in the wet sheet, and is closely packed from neck to toe and covered with a number of other blankets . . . having duly sweated, the patient is unpacked, and steps into a shallow bath, preferably a plunge bath . . . this transition from copious perspiration to cold water is not only perfectly innocuous, but highly salutory. A powerful reaction. and a high degree of exhilaration and vigor are the result (1, no. 3 [1 January 1846]: 41).

Leslie Fiedler, *Love and Death in the American Novel*, pp. 293, 336, discussed the division in American literature between light and dark heroines as another manifestation of the American denial of sexuality to "good" women and its attribution to "evil" women only. Thus a woman who expressed sexuality was threatening to men. Fiedler suggested that women were kept "pure" to enable men to retain their youthful mother–son relationship to women; youth and potentiality being so highly valued in American society, and maturity feared.

The strong link between health and sexuality in the minds of many nineteenth-century Americans was demonstrated most dramatically in the life and work of Sylvester Graham. See Stephen Nissenbaum, "Careful Love: Sylvester Graham and the Emergence of Victorian Sexual Theory in America, 1830–1840," Ph.D. diss., University of Wisconsin, 1968. Graham's experience and that of Catharine Beecher seems to have been dissimilar insofar as Graham believed that a healthy person was conscious of no internal sensations whatever, although he was very sensitive to the threatening forces around him. CB was on the contrary highly conscious of the connection between her inner feelings and outer forces and mainly feared that she could not control the links between the two. Thus she feared "animal magnetism" and the uncontrollable attraction of one person for another in general: "Since many of my pupils have become matrons, I have been told by them of liabilities which perfect purity and innocence involve, which ought to be considered in regulating protecting customs for the young. They have told me, what I also had occasion to observe frequently myself, of the power which a teacher, even of the same sex, may exert on the affections and susceptibilities of pupils, so that in some cases they may become morbid and excessive" (CB, *Letters on Health and Happiness*, p. 160). CB may have feared the power her own personality exercised over others as much as she feared the response such a power elicited from the young. Contrary to Graham, CB was trying not so much to express her sense of isolation from others as she was trying to order and define and reduce the complexities of her relationships with others.

8   *Water Cure Journal* 1, no. 7 (1 March 1846) : 136 discusses the phenomenon of *prolapsis uteri.* A typical water-cure attitude toward childbirth was this: "It is very certain that woman's suffering in labor can be in a great degree prevented, and that she need not endure that weakness after childbirth which is so common. Under the water treatment the constitution is not injured from bearing children . . . we have long felt that it was unnatural for woman to be so injured, so torn to pieces, *so wrecked by natural pain*" (*Water Cure Journal* 2, no. 2 [1 November 1846] : 168–96). Whether pains were milder because women expected them to be, or whether the water helped, the *Journal* is laden with testimonies to the effectiveness of the water treatment (mainly sitzbaths) before and after childbirth. The December 1848 issue, p. 164, prescribes twelve months of celibacy for married women with fallen wombs. The water cure thus enabled women to adjust their sexual and sensual lives in a variety of ways. Through it they could eliminate unrewarding marital sexuality or increase sensual pleasures of a different sort, depending on their individual needs. The *Water Cure Journal* had no analogous concern for the sexual problems experienced by men, although they too must have found sensual release in the regular cure treatments.

9   Many allopathic doctors endorsed the water cure (CB, *Letters on Health and Happiness,* pp. 149–50). One of the advantages of water cure was that many establishments maintained women hydropathic doctors. One of the most interesting of these was Mary Walker, a feminist who graduated from the New York Hygeio-Therapeutic College in 1862 (having earned a regular medical degree at Syracuse Medical College in 1855), and was apparently connected with one of Trall's water-cure establishments at Florence, New Jersey. (Weiss and Kemble, *Water-Cure Craze,* p. 88; Mary Walker biographical sketch in James et al., *Notable American Women,* 3 : 532–33.) Another more important woman was Mary Gove Nicholas (Weiss and Kemble, pp. 72–77), who operated her own water-cure establishment in New York in the 1840s and went on to become one of the central figures in hydropathy. See her biographical sketch in *Notable American Women.*

10 Charles West, M.D., *Lectures on the Diseases of Women,* p. 89.

11 See *Water Cure Journal* 1, no. 1 (1 December 1845) : 55 for hemorrhage treatment; Edward Mansfield, *The Legal Rights, Liabilities, and Duties of Women,* p. 34, for abortion laws. Mansfield warned women:

The progress of population, wealth, and fashion in our country has made this crime [abortion] quite common. In the large cities it is, we fear, practiced frequently, as it has been in the large cities of the Old World. Indeed, public advertisements, sshameless as they are, have been published in the newspapers. directing the child of fashion, or of vice, where she might find a woman to perform that service! It is presumed, that many persons who have practiced this crime have done so in ignorance of the law, and with a belief that it is a comparatively innocent offence. Women should therefore know, and teach others, that the law considers such an art as a high offence and punishes it, when detected, with severity. They should teach, also, that it is a crime which reflects shame and dishonor on their sex.

Two examples of advertisements for abortive pills read:

The Great English Remedy, Sir James Clarke's CELEBRATED FEMALE PILLS. Prepared from a prescription of Sir. J. Clarke M.D., Physician extraordinary to the queen. This invaluable medicine is unfailing in the cure of all those painful and dangerous diseases incident to the female constitution. It moderates all excess, removes all obstructions, and brings on the monthly period with regularity. These pills should not be taken by females that are pregnant, during the FIRST THREE MONTHS, as they are sure to bring on MISCARRIAGE: but at every other time and in every other case, they are perfectly safe (*Milwaukee Sentinel,* 2 February 1857).

DR. CHESSMAN'S PILLS. The combinations of Ingredients in these Pills are the result of a long and extensive practice. They are mild in their operation, and certain in correcting all irregularities, Painful Menstruations, removing all obstructions, whether from cold or otherwise, headache, pain in the side, palpitation of the heart, disturbed sleep, which arise from the interruption of nature. To MARRIED LADIES they are invaluable, as they will bring on the monthly period with regularity. NOTICE: They should not be used during pregnancy, as a miscarriage would certainly result therefrom (*Milwaukee Sentinel,* 21 March 1857).

One of the best discussions of contraception in the nineteenth century is in Andrew Sinclair, *The Emancipation of the American Woman,* chap. 11, where he points out that until 1849 Americans believed that conception could only occur immediately following the menstrual period (p. 133).

12 Russell T. Trall, *The Hydropathic Encyclopedia,* p. 205; Norman Himes, *Medical History of Contraception,* p. 269; a typical representation of hydropathy's attitude is summed up in *Water Cure Journal:* "Some, we presume, will be anxious to learn our views on water treatment, as applicable to pregnancy . . . poor, suffering women, as things are, how much art thou doomed to endure! Heaven grant, that now in another sense as well as in the moral 'the truth shall make you free' " (1, no. 4 [15 January 1846] : 58). For the American attitude toward contraception during this period, see Carl Bode's excellent summary in "Columbia's Carnal Bed," *American Quarterly* 15, no. 1 (Spring 1963) : 52–64.

HBS may have made attempts at contraception. CB wrote Mary Perkins in 1837: "Harriet has one baby put out for the winter, the other at home, and number three will be here the middle of January. Poor thing, she bears up wonderfully well, and I hope will live through this first tug of matrimonial warfare, and then she says she shall not have any more *children, she knows for certain* for one while. Though how she found this out I cannot say, but she seems quite confident about it" (CB to Mary Beecher Perkins, Fall 1837, Beecher–Stowe Collection, folder 17).

13 Hugh L. Hodge, M.D., *Foeticide, or Criminal Abortion,* p. 32. Hydropathy began to decline in the 1890s when state licensing and medical profession reforms began to transform the profession and place it exclusively in the hands of allopathic physicians (Kett, *American Medical Profession,* p. vii).

14 CB, *Letters on Health and Happiness,* pp. 136–38. CB may have been referring to the work of Mary Gove and her husband Thomas Nichols, both prominent water-cure specialists who in 1853 planned a community at Modern Times, Long Island, devoted to "complete freedom, including free love, or the right of every woman to choose the father of her child." This community never opened, but Mary Gove Nichols's and her husband's joint book *Marriage,* published in 1854, analyzed marriage as the root of all evil. The couple were read out of the water-cure movement the next year. See biographical sketch of "Mary Sargent Neal Gove Nichols" in *Notable American Women,* 2 : 627–29.

15 For the brief relationship between Elizabeth Blackwell and CB, see Ishbel Ross, *Child of Destiny* and Elizabeth Blackwell, *The Laws of Life.* Like CB, Dr. Blackwell warned against the periods of leisure for women. "Who can describe the fearful void of such an existence; yearning for an object, the self-reproach for wasted powers; weariness of daily life, loathing of pleasure of frivolity, and the fearful consciousness of deadening life" (p. 59). Blackwell also emphasized that "diseases of the generative organs make children hard to bear and the 'marriage relation' destroyed" (p. 138). Although she mentions prostitution, by "generative" diseases she does not seem to mean venereal disease, but a more generalized set of disabilities arising from women's ignorance in seeking diagnosis and treatment for what might have initially been a simple ailment.

16 CB, *Letters on Health and Happiness,* p. 161.

17 Ibid., pp. 91, 158, 160.

18 Ibid., pp. 158–63. Carroll Smith Rosenberg's "Puberty to Menopause: The Cycle of Femininity" (Paper delivered at The Berkshire Conference of Women Historians at Douglass College, New Brunswick, N.J., 3 March 1973) made three important points relating female

physiology to emotions of fear from 1840 to 1890. First, she said, medical views of nineteenth-century female physiology saw the woman's body as qualitatively different from the man's because it was subject to cyclical forces that could not be controlled by the human will. The nonrational nature of the female physiological system was thus seen as the central fact of female life from puberty to menopause. Second, these threatening irrational powers of generative processes were used to rationalize and justify social roles limiting women's activities. To exert themselves beyond their body's capacities was to run the risk of unleashing these internal irrational forces. Third, these medical attitudes functioned as an interface between women and their culture, fostering a general fear of female sexuality on the one hand, and romanticizing all that had to do with the nongenerative aspects of womanhood on the other. CB was then responding to this increased tendency to associate the female body with fearful, irrational forces. Her "protective customs" thus seem designed to act as a barrier between the irrational forces contained within the female body and those present in the external society. Human intelligence alone was not powerful enough to restrain physiological imperatives, and thus one needed to employ new measures of social control. It was at this midcentury point that adolescence was identified as a time of ominous sexual awakening, and looking back over her career CB was retrospectively wary of emotions she had deemed quite innocent in the 1820s:

Since many of my pupils have become matrons, I have been told by them of liabilities which perfect purity and innocence involve, which ought to be considered in regulating protecting customs for the young. They have told me, what I also had occasion to observe frequently myself, of the power which a teacher, even of the same sex, may exert on the affections and susceptibilities of pupils, so that in some cases they may become morbid and excessive. There is a period when the young, especially if highly gifted, find an outbursting of sensibilities that they have not learned to control (*Letters to the People,* p. 160).

19 Ibid., pp. 88, 183–84.
20 Ibid., pp. 183–84.
21 Ibid., pp. 162, 178.
22 Theodore Cianfrani, *A Short History of Obstetrics and Gynecology,* pp. 300, 314. Cianfrani pointed to the large part played by infection and contagion in gynecological medicine and the importance of the discovery of streptococci as a source of puerperal fever. Puerperal fever was beginning to be well understood in the late nineteenth century as a chief source of death in childbirth, but gynecologists "were slow to adopt and apply the principles of antisepsis." Although

Lister diagnosed the bacterial origin of infection in the 1860s, his discoveries were ignored in obstetrical surgery through the 1870s and only slowly adopted in the 1880s and 1890s. Thus the period of "Victorianism" coincides with the period when women were conscious of the hazards connected with their physiology, were unwilling to die because of them, but were as yet unable to obtain effective medical cures.

23 CB, *Treatise*, pp. 42–43.

24 HBS and CB to Calvin Stowe, 14 August 1846, Beecher–Stowe Collection, folder 71.

25 HBS to Calvin Stowe, 7 January 1847, Beecher–Stowe Collection, folder 72.

26 CB, *Letters on Health and Happiness*, pp. 185–89.

27 CB to Beecher family, 3 February 1855, White Collection.

Chapter 15

1 CB, *True Remedy*, pp. 206–11; CB, *Letter to Benevolent Ladies in the United States*, p. 15.

2 Minerva Brace Norton, *A True Teacher, Mary Mortimer*, pp. 119–20.

3 CB, *True Remedy*, appendix, pp. 249–51.

4 American Woman's Educational Association (AWEA), *Report* (New York, 1853), p. 40; CB, *True Remedy*, p. 201.

5 Bayrd Still, *Milwaukee*, pp. 151–224.

6 The John Tweedy family and the Increase Lapham family were examples of the socially ambitious in Milwaukee who practiced genteel manners but felt inferior to the new immigrants from the East. See Mrs. Increase Lapham to Mrs. Jacob Gould, March 1852, Increase Lapham Papers, box 9, State Historical Society of Wisconsin. Margaret Fuller visited Milwaukee in 1842 and observed the efforts of parents to bring their daughters up to the refined standards of the East. Margaret Fuller Ossoli, *At Home and Abroad*, pp. 46–76.

7 Biographical sketch of Increase Lapham, Increase Lapham Papers.

8 Increase Lapham, "Address Delivered in the Unitarian Church," 4 February 1848, Increase Lapham Papers, box 8; Increase Lapham to Lapham family, 24 April 1848, Increase Lapham Papers, box 3.

9 CB, *True Remedy*, pp. 151–52; see Grace Norton Kieckhefer, *The History of Milwaukee-Downer College, 1851–1951* for the varieties of name changes during the college's early years.

10 Mary Mortimer to her sisters, May 1850, in Norton, *A True Teacher*, p. 126.

11 Fredrika Bremer, *The Homes of the New World*, 1 : 615. CB referred to the normal department of Milwaukee Female College as a "Mother-

House" where teachers could always find a temporary home. AWEA, *Report,* (New York, 1853), p. 23.

12 CB to Lydia Beecher, 30 April 1851, White Collection.

13 William W. Wight, *Annals of Milwaukee College, 1848–1891,* p. 7.

14 Mary Mortimer to Morilla Hill, 8 June 1852, in Norton, *A True Teacher,* p. 144.

15 AWEA, *Second Annual Report* (New York, 1854), p. 15.

16 AWEA, *Report* (New York, 1853), p. 11.

17 CB, *True Remedy,* pp. 59, 241; AWEA, *Third Annual Report* (New York, 1855), pp. 15–16.

18 Several other cities appealed to CB and her organization for aid, and colleges on the Milwaukee plan were begun at Dubuque, Iowa; Quincy, Illinois; and Kalamazoo, Michigan. The association gave money to the first two of these. CB visited Dubuque and Quincy on her frequent western trips, but she did not give them the same attention she gave Milwaukee Female College, and they lasted only a few academic terms.

19 Samuel Carter, *Cyrus Field, Man of Two Worlds,* p. 73; Benjamin Bonney to G. C. Verplanck, December 1857, Gulian Verplanck Papers, box 1, New York Historical Society; *Appleton's Cyclopaedia of American Biography,* s.v. "Tracy, Charles (1810–1885)," "Van Norman, Daniel C. (1815–1886)," and "Webster, Horace (1794–1871)."

20 AWEA, Annual Reports, 1853–1856.

21 *Annals of Milwaukee College,* p. 23.

22 CB to Beecher family, 3 February 1855, White Collection.

23 CB to LB, 12 October 1855, White Collection; ibid.

24 CB to Increase Lapham, 6 November 1855 and 18 February 1856, Milwaukee–Downer College Papers, series 10, box 10, Milwaukee Library. All subsequently cited correspondence between CB and Lapham comes from this collection.

25 Increase Lapham to CB, 27 February 1856.

26 CB to Increase Lapham, 13 March 1856; AWEA, *Fourth Annual Report* (New York, 1856); Increase Lapham to CB, 19 March 1861; CB to Increase Lapham, 25 March 1861.

Chapter 16

1 L. B. Stowe *Saints, Sinners and Beechers,* pp. 271, 169, 142, 339, 152, 149–50 can confirm the Beechers' movements during these years.

2 Thomas K. Beecher, born 1824, innovated techniques for bringing the people into his Elmira church by providing them with a theater, dances, and pool tables in the late 1870s. See Max Eastman, *Heroes I Have Known,* for a loving sketch of Thomas Beecher. Isabella

Beecher Hooker devoted herself wholeheartedly to the women's suffrage movement.

3 CB to Eunice Beecher, 15 January 1851, Beecher Family Papers, Sterling Memorial Library.

4 Charles Beecher's description in LB, *Autobiography,* 2 : 412.

5 Charles Beecher to Henry Ward Beecher, 12 April 1857, Beecher Family Papers, Sterling Memorial Library.

6 Ibid.

7 LB to Lydia Jackson Beecher, 3 July 1844, White Collection.

8 HBS to Henry Ward Beecher, 29 January [1845], Beecher Family Papers, Sterling Memorial Library; CB to Mary Beecher Perkins, 27 September 1851.

9 HBS to LB and Henry Ward Beecher, 9 September 1851, Beecher Family Papers, Sterling Memorial Library.

10 Ibid.

11 Ibid. CB did explore the possibility of working for Greeley in 1854. She volunteered to send him a series of articles on the South if he would help finance a southern tour for her "to observe the situation and prospects of *my own sex* as it relates to health, education and domestic interests" (CB to Horace Greeley, 17 September 1854, Stauffer Collection, New York Public Library). Although it seems unlikely that Greeley declined her offer, he may have done so, or CB may have changed her mind about the southern trip since she was so preoccupied with Milwaukee at the time.

12 CB to Eunice Beecher, 15 January 1851, Beecher Family Papers, Sterling Memorial Library; Horace Greeley, *Hints Toward Reforms.*

13 HBS to the editor of the *New York Observer* [May 1852], Beecher Family Papers, Sterling Memorial Library; The Rev. Joel Parker to HBS, 19 May 1852, ibid. The entire context of the quotation was: "Tom had watched the whole transaction from first to last, and had a perfect understanding of its results. To him it looked like something unutterably horrible and cruel, because, poor ignorant black soul! he had not learned to generalize, and to take enlarged views. If he had only been instructed by certain ministers of Christianity he might have thought better of it, and seen in it an everyday incident of a lawful trade; a trade which is the vital support of an institution which an American divine* tells us has no evils but 'such as are inseparable from any other relations in social and domestic life.' But, Tom, as we see, being a poor ignorant fellow whose reading had been confined entirely to the New Testament could not comfort and solace himself with views like these. His very soul bled within him, for what seemed to him the wrongs of the poor suffering thing that lay like a crushed seed on the boxes." Parker was identified by name,

title, and place of residence with an asterisk at the bottom of the page. HBS to the editor of the *New York Observer* [May 1852] for Cato quote, Beecher Family Papers, Sterling Memorial Library.

14   Calvin Stowe to Joel Parker, 11 May 1852; Henry Ward Beecher to HBS, 11 June 1852; HBS to Joel Parker, 2 July 1852, all from Beecher Family Papers, Sterling Memorial Library.

Possibly conscious of playing on the title of CB's *Truth Stranger than Fiction,* HBS wrote that her novel was *"fiction truer than fact"* [HBS's emphasis]. HBS to Rev. T. C. Webster, 25 September 1852, in Doheny Memorial Library, St. John's Seminary, Camarrillo, California. In another letter to the *New York Observer,* HBS quoted Dr. Albert Burns: " 'What is it that lends the most efficient sanction to Slavery in the United States? What is it that does most to keep the public conscience at ease on the subject? What is it that renders abortive all efforts to remove the evil? . . . It is the fact that the System is countenanced by good men; that Bishops and Priests and Deacons, that Ministers and Elders, that Sunday-School teachers, and Exhorters, that pious matrons and heiresses, are the holders of Slaves, and that the Ecclesiastical bodies of the Land address no language of rebuke or entreaty to their consciences!' " (HBS to the editor of the *New York Observer* [May 1852] Beecher Family Papers, Sterling Memorial Library.) For works that discuss HBS's domesticity-based feminism, and/or her conscious adoption of themes from CB, see Constance Rourke, *Trumpets of Jubilee,* chap. on HBS; Kenneth Lynn, Introduction to the John Harvard Library edition of *Uncle Tom's Cabin* (Cambridge, 1962); Edward Wagenknecht, *Harriet Beecher Stowe,* pp. 36, 96, 144; Charles Foster, *The Rungless Ladder,* pp. 23, 25, 89, 91, 94–97, 111–16, 179–80, 221.

15   Isabella Beecher Hooker to John Hooker, 26 June 1852, Isabella Hooker Collection, Stowe–Day Foundation, noted the beginning of CB's attack on Jewett; CB to Rev. E. N. Kirk, 4 July 1855, Day Collection, records CB's continuing effort to discredit Jewett. CB expected Kirk, as Jewett's clergyman, to urge him to make more lenient terms with HBS, and she threatened Kirk: "I am about commencing a volume, probably to be entitled *'Letters to the People on Religion and Common Sense'* in which I shall present my views on this as well as on other subjects. . . . Should they [Jewett and Proctor] decline, or should you decline to act in the matter, I should feel that I have fulfilled all the preliminaries that the Gospel requires, previous to such an exposure as may result from the course I expect to pursue." CB did not, however, carry through with this threat. L. B. Stowe, *Saints, Sinners and Beechers,* p. 183, described the contract options; Mary Beecher Perkins to LB, Hartford, 22 January 1853, Day Collec-

tion, expressed the family's fear that CB was writing "another book after the manner of 'Fact Stranger than Fiction [*sic*].' " HBS did briefly consider suing Jewett, but dropped the matter when she concluded her case was too weak to be upheld in court.

16 HBS, *The Mayflower, or Sketches of the Descendents of the Pilgrims,* pp. xi, xvii; L. B. Stowe, *Saints, Sinners and Beechers,* p. 182, for HBS's fulfillment of a promise to "sister Katy" with the writing of *Uncle Tom's Cabin.*

17 CB, *Essay on Slavery and Abolitionism,* pp. 100–01.

18 LB began to review his papers at Brunswick in 1851 when both HBS and CB were present. Then he continued the process in Andover when Calvin moved the family there in 1853 to assume a professorship at Andover Theological Seminary. LB, *Autobiography,* 2 : 408–09. HBS's letter and CB's response of 1827 cited in L. B. Stowe, *Saints, Sinners and Beechers,* pp. 159–60; CB to Rebecca Wetherell, 1 February 1861, Berg Collection, New York Public Library. "So through her married life I have shared her cares and sorrows as well as her pleasures," CB concluded. HBS confirms CB's maternal role from 1816 to 1836. (Charles E. Stowe, *The Life of Harriet Beecher Stowe Compiled from Her Letters and Journals,* p. 509.)

19 For CB's organizational role, as well as the cited quotation, see CB to LB, 12 October 1855, White Collection.

20 Although HBS would not have had time to read the book, she was familiar with its contents since CB had been working on it since 1855.

21 HBS to CB, n.d., cited in C. E. Stowe, *Life of Harriet Beecher Stowe,* pp. 320–21 as being written "shortly after" HBS learned of Henry's death.

22 HBS, *The Minister's Wooing,* pp. 17, 19 passim. (Originally published, Boston, 1859.)

23 Ibid., p. 356. I am indebted to Charles Foster's fine work of criticism, *The Rungless Ladder,* for the basic outlines of this interpretation of *The Minister's Wooing.*

24 HBS, *The Minister's Wooing,* pp. 311–12.

25 CB to Leonard Bacon, 28 September 1857, Collection of American Literature, Beinecke Library.

Chapter 17

1 Michael Walzer, *The Revolution of the Saints,* describes Puritanism in these terms; for the easy adoption of Darwinism in the United States, see Richard Hofstadter, *Social Darwinism in American Thought.*

2 George M. Frederickson, *The Inner Civil War,* describes the widespread adoption of the ethic of suffering by Northern leaders during

and after the 1850s. CB certainly fits the phenomenon Frederickson describes.

3   CB's other work of the same kind during this period was *The Religious Training of Children in the School, the Family, and the Church.*

4   Walter Houghton, *The Victorian Frame of Mind,* pp. 218–80.

5   CB, *Common Sense,* pp. 330–32.

6   Ibid., pp. 281, 337.

7   CB, *Common Sense,* p. xi; CB, *Appeal to the People,* pp. 343, 368.

8   Ibid., pp. 33–38.

9   Ibid., p. 203.

10 Ibid., pp. 254–55.

11 Ibid., pp. 165, 186–89; CB, *Common Sense,* p. 215.

12 CB, *Common Sense,* p. 37.

13 CB, *Appeal to the People,* p. 160; CB, *Religious Training of Children,* p. 219.

14 CB, *Religious Training of Children,* p. 219; CB, *Common Sense,* p. 30; CB, *Appeal to the People,* p. 52.

15 CB, *Common Sense,* p. 36.

16 Ibid., p. 37.

17 Ibid., p. 9.

18 CB, *Appeal to the People,* p. 186.

19 Ibid., pp. 210–11.

20 CB, *Common Sense,* p. 152.

21 CB, *Appeal to the People,* pp. 133–34.

22 CB, *Common Sense,* pp. 142, 203.

23 Ibid., p. 46.

24 Ibid., pp. 46, 239, 39.

25 Timothy L. Smith, *Revivalism and Social Reform,* pp. 63–65.

26 CB, *Appeal to the People,* p. 160.

27 See especially Oliver Wendell Holmes, *An Address by Oliver Wendell Holmes on Memorial Day, May 30, 1895* and his Civil War letters, *Touched With Fire: Civil War Letters and Diaries of Oliver Wendell Holmes, Jr.,* ed. Mark De Wolfe Howe. See Ann Douglas Wood, "The War Within a War : Women Nurses in the Union Army," *Civil War History* 18, no. 3 (September 1972) for examples of women who chose active engagement rather than passive suffering, yet who were inspired by the cultural image that linked women to suffering and the relief of suffering.

28 CB, *Religious Training of Children,* p. 220.

29 *The Christian Examiner* 15, no. 3 (November 1865). The review went on to say: "Miss Beecher comes to her subject with rare qualifications, at least for negative criticism. With a nature of ardent aspirations and clear intellectual activity. . . . with great moral earnestness, in a style

perfectly free from all scholasticism, appealing with boldness and
vigor to the plain sense and understanding of common minds, she
deals a most destructive criticism against the theories that had
troubled her so long, and presents ideas of Christianity which she
deems accordant with the character of God, with the plain meaning
of the New Testament, with the wants of the soul and the common
sense of mankind. The negative, or more properly the destructive
portion of her work, is admirably done. Sometimes by invincible logic,
sometimes by apt illustration more telling than argument, sometimes
by personal narrative calculated to touch the pity and indignation
even of theologians who have any dregs of manhood left in them,
she succeeds in making Calvinism not only absurd, but utterly hateful." Although the reviewer objected at length to CB's "Pelagianism"
and her elimination of conversion as an essential element of Christianity, he evidently found nothing objectionable or even unusual in her
discussion of sacrifice.

30   CB, *Common Sense*, pp. xii, 261, 319.

Chapter 18

1   CB to Henry Ward Beecher, 26 March 1860, Beecher Family Papers,
Sterling Memorial Library.

2   L. B. Stowe, *Saints, Sinners and Beechers*, pp. 129–30.

3   Minutes of the AWEA, New York, 10 May 1862, Schlesinger Library.
CB traveled to Philadelphia and Boston on behalf of the organization
in 1862. CB to Rebecca Wetherell, 21 April 1862, Berg Collection,
New York Public Library.

4   Records of the AWEA, 1870, Schlesinger Library. The organization
only officially terminated with CB's death in 1878.

5   CB to Nathaniel Wright, 20 December 1859, Nathaniel Wright Papers,
box 34; Henry Ward Beecher to Eunice Beecher, 6 May [1862],
Beecher Family Papers, Sterling Memorial Library; CB to Nathaniel
Wright, 30 May 1861, Nathaniel Wright Papers, box 35. Wright was
president of the Little Miami Railroad at the time. "I return this and
others on the supposition that I should do so if it is not used," CB
explained. CB to Increase Lapham, May 1864, Increase Lapham
Papers, box 7. Isabella Hooker to John Hooker, 10 March 1863,
Hooker Collection. CB to James Beecher and family, 1 January 1867,
James Beecher Family Papers, Schlesinger Library, folder 30.

6   HBS [to her daughters], 17 January 1863, Beecher–Stowe Collection,
folder 121.

7   CB to Leonard Bacon, 31 March 1862; CB to Leonard Bacon, 24
April 1862, Collection of American Literature, Beinecke Library.

8   Mrs. H. O. Ward, *Sensible Etiquette of the Best Society Customs, Manners, Morals, and Home Culture, Compiled from the Best Authorities*, pp. 379–81. This book went through more than 18 printings.

9   CB, *Religious Training of Children*, pp. 29, 212, 216, 239.

10 HBS [to her daughters], 24 August 1869, Beecher–Stowe Collection, folder 148; Stowe, *Saints, Sinners and Beechers*, p. 229.

11 CB and HBS *The American Woman's Home, or Principles of Domestic Science*, pp. 454–59, illustrations no. 75, 76, 77.

12 Ibid., p. 470.

13 Ibid., pp. 18–19.

14 Ibid., p. 19.

15 CB, miscellaneous writings and mementos, Beecher–Stowe Collection, folder 317.

16 Grace Royce, "Recollections of the Beecher Family," 18 January 1932, Day Collection.

17 CB to Roswell Smith, 20 March 1871, MS division, New York Public Library. Throughout 1873 CB tried unsuccessfully to recover her financial losses entailed in the seminary, but the trustees, unsympathetic to CB's pleas, refused to repay her even after she hinted that they would not appear honest when future historians described the episode. Indeed the trustees seemed willing to take advantage of CB's 1870 generosity, and although she and they clearly agreed at the time that she should be repaid, she never was. The year before her death she threatened to organize a student protest against the trustees in her behalf, but that still did not move them (Hartford Female Seminary Papers, Connecticut Historical Society, Hartford).

18 CB, *Woman's Profession as Mother and Educator with Views in Opposition to Woman Suffrage*, pp. 4–5.

19 CB, *True Remedy*, pp. 29, 31, 59–60; Charlotte Perkins Gilman, *Woman and Economics*.

20 CB, *True Remedy*, pp. 142–44.

21 CB and HBS unpublished pamphlet on women's medical education proposed for implementation in a women's university to be founded in Hartford and operated by CB and HBS (New York Historical Society).

22 "Circular" in CB's scrapbook, Day Collection.

23 CB to Elizabeth Cady Stanton, 16 May 1870, Henry E. Huntington Library, San Marino, Calif.: Aileen Kraditor, *Ideas of the Woman Suffrage Movement, 1890–1920*, p. 4.

24 CB, *Woman's Profession*, pp. 112–13.

25 Ibid., pp. 190–92.

26 Ibid., p. 134.

27 Ibid., pp. 86–87.

28 CB to Emma Willard, 18 July 1873, and CB to "My Dear Lady President," 10 October 1877, Day Collection.

29 CB's *Educational Reminiscences and Suggestions* was more an institutional than a personal memoir and in large part was a continuation of her effort to revitalize the AWEA.

30 CB, *Reminiscences*, p. 10.

31 L. B. Stowe, *Saints, Sinners and Beechers*, p. 135, drawn from the memory of Willard Fisher's son.

32 CB, *Reminiscences*, p. 14.

33 Julia Beecher to Olivia Langdon, 28 April 1877, Langdon Collection, Stowe–Day Foundation; for a description of Julia Beecher, see L. B. Stowe, *Saints, Sinners and Beechers*, pp. 364–67.

34 HBS to [CB] n.d., Beecher–Stowe Collection, folder 100.

35 Memorial about CB, describing her last year in Elmira, her death, and funeral, by "R," MS, Mt. Holyoke College Archives.

36 L. B. Stowe, *Saints, Sinners and Beechers*, pp. 135–37.

37 Obituary in CB's "Sketchbook," Day Collection; Henry Ward Beecher composed a tribute to CB, concluding: "Her religious feelings were strong and intense and her views have been somewhat fluctuating. For the past few years however she had settled down to the Protestant Episcopal faith, thus returning to the faith of her mother. . . . Her influence was very great. Few persons, even in the ministry had influenced as many minds as she had, because she reached the mother mind, and whoever carried the mother mind moves the world. Although she was motherless, she had reached and influenced millions" (Beecher Family Papers, Sterling Memorial Library). By "motherless" Henry referred to Roxana's early death, a death he felt far more than CB. Henry's tribute may have been in part a grateful response to CB's complete loyalty to him during his scandalous trial for alienating the affections of the wife of his best friend (CB to Leonard Bacon, 5 October 1874, Collection of American Literature). Other obituary notices remembered CB's role as a Great Aunt: "She was always bright, witty, and sympathetic, a jolly companion, and at Christmastime she was sought for in gay houses that her presence might add to the festivity. She would play for the children to dance, help them get up entertainments, and write their speeches. . . . Her voice retained much of its sweetness and she was fond of the old hymns of which she knew sixty by heart." CB receded quickly in the family memory, emerging only briefly in a recollection by Isabella who tried in 1892 to organize a memorial sketch "to bring out sister Cate as the really remarkable woman she was in those early days" (Isabella Hooker to Alice Day, 11 April 1892, Day Collection).

Bibliography

Manuscript Collections

Arthur and Elizabeth Schlesinger Library on the History of Women in America. Radcliffe College, Cambridge, Mass.
  Beecher–Stowe Collection
  Bradley–Hyde Papers
  James C. Beecher Family Collection
Beinecke Rare Book and Manuscript Library. Yale University, New Haven, Conn.
  Alexander Metcalf Fisher Collection
  Collection of American Literature: Leonard Bacon–Beecher Letters, Mary Dutton–Beecher Letters
Cincinnati Historical Society
  Beecher–Perkins Letters
  Kemper Family Letters
  King Family Papers
  Semi-Colon Club Papers
  Torrence Family Papers
Clements Library. University of Michigan, Ann Arbor, Mich.
  Phoenix Family Papers
  Weld-Grimké Papers
Clifton Waller Barrett Library. University of Virginia, Charlottesville.
  Harriet Beecher Stowe Papers
Connecticut Historical Society. Hartford.
  David Johnson Papers
  Hartford Female Seminary Papers
Historical Society of Pennsylvania. Philadelphia.
  American Prose Writers
  Dreer Collection
Historical Society of Philadelphia.
  American Literary Duplicates
Library of Congress. Washington, D.C.
  Blackwell Family Papers
  Nathaniel Wright Papers
Massachusetts Historical Society. Boston.
  Horace Mann Papers
New York Historical Society. New York, N.Y.
  Guilian Verplanck Papers

New York Public Library. New York, N.Y.
  Berg Collection
  Stauffer Collection
Olin Library. Cornell University, Ithaca, N.Y.
  Collection of Regional History and University Archives
  Andrew D. White Papers
Rutherford B. Hayes Library. Fremont, Ohio.
  Ebenezer Lane Papers
State Historical Society of Wisconsin. Madison.
  Increase Lapham Papers
Sterling Memorial Library. Yale University, New Haven, Conn.
  Beecher Family Papers
  Hillhouse Family Papers
  Strong Family Papers
Stowe–Day Foundation. Hartford, Conn.
  Isabella Hooker Collection
  Katharine Day Collection
  Langdon Collection
  White Collection
University of Wisconsin–Milwaukee Library. Area Research Center, Milwaukee.
  Milwaukee-Downer College Papers
Williston Memorial Library. Mt. Holyoke College, South Hadley, Mass.
  Beecher Family Papers

Other Unpublished Works

Aaron, Daniel. "Cincinnati, 1818–1838 : A Study of Attitudes in the Urban West." Ph.D. dissertation, Harvard, 1942.

Glazer, Walter. "Cincinnati in the 1840's : A Community Profile." Ph.D. dissertation, University of Michigan, 1968.

Kett, Joseph. "The Cult of Youth and the Crisis of 'Middle Age.'" Paper delivered at the American Historical Association, New York, 1971.

Lockridge, Kenneth. "Literacy in Colonial New England : A Summary of Preliminary Researches." Paper written at the University of Michigan, 1973.

Melder, Keith. "The Beginnings of the Women's Rights Movement in the United States, 1800–1840." Ph.D. dissertation, Yale University, 1963.

Nissenbaum, Stephen. "Careful Love : Sylvester Graham and the Emergence of Victorian Sexual Theory in America, 1830–1840." Ph.D. dissertation, University of Wisconsin, 1968.

Rosenberg, Carroll Smith. "Puberty to Menopause : The Cycle of Femininity." Paper delivered at The Berkshire Conference of Women Historians, Douglass College, 3 March 1973.

Ryan, Mary Patricia. "American Society and the Cult of Domesticity, 1830–1860." Ph.D. dissertation, University of California at Santa Barbara, 1971.

Smith, Daniel Scott. "Child-Naming Patterns and Family Structure Change : Hingham, Massachusetts, 1640–1880." Paper prepared for the Clark University Conference on the Family and Social Structure, 27–29 April 1972.

Published Works

Abbott, John S. C. *The Mother at Home.* Boston : Crocker & Brewster, 1833.
———. *The School Boy.* Boston : Crocker & Brewster, 1839.
Abercrombie, John. *Inquiries Concerning the Intellectual Powers, and the Investigation of Truth.* Edited by Jacob Abbot. New York : Collins & Bros., 1833.
Agnew, J. H. "Woman's Offices and Influence," *Harpers New Monthly Magazine* 3, October, 1851.
Ahlstrom, Sydney. "The Scottish Philosophers and American Theology." *Church History* 25 (September 1955) : 257–72.
American Album. Edited by American Heritage editors. New York : Simon & Schuster, 1968.
American Woman's Educational Association. *Reports* 1–4. New York, 1853–56.
Aries, Philippe. *Centuries of Childhood.* New York : Alfred Knopf, 1962.
Barnard, Henry. "Report to the Secretary of the Board." *Connecticut Common School Journal* 1, no. 13 (1839).
———. *A Tribute to Gallaudet.* Hartford : Brockett & Hutchinson, 1852.
Beecher, Catharine. *An Address to the Protestant Clergy of the United States.* New York : Harper & Bros., 1846.
———. An *Appeal to the People on Behalf of Their Rights as Authorized Interpreters of the Bible.* New York : Harper & Bros., 1860.
———. *Arithmetic Simplified.* Hartford : D. F. Robinson & Co., 1832.
———. *The Biographical Remains of Rev. George Beecher.* New York : Leavitt, Trow, & Co., 1844.
———. *Common Sense Applied to Religion, or the Bible and the People.* New York : Harper & Bros., 1857.
———. *The Duty of American Women to Their Country.* New York : Harper & Bros., 1845.
———. *Educational Reminiscences and Suggestions.* New York : J. B. Ford & Co., 1874.
———. *The Elements of Mental and Moral Philosophy, Founded upon Experience, Reason, and the Bible.* Hartford, 1831.
———. "An Essay on Cause and Effect in Connection with the Difference of Fatalism and Free Will." *American Biblical Repository* 2, no. 4 (October 1839).
———. *An Essay on Slavery and Abolitionism with Reference to the Duty of American Females.* Philadelphia : Henry Perkins, 1837.
———. *An Essay on the Education of Female Teachers.* New York : Van Nostrand & Dwight, 1835.

————. "The Evening Cloud." *The Christian Spectator* 2, no, 1 (January 1820).

————. *The Evils Suffered by American Women and American Children : The Causes and the Remedy*. New York : Harper & Bros., 1846.

————. "Female Education." *American Journal of Education* 2, nos. 4 and 5 (April & May 1827) : 219–23, 264–69.

————. Letter in *Common School Journal* 5 (Boston, 1843).

————. *Letter to Benevolent Ladies in the United States*. New York, 1849.

————. *Letters on the Difficulties of Religion*. Hartford : Belknap & Hammersley, 1836.

————. *Letters to Persons Who Are Engaged in Domestic Service*. New York : Leavitt & Trow, 1842.

————. *Letters to the People on Health and Happiness*. New York : Harper & Bros., 1855.

————. *The Lyceum Arithmetic*. Boston : W. Pierce, 1835.

————. *Miss Beecher's Housekeeper and Healthkeeper*. New York : Harper & Bros., 1873.

————. *The Moral Instructor for Schools and Families : Containing Lessons on the Duties of Life, Arranged for Study and Recitation, Also Designed as a Reading Book for Schools*. Cincinnati : Truman & Smith, 1838.

————. *Physiology and Calisthenics for Schools and Families*. New York : Harper & Bros., 1856.

————. *The Religious Training of Children in the School, the Family, and the Church*. New York : Harper & Bros., 1864.

————. *Suggestions Respecting Improvements in Education, Presented to the Trustees*. Hartford : Packard & Butler, 1829.

————. *Treatise on Domestic Economy for the Use of Young Ladies at Home and at School*. Boston : T. H. Webb & Co., 1843.

————. *The True Remedy for the Wrongs of Women*. Boston : Phillips, Sampson, 1851.

————. *Truth Stranger than Fiction : A Narrative of Recent Transactions involving Inquiries in regard to the Principles of Honor, Truth and Justice which obtain in a distinguished American University*. New York : printed for the author, 1850.

————. *Woman's Profession as Mother and Educator with Views in Opposition to Woman Suffrage*. Philadelphia : George Maclean, 1872.

Beecher, Catharine, and Stowe, Harriet B. *The American Woman's Home, or Principles of Domestic Science*. New York : J. B. Ford & Co., 1869.

————. *The New Housekeeper's Manual : Embracing a New Revised Edition of the American Woman's Home; or, Principles of Domestic Science. Being a Guide to Economical, Healthful, Beautiful, and Christian Homes*. New York : J. B. Ford & Co., 1873.

————. *Principles of Domestic Science; As Applied to the Duties and Pleasures of the Home. A Text Book for the Use of Young Ladies in Schools, Seminaries, and Colleges*. New York : J. B. Ford & Co., 1870.

Beecher, Edward. *The Conflict of Ages*. Boston : Crosby & Nichols, 1852.

Beecher, Lyman. *The Autobiography of Lyman Beecher*. Edited by Barbara

Cross. 2 vols. Cambridge : Harvard University Press, Belknap Press, 1961.
———. *The Bible a Code of Laws.* Andover, Mass.: Flagg & Gould, 1818.
———. *The Practicality of Suppressing Vice by Means of Societies Instituted for that Purpose : A Sermon Delivered Before the Moral Society in East Hampton, September 21, 1803, by Lyman Beecher, Pastor.* New London : Samuel Green, 1804.

Bixby, James Thompson. *The Ethics of Evolution.* Boston : Small, Maynard, & Co., 1900.

Blackwell, Elizabeth. *The Laws of Life : Lectures Delivered to a Class of Ladies.* New York : George P. Putnam, 1852.

Blau, Joseph, ed. *Social Theories of Jacksonian Democracy.* New York : Hafner Publishing Co., 1947.

Board of National Popular Education. *Reports of the General Agent of the Board of National Popular Education.* Hartford, 1848–57.

Bode, Carl. "Columbia's Carnal Bed." *American Quarterly* 15, no. 1 (Spring 1963).

Boone, Richard G. *A History of Education in Indiana.* New York : D. Appleton & Co., 1892.

Bremer, Fredrika. *The Homes of the New World.* 2 vols. New York: Harper & Bros., 1853.

Brownson, Orestes A. "The Laboring Classes." *The Boston Quarterly Review* 3 (July 1840) : 366–95.

Buell, Samuel. *A Faithful Narrative of the Remarkable Revival of Religion in the Congregation of East Hampton on Long Island in the Year of Our Lord 1764; with Some Reflections, to Which Are Added Sketches of the Author's life, and Also an Account of the Revival of Religion in Bridgehampton and Easthampton in 1800.* Sag Harbor : Alden Spooner, 1808.

Bushman, Richard. *From Puritan to Yankee : Character and Social Order in Connecticut, 1690–1765.* Cambridge : Harvard University Press, 1967.

Bushnell, Horace. "American Politics." *The American National Preacher* 14 (1840).

Bushnell, Horace. *Christian Nurture.* New York : Scribner, Armstrong & Co., 1876.

Cabot, Mary R., ed. *Annals of Brattleboro, 1681–1895.* 2 vols. Brattleboro, Vt., 1921.

Calhoun, Arthur W. *A Social History of the American Family.* 3 vols. New York : Barnes & Noble, 1945.

Campbell, Helen. *Household Economics : A Course of Lectures in the School of Economics at the University of Wisconsin.* New York : G. P. Putnam's Sons, 1898.

Carter, Samuel. *Cyrus Field, Man of Two Worlds.* New York : G. P. Putnam's Sons, 1968.

Child, Lydia Maria. *The American Frugal Housewife.* Boston : Charter, Hendee & Co., 1832.

Cianfrani, Theodore. *A Short History of Obstetrics and Gynecology.* Springfield, Mass. : Charles C. Thomas, 1960.

Clark, Alice. *Working Life of Women in the Seventeenth Century.* New York : Harcourt, Brace & Howe, 1920.

Clark, Rev. John A., ed. *The Christian Keepsake and Missionary Annual.* Philadelphia, 1837.

Cohen, Yehudi A. "Social Boundary Systems." *Current Anthropology* 10, no. 1 (February 1969).

Coxe, Margaret. *Claims of the Country on American Females.* Columbus, Ohio : Isaac N. Whitney, 1842.

Crofut, Florence. *Guide to the History and Historical Sites of Connecticut.* New Haven : Yale University Press, 1937.

Cross, Barbara. *Horace Bushnell, Minister to a Changing America.* Chicago : University of Chicago Press, 1958.

Culver, Raymond B. *Horace Mann and Religion in the Massachusetts Public Schools.* New Haven : Yale University Press, 1929.

Current, Richard N. *Daniel Webster and the Rise of National Conservatism.* Boston : Little, Brown & Co., 1955.

Doddridge, Philip. *The Rise and Progress of Religion in the Soul Illustrated in a Course of Serious and Practical Addresses Suited to Persons of Every Character and Circumstance with a Devout Meditation, or Prayer Subjoined to Each Chapter.* New York : American Tract Society, 1847.

Donald, David. "The Autobiography of James Hall, Western Literary Pioneer." *Ohio State Archaeological and Historical Quarterly* 56, no. 3 (July 1947).

Downing, Andrew Jackson. *Cottage Residences.* New York : Wiley & Putnam, 1842.

Dwight, Sereno E., ed. *The Works of President Edwards.* Vol. 1 New York : G & C & H Carville, 1830.

Dwight, Theodore. *The Father's Book.* Springfield, Mass. : G. & C. Merriam, 1834.

Eastman, Max. *Heroes I Have Known : Twelve Who Lived Great Lives.* New York : Simon & Schuster, 1942.

Edwards, Jonathan. *The Nature of True Virtue.* Ann Arbor : University of Michigan Press, 1960.

Ekirch, Arthur, Jr. *The Idea of Progress in America, 1815–1860.* New York : Columbia University Press, 1944.

Eliot, Charles William. *American Contributions to Civilization.* New York : The Century Co., 1897.

Eliot, Charles William. "Wise and Unwise Economy in Schools." *Atlantic Monthly,* no. 35 (June 1875).

Ellul, Jacques. *The Technological Society.* New York : Alfred Knopf, 1964.

Elson, Ruth. *Guardians of Tradition American Schoolbooks of the Nineteenth Century.* Lincoln, Nebr. : University of Nebraska Press, 1964.

Ernst, Robert. *Rufus King, American Federalist.* Chapel Hill : University of North Carolina Press, 1968.

Exman, Eugene. *The Brothers Harper.* New York : Harper & Row, 1965.

Fiedler, Leslie. *Love and Death in the American Novel.* New York : Dell Publishing Co., 1966.

Foote, John P. *Memoirs of the Life of Samuel F. Foote, by His Brother, John P. Foote.* Cincinnati : R. Clarke & Co., 1860.

———. *The Schools of Cincinnati and Its Vicinity.* Cincinnati : C. F. Bradley, 1856.

Foster, Charles H. *An Errand of Mercy : The Evangelical United Front, 1790–1837.* Chapel Hill : University of North Carolina Press, 1960.

———. *The Rungless Ladder : Harriet Beecher Stowe and New England Puritanism.* Durham, N.C. : Duke University Press, 1954.

Fowler, William Chauncey. *Essays.* Hartford : Case, Lockwood, & Brainard Co., 1876.

Fredrickson, George M. *The Inner Civil War : Northern Intellectuals and the Crisis of the Union.* New York : Harper & Row, 1965.

Gardiner, John Lyon. "Notes and Observations of the Town of East Hampton at the East End of Long Island Written by John Lyon Gardiner of the Isle of Wright in April 1798 at the Request of the Revd. Samuel Miller of N : York." *Collections of the New York Historical Society.* New York, 1870.

Gallaudet, Thomas H. *The Youth's Book on Natural Theology.* New York : American Tract Society, 1832.

Giedion, Siegfried. *Mechanization Takes Command : A Contribution to Anonymous History.* New York : Oxford University Press, 1948.

Gilman, Charlotte Perkins. *Woman and Economics : The Economic Factor Between Men and Women as a Factor in Social Evolution.* Boston : Small, Maynard, & Co., 1898.

Godey, L. A. and Hale, Sarah Josepha, eds. *Godey's Lady's Book.* New York : The Godey Co.

Grave, S. A. *The Scottish Philosophy of Common Sense.* Oxford : Clarendon Press, 1960.

Graves, Margaret. *Women in America.* New York : Harper & Bros., 1855.

Greeley, Horace. *Hints Toward Reforms.* New York : Harper & Bros., 1850.

Greve, Charles T. *Centennial History of Cincinnati.* Chicago : Biographical Publishing Co., 1904.

Grimké, Angelina. *Appeal to the Christian Women of the Southern States.* New York : American Anti-Slavery Society, 1836.

———. *An Appeal to the Women of the Nominally Free States; Issued by an Anti-Slavery Convention of American Women and Held by Adjournment from the 9th to the 12th of May, 1837.* New York, 1837.

———. *Letters to Catharine Beecher, in Reply to an Essay on Slavery and Abolitionism, Addressed to A. E. Grimké.* Boston : I. Knapp, 1838.

Guilford, Linda Thayer. *The Use of a Life : Memorials of Mrs. Z. P. Grant Banister.* New York : American Tract Society, 1885.

Haight, Gordon S. *Mrs. Sigourney, the Sweet Singer of Hartford.* New Haven : Yale University Press, 1930.

Hale, Sarah Josepha. *Housekeeping and Keeping House.* New York : Harper & Bros., 1845.

Hall, G. Stanley. "On the History of American College Textbooks and Teaching in Logic, Ethics, Psychology, and Allied Subjects." (American Antiquarian Society) *Proceedings*, n.s, 9, Worcester, Mass., 1895.

Handlin, Oscar. *Race and Nationality in American Life.* Boston : Little, Brown & Co. 1950.

Hansen, Allen Oscar. *Early Educational Leadership in the Ohio Valley.* Bloomington, Illinois : Public School Publishing Co., 1923.

Haroutunian, Joseph. *Piety Versus Moralism : The Passing of the New England Theology.* New York : H. Holt & Co., 1932.

Hartford Female Seminary. *The Annual Catalogue of Hartford Female Seminary.* Hartford, 1831.

————. *Catalogue of the Officers, Teachers, and Pupils of the Hartford Female Seminary.* Hartford, 1827–28.

Hartford Female Seminary Papers. *Hartford Female Seminary Reunion.* Hartford, Conn. : Connecticut Historical Society, 1892.

Harveson, Mae Elizabeth. *Catharine Esther Beecher, Pioneer Educator.* Philadelphia : University of Pennsylvania, 1932.

Hawes, Joel. *Lectures Addressed to the Young Men of Hartford and New Haven.* Hartford : O. D. Cooke & Co., 1828.

Higham, John. *From Boundlessness to Consolidation : The Transformation of American Culture, 1884–1860.* Ann Arbor : William L. Clements Library, 1969.

Himes, Norman. *Medical History of Contraception.* New York : Gamut Press, Inc., 1963.

History of the Foundation and Endowment of the Lane Theological Seminary. Cincinnati : Ben Franklin printing house, 1848.

Hobson, Elsie Garland. "Educational Legislation and Administration in the State of New York from 1772 to 1850." *Supplementary Educational Monographs* 3, no. 1, (1918).

Hodge, Hugh L., M. D. *Foeticide, or Criminal Abortion : A Lecture Introductory to the Course on Obstetrics, and Diseases of Women and Children, University of Pennsylvania, Session 1830–1840.* Philadelphia : Lindsay & Blakiston, 1869.

Hofstadter, Richard. *Social Darwinism in American Thought.* Philadelphia : University of Pennsylvania Press, 1944.

Holmes, Oliver Wendell. *An Address by Oliver Wendell Holmes on Memorial Day, May 30, 1895.* Boston : Little, Brown & Co., 1895.

Hopkins, Vivian C. *Prodigal Puritan : A Life of Delia Bacon.* Cambridge : Harvard University Press, Belknap Press, 1959.

Houghton, Walter. *The Victorian Frame of Mind.* New Haven : Yale University Press, 1957.

Howe, Daniel Walker. *The Unitarian Conscience, Harvard Moral Philosophy, 1805–1861.* Cambridge : Harvard University Press, 1970.

Howe, Mark De Wolf, ed. *Touched with Fire : Civil War Letters and Diaries of Oliver Wendell Holmes, Jr.* Cambridge : Harvard University Press, 1946.

Humphrey, Herman. *Domestic Education.* Amherst, Mass.: J. S. & C. Adams, 1840.

Huntington, David. *Thomas Cole, Poet–Painter.* New York : Praeger, 1973.

James, Edward, ed. *Notable American Women 1607–1950.* 3 vols. Cambrige : Harvard University Press, 1971.

James, William. *The Varieties of Religious Experience.* New York : Longmans, Green & Co., 1902.

Johnson, Allen, ed. *Dictionary of American Biography.* New York: Charles Scribner's Sons, 1957.

Katz, Michael. *The Irony of Early School Reform : Educational Innovation in Mid-Nineteenth Century Massachusetts.* Cambridge : Harvard University Press, 1968.

Keagy, W. R. "The Lane Seminary Rebellion." *Bulletin of the Historical and Philosophical Society of Ohio* 9 (April 1951).

Keller, Charles Ray. *The Second Great Awakening in Connecticut.* New Haven : Yale University Press, 1942.

Kett, Joseph F. *The Formation of the American Medical Prefession : The Role of Institutions, 1780–1860.* New Haven : Yale University Press, 1968.

Kieckhefer, Grace Norton. *The History of Milwaukee–Downer College, 1851–1951.* Milwaukee : Centennial Publication of Milwaukee–Downer College, 1950.

Kingsley, James Luce. *Yale College : A Sketch of Its History.* Boston : Perkins, Marvin & Co., 1835.

Kraditor, Aileen. *The Ideas of the Woman Suffrage Movement 1890–1920.* New York : Doubleday & Co., 1971.

———. *Means and Ends in American Abolitionism : Garrison and His Critics on Strategy and Tactics, 1834–1850.* New York : Pantheon Books, 1967.

Kuhn, Anne. *The Mother's Role in Childhood Education.* New Haven : Yale University Press, 1947.

Lawrence, Edward A. *The Life of Rev. Joel Hawes, D.D.* Hartford : Hamersley & Co., 1871.

Lerner, Gerda. *The Grimké Sisters from South Carolina : Pioneers for Women's Rights and Abolition.* Boston : Houghton Mifflin Co., 1967.

———. "The Lady and the Mill Girl : Changes in the Status of Women in the Age of Jackson." *Mid-Continent American Studies Journal* 10 (1969).

Levi-Strauss, Claude. *The Elementary Structure of Kinship.* Boston : Beacon Press, 1969.

Lutz, Alma. *Emma Willard, Daughter of Democracy.* New York : Houghton Mifflin Co., 1929.

Lynn, Kenneth. Introduction to *Uncle Tom's Cabin* by Harriet Beecher Stowe. John Harvard Library edition. Cambridge : Harvard University Press, 1962.

McLachlan, James. *American Boarding Schools.* New York : Scribner's, 1970.

McLoughlin, William G. *The Meaning of Henry Ward Beecher : An Essay on the Shifting Values of Mid-Victorian America, 1840–1870.* New York : Alfred Knopf, 1970.

Mansfield, E. D. *Personal Memories, Social, Political and Literary Sketches of Many Noted People, 1803–1843.* Cincinnati : R. Clarke & Co., 1879.
———. *The Legal Rights, Liabilities, and Duties of Women.* Salem, Mass.: John P. Jewett & Co., 1845.
Martineau, Harriet. *Household Education.* Philadelphia : Lea & Blanchard, 1849.
Mathews, Donald G. "The Second Great Awakening as an Organizing Process, 1780–1830 : An Hypothesis." *American Quarterly* 21, no. 1 (Spring 1969) : 23–44.
Mead, Sidney Earl. *Nathaniel William Taylor, 1786–1858 : A Connecticut Liberal.* Chicago : University of Chicago Press, 1942.
Melder, Keith. "Forerunners of Freedom : The Grimké Sisters in Massachusetts." *Essex Institute Historical Collections* 3, no. 3 (July 1967).
———. "Ladies Bountiful : Organized Women's Benevolence in Early 19th Century America," *New York History* 68, no. 3 (July 1967) : 231–54.
Meltzer, Milton. *Tongue of Flame : The Life of Lydia Maria Child.* New York : T. Y. Crowell, 1965.
Meyer, Donald. *The Positive Thinkers : A Study of the American Quest for Health, Wealth, and Personal Power from Mary Baker Eddy to Norman Vincent Peale.* New York : Doubleday & Co., 1965.
Meyers, Marvin. *The Jacksonian Persuasion : Politics and Belief.* Stanford : Stanford University Press, 1957.
Miller, Charles G. "The Background of Calvin E. Stowe's 'Report on Elementary Public Instruction in Europe.'" *Ohio State Archeological and Historical Quarterly* 29, no. 2 (April 1940).
Minnich, Harvey. *William Holmes McGuffey and His Readers.* New York : American Book Co., 1936.
Mohr, Ropert Landis. *Thomas Henry Burrowes, 1805–1871.* Philadelphia : University of Pennsylvania Press, 1946.
Monroe, Paul. *Founding of the American Public School System : A History of Education in the United States from the Early Settlements to the Close of the Civil War Period.* New York : Macmillan Co., 1940.
Mosier, Richard David. *Making the American Mind : Social and Moral Ideas in McGuffey Readers.* New York : Russell & Russell, 1947.
Norton, Minerva Brace. *A True Teacher, Mary Mortimer : A Memoir.* Chicago: Fleming H. Revell Co., 1894.
Nuttall, Geoffrey F. *Philip Doddridge 1702–51 : His Contribution to English Religion.* London : Independent Press, 1951.
Ossoli, Margaret Fuller. *At Home and Abroad : Or Things and Thoughts in America and Europe.* Boston : Crosby, Nichols, & Co., 1856.
———. *Summer in the Lakes.* Boston : C. C. Little & J. Brown, 1843.
Papashvily, Helen. *All the Happy Endings.* New York: Harper & Row, 1956.
Park, Edwards A. *Memoir of Nathanael Emmons.* Boston : Congregational Board of Publication, 1861.
Pattee, Fred Lewis. *The Feminine Fifties.* New York : D. Appleton–Century Co., Inc., 1940.
Phelps, Almira. *The Female Student.* New York : Leavitt & Lord, 1836.

Pilkington, Mrs. [Mary Hopkins]. *A Mirror for the Female Sex*. Hartford : Hudson & Goodwin, 1799.

Price, C. Matlack. "Historic Houses of Litchfield." *The White Pine Series of Architectural Monographs* 5, no. 3 (June 1919).

Purcell, Richard J. *Connecticut in Transition : 1775–1818*. Washington, D.C.: American Historical Association, 1918.

Randall, Randolph C. *James Hall, Spokesman of the New West*. Columbus : Ohio State University Press, 1964.

Riley, Glenda Gates. "The Subtle Subversion : Changes in the Traditionalist Image of the American Woman." *Historian* 22, no. 2 (February 1970).

Robinson, Solon. *How to Live*. New York : Fowler and Wells, 1860.

Rosenberg, Carroll Smith. "The Hysterical Woman : Sex Roles and Role Conflict in Nineteenth-Century America." *Social Research* 39, no. 4 (Winter 1972).

Ross, Ishbel. *Child of Destiny*. New York : Harper, 1949.

Rourke, Constance. *Trumpets of Jubilee*. New York : Harcourt, Brace & Co., 1927.

Rozwenc, Edwin C. *Ideology and Power in the Age of Jackson*. New York : New York University Press, 1964.

Schneider, Herbert W. *A History of American Philosophy*. New York : Columbia University Press, 1963.

Sedgwick, Catharine M. *A New England Tale : or Sketches of New England Character and Manners*. New York : Bliss & White, 1822.

Sigourney, Lydia. *Letters to Mothers*. New York : Harper & Bros., 1846.

Sinclair, Andrew. *The Emancipation of the American Woman*. New York : Harper & Row, 1966.

Smith, H. Shelton. *Changing Conceptions of Original Sin : A Study in American Theology Since 1750*. New York : Scribner's, 1955.

Smith, Henry Nash. *Virgin Land : The American West as Symbol and Myth*. Cambridge : Harvard University Press, 1950.

Smith, Timothy L. *Revivalism and Social Reform : American Protestantism on the Eve of the Civil War*. New York : Abingdon Press, 1957.

Smith, Wilson. *Professors and Public Ethics : Studies of Northern Moral Philosophers Before the Civil War*. Ithaca : Cornell University Press, 1956.

Stansbury, Arthur Joseph. *Trial of the Reverend Lyman Beecher Before the Presbytery of Cincinnati on the Charge of Heresy, Reported for the "New York Observer."* New York : The New York Observer, 1835.

Stanton, Elizabeth Cady. *Eighty Years and More : Reminiscences, 1815–1897*. New York : European Publishing Co., 1898.

Stears, Peter. "Working Class Women in Britain," in *Suffer and Be Still : Women in the Victorian Age,* edited by Martha Vicinus. Bloomington : Indiana University Press, 1972.

Stewart, Dugald. *Elements of the Philosophy of the Human Mind.* Albany : E & E Hosford, 1822.

Still, Bayrd. *Milwaukee : The History of a City*. Madison : State Historical Society of Wisconsin, 1948.

Stowe, Calvin. *Report on Elementary Instruction in Europe.* Columbus :
S. Medary, 1837.

Stowe, Charles E. *The Life of Harriet Beecher Stowe Compiled from Her
Letters and Journals.* Boston : Houghton Mifflin Co., 1889.

Stowe, Harriet Beecher [Christopher Crowfield]. *House and Home Papers.*
Boston : Fields, Osgood & Co., 1869.

———. *The Mayflower, or Sketches of the Descendents of the Pilgrims.*
New York : Harper & Bros., 1843.

———. *The Minister's Wooing.* Boston : Ticknor & Fields, 1866. Originally
published by Derby & Jackson, Boston, 1859.

———. *Uncle Tom's Cabin.* Boston : John P. Jewett & Co., 1851.

Stowe, Harriet Beecher et al. *Our Famous Women.* Hartford : A. D.
Worthington & Co., 1884.

Stowe, Lyman Beecher. *Saints, Sinners and Beechers.* Indianapolis : The
Bobbs-Merrill Co., 1934.

Taylor, William R. *Cavalier and Yankee : The Old South and American
National Character.* New York : Harper & Row, 1961.

Taylor, William R., and Lasch, Christopher. "Two 'Kindred Spirits' :
Sorority and Family in New England, 1839–1846." *New England
Quarterly* 36 (March 1963).

Tocqueville, Alexis de. *Democracy in America.* New York : Harper &
Row, 1966.

Trall, Russell T. *The Hydropathic Encyclopedia.* New York : Fowler &
Wells, 1853.

Tyler, Alice Felt. *Freedom's Ferment : Phases of American Social History
from the Colonial Period to the Outbreak of the Civil War.* Minneapolis : University of Minnesota Press, 1944.

Upham, Thomas C. *Elements of Intellectual Philosophy.* Portland, Me. :
W. Hyde & Co., 1827.

———. *Elements of Mental Philosophy, Intellect, and Sensibilities.* Portland, Me. : W. Hyde & Co., 1831.

Vanderpoel, Emily Noyes. *Chronicles of a Pioneer School from 1792 to
1833, Being the History of Miss Sarah Pierce and Her Litchfield School.*
Cambridge : Harvard University Press, 1903.

———. *More Chronicles of a Pioneer School, from 1792 to 1833.* New
York : The Cadmus Book Shop, 1927.

Veblen, Thorstein. "The Barbarian Status of Women." *American Journal
of Sociology* 4 (January 1899).

Venable, W. H. *Beginnings of Literary Culture in the Ohio Valley.*
Cincinnati : R. Clarke & Co., 1891.

Vicinus, Martha, ed. *Suffer and Be Still : Women in the Victorian Age.*
Bloomington : Indiana University Press, 1972.

Wade, Richard C. *The Urban Frontier : The Rise of Western Cities, 1790–
1830.* Cambridge : Harvard University Press, 1959.

Wagenknecht, Edward. *Harriet Beecher Stowe : The Known and the
Unknown.* New York : Oxford University Press, 1965.

Walker, George Leon. *Address at the Two Hundred and Fiftieth Anni-*

versary of the First Church of Christ, Hartford. Hartford : Case, Lockwood, & Brainard Co., 1883.

Walzer, Michael. *The Revolution of the Saints : A Study in the Origins of Radical Politics.* Cambridge : Harvard University Press, 1965.

Ward, H. O. *Sensible Etiquette of the Best Society Customs, Manners, Morals, and Home Culture, Compiled from the Best Authorities.* Philadelphia : Porter & Coates, 1878.

Ward, John W. "The Age of the Common Man" in *The Reconstruction of American History,* edited by John Higham. London : Hutchinson, 1963.

Wasserstrom, William. *Heiress of All the Ages : Sex and Sentiment in the Genteel Tradition.* Minneapolis : University of Minnesota Press, 1959.

The Water Cure Journal 1, nos. 1, 3, 4, 5, 7; 2, nos. 1, 2. New York, 1845–48.

Wayland, Francis. *Elements of Moral Science with Questions for Examinations.* London : The Religious Tract Society, 1835.

Webster, Thomas, and Parkes, Mrs. *An Encyclopaedia of Domestic Economy.* New York : Harper & Bros., 1845.

Weiss, Harry B. and Kemble, Howard R. *The Great American Water-Cure Craze.* Trenton : The Past Times Press, 1967.

Welter, Barbara. "Anti-Intellectualism and the American Woman : 1800–1860." *Mid-America* 48 (October 1966).

———. "The Cult of True Womanhood, 1820–1860." *American Quarterly* 18 (1966) : 151–74.

Wesselhoeft Conrad, *The Water Cure in Amercia.* New York : Fowler & Wells, 1852.

West, Charles, M. D. *Lectures on the Diseases of Women.* Philadelphia : Blanchard and Lea, 1858.

Western Literary Institute. *Transactions* 3 (October 1836) : 61–67.

White, Alden C. *The History of the Town of Litchfield, Connecticut, 1720–1920.* Litchfield : Enquirer Print, 1920.

Wight, William. *Annals of Milwaukee College, 1848–1891.* Milwaukee, 1891.

Willard, Emma. *An Address to the Public : Particularly to the Members of the Legislature of New York, Proposing a Plan for Improving Female Education.* New York : J. W. Copeland, 1819.

Wilson, Edmund. *Patriotic Gore.* New York : Oxford University Press, 1962.

Wilson, James Grant and Fiske, John. *Appleton's Cyclopaedia of American Biography.* New York : D. Appleton & Co., 1888.

Wishy, Bernard. *The Child and the Republic : The Dawn of Modern American Child Nurture.* Philadelphia : University of Pennsylvania Press, 1968.

Wood, Ann Douglas. "Mrs. Sigourney and the Sensibility of the Inner Space." *New England Quarterly* 45, no. 2 (Spring 1971).

———. "The 'Scribbling Women' and Fanny Fern : Why Women Wrote." *American Quarterly* 23, no 1 (Spring 1971).

————. "The War Within a War : Women Nurses in the Union Army." *Civil War History* 18, no. 3 (September 1972).

Woodbridge, William, ed. *American Annals of Education and Instruction* 3 (August 1833) : 380.

Woods, Leonard. "Inquiries Respecting Free Agency." *American Biblical Repository* 5, no. 37 (January 1840).

Woody, Thomas. *A History of Women's Education in the United States.* 2 vols. New York : Octagon Books, 1966.

Index